D0203005

The Critical Response to Dashiell Hammett

Recent Titles in
Critical Responses in Arts and Letters

The Critical Response
to Dashiell Hammett

Edited by
Christopher Metress

Critical Responses in Arts and Letters, Number 15
Cameron Northouse, Series Adviser

GREENWOOD PRESS
Westport, Connecticut • London

Library of Congress Cataloging-in-Publication Data

The critical response to Dashiell Hammett / edited by Christopher
   Metress.
            p.   cm.—(Critical responses in arts and letters, ISSN
   1057–0993 ; no. 15)
      Includes bibliographical references (p.   ) and index.
      ISBN 0–313–28938–7 (alk. paper)
      1. Hammett, Dashiell, 1894–1961—Criticism and interpretation.
   2. Hammett, Dashiell, 1894–1961. I. Metress, Christopher.
   II. Series.
   PS3515.A4347Z6   1994
   813'.52—dc20   94–28713

British Library Cataloguing in Publication Data is available.

Copyright © 1994 by Christopher Metress

All rights reserved. No portion of this book may be
reproduced, by any process or technique, without the
express written consent of the publisher.

Library of Congress Catalog Card Number: 94–28713
ISBN: 0–313–28938–7
ISSN: 1057–0993

First published in 1994

Greenwood Press, 88 Post Road West, Westport, CT 06881
An imprint of Greenwood Publishing Group, Inc.

Printed in the United States of America

∞™

The paper used in this book complies with the
Permanent Paper Standard issued by the National
Information Standards Organization (Z39.48–1984).

10 9 8 7 6 5 4 3 2 1

Copyright Acknowledgments

The editor and publisher gratefully acknowledge permission for use of the following material:

Review of *Red Harvest*, *New Statesman* 27 July 1929: 500. Reprinted by permission.

John G. Cawelti, *Adventure, Mystery, and Romance* (U of Chicago P, 1976) 168-173. Reprinted by permission.

Carl Freedman and Christopher Kendrick, "Forms of Labor in *Red Harvest*." Reprinted by permission of the Modern Language Association of America from *PMLA* 106 (1991), 209-221.

Review of Dashiell Hammett's *The Dain Curse*, August 1929. Copyright © 1929 by The New York Times Company. Reprinted by permission.

Will Cuppy. Review of *The Dain Curse. New York Herald Tribune*, 11 August 1929, 11; © 1929, New York Herald Tribune Inc. All rights reserved. Reprinted by permission.

Sinda Gregory, "*The Dain Curse*: The Epistemology of the Detective Story." *Private Investigations: The Novels of Dashiell Hammett* (Southern Illinois UP, 1985) 61-87. Reprinted by permission.

Bruce Gatenby. "'A Long and Laughable Story': Hammett's *Dain Curse* and the Postmodern Condition." Printed by the permission of the author.

Donald Douglas, "Not One Hoot for the Law," *The New Republic* 9 April 1930: 226.

Irving Malin, "Focus on *The Maltese Falcon*: The Metaphysical Falcon." *Tough Guy Writers of the Thirties*. ed. David Madden (Southern Illinois UP, 1968) 104-109. Copyright © Southern Illinois UP. Reprinted by permission.

Jasmine Yong Hall, "Jameson, Genre, and Gumshoes: *The Maltese Falcon* as Inverted Romance," *The Cunning Craft: Original Essays on Detective Fiction*. Essays in Literature Book Series (Macomb: Western Illinois UP, 1990) 109-119. Reprinted by permission.

Christopher Metress, "Dashiell Hammett and the Challenge of New Individualism: Rereading *Red Harvest* and *The Maltese Falcon*," *Essays in Literature* 17 (Fall 1990) 242-260. Reprinted by permission.

Bruce Rae, Review of Dashiell Hammett's *The Glass Key*, May 3, 1931. Copyright © 1931 by The New York Times Company. Reprinted by permission.

Will Cuppy. Review of *The Glass Key*. From *New York Herald Tribune*, 26 April 1931, 13; © 1931, New York Herald Tribune Inc. All rights reserved. Reprinted by permission.

Joseph T. Shaw, Letter to the Editor of *Writer's Digest*, September 1930. Reprinted by permission of *Writer's Digest*.

Will Murray. "The Riddle of the Key." *The Armchair Detective* 22 (Summer 1989): 290-95. Reprinted by permission.

Jon Thompson, "Dashiell Hammett's Hard-Boiled Modernism," *Fiction, Crime, and Empire* (University of Illinois P, 1993) 134-147. Copyright The U of Illinois Press. Reprinted by permission The University of Illinois Press and the author.

Peter Quennell, Review of *The Thin Man*, *New Statesman* 7 (26 May 1934): 801. Reprinted by permission.

T.S. Matthews, "Mr. Hammett Goes Coasting," *The New Republic* 77 (24 January 1934): 316.

Hershell Brickell, Review of *The Thin Man*, *The North American Review* 237.3 (March 1934) 283. Reprinted by permission.

George J. Thompson, "The Problem of Moral Vision in Dashiell Hammett's Detective Novels—Part IV: *The Thin Man*: The End Game," *The Armchair Detective* (1974) 27-35. Reprinted by permission.

Peter Wolfe. From Chapter 7 of *Beams Falling: The Art of Dashiell Hammett's Novels* (Bowling Green U Popular P, 1980) 148-149, 158-163. Reprinted by permission.

Howard Haycraft. From *Murder for Pleasure* by Howard Haycraft. Copyright 1941 by D. Appleton-Century Co. Inc. Renewed copyright © 1968 by Howard Haycraft. Used by permission of Dutton Signet, a division of Penguin Books USA Inc.

Raymond Chandler. Excerpt from "The Simple Art of Murder" by Raymond Chandler. Copyright 1950 by Raymond Chandler, © renewed 1978 by Helga Greene. Reprinted by permission of Houghton Mifflin Company. All rights reserved. Also reproduced by permission of Hamish Hamilton Ltd.

David T. Bazelon, "Dashiell Hammett's Private Eye: No Loyalty Beyond the Job." Reprinted from *Commentary*, May 1949, by permission; all rights reserved.

A. Alvarez, "The Thin Man," *The Spectator* 7181 (11 February 1966): 169-170. Reprinted by permission.

Robert I. Edenbaum, "The Poetics of the Private-Eye: The Novels of Dashiell Hammett." *Tough Guy Writers of the Thirties*. ed. David Madden (Southern Illinois UP, 1968) 80-103. Copyright © Southern Illinois UP. Reprinted by permission.

Steven Marcus, "Dashiell Hammett and the Continental Op," *Partisan Review* 41 (1974) 366-377. Reprinted by permission.

Ross Macdonald. From *Self-Portrait: Ceaselessly Into the Past*, copyright © 1981 by Ross Macdonald; reprinted with permission from Capra Press, Santa Barbara.

David J. Herman, "Finding Out about Gender in Hammett's Detective Fiction: Generic Constraints or Transcendental Norms?" *Genre* 24 (Spring 1991) 1-23. Reprinted by permission.

Larry Anderson, "Dangerous Romance as Prelude to Love: Hammett's *Woman in the Dark*." Printed by permission of the author.

Permission to reprint excerpts from *Red Harvest*, *The Dain Curse*, *The Maltese Falcon*, *The Glass Key*, and *The Thin Man* granted by Random House Inc.

Every reasonable effort has been made to trace the owners of copyright materials in this book, but in some cases this has proven impossible. The author and the publisher will be glad to receive information leading to more complete acknowledgments in subsequent printings of the book and in the meantime extend their apologies for any omissions.

Contents

Series Foreword

Critical Responses in Arts and Letters is designed to present a documentary history of highlights in the critical reception to the body of work of writers and artists and to individual works that are generally considered to be of major importance. The focus of each volume in this series is basically historical. The introductions to each volume are themselves brief histories of the critical response an author, artist, or individual work has received. This response is then further illustrated by reprinting a strong representation of the major critical reviews and articles which collectively have produced the author's, artist's, or work's critical reputation.

The scope of *Critical Responses in Arts in Letters* knows no chronological or geographical boundaries. Volumes under preparation include studies of individuals from around the world and in both contemporary and historical periods.

Each volume is the work of an individual editor, who surveys the entire body of criticism on a single author, artist, or work. The editor then selects the best material to depict the critical response received by an author or artist over his/her entire career. Documents produced by the author or the artist may also be included when the editor finds that they are necessary to a full understanding of the materials at hand. In circumstances where previous, isolated volumes of criticism on a particular individual or work exist, the editor carefully selects material that better reflects the nature and directions of the critical response over time.

In addition to the introduction and the documentary section, the editor of each volume is free to solicit new essays on areas that have not been adequately dealt with in previous criticism. Also, for volumes on living writers and artists, new interviews may be included, again at the discretion of the volume's editor. The volumes also provide a supplementary bibliography and are fully indexed.

While each volume in *Critical Responses in Arts and Letters* is unique, it is also hoped that in combination they form a useful, documentary history of the critical response to the arts, and one that can be easily and profitably employed by students and scholars.

Cameron Northouse

Introduction

In 1944, a full decade after Dashiell Hammett published his last novel, three important critics assessed the achievement of detective fiction's once-prolific but by then long-silent innovator. In the February 7th issue of the *New Republic*, André Gide praised Hammett's first novel, *Red Harvest*, as "a remarkable achievement," and concluded that "Dashiell Hammett's dialogues, in which every character is trying to deceive all the others and in which the truth slowly becomes visible through a fog of deception, can be compared only with the best of Hemingway" ("An Imaginary Interview" 186). Edmund Wilson, writing in the October 14th issue of the *New Yorker*, was less enthusiastic. In "Why Do People Read Detective Stories?" Wilson took an entire genre to task, belittling the public's endless fascination with such writers as Agatha Christie, Ngaio Marsh, and Rex Stout. Eventually, Wilson turned his sights on Hammett and *The Maltese Falcon*, which he "assumed to be a classic in the field." But where so many others had found merit, Wilson found only incompetence:

> As a writer, [Hammett] is surely almost as far below the rank of Rex Stout as Rex Stout is below that of James Cain. *The Maltese Falcon* today seems not much above those newspaper picture-strips in which you follow from day to day the ups and downs of a strong-jawed hero and a hardboiled but beautiful adventuress. (235-236)

Before year's end, Raymond Chandler proffered his own assessment, one that fell midway between Gide's admiration and Wilson's denunciation. In "The Simple Art of Murder," Chandler praised Hammett as "the ace performer" in a school of writers who transformed the classical detective story, but he issued the following caveat: "I doubt that Hammett had any deliberate artistic aims whatever; he was [simply] trying to make a living by writing something he had firsthand information about." Yes, Chandler observed, Hammett did have a "literary style," and while this style "at its best . . . could say anything," it was "at its worst . . . as formalized as a page of *Marius the Epicurean*." Moreover, "How original a writer Hammett really was isn't easy to decide now," Chandler reflected, "[but] there is nothing in his work that is not implicit in the early novels and stories of Hemingway" (57). Yet despite such reservations about Hammett's style and originality, Chandler in the end confessed that, whatever his shortcomings, Hammett "did over and over again what only the best writers can ever do at all. He wrote scenes that seemed never to have been written before" (58).

With his reputation as both a daring original and a mere pulpster, Dashiell Hammett has long held a peculiar position in American letters. Few writers can be dismissed one month as a creator of derivative "newspaper picture-strips" and then two months later be hailed as an artist who "wrote scenes that seemed never to have been written before." The Gide-Wilson-Chandler colloquy of 1944 is but one example of the eclectic and often contentious estimations that have long characterized the critical response to Dashiell Hammett. 1966 offers a similar illustration. Reviewing the reissued *Novels of Dashiell Hammett* in the January 8th issue of the *New Republic*, Leonard Moss found little to praise. Like Wilson more than twenty years before, Moss was extremely disappointed by Hammett's most famous work. Calling *The Maltese Falcon* Hammett's "worst novel," one full of "insipid dialogue," Moss concluded that "Dashiell Hammett cannot through any generosity be considered a complex author. It would be fatuous to search for profound ethical, sociological, or psychological implications" (34) in his fiction. Yet one month later, in the *Spectator*, A. Alvarez extended to Hammett the very generosity Moss so grudgingly withheld, arguing that Hammett's five novels "tell you more about the United States than many with more high-minded intentions, like Upton Sinclair's" (169). Hailing Hammett's art as "meticulous, witty, authentic, and utterly nihilistic" (170), Alvarez insisted that, with "their elegant plots and stripped, clean writing," Hammett's novels "have their own unwavering kind of perfection" (169). As more recent examples bear out, Hammett's fiction continues to be both embraced and rejected by the critical community. In 1986, for instance, French scholars placed *The Glass Key* on the Syllabus of Agrégation, the highest competitive examination for teachers in France. The other American writer featured on that year's syllabus was Walker Percy, and the following year the Sorbonne published a collection of critical essays devoted solely to these two writers. On the other hand, back in America, the 1250 page *Columbia Literary History of the United States* (1988) contained only a few brief mentions of Hammett—including an unfortunate mischaracterization of *Red Harvest* as an example of 1920s "leftist literature" (864). Thus, in one year and on one side of the Atlantic, Hammett was presented to a generation of teachers as a major American writer. Two short years later, however, he was all but ignored in the most ambitious work of American literary history in the last forty years.

Critical responses to Dashiell Hammett have not always been as extreme as the previous examples suggest. During the five years in which he published his five novels, the response to his work was fairly uniform, and where there was disagreement it was not about whether to praise his achievement, but how far to go in one's praise of it. From 1929 to 1934, few doubted Hammett's supremacy in the field of detective fiction. Here, the critics agreed, was an American original, a distinctive voice that was revitalizing a tired genre. Others, however, went further in their praise, demanding that Hammett be placed not only at the top of his genre but also at the top of American literature. Whether Hammett was a better artist than S.S. Van Dine was not an issue. Whether Hammett was the equal of Hemingway, Lardner, and Fitzgerald, this was perhaps the one point of serious critical contention between 1929 and 1934. In fact, the only critic who continually remained unimpressed by Hammett's achievement was Hammett himself. In a 1932 interview with the author, Elizabeth Sanderson recounted Hammett's critical response to his own work: "He considers *The Dain Curse* a silly story, *The Maltese Falcon* 'too manufactured,' and *The Glass Key* not so bad—that the clews were nicely placed there, although nobody seemed to see them" (518).

Fortunately, the critics were more willing to trust the tales than the teller. Although a reviewer for the *Boston Evening Transcript* observed that "when [*Red Harvest*] is all over the reader wonders just what it was all about" (3), Hammett's first novel was generally well-received. Walter Brooks claimed that he and his colleagues at *Outlook and Independent* gave it an "A plus before we'd finished the first chapter" (274). In *Bookman*, Herbert Asbury doubted "if even Ernest Hemingway has ever written more effective dialogue than may be found within the pages of [*Red Harvest*]." According to Asbury, Hammett's novel was "the liveliest detective story that has been published in a decade" (92). *The Dain Curse*, published in the same year as *Red Harvest*, fared just as well. In the *New York Herald Tribune*, Will Cuppy recommended the novel for "its weird characters and really astonishing speed" (11), and in the *New York Times* Bruce Rae praised "the racy narrative style of the author's detective mouthpiece" (16). Moreover, Walter Brooks and his colleagues once again chimed in with high praise: "We can think of only one story of the kind better than this second book of Mr. Hammett's, and that is his first" (552).

With the 1930 publication *The Maltese Falcon* Hammett secured his most enthusiastic contemporary response. Brooks not only reshuffled his ordering of Hammett's novels, moving *The Maltese Falcon* ahead of *Red Harvest*, but he also argued for the larger merits of the work: "This is not only probably the best detective story we have ever read, but it is an exceedingly well-written novel. There are few contemporaries who can write prose as clean-cut, vivid and realistic" (350). In the upscale *Town and Country*, William Curtis concurred, claiming that "Mr. Hammett has something quite as definite to say, quite as decided an impetus to give the course of newness in the development of the American tongue, as any man now writing" (qtd. in Layman 113). "There is nothing like [Hammett's] books in the whole range of detective fiction," wrote Donald Douglas in the *New Republic*. "The plots don't matter so much," Douglas contended, "[but] the art does; and there is an absolute distinction of real art" (226).

While never quite generating the same kind of unreserved enthusiasm as *The*

Maltese Falcon, Hammett's next two novels, *The Glass Key* and *The Thin Man*, continued to increase his reputation. Despite Will Cuppy's claim that *The Glass Key* was "about twice as good as *The Maltese Falcon*" (13), most critics concurred with Bruce Rae, who predicted that "Mr. Hammett's new book is bound to find favour, although probably not as much as was accorded . . . *The Maltese Falcon*" (23). In the *New Yorker*, Dorothy Parker confirmed Rae's suspicion when she admitted that *The Glass Key*, while a "good and enthralling" novel, "seems to me nowhere to touch its predecessor" (84). In responding to *The Thin Man*, most critics agreed with Peter Quennell, who characterized Hammett's final novel as "not only an absorbing and extremely ingenious 'thriller,' but [also a work that] contains portraits, snatches of dialogue . . . that Hemingway himself could not have improved on." For Quennell, "*The Thin Man*—unusually brilliant read as a detective story—has every right to consideration on its literary merits" (801). T.S. Matthews, however, argued against the brilliance of *The Thin Man*. While noting that Hammett's latest novel was "still head-and-shoulders above any other murder mystery published since" *The Glass Key*, Matthews declared that *The Thin Man* "seems a less excitingly fresh performance than, say, *The Maltese Falcon*." "Now that Dashiell Hammett is beginning to be taken seriously by the highbrows," Matthews confessed, "my first enthusiasm for him is beginning to cool a little" (395).

It is only after we move away from contemporary responses to Hammett's fiction do we see, if not a cooling of enthusiasm, then at least a warming up of critical dissent. Early on characterized almost exclusively by praise for Hammett's achievement, the critical response since then has generated an engaging, and sometimes maddening, disagreement as to the respective merits of the five novels. As noted earlier, André Gide considered *Red Harvest* a "remarkable achievement," and elsewhere, against popular opinion, he hailed the novel as "far superior to *The Falcon*." For Gide, *Red Harvest* is Hammett's greatest achievement, a novel which could "give pointers to Hemingway or even to Faulkner" (*Journals* 191). In the early 1940s, Robert Graves, while not as rhapsodic as Gide, tabbed *Red Harvest* as "an acknowledged literary landmark" (qtd. in Nolan, *Casebook* 46), and the general consensus is that *Red Harvest* is a carefully-crafted and innovative novel. As Geoffrey O'Brien put it in 1981, "The hardboiled novel was born complete in *Red Harvest* in 1929, after a decade of experiments in the pages of *Black Mask*. . . . [and it remains] a remarkably original and brilliant exercise in the American language" (68). Where there is dissent about the novel, it usually echoes the sentiments of Peter Wolfe: "Too many bullets fly; too many bombs explode; too much blood is spilled. [The] brutality [of *Red Harvest*] is numbing, not exciting" (91).

The critical assessment of *The Dain Curse* is more varied than that of *Red Harvest*. Gide, who loved everything else Hammett ever wrote, could not recall the title of this second novel. All he could remember was that it seemed "obviously written on order" (*Journals* 191). In turn, Alvarez characterizes *The*

Dain Curse as "wandering, melodramatic, a bit silly, and, with its supernatural trimmings, not at all typical" (169), and Wolfe, while he sees *The Dain Curse* as a "notable advance from *Red Harvest*" (94), still warns us that the work never becomes a "solid, serious novel" (110). For William Nolan, *The Dain Curse* is not as bad as many critics have contended, but it indeed "marked a plateau, not an upward step" (*Casebook* 51) in Hammett's artistic development. On the other hand, William Marling defends *The Dain Curse* as "a novel of sophisticated intent" (57), Sinda Gregory argues persuasively for its "innovative cleverness" (175), Robert Edenbaum considers in "by far the most complicated of the novels," and Philip Durham praises it as the work in which "Hammett reached his peak" (70).

Durham's pronouncement aside, most critics consider *The Maltese Falcon* the peak of Hammett's achievement. William Patrick Kenney hails *The Maltese Falcon* as "one of the remarkable achievements in American crime fiction" (108), Robert Schulman calls it Hammett's "most precise and suggestive work" (401), Sinda Gregory characterizes it as "a brilliantly unified novel whose imagery, character development, style, and theme are closely interwoven" (88), and Bernard Schopen believes *The Maltese Falcon* "demands that [Hammett] be ranked among the important writers of the period" (180). Moreover, Hammett's two most important disciples, Chandler and Ross Macdonald, consider *The Maltese Falcon* the pinnacle of Hammett's career. While Chandler had high praise for the book—"*The Maltese Falcon* may or may not be a work of genius, but an art which is capable of it is not 'by hypothesis' incapable of anything" (58)—perhaps Macdonald best expresses the immediate and continued admiration critics have had for Hammett's third novel: "*The Maltese Falcon* broke the barrier of the genre; it was, and is, a work of art."

The Glass Key and *The Thin Man* were both well-received upon publication, but since then they, like *The Dain Curse*, have met with disparate critical assessments. Nolan, for instance, describes *The Glass Key* as "a perplexing, frustrating book" (*Casebook* 69), Wolfe labels it a "scamped, evasive novel" (146), and Gregory marks it as "Hammett's most frustrating and puzzling work . . . a less artistically satisfying book" (116) than his first three novels. Furthermore, Edenbaum, in one of the most influential essays on Hammett, judges *The Glass Key* to be "Hammett's least satisfactory novel" (100). On the other hand, William Marling hails *The Glass Key* as "one of Hammett's best novels" (97), Julian Symons considers it "the peak of Hammett's achievement" (*Mortal Consequences* 139), and fellow crime novelist Rex Stout praises the novel as "more pointed and profound . . . than anything Hemingway ever wrote" (Lochte 213). According to Paul Gray, *The Glass Key*, along with *The Maltese Falcon*, is responsible for Hammett's "international reputation" (73), and biographer Diane Johnson believes it to be "as elegant and controlled in style as anything [Hammett] ever wrote" (85).

When *The Thin Man* first appeared, Alexander Woollcott and Sinclair Lewis were among the many voices to praise Hammett's final novel. Woollcott called *The Thin Man* "the best detective story yet written in America" and Lewis proclaimed that "*The Thin Man* is certainly the most breathless of [Hammett's] stories" (qtd. in Nolan, *Casebook* 86). Since then, however, such praise for *The Thin Man* as been, well, thin. According to the usually sympathetic Howard Haycraft, Hammett's last novel is "his least typical and least important contribution" (171), showing "a distinct softening of the author's talents" (170). Roger Sale agrees, characterizing the novel as "an inconsequential effort" (20), and Wolfe takes this all a step further by professing that "*The Thin Man* robs Hammett's career of a sense of artistic growth or deepening vision" (162). Russell Nye concurs, claiming that "the heart of Hammett's work lies in his first four novels" (259) and, Richard Layman, in a very direct assessment, proclaims that "After *The Glass Key*, Hammett was ruined as a novelist" (115). And yet *The Thin Man* has found a few champions. Gregory suggests that *The Thin Man* "may be [Hammett's] most subtle and, in certain ways, his most controlled work" (177), Alvarez characterizes Hammett's last novel as "smarter, more deliberately sophisticated" (169) than the rest, and Julian Symons praises it as "a continually charming and sparkling performance" (*Mortal Consequences* 140). Moreover, George J. Thompson declares that "Because the critics have been more interested in determining what the novel is not rather than what it is, they have isolated weaknesses that should more properly be seen as strengths, strengths that are intrinsically connected with Hammett's intention to render a dark vision" (28). According to Thompson, *The Thin Man* does not, as Wolfe would have us believe, rob Hammett's career of a sense of artistic growth or deepening vision. It is not, as crime-novelist Robert Parker has suggested, "Hammett's weakest effort" (118); rather, *The Thin Man* is an indispensable novel, without which Hammett's career, achievement, and vision cannot be fully appreciated.

Similarly, we cannot fully appreciate Hammett's critical reputation by merely discussing contemporary book reviews and subsequent responses to individual works. Certainly, all critical reputations begin with book reviews, and, as we have seen, the immediate response to Hammett was, for the most part, laudatory. But critical reputations are only begun, not made, by contemporaries. One of America's most talked about writers from 1929 to 1935, Hammett fell out of critical discourse for the remainder of the decade. Whereas in his 1932 memoir, *Death in the Afternoon,* Ernest Hemingway was telling the world that he had once asked his wife to read aloud to him from *The Dain Curse,* and whereas in 1935 Gertrude Stein proclaimed that in all of California there were only two people she would like to meet, Charlie Chaplin and Dashiell Hammett, by decade's end critics were ignoring Hammett's work. They, like he, had lapsed into silence.

By the early 1940s, however, critical appreciation of Hammett began to re-emerge. Overseas, in *The Long Week-end: A Social History of Great Britain 1918-1939* (1940), Robert Graves and Alan Hodge determined that "Of all the detective novelists of the period only one, the American Dashiell Hammett, happened to be . . . a first-rate writer" (301). In 1941, back here in the States, Howard Haycraft wrote the first sustained commentary on Hammett's fiction. In *Murder for Pleasure: The Life and Times of the Detective Story*, Haycraft devoted five-plus pages to Hammett, offering an assessment that would be repeated many times by later critics:

> Because of their startling originality, the Hammett novels virtually defy exegesis even to-day—though their external pattern is by now all too familiar by process of over-much imitation. As straightway detective stories they can hold their own with the best. They are also character studies of close to top rank in their own right, and are penetrating if often shocking novels of manners as well. They established new standards for realism in the genre. Yet they are as sharply stylized and deliberately artificial as Restoration Comedy, and have been called an inverted form of romanticism. They were commercial in inception; but they miss being Literature, if at all, by the narrowest margins. (171)

By 1944, Gide, Wilson, and Chandler were submitting their own assessments—Gide and Chandler concurring with Haycraft that Hammett's work missed being literature, if at all, by the narrowest margins; Wilson professing that Hammett's most admired novel missed being even good detective fiction (and that, if it belonged anywhere, it belonged not in the margins of literature but in the middle of the comics page).

At the close of the decade, David T. Bazelon published in *Commentary* magazine the first critical essay devoted solely to Hammett's work. In "Dashiell Hammett's Private Eye: No Loyalty Beyond the Job" (1949), Bazelon discovers "the chief concern of Dashiell Hammett's art" to be the "ascendancy of the job in the lives of Americans" (468). Furthermore, he senses an abdication of moral responsibility in Hammett's fiction, complaining that "the question of doing or not doing a job competently seems to have replaced the whole larger question of good and evil" (470). Bazelon's conservative politics no doubt inform his dislike for Hammett's fiction, but his mostly unsympathetic essay marks Hammett as worthy of serious critical attention. Until this essay, critical discourse about Hammett focused on little else but his innovations within the detective genre. While Bazelon does not particularly like what he sees in Hammett's fiction, he finds in it something more than generic innovation and cleverness—he finds a social, political, and moral vision that, however distasteful, deserves—and can sustain—thoughtful commentary.

In the 1950s, however, critics did not follow Bazelon's example. The silence and misprision that characterize the critical response to Hammett during this decade can be attributed, in part at least, to politics. Hammett's association with the Communist party drew scorn upon him and his work, a scorn that, more often than not, resulted in critical silence. Where attention was paid, it was mixed and, unfortunately, misleading. In "The Decline and Fall of the Detective

Story" (1953), Somerset Maugham praised Hammett as "an inventive and original writer," and reserved special recognition for *The Maltese Falcon*, Hammett's "most convincing novel," and Sam Spade, "a nasty bit of goods, but . . . admirably depicted" (126). But in *The Development of the Detective Story* (1958), A.E. Murch had little to say about Hammett, except that his novels began a kind of "vogue for over-emphasis, a cult of exaggerated realism" (227). Leo Gurko was even more hostile. In *Heroes, Highbrows and the Popular Mind* (1953), Gurko labelled the private eye "begotten" by Hammett in *Red Harvest* as "sensual and amoral," a man who "survived in a bloody world, only because he lost less blood than the opposition and because he had mastered better than they the fine points of Darwinian ethics" (187). Gurko's attack on the amorality of the genre, and by extension the amorality of Hammett's vision, echoes Bazelon's earlier charge, but whereas Bazelon's critique stemmed from a careful reading of Hammett's work, one suspects—at least when reading the following misrepresentation of *Red Harvest*—that Gurko is more familiar with Hammett's imitators than with Hammett himself:

> In that early book, at any rate, the private eye went through maneuvers soon destined to become a classic. Hired to find some important object (a jade necklace, an I.O.U., an incriminating photograph) our hero, aged thirty to forty and in excellent physical condition, finds himself at the beginning of a maze. He lives from incident to incident with no clear notion until the very end where they are leading him and who the major criminal is. As in the adventures of [Dreiser's] Cowperwood, slices of erotica and slices of violence are pasted together as far as the eye can reach. On the average he makes love to three or four sexually magnetic women, consumes four or five quarts of hard liquor, smokes cartons of cigarettes, is knocked on the head, shot, and bruised in fist fights from seven to ten times—while groping his way through a fog as far as breaking the case is concerned. . . . He is no more hampered by scruples than Dreiser's robber baron, and is playing for high stakes (if not money, then in life) in the same kind of dangerous universe. (187-188)

There is more Mike Hammer in this description than Continental Op. Yes, the Op does move through events with little clear notion where events are leading him (he is, in his own words, simply "stirring things up"), and, yes, fist fights and shoot-outs are plenty in *Red Harvest*. But the Op never makes love to any woman (much less four or five "sexually magnetic women") and while Poisonville gets the best of the Op (he does indeed go "blood-simple") it is only because his scruples fail him, not because he is unhampered by them.

Gurko's misreading of Hammett gives credence to Haycraft's contention that "Like all originators, Dashiell Hammett has suffered at the hands of his imitators" (173). With the emergence of Mickey Spillane and his masochistic Mike Hammer in the late 40s and early 50s, Dashiell Hammett's reputation suffered a serious setback. In this case of literary kinship, it seems, the sins of the son were visited upon the father. Leslie Fielder's discussion of hardboiled fiction in *Love and Death in the American Novel* (1960) is evidence of this. Fiedler begins: "As it has descended the long way from Sam Spade to Mike Hammer, the proletarian thriller has come to treat the riddle of guilt and innocence more and more perfunctorily, as its occasion rather than its end. . . Murder laced with lust, mayhem spiced with nymphomania: this is the formula for the chief surviving form of the murder mystery in America" (476-477). To his credit, Fiedler is in this passage distinguishing between Hammett and Spillane, suggesting a corruption of the genre as it moves from father to son. But if we continue on in the same paragraph we notice that the distinction between Hammett and Spillane is not simply blurred, but erased—first by eliding the difference between Spillane and Chandler, and then the difference between Chandler and Hammett. Eventually the "crude" Spillane and the "pretentious" Chandler are subsumed within Hammett's "own school":

> Not only in the cruder and more successful books of Mickey Spillane, but in the more pretentious ones of Raymond Chandler, the detective story has reverted to the kind of populist semi-pornography that once made George Lippard's *The Monks of Monk Hall* a black-market best-seller. . . .[E]ven as a hundred years ago, such readers relish thinking that the sadist fantasies in which they find masturbatory pleasure are revelations of social disorder, first steps toward making a better world. "The realist in murder," Hammett writes of his own school, "writes of a world in which gangsters can rule nations and almost rule cities, in which hotels and apartment houses and celebrated restaurants are owned by men who made their money out of brothels, and in which a screen star can be the finger-man for a mob . . . ." And through this world, he continues, walks the private eye, the man of honor who is also the poor man, the common man. "If there were enough like him," Chandler concludes, "the world would be a safe place to live in. . . " (477)

Fortunately, most critics no longer lump together Hammett and Hammer, Spade and Spillane, though at first the temptation appears to have been great. Several important publishing events in the 1960s helped to correct the misreadings of the 1950s. First, in 1965 Knopf reset the 1942 *Complete Dashiell Hammett* and republished it as *The Novels of Dashiell Hammett*. More significantly, the following year Random House published *The Big Knockover*, a collection of ten tales, including the never before published "Tulip," Hammett's unfinished novel. With an introduction by Lillian Hellman, this collection received much critical attention, garnering significant laudatory reviews in the *Nation*, the *National Review*, *Book Week*, the *Atlantic*, the *New York Times Book Review*, and *Newsweek*. For instance, Anthony Boucher professed that "It is impossible to overstate the importance of Dashiell Hammett to the American detective story (or, I believe, to American literature)," and he hailed the collection as "one of the year's major books" (22). In his own review, Frederick Gardner bemoaned the fact that soon after Hammett started writing "imitators proliferated and Hammett . . . became typecast as the founder of the hard-boiled school of detective fiction" (455). Gardner insisted on Hammett's distinctiveness, confessing that "Hammett is due for a renaissance and I hope *The Big Knockover* hastens it" (456).

With its focus on the Continental Op, *The Big Knockover* reminded critics that Hammett's achievement extended well beyond Sam Spade and Nick and Nora Charles. More importantly, however, the collection challenged many readers to recognize the vast differences between Hammett and his imitators, differences which had been all but forgotten in the previous decade. For instance, in his review of *The Big Knockover*, Richard Schickel first remarked on the difference between Hammett and the writer he supposedly imitated: "Hammett has been frequently put down as an imitation of Hemingway, but reading these early stories, one is impressed by how much Hammett was his own man." While admitting that Hammett was "not, of course . . . Hemingway's equal," Schickel does observe that there is "less affectation, less self-consciousness than in the average Hemingway piece. And in Hammett the lines never go limp with sentiment and only rarely become overly mannered in their cadences" (14). After noting the differences between Hammett and Hemingway, Schickel takes a more important step, highlighting the significant differences between Hammett and the writers who supposed imitated him. In the following passage we hear a rebuke not only of Spillane and his "school" but also of critics like Gurko and Fielder:

> The Op neither strips nor tortures women; he fights only after someone else fires the first punch or shot; and in the cool description of the ensuing action, the nastier details are never lingered over. . . . As for the masochistic delights a James Bond appears to feel when a Goldfinger or a Blofeld is working him over, The Op would suspect his mind of failure if he felt such weird emotions welling up within him. In short, there is a purity in these stories that is now quite lost to the adventures and mysteries that are currently derived from the tradition Hammett established. (15)

The Novels of Dashiell Hammett and *The Big Knockover* gave readers in the 1960s easy access to almost all of Hammett's fiction, and thus helped to ready him for the "renaissance" Gardner predicted. *Tough Guy Writers of the Thirties* (1968), a collection of critical essays issued by Southern Illinois University Press, included three essays on Hammett's fiction, and intimated that this renaissance was indeed underway. It is difficult to overstate the importance of these three pieces. Philip Durham's "The *Black Mask* School" was the first essay to survey the achievement of Hammett's short fiction; Irving Malin's "Focus on *The Maltese Falcon*: The Metaphysical Falcon" was the first essay devoted solely to a single Hammett novel; and Robert Edenbaum's "The Poetics of the Private Eye: The Novels of Dashiell Hammett" was the first essay to consider how Hammett's fiction contained within it a critique of the very values it seemed to promote. The pieces by Malin and Edenbaum have proven especially important to later critics, the first for its emphasis on mutability and ambiguity as the foundation of Hammett's fiction, and the latter for its insights into how

Hammett's novels, while portraying a hero "free of sentiment, of the fear of death, of the temptations of money and sex," nonetheless "present a 'critique' of the tough guy's freedom as well" (81). 1968, then, marks the year that Hammett's fiction entered the domain of academic discourse (with apologies to Walter Blair, whose "Dashiell Hammett: Themes and Techniques" appeared in 1967, but whose work has had less of an impact than Durham, Malin, and Edenbaum).

The renaissance of the 1960s was capped off with the publication of William Nolan's *Dashiell Hammett: A Casebook* (1969), the first book devoted solely to Hammett. Nolan himself recognized the limited scope of his work, warning the reader that his study "is not, nor does it pretend to be, a definitive treatment. Until Lillian Hellman, who controls [Hammett's] estate, releases the full Hammett papers, including now-restricted letters, unpublished manuscripts, and various personal documents, no comprehensive study can be successfully undertaken" (vii). Still, Nolan's work—which received an Edgar Allan Poe Special Award in 1970 from the Mystery Writers of America—blends biography and criticism (much more of the former than the latter) in an informative and perceptive manner. The most valuable aspect of Nolan's study, however, was his "Dashiell Hammett Check-List." Here, for the first time, was a complete list of primary materials, a list which included all of Hammett's novels and story collections, as well as his magazine fiction, magazine articles, book introductions, book reviews, poetry, *Black Mask* letters, newspaper articles, anthology appearances, and radio work. Nolan's checklist remained the definitive bibliography until 1979, when Richard Layman published his *Dashiell Hammett: A Descriptive Bibliography*.

The momentum of the late 1960s carried over into the next decade. In 1972, *The Armchair Detective* began serializing George J. Thompson's seven part dissertation, "The Problem of Moral Vision in Dashiell Hammett's Novels." With an introduction, a chapter apiece on the five novels, and a conclusion, Thompson's study was the first extensive critical analysis of Hammett's fiction (the first dissertation on Hammett, William Patrick Kenney's 1965 "The Dashiell Hammett Tradition and the Modern Detective Novel," devoted less than one third of its pages to Hammett). Thompson's study pays careful attention to previous critical responses to Hammett (especially those forwarded by Durham, Malin, and Edenbaum), thus making him the first critic to manifest an interest in both Hammett's fiction and the critical discourse concerning that fiction. According to Thompson, "even Raymond Chandler, who was one of Hammett's most ardent admirers, failed finally to perceive the full complexity and artistry in [Hammett's] works. Too often what one comes away with after reading the critical material on Hammett—reviews, critiques, and analyses—are rather stereotyped notions that he is the founder of the so-called hardboiled detective novel, that his style is bare-boned, hard, muscular, realistic prose, and that his heroes are coldly methodical, machine-like creations." Such stereotypes are "unfair or misleading"; furthermore "they encourage us to see him as a static writer, repeatedly employing the same formulas in only slightly varying patterns" ("Problem" 155). The intent of Thompson's dissertation is to correct this image of Hammett as a "static writer," forwarding instead the assertion that Hammett's five novels reveal a "developing artistic pattern of moral and social vision" ("Problem" 155). In his final chapter, Thompson concludes that with each novel "we increasingly become aware of a darkening authorial vision" ("Conclusion" 126), a vision that eventually drove Hammett into silence. More than twenty years after its publication, Thompson's dissertation remains an often-cited source, and his attempt to read the novels as a narrative of darkening authorial vision has encouraged other critics to proffer their own interpretations of Hammett's evolving poetics.

The 1970s also saw the publication of other important critical responses. In "The First Thin Man" (1972), Donald K. Adams offered an intriguing analysis of Hammett's aborted 1931 draft of *The Thin Man*, which exists today as an unpublished sixty-five page typescript housed in the E.T. Guymon, Jr. Collection of Detective and Mystery Fiction at Occidental College. William Ruehlman devoted a chapter to Hammett in his *Saint with a Gun: The Unlawful American Private Eye* (1974), and John G. Cawelti, in his landmark *Mystery, Adventure and Romance: Formula Stories as Art and Popular Culture* (1976), praised Hammett's work as manifesting "both an awareness of earlier literary models and a continual interest in such literary effects as irony and paradox" (164). In "Dashiell Hammett in the Wasteland" (1978), H. H. Morris compared Hammett to the high modernists, concluding, however, that "while Eliot holds out the hope of the impending rescue by Parsifal, Hammett never suggests that any man can enter the ruined tower and find the Holy Grail" (202). For Paul F. Kress the point of comparison was A. Conan Doyle rather than T.S. Eliot. In "Justice, Proof, and Plausibility in Conan Doyle and Dashiell Hammett" (1977), Kress examined "the considerable distance that separates [the] moral and intellectual universes" of Conan Doyle and Hammett, concluding that "our loss of faith in the ontology of 1895 which supported Doyle's belief in an 'objectivist' science of detection and demonstration has a parallel in the erosion of confidence in our public institutions to render justice" (131-32), an erosion that is borne out in the novels of Dashiell Hammett. Other important contributions from the decade include George Grella's comparison of Henry James and Hammett in "The Wings of the Falcon and the Maltese Dove," Kathleen Hulley's "From Crystal Sphere to Edge City: Ideology in the Novels of Dashiell Hammett," and David Glover's carefully argued interdisciplinary venture, "Sociology and the Thriller: The Case of Dashiell Hammett."

But no discussion of Hammett's critical reception in the 1970s would be complete without mention of two other events: the serial appearance of Lillian Hellman's three part autobiography (*Unfinished Woman* [1969], *Pentimento* [1973], and *Scoundrel Time* [1976]) and the 1974 publication of *The Continental Op*, with its enormously influential introduction by Steven Marcus. Hellman's memoirs helped to make Hammett, more than a decade after his death, something of a *cause célèbre*. *Unfinished Woman*, winner of the 1969 National Book Award, included a revised version of Hellman's introduction to *The Big Knockover*, and thus brought even wider attention to Hammett's work. 1973's *Pentimento* not only continued to keep Hammett fresh in the public imagination but it also continued to add to the posthumous mystique that Hellman was carefully cultivating about her longtime companion. As one critic said in her review of the memoir, "Though he appears infrequently [in *Pentimento*], Hammett steals every scene he is dragged into" (Duffy 114). Moreover, when *Pentimento* was made into the 1977 film *Julia*, millions of Americans were treated to Jason Robards's Oscar-winning performance as Hammett.

Random House's decision to publish *The Continental Op* in 1974 may have indeed been influenced by the growing interest in Hammett that Hellman's memoirs were creating. The seven stories in *The Continental Op* had all previously appeared in the 1966 hardcover issue of *The Big Knockover*. Curiously, however, whereas *The Big Knockover* was well-received, *The Continental Op*, which contained no story that was not in *The Big Knockover*, was met with some disfavor. Leonard Michaels thought many of the stories "absurd—unintentionally absurd," and predicted that "Sooner or later someone will compare them to the fiction of Kafka, Beckett, Handke, et al., if somebody hasn't already made that mistake" (1). Moreover, Roger Sale argued that "the stories are inferior work . . . and [that] those who come to Hammett for the first time via this volume will get only snatches that show why anyone should read him. With a writer who is very limited at his best, this kind of exposure is especially unwelcome" (74). The merits of the stories aside, the lasting importance of *The Continental Op* is to be found in its introduction. Here, in twenty pages, Steven Marcus changed the direction of Hammett studies, bringing to his analysis of Hammett's work a sensibility shaped by recent developments in literary theory. In what has become perhaps the most influential approach to Hammett's fiction, Marcus set out "to construct a kind of 'ideal type' of a Hammett or Op story" (xviii). Here is what he discovers:

> The Op is called in or sent out on a case. Something has been stolen, someone is missing, some dire circumstance is impending, someone has been murdered—it doesn't matter. The Op interviews the person or persons most immediately accessible . . . Guilty or innocent, they provide the Op with an account of what they know, of what they assert really happened. . . . What [the Op] soon discovers is that the "reality" that anyone involved will swear to is in fact itself a construction, a fabrication, a fiction, a faked and alternate reality—and that it has been gotten together before he ever arrived on the scene. And the Op's work therefore is to deconstruct, decompose, deplot and defictionalize that "reality" and to compose or reconstruct out of it a true fiction, i.e., an account of what "really" happened. (xix)

But were this all, Marcus contends, the Op—and Hammett—would be doing nothing different than what we find in the classical detective story. Called in to "deconstruct, decompose, deplot, and defictionalize," however, the Op never achieves the kind of "disambiguation" arrived at by the classical detective. Instead, the Op replaces the "fictions" of the criminals with his own "fiction," which "may also be 'true' or mistaken, or both at once." Thus Hammett, through the Op, is not only trying to "make the fictions of others visible as fictions, inventions, concealments, falsehoods, and mystifications," but he is also trying to suggest that "what is [finally] revealed as 'reality' is still a further fiction-making activity. . . . [nothing but] a narrative, a coherent yet questionable account of the world" (xxi). Several reviewers of *The Continental Op* found these conclusions a bit pretentious—Sale called Marcus's observations a "fancy way to say something pretty obvious" (75) and another reviewer called them simply "pompous" (Review of *The Continental Op* 74)—but the ideas expressed in this introduction have exerted enormous influence ever since. Marcus's metafictional and mildly-deconstructionist approach to Hammett has been embraced and developed further by a number of perceptive critics, including Sinda Gregory, Jasmine Yong Hall, David J. Herman, Carl Freedman, Christopher Kendrick, and, most recently, Bruce Gatenby. Two decades after its publication, Marcus's introduction continues to suggest productive avenues for inquiry, and no understanding of the critical reception of Dashiell Hammett is complete without it.

   Despite these advances in critical response and exegesis, Hammett entered the 1980s as a neglected figure in American literary studies. But if he entered the decade as such, he exited it in a completely different fashion. During the 1980s, three major biographies were published: Richard Layman's *The Shadow Man: The Life of Dashiell Hammett* (1981), Nolan's *Hammett: A Life at the Edge* (1983), and Diane Johnson's *Dashiell Hammett: A Life* (1983). Moreover, within five years five book-length studies appeared: Peter Wolfe's *Beams Falling: The Art of Dashiell Hammett* (1980), William Marling's *Dashiell Hammett* (1983), Dennis Dooley's *Dashiell Hammett* (1984), Julian Symons's *Dashiell Hammett* (1985), and Sinda Gregory's *Private Investigations: The Novels of Dashiell Hammett* (1985). In addition, John S. Whitley and Paul Skenazy each issued monographs comparing Hammett and Chandler (*Detectives and Friends: Dashiell Hammett's "The Glass Key" and Raymond Chandler's "The Long Goodbye"* [1981] and *The New Wild West: The Urban Mysteries of Dashiell Hammett and Raymond Chandler* [1982]), and several books contained helpful chapters or essays on Hammett (Edward Margolies's *Which Way Did He Go? The Private Eye in Dashiell Hammett, Raymond Chandler, Chester Himes, and Ross Macdonald* [1982], Stoddard Martin's *California Writers* [1983], Bernard Benstock's *Art in Crime Writing* [1983], Cynthia Hamilton's *Western and Hardboiled Detective Fiction in America* [1987], and Brian Docherty's *American Crime Fiction:* [1988]). Furthermore, articles on Hammett appeared in academic journals as diverse as the *Centennial Review*, the *Southwest Review*, *Proteus*, and the *Journal of American Studies*, and Robert F. Skinner published an important secondary bibliography, *The Hardboiled Explicator: A Guide to the Study of Dashiell Hammett, Raymond Chandler, and Ross Macdonald* (1985).

The three biographies were met with everything from high praise to outright disdain. Like Nolan's 1969 casebook, Layman's *Shadow Man* was written without Lillian Hellman's assistance—or, as Layman puts it, "written without her assistance and without hindrance from her" (x). In his preface, Layman promises his readers that "Facts are important things," and that "Research has taken precedence over invention and speculation" in the preparation of his biography. As a result, of the three biographies *Shadow Man* contains the most accurate and thorough information. Several reviewers, however, lamented the fact that, in sticking only to facts, Layman never really tried to get at Hammett's true character. According to Mary Cantwell, "Mr. Layman's biography is a stream of facts and critical exegeses, but it is devoid of interpretation. Hammett remains opaque, less a celebrity in need of a biographer than a character in need of a novelist" (20). Paul Grey agrees in part, but he is more accurate in his assessment of *Shadow Man*: "Layman avoids speculation and sticks to the facts. This approach inspires both trust and a question: What kind of man, finally, was Hammett? . . . . *Shadow Man* tells a fascinating and tantalizing story. It also suggests just how cleverly the old detective covered his tracks" (73). Despite its self-imposed limitations, *Shadow Man* provides detailed information about many lesser-known parts of Hammett's life (for instance, his stint as advertising manager at Samuel's Jewelry Company in 1926, or his role as editor-in-chief of *The Akadian* during the Second World War). In addition, Layman proves to be a perceptive and opinionated critic of Hammett's fiction, especially the short stories. Layman's title suggests he was well aware that his subject would be, in the end, elusive, and, if one considers the speculative excesses of Diane Johnson's later biography, Layman's decision to err on the side of caution makes his work, while limited, certainly the most reliable to date.

Nolan's *Dashiell Hammett: A Life at the Edge* is not a mere updating of his 1969 volume. As Nolan said of his first book, "Its purpose was to serve as a basic reference on Hammett's writing." The new book, however, is an attempt "to bring Hammett, the man as well as the writer, out of the shadows, to render him in full dimension for the reader" (xii). Nolan's biography is less scholarly than Layman's and, as can be expected, there is a good deal of overlapping information, but the two books complement each other well. Nolan's biography has more of a narrative turn than Layman's, and its lighter tone and style do allow for a somewhat different portrait of Hammett to emerge. Like Layman, Nolan is careful with his facts and reads the fiction with an appreciative but discerning eye. And yet, as one reviewer observed, "[While] Mr. Nolan writes perceptively of the novels . . . [and] exhaustively of the events in Hammett's life . . . Hammett himself remains a shadowy figure. It is as if one knew everything, and nothing, about this strange and gifted man" (Review of *Dashiell Hammett: A Life at the Edge* 97). The problem, of course, is less with Nolan or Layman than with their elusive subject. If Hammett somehow escapes these two biographers it is not because they have not done their research, but rather because Hammett seems to have wanted it this way. Read in tandem, however, these two biographies give us the best picture of Hammett we have and, we may have to admit, the best picture we are likely to get.

Neither Layman nor Nolan had access to the letters and manuscripts possessed by Lillian Hellman. Diane Johnson did. According to Johnson, *Dashiell Hammett: A Life* "could not have been written without the cooperation of Hammett's friend and executrix, Lillian Hellman" (xiii). Because of this, many expected Johnson's work to be the definitive biography, the study that would finally bring the shadow man into the light. For the first time Hammett's letters—both professional and personal—were to be made public, and because of the special access provided to her by Hellman's blessing, Johnson was able to solicit interviews with many people who had heretofore remained silent. But of all the biographies, Johnson's is the most disappointing. Certainly, the biography has its champions. In a front page appraisal in the *New York Times Book Review*, George Stade hailed it as "cool, steady-eyed, and engrossing" (1), concluding that "This biography is better written and more shapely than its predecessors . . . . [Johnson] adds many new facts and gets very few of the old ones wrong" (35). In *Newsweek*, Peter Prescott agreed, noting that "Johnson has done her research well . . . [and] she writes her biography as a fiction writer would—which is to say with appropriate twists and a breezy style" (86). Others, however, attacked Johnson for both her facts and her style. Julian Symons called Johnson's biography a "deeply disappointing book" whose "failure springs from Johnson's inability to order and shape the material at under hand." "The book's chief weakness, apart from the sloppiness of the writing," Symons concludes, "is that it is a portrait of Nick Charles rather than of Dashiell Hammett" ("The Daring" 8). In his own review, William Nolan had fewer problems with the style of the biography than with the facts it contained. In "Setting the Record Straight on *Dashiell Hammett: A Life*," Nolan lists more than two dozen factual errors in the work, claiming that Johnson has written a "biography that distorts rather than illuminates, a book riddled with factual errors and wrong-headed conjectures" (38). Even a sympathetic reviewer such as Constance Casey, who prefers Johnson's biography to either Layman's or Nolan's, feels compelled to draw attention to the errors in the biography (639). In the end, Johnson's book reads too often like a collage of primary materials (sometimes chapters appear to be nothing more than a compilation of one letter or one interview after another). In addition, she has little to say about Hammett's fiction—at times, in fact, she seems determined to ignore it—and when she does discuss it she gets some fundamental facts wrong (such as her assertion that Donald Willsson in *Red Harvest* is killed by his father). But the most disturbing fact of her biography is her decision to move freely in and out of the minds of her subjects, like a third-person omniscient narrator. Such movements lead her to repeatedly speculate on what it was this or that person must have been thinking at this or that given moment. For a novelist, this is fine; for a biographer, it is very risky.

This is not to say Johnson's biography is without merit—there is information here that one cannot get anywhere else, letters and draft fragments and personal notes that, in the right hands, may lead to some perceptive reevaluations of Hammett's fiction. But the general reader must approach this biography with great care.

Dealing with the work rather than the man, the five critical studies from the 1980s exhibit diverse ambitions, concerns and conclusions. Both Wolfe and Dooley devote nearly half their studies to Hammett's short fiction, Wolfe because the stories "remain the least read and least understood of the canon" (44), Dooley because "It was here [in the short stories] that Hammett honed his craft as a writer and first explored many of the themes and techniques and fictional situations that were too preoccupy him throughout his career" (xiii). Both books, of course, discuss the five novels (Wolfe in greater detail than Dooley) but, unlike Wolfe, Dooley is guided by a specific premise, an attempt to elaborate Hammett's "moral perspective." For Dooley "Hammett's deeper concerns . . . are essentially spiritual in nature—a fact that has not sufficiently been noted" (xv) by previous critics. Dooley and Wolfe differ not only in their approaches, but also their conclusions. Dooley claims that "As a writer [Hammett] asked important questions and ventured some bold answers . . . and he showed us things about our society and our very language—the way we talk and they way we think about our lives—that have become a permanent part of what we know" (xv). Wolfe, while still admiring Hammett's achievement, reaches a less laudatory conclusion, stressing not what Hammett was able to say, but what he refused to say, focusing not on Hammett's moral perspective but on his lack of moral vision:

> He would write about his experiences, but not about how they touched his heart. His feelings he kept to himself, but at the cost of relegating his works to the ranks of minor fiction. Major literature, always a combined self-exploration and self-discovery, conveys the author's feelings about both himself and his environment. Hammett didn't test himself deeply enough to give his work this finality and scope. Moral vision *qua* psychological thrust exists but marginally in the canon. (4)

In his 1983 study, William Marling reaches a conclusion somewhere between Dooley and Wolfe, positioning Hammett just below the major writers but well above the minor ones. According to Marling, Hammett "stands, as Malraux tried to argue, between the realism of Dreiser and Crane and the modernism of Hemingway and Pound. Though not the equal of these writers, he stands above James M. Cain, John O'Hara, or James T. Farrell. He had the ability, as major writers do, to break genres and make something new of them" (128). Marling's study was the first to benefit from Layman's *Shadow Man*, and the opening and closing chapters of his work have a biographical focus. The middle four chapters—"The Short Stories," "The *Black Mask* Novels," "The Falcon and The Key," and "Lillian and *The Thin Man*"—focus on the fiction. While the format of the Twayne Series usually demands a good deal of plot summary, Marling manages to offer insightful readings of the fiction while still giving the plot coverage his format calls for. His section on the short stories is limited to what he terms "the best of the anthologized pieces," but in limiting his scope he allows himself the space to elaborate on the merits of the stories he has chosen. In this chapter, his reflections on Hammett's style are especially keen, and in a few short pages he makes a strong case that Hammett's "was a made, not a found, style" (46). Overall, Marling's study mixes biography and criticism, coverage and close reading, in a concise and persuasive manner.

Sprinkled throughout with movie stills, news photos, and handsome snapshots of first editions and paperback reissues, Julian Symons's *Dashiell Hammett* is intended for a popular audience. Though little concerned with Hammett's life before he became a writer, Symons's study is still more biography than criticism, and although there is little new information in this book, its lucid and occasionally witty prose make it perhaps the best general introduction to Hammett. On the other hand, Sinda Gregory's *Private Investigations* is clearly intended for an academic audience. Unlike the other book-length critical works from this decade, Gregory's study focuses only on the novels, contains only cursory biographical information, and concerns itself primarily with aesthetic and metafictional issues. Examining "the interplay between form and content" (28) in Hammett's novels, Gregory follows an "analysis of the principle formal features of the novels" with an analysis of "how these features contribute to the development of Hammett's main thematic interests—the nature of personal relationships, the limits of reason, the concept of order, and various metafictional issues" (29). With such an approach, Gregory reads *Red Harvest* as "an ethical inquiry into system making" (60), *The Dain Curse* as "a novel about how we impose a fictional sense of order in our lives and in our literature" (61), *The Maltese Falcon* as "a declaration of the omnipotence of mystery and of the failure of human effort . . . to ever dispel it" (88) *The Glass Key* as an unsuccessful attempt to "affirm the circumfluent quality of mystery that must always overpower our attempts to order and interpret our lives" (116), and *The Thin Man* as a work of "metaphysical skepticism" (171). Informed but not overwhelmed by literary theory, Gregory's work is the most accomplished of all the book-length studies. Moreover, in her conclusion Gregory asks, and then answers persuasively, a series of suggestive questions about Hammett.

[G]iven the predisposition to dismiss [the hard-boiled detective story] as inconsequential literature, why did Hammett write only in this form? Was he hesitant to attempt a "serious" novel because he doubted his skill? Most puzzling of all, why would a writer who insisted so resolutely on the ultimate mystery of the human experience work within the very medium most committed to solving and eliminating mystery? The answer seems to lie in Hammett's conviction that the notion of mystery's supremacy is best illustrated by showing its power to withstand our attempts to dismantle it. (178)

In addition to all these biographies and book-length studies, the 1980s produced a nearly a dozen important journal articles and book chapters that deserve more attention than can be given here. These studies include John S. Whitley's "Stirring Things Up: Dashiell Hammett's Continental Op" and David Glover's rebuttal "The Frontier of Genre: Further to John S. Whitley's 'Stirring Things Up: Dashiell Hammett's Continental Op'" (1980-81), James F. Maxfield's "Hard-Boiled Dicks and Dangerous Females: Sex and Love in the Detective Fiction of Dashiell Hammett" (1985), Robert Schulman's "Dashiell Hammett's Social Vision" (1985), John Anderson's "The World of *The Maltese Falcon*" (1988), Gary Day's "Investigating the Investigator: Hammett's Continental Op" (1988), Christopher Bentley's "Radical Anger: Dashiell Hammett's *Red Harvest*" (1988), William Murray's "Riddle of the Key" (1989), and two pieces by William Marling ("The Hammett Succubus" [1982] and "The Style and Ideology of *The Maltese Falcon*" [1989]).

The 1990s have yet to produce any book-length studies or new biographies, but an important body of work reflecting diverse critical approaches has already emerged in the first few years of the decade. For instance, in "Forms of Labor in Dashiell Hammett's *Red Harvest*" (1991), Carl Freedman and Christopher Kendrick combine Marxism and post-structuralism in their attempt to show not only how the Op's primary "labor" is "dialogic" but also how "the generic composition of the novel" has "political resonances and implications" (210). In "Jameson, Genre, and Gumshoes: *The Maltese Falcon* as Inverted Romance" (1990), Jasmine Yong Hall blends Northrop Frye's archetypal structuralism with Fredric Jameson's speculative Marxism. As a result, she looks at the novel "through the filter of romance in order to highlight the historical differences between the romance structure which originates in a Christian, feudal society, and the novel which is produced in a capitalist, monied one" (110). David J. Herman approaches Hammett's fiction from a feminist perspective informed by deconstruction. In "Finding out about Gender in Hammett's Fiction: Generic Constraints or Transcendental Norms?" (1991), Herman examines Hammett's "syntactic laws of gender," especially the ideologically complex images of androgyny in the early fiction, and makes a strong case that "the absence of androgyny in the later works represents not an increased conservatism about gender, but rather an interpretive code according to which gender itself becomes multiple and complex" (6). In "Dashiell Hammett and the Challenge of New Individualism: Rereading *Red Harvest* and *The Maltese Falcon*" (1990), Christopher Metress situates Hammett's novels within the cultural discourse about individualism that dominated the first three decades of this century. Placed alongside such works as Herbert Croly's *The Promise of American Life*, Herbert Hoover's *American Individualism*, and John Dewey's *Individualism Old and New*, *Red Harvest* and *The Maltese Falcon* emerge as texts in which Hammett, like the social and political philosophers of his day, "examines the possibility of refashioning the inherited impulses of nineteenth-century individualism into a 'better, brighter, broader [new] individualism' which seeks, either through allegiance and/or willing submission, to promote collective rather than individual needs" (246-47). Finally, in two essays written specifically for this collection, Bruce Gatenby reexamines *The Dain Curse* through the postmodernism of Lyotard and Derrida, and Larry Anderson, in the only essay to date on *Woman in the Dark*, investigates Hammett's manipulation of romance and convention in this unjustly-forgotten 1933 novella.

The Critical Response to Dashiell Hammett is the first collection of critical essays devoted solely to Hammett. Containing almost twenty complete essays, as well as more than thirty reviews and short commentaries, this collection surveys sixty-five years of critical response to one of America's most widely-read authors. The collection is divided into six chapters (followed by a selected bibliography of further criticism). Each of the first five chapters focuses on a specific Hammett novel, while the sixth chapter contains more general essays. This sixth chapter is arranged chronologically, beginning with an excerpt from Howard Haycraft's 1941 *Murder for Pleasure* and ending with Anderson's 1994 essay on *Woman in the Dark*. The five chapters which focus on the novels open with selected book reviews. Following these reviews, I have placed short commentaries lifted from larger works. Sometimes I have selected these commentaries because they happen to come from important writers (Gide, Wilson, Rex Stout, James M. Cain, Donald Westlake, etc.) but more often than not these passages have a thematic focus. For instance, the short commentaries on *Red Harvest* each discuss the extent of the novel's Marxist politics, the selections concerning *The Maltese Falcon* focus on the heroism or anti-heroism of Sam Spade, the passages on *The Thin Man* defend or attack the artistic merits of the novel. These short commentaries are followed by two, sometimes three, full-length essays which represent the best in Hammett criticism. While the present volume stands as the most comprehensive collection to date, various limitations prohibit inclusion of many worthy critical pieces, most notably David Glover's "Sociology and the Thriller: The Case of Dashiell Hammett," Philip Durham's "The *Black Mask* School," and two pieces by William Marling, "The Style and Ideology of *The Maltese Falcon*" and "The Hammett Succubus." Bibliographical information about these and other works is included in the "Additional Readings" section at the end of the collection.

When André Gide praised Dashiell Hammett in the 1944 essay cited at the very beginning of this introduction, he offered the following apology: "If I speak of Hammett it is because I seldom hear his name mentioned" (186). Today, of course, no such apology is necessary. With three biographies, five critical studies, and more than fifty book chapters and journal articles devoted to his work in the last fifteen years, there is no longer a shortage of critical response to Dashiell Hammett. But this increase in attention has by no means secured him a place within the American canon. Despite all the recent gestures toward diversity and inclusiveness in literary studies, and despite the fact that more than ninety percent of his work remains in print, Hammett is, at best, a shadow man in the American academy. For instance, none of the major college anthologies—Norton, Heath, McMillian, etc.—include a single selection by Hammett. However, as courses in genre fiction continue to increase in popularity on American campuses, the deceptively simple art of Dashiell Hammett should begin to reach a wider academic audience. And as this art is studied in greater detail, teachers may come to realize that *The Maltese Falcon* belongs not beside *The Murder of Roger Ackroyd* but *The Great Gatsby*, that *The Dain Curse* explores the same epistemological issues as *The Crying of Lot 49*, that *The Glass Key* predates by more than two decades the themes and techniques of the French *nouveau roman*. Whatever the outcome of his critical reputation, we can, with apologies to Raymond Chandler, know one thing for certain: the last sixty years have shown us that Dashiell Hammett is both a common writer and an unusual writer, the best in his genre, and a good enough writer for any genre, any time, any place.

WORKS CITED

Alvarez, A. "The Thin Man." *Spectator* 11 February 1966: 169-170.

Asbury, Herbert. Review of *Red Harvest. Bookman* March 1929: 92.

Bazelon, David T. "Dashiell Hammett's Private Eye: No Loyalty Beyond the Job." *Commentary* 7 (1949): 467-72.

Boucher, Anthony. Review of *The Big Knockover. New York Times Book Review* 26 June 1966: 22.

Brooks, Walter. Review of *Red Harvest. Outlook and Independent* 13 February 1929: 274.

_____. Review of *The Dain Curse. Outlook and Independent* 31 July 1929: 552.

_____. Review of *The Maltese Falcon. Outlook and Independent* 26 February 1930: 350.

Cantwell, Mary. "The Lady and the Pinkerton." *New York Times Book Review* 23 August 1981: 9.

Casey, Constance. "Downhill All the Way." *Nation* 17 December 1983: 639-41.

Cawelti, John G. *Adventure, Mystery and Romance*. Chicago: U of Chicago P, 1976.

Chandler, Raymond. "The Simple Art of Murder." *Atlantic Monthly* December 1944: 53-59.

Cuppy, Will. Review of *The Dain Curse. New York Herald Tribune* 11 August 1929: 11.

_____. Review of *The Maltese Falcon. New York Herald Tribune* 26 April 1931: 13.

Dooley, Dennis. *Dashiell Hammett*. New York: Ungar, 1984.

Douglas, Donald. "Not One Hoot For the Law." *New Republic* 9 April 1930: 226.

Duffy, Martha. Review of *Pentimento* by Lillian Hellman. *Time* 1 October 1973: 114.

Durham, Philip. "The *Black Mask* School." *Tough Guy Writers of the Thirties*. Ed. David Madden. Carbondale: Southern Illinois UP, 1968. 51-79.

Edenbaum, Robert I. "The Poetics of the Private Eye: The Novels of Dashiell Hammett." *Tough Guy Writers of the Thirties*. Ed. David Madden. Carbondale: Southern Illinois UP, 1968. 80-103.

Elliott, Emory (ed). *Columbia Literary History of the United States*. New York: Columbia UP, 1988.

Fiedler, Leslie. *Love and Death in the American Novel*. New York: Stein and Day, 1966.

Freedman, Carl and Christopher Kendrick. "Forms of Labor in *Red Harvest.*" *PMLA* 106 (1991): 209-221.

Gardner, Frederick. "The Return of the Continental Op." *Nation* 31 October 1966: 454-56.

Gide, André. "An Imaginary Interview." Trans. by Malcolm Cowley. *New Republic* 7 February 1944: 184, 186.

_____. *The Journals of André Gide*. Chicago: Northwestern UP, 1987.

Graves, Robert and Alan Hodge. *The Long Week-end: A Social History of Great Britain 1918-1939*. London: Faber, 1941.

Gray, Paul. "He Was His Own Best Whodunit." *Time* 20 July 1981: 73.

Gregory, Sinda. *Private Investigations: The Novels of Dashiell Hammett*. Southern Illinois UP, 1985.

Gurko, Leo. *Heroes, Highbrows and the Popular Mind*. New York: Bobbs-Merril, 1958.

Hall, Jasmine Yong. "Jameson, Genre, and Gumshoes: *The Maltese Falcon* as Inverted Romance." *The Cunning Craft: Original Essays on Detective Fiction*. Macomb: Western Illinois UP, 1990. 109-19.

Haycraft, Howard. *Murder for Pleasure: The Life and Times of the Detective Story*. New York: Appleton-Century, 1941.

Herman, David J. "Finding out about Gender in Hammett's Detective Fiction: Generic Constraints or Transcendental Norms?" *Genre* 24 (Spring 1991): 1-23.

Johnson, Diane. *Dashiell Hammett: A Life*. New York: Random, 1983.

Kenney, William Patrick. "The Dashiell Hammett Tradition and the Modern Detective Novel." Diss. University of Michigan, 1964.

Kress, Paul F. "Justice, Proof, and Plausibility in Conan Doyle and Dashiell Hammett." *Occasional Review* 7 (Winter 1977): 119-43.

Layman, Richard. *Shadow Man: The Life of Dashiell Hammett*. New York: Harcourt, 1981.

Lochte, Richard S. "Who's Afraid of Nero Wolfe?: An Interview with Rex Stout." *The Armchair Detective* 3 (1970): 211-14.

Marcus, Steven. Introduction to *The Continental Op* by Dashiell Hammett. New York: Random, 1974.

Marling, William. *Dashiell Hammett*. Boston: Twayne, 1983.

Matthews, T.S. "Mr. Hammett Goes Coasting." *The New Republic* 24 January 1934: 316.

Maugham, Somerset. "The Decline and Fall of the Detective Story." *The Vagrant Mood*. Garden City: Doubleday, 1953. 101-132.

Metress, Christopher. "Dashiell Hammett and the Challenge of New Individualism: Rereading *Red Harvest* and *The Maltese Falcon*." *Essays in Literature* 17 (1990): 242-60.

Michaels, Leonard, "The Continental Op." *New York Times Book Review* 8 December 1974: 1, 20, 22, 26.

Morris, H.H. "Dashiell Hammett in the Wasteland." *Midwest Quarterly* 19 (Winter 1978): 196-202.

Moss, Leonard. "Hammett's Heroic Operative." *New Republic* 8 January 1966: 32-34.

Murch, A.E. *The Development of the Detective Story*, 1958.

Nolan, William. *Dashiell Hammett: A Casebook*. Santa Barbara: McNally & Loftin, 1969.

_____. *Hammett: A Life at the Edge*. New York: Congdon & Weed, 1983.

_____. "Setting the Record Straight on *Dashiell Hammett: A Life*." *The Armchair Detective* 17 (1984): 360-367.

Nye, Russell. *The Unembarrassed Muse*. New York: Dial, 1970.

O'Brien, Geoffrey. *Hardboiled America: The Lurid Years of the Paperbacks*. New York: Van Nostrand Reinhold, 1981.

Parker, Dorothy. "Oh Look—Two Good Books!" *New Yorker* 25 April 1931: 83-84.

Parker, Robert B. "The Violent Hero, Wilderness Heritage and Urban Reality: A Study of the Private Eye in the Novels of Dashiell Hammett, Raymond Chandler and Ross Macdonald." Diss. Boston University, 1971.

Prescott, Paul. "The Original Thin Man." *Newsweek* 17 October 1983: 86.

Quennell, Peter. Review of *The Thin Man*. *New Statesman* 26 May 1934: 801.

Rae, Bruce. Review of *The Dain Curse*. *New York Times Book Review* 18 August 1929: 16.

_____. Review of *The Maltese Falcon*. *New York Times Book Review* 3 May 1931: 23.

[Review of *The Continental Op* by Dashiell Hammett. Intro. by Steven Marcus]. *The Critic* 33 (March-April 1975): 74.

[Review of *Hammett: A Life at the Edge* by William F. Nolan]. *Economist* 17 September 1983: 97.

Sale, Roger. "The Hammett Case." *On Not Being Good Enough*. London: Oxford UP, 1979. 73-80.

Sanderson, Elizabeth. "Ex-detective Hammett." *Bookman* Jan-Feb 1932: 516-18.

Schickel, Richard. "Dirty Work." *Book Week* 28 August 1966: 14-15.

Schopen, Bernard. "From Puzzles to People: The Development of the American Detective Novel." *Studies in American Fiction* 7 (1979): 175-89.

Schulman, Robert. "Dashiell Hammett's Social Vision." *Centennial Review* 29 (Fall 1985): 400-19.

Stade, George. "Mysteries of a Hardcase." *The New York Times Book Review* 16 October 1983: 1, 34-35.

Symons, Julian. *Mortal Consequences*. New York: Schocken, 1973.

_____. "The Daring and the Chatter." *Times Literary Supplement* 27 January 1984: 78.

Thompson, George J. "The Problem of Moral Vision in Dashiell Hammett's Detective Novels." *Armchair Detective* 6 (1972): 153-56.

_____. "Conclusion: The Problem of Moral Vision in Dashiell Hammett's Detective Novels." *Armchair Detective* 8 (1974): 124-30.

Wilson, Edmund. "Why Do People Read Detective Stories?" *New Yorker* 14 October 1944.

Wolfe, Peter. *Beams Falling: The Art of Dashiell Hammett*. Bowling Green: Bowling Green U Popular Press, 1980.

Chronology

1894 Born to Richard and Annie Bond Hammett, May 27, St. Mary's County.

1908 Drops out of Baltimore Polytechnic Institute.

1915 Joins Pinkerton Detective Agency.

1918 Enlists in Motor Ambulance Corps, US Army, Camp Mead, Maryland.

1919 Discharged honorably from the army.

1920 In May, moves to Spokane, Washington, and rejoins the Pinkertons.
November, hospitalized for tuberculosis. Meets Josephine Dolan, a nurse.

1921 In June, moves to San Francisco. Joins the local Pinkerton branch.
Marries Josephine Dolan, July 7.
Mary Jane Hammett, daughter, is born, October 15.
December 1, Hammett resigns from Pinkertons.

1922 October, first story, "The Parthian Shot," published in *Smart Set*.
First *Black Mask* story, "The Road Home," published.

1923 October 1, first Op story, "Arson Plus," published in *Black Mask*.

1926 March, becomes ad manager at Samuels Jewelry Co. in San Francisco.
May 24, second daughter, Josephine, born.
July 20, resigns position at Samuels.

1927 Begins two-year stint reviewing mysteries for *The Saturday Review*.
November, serialization of *Red Harvest* begins in *Black Mask*.

1928 November, serialization of *The Dain Curse* begins in *Black Mask*.

1929 February 1, *Red Harvest* published by Knopf.
July 19, *The Dain Curse* published by Knopf.
September, serialization of *The Maltese Falcon* begins in *Black Mask*.
Marriage breaks-up. Hammett moves to New York.

1930 February 14, *The Maltese Falcon* published by Knopf.
February, Paramount releases *Roadhouse Nights*, based on *Red Harvest*.
March, serialization of *The Glass Key* begins in *Black Mask*.
April, begins six-month stint reviewing for the *New York Evening Post*.
Signs with Paramount. Moves to Hollywood and meets Lillian Hellman.

1931 January 20, *The Glass Key* is published by Knopf.
Writes screenplay for *City Streets*.
Begins, then abandons, *The Thin Man*.
May, Warner Brothers releases first *Maltese Falcon* film.

1933 December, *The Thin Man* is published in *Redbook*.

1934 January 8, *The Thin Man* published by Knopf.
Writes screenplay for *Woman in the Dark*.
Begins writing the comic strip *Secret Agent X-9*.
March 24, *Collier's* publishes "This Little Pig," Hammett's last story.
June, MGM's *The Thin Man*, released.

1935 May, Universal releases *Mr. Dynamite*, based on Hammett's screen story
"On the Make."
June, *The Glass Key* released by Paramount.

1936 July, Warner Brothers releases *Satan Met a Lady*, a second film version
of *The Maltese Falcon*.
December, *After the Thin Man*, based on a Hammett story, released.

1937 February, Hammett sells MGM all rights to *The Thin Man* characters for
$40,000.
August, a Mexican court grants Josephine Hammett a divorce.

1939 Random House announces a new Hammett novel, *There Was a Young
Man*. Novel is never published.
November, *Another Thin Man*, based on an original Hammett story,
released by MGM.
Fired by MGM.

1940 Named national chairman of Committee on Election Rights.

1941 October, John Huston's *The Maltese Falcon* released by Warner Brothers.

1942 September, enlists in the US Army. Stationed at Fort Monmouth, NJ.
     November, *The Shadow of the Thin Man* is released by MGM.
     October, Paramount releases a second movie version of *The Glass Key*.

1943 September, transferred to Alaska.
     Screenplay of Lillian Hellman's *Watch on the Rhine* filmed by MGM.

1944 January 19, edits first issue of *The Adakian*, a daily newspaper for army.
     Continues editing newspaper until April of 1945.

1945 January, *The Thin Man Goes Home* is released by MGM.
     September, honorably discharged from US Army.

1946 Begins working on radio series *The Adventures of Sam Spade* and
          The Fat Man.
     June, elected president of New York Civil Rights Congress.

1947 *Song of the Thin Man*, last of the *Thin Man* series, filmed.

1951 July, testifies in United States District Court about the activities of the
     Civil Rights Congress bail fund. Sentenced to six months in prison for
     contempt of court.

1952 Begins *The Tulip*, an unfinished novel.

1953 March 26, Hammett testifies before Joseph McCarthy's House Committee
          on un-American Activities.
     Abandons *The Tulip*.

1955 August, sufffers a heart attack at Lillian Hellman's house in Martha's
     Vineyard.

1956 Sued by government for back taxes.

1961 Dies, January 10, at Lennox Hill Hospital, New York City.
     Buried, January 13, Arlington National Cemetary.

The Critical Response
to Dashiell Hammett

Red Harvest

Reviews

It is doubtful if even Ernest Hemingway has ever written more effective dialogue than may be found within the pages of this extraordinary tale of gunmen, gin and gangsters. The author displays a style of amazing clarity and compactness, devoid of literary frills and furbelows, and his characters, who race through the story with the rapidity and destructiveness of machine guns, speak the crisp, hard-boiled language of the underworld. Moreover, they speak it truly, without a single false or jarring note, for Mr. Hammett, himself an old-time Pinkerton detective, knows his crime and criminals through many years of personal contact. Those who begin to weary of the similarity of modern detective novels, with their clumsily involved plots and their artificial situations and conversations, will find their interest revived by this realistic, straightforward story, for it is concerned solely with fast and furious action and it introduces a detective who achieves his purposes without recourse to higher mathematics, necromancy or fanciful reasoning. It reads like the latest news from Chicago.

Mr. Hammett's hero, an operative of a private detective agency, who tells the story, is confronted by a mystery when he arrives in Personville, a western town so wicked that its citizens call it Poisonville, but it is a mystery of no particular consequence and he quickly gets to the bottom of it by simply employing common sense and his powers of observation.

Thereafter, he performs no miracles whatsoever. But in a moment of panic, soon regretted, Personville's big political and business boss hires him to rid the town of its gunmen and gangsters, and he proceeds to do the job by acting as a sort of "agent provocateur" among the criminal cliques, inciting one against the other by superb manoeuvering until in successive bursts of blazing fury they have destroyed themselves. He thus sets the local underworld by the ears and, in one way or another, he is concerned with no fewer than a score of killings. For a considerable period the detective is in doubt whether he may have committed one of the murders himself, for he awakens from a laudanum-and-gin debauch with the handle of an ice pick clutched in his hand and the steel sliver buried in a girl's breast. The chapter in which this excellent crime occurs is one of the high spots of the liveliest detective story that has been published in a decade. [Herbert Asbury, *The Bookman* March 1929: 92]

A thriller that lives up to the blurb on the jacket is unusual enough to command respect. When, in addition, it is written by a man who plainly knows his underworld and can make it come alive for his readers, when the action is exciting and the conversation racy and amusing—well, you'll want to read it. A detective from San Francisco goes to the city of Personville to break up the ring of thugs who control the town. He splits them into factions which turn the town into a battlefield. Knives and blackjacks and pistols and bombs and machine-guns have accounted for some twenty-five or thirty people by the time he finishes his job. And the book is full of vivid writing. The storming of Pete the Finn's stronghold in Whiskeytown is as real a fiction battle as we've ever attended.

We recommend this one without reservation. We gave it A plus before we'd finished the first chapter. [Walter Brooks, *Outlook and Independent* 13 February 1929: 274]

Red Harvest takes us to America again and to an almost inconceivable world. The English novelist who wants to write a story of peril and adventure has to go some distance from ordinary life. The municipal troubles of a small town would be of no service to him. The American novelist is luckier, for he can take the train from New York or Chicago and, if Mr. Hammett is to be believed, find mediaeval violence and uncertainty co-existent with a good tram service. What troubles me about Mr. Hammett's book is that his hero is so often shot at without being hit. This, in the romantic stories which transport us to Ruritanisa or some such neighbourhood, seems reasonable enough. When we begin to read such a book we consent to being transported into a fairy-tale atmosphere, where the eventual safety and triumph of the hero are, as it were, certified on the title-page. But it is not easy to reconcile this convention with the realistic atmosphere of the modern American story of adventure. Mr. Hammett's hero seems to me to come alive out of page after page by sheer good luck, and if his luck had ever failed, then there would have been an end to Mr. Hammett's story. But the mere fact that an author of obvious intelligence can write such a tale and persuade an American publisher to print it throws a valuable light on American conditions. If there is anywhere on the North American continent a town even remotely like Personville, then it is a sociological phenomenon which we must take into our reckoning, and I cannot believe that Mr. Hammett has made up Personville purely out of his desire to have a background for sensational happenings. [*New Statesman* 27 July 1929: 500]

From *The Journals of André Gide*

André Gide

Read with very keen interest (and why not dare to say with admiration) *The Maltese Falcon* by Dashiell Hammett, by whom I had already read last summer, but in translation, the amazing *Red Harvest*, far superior to the *Falcon*, to *The Thin Man*, and to a fourth novel, obviously written on order, the title of which escapes me. In English, or at least in American, many subtleties of the dialogues escape me; but in *Red Harvest* those dialogues, written in a masterful way, are such as to give pointers to Hemingway or even to Faulkner, and the entire narrative ordered with skill and an implacable cynicism. . . . In that very special type of thing it is, I really believe, the most remarkable I have read. Curious to read *The Glass Key*, which Malraux recommended so strongly to me, but which I cannot find.

From *The Pursuit of Crime*

Dennis Porter

Hammett's Poisonville resembles the cityscape of American naturalism, which is also that of the "valley of ashes" in *The Great Gatsby*. That is to say, it appears as the typical environment of an unregulated industrial capitalism, which acknowledges no limits to the pursuit of private wealth. Both detective hero and reader are, therefore, faced with the alienated product of human labor on the level of a total environment. Moreover, Hammett's example in this became a model for the hard-boiled genre, whether subsequent writers shared his radical tendencies or not. The cityscapes of his early writings are represented as perverted fiefdoms of the owners of capital and of those strong-arm men who support them and live off their greed. And the victims are ordinary citizens who have recourse neither to their political leaders nor to the law because both politics and law enforcement are part of the corrupt system. [Yale UP 1981: 198]

From *Shadow Man: The Life of Dashiell Hammett*

Richard Layman

After Hammett became active in leftist politics in the mid-1930s, it became fashionable to read *Red Harvest* as a Marxist statement on political corruption and the abuse of power by governmental officials who have no concern for their democratic responsibilities. That is an imaginative approach to Hammett's novel—or, in fact, to any of his writings—but a misguided one. Bill Quint, the IWW leader in Personville, is a hollow idealist whose arguments are unpersuasive. When he had an affair with Dinah Brand, she used information she got from him about planned IWW disruptions to play the stock market.

There are no masses of politically dispossessed people in *Red Harvest*—only a detective and a group of crooks. Hammett never used his fiction as a forum for his political beliefs. Indeed, he kept whatever political convictions he had in 1929 to himself. [Harcourt Brace Jovanovich 1981: 96]

From *Hammett: A Life at the Edge*

William F. Nolan

Some critics have described [*Red Harvest*] as a Marxist assault on capitalism, and certainly Hammett forcefully dramatized the evils of a system driven by greed. His message, however, was not overt. Hammett mixed his politics with his fiction, and he often dealt with the theme of political corruption, but his primary purpose was to tell a story, not to convert his readers. He was several years away from active political commitment—and by the time he entered the political arena he was no longer writing crime fiction. [Congdon & Weed 1983: 77-78]

From "Radical Anger: Hammett's *Red Harvest*"

Christopher Bentley

In *Red Harvest* Hammett implicitly attacks both free enterprise and democracy. The one is presented as exploitation and the other as corruption. But these flawed structures apparently evolved outside history, and they are unchanging realities. The Op moves in a fallen world, but we never learn how or when it fell; and Hammett offers no political formula that will redeem it. A contemporary wrote of one factual analogue of *Red Harvest*, a protracted employer-union-labour war in that part of southern Illinois called "Egypt":

"Socialism, communism, and other doctrines have played no part in the violence and murder which have brought such ill fame to this 'queen of Egypt.' The issues are strictly American, and the wrongs done are the native products of the United States." Whatever Hammett's political allegiance in later life, this is his attitude in *Red Harvest*. Without doctrine he can neither explain Personville (and the later Poisonville of which it is a part) nor cure it, and he remains an angry observer, his frustration finding some release in his detective's violence. Perhaps the eventual attraction of Communism for Hammett was that it claimed to provide the explanation and the cure. [*American Crime Fiction: Studies in the Genre*. Ed. by Brian Docherty. St. Martin's 1988: 68-69]

From *Adventure, Mystery, and Romance*

John G. Cawelti

Hammett's first full-length novel, *Red Harvest,* presents the confrontation of the Hammett hero with a world of crazy, irrational violence that nearly catches him up in an orgy of destruction. Only his common sense, his brutal cynicism and disillusion, and his technical skills as a manhunter save him from the torrent of chaos unleashed in the town of Personville by his own investigations. *Red Harvest* is a prime example of that rhythm of exposure and temptation that was designated in the preceding chapter as one of the major characteristics of the hard-boiled formula. The Op is called to Personville—known as Poisonville to many—by a newspaper editor, Donald Willsson. Before the Op can even see his client, Willsson is murdered. The Op soon discovers that Willsson had sent for a detective in connection with a paper crusade he planned to launch against the rampant corruption in Personville. At the center of this corruption lies Willsson's own father, the violent old mining baron Elihu Willsson. The older Willsson had run the town of Personville like a little kingdom of his own until challenged by the IWW. To break the power of organized labor, Willsson had brought in criminal-dominated gangs of strike-breakers. But, as a former labor leader tells the Op,

> old Elihu didn't know his Italian history. He won the strike, but he lost his hold on the city and the state. To beat the miners he had to let his hired thugs run wild. When the fight was over he couldn't get rid of them. He had given his city

to them and he wasn't strong enough to take it away from them.[1]

Finding his city dominated by such disreputable characters as "Whisper" Thaler, Pete the Finn, and Lew Yard, old Willsson gives his idealistic son the *Morning Herald* in the belief that a newspaper crusade against crime will help him to regain his old power. Willsson's gangster allies, suspecting his intentions, have apparently murdered his son to stop the crusade. Old Elihu doesn't show much interest in the connection between his son's murder and Personville's rampant corruption until, the next evening, a gangster named Yakima Shorty breaks into his home. At this point, Willsson decides that his former gangster allies are determined to kill him as well. He commissions the Op to clean up Personville.

The Op proceeds to apply the principle of divide and conquer. With information provided by a woman named Dinah Brand who has been the mistress of several of the men involved in Personville's gangs, the Op splits the various forces and brings them to a state of open war against each other. Explaining his technique to Dinah, the Op reveals the kind of stoical self-reliance that marks the Hammett hero:

> "The closest I've got to an idea is to dig up any and all the dirty work I can that might implicate the others, and run it out. Maybe I'll advertise—*Crime Wanted—Male or Female*. If they're as crooked as I think they are I shouldn't have a lot of trouble finding a job or two that I can hang on them." . . .
>
> "So that's the way you scientific detectives work. My God! for a fat, middle-aged, hard-boiled, pig-headed guy, you've got the vaguest way of doing things I ever heard of."
>
> "Plans are all right sometimes," I said. "And sometimes just stirring things up is all right—if you're tough enough to survive, and keep your eyes open so you'll see what you want when it comes to the top."[2]

The Op's stirring-up technique works beautifully at first. As he hears shooting break out all over the city, the Op purrs with satisfaction:

> Off to the north some guns popped.
>
> A group of three men passed me, shifty-eyed, walking pigeon-toed.
>
> A little farther along, another man moved all the way over to the curb to give me plenty of room to pass. I didn't know him and didn't suppose he knew me.
>
> A lone shot sounded not far away.
>
> As I reached the hotel, a battered black touring car went down the street hitting fifty at least, crammed to the curtains with men.
>
> I grinned after it. Poisonville was beginning to boil out under the lid, and I felt so much like a native that even the memory of my very un-nice part in the boiling didn't keep me from getting twelve solid end-to-end hours of sleep.[3]

If this represented the Op's final attitude toward the Personville situation only Hammett's style would differentiate his hero from a bloodthirsty manhunter like Mickey Spillane's Mike Hammer. But legitimating brutal aggression in the name of justice is not exactly Hammett's intention. Instead, as the violence in Personville mounts, driven on by his own machinations, the Op himself begins to lose his grip, caught up in the bloodlust.

> "This damned burg's getting me. If I don't get away soon I'll be going blood-simple like the natives. There's been what? A dozen and a half murders since I've been here. . . . I've arranged a killing or two in my time, when they were necessary. But this is the first time I've ever got the fever. . . . Play with murder enough and it gets you one of two ways. It makes you sick, or you get to like it."[4]

Additional ironies compound the ambivalence of the Op's position. It turns out that the killing of Donald Willsson, which initiated the slaughter, was committed by a bank clerk, jealous of Willsson's attentions to Dinah Brand. Thus it had nothing to do with underworld intrigue. When Elihu Willsson realizes this, he attempts to call the Op off the case. Moreover, the gangsters soon discover that internecine warfare can only lead to ruin. All parties concerned would like to bury the hatchet. The Op arranges a "peace conference" at old Willsson's house where he plays so effectively on the fears and jealousies of the assembled gangsters that a new orgy of violence breaks out almost before the meeting is over. Unlike most of the hard-boiled writers, Hammett does not ignore or evade the vicious implications of his hero's actions. The Op senses that he, too, is becoming a murderer. Speaking to Dinah Brand, who has become his ally, the Op bitterly explains the significance of what he did at the "peace conference."

> "I could have gone to [Elihu Willsson] this afternoon and showed him that I had them ruined. He'd have listened to reason. He'd have come over to my side, have given me the support I needed to swing the play legally. I could have done that. But it's easier to have them killed off, easier and surer, and, now that I'm feeling this way, more satisfying. I don't know how I'm to come out with the agency. The Old Man will boil me in oil if he ever finds out what I've been doing. It's this damned town. Poisonville is right. It's poisoned me.
>
> "Look. I sat at Willsson's table tonight and played him like you'd play trout, and got just as much fun out of it. I looked at Noonan and knew he hadn't a chance in a thousand of living another day because of what I had done to him, and I laughed, and felt warm and happy inside. That's not me. I've got hard skin all over what's left of my soul, and after twenty years of messing around with crime I can look at any sort of a murder without seeing anything in it but my bread and butter, the day's work. But this getting a rear out of planning deaths is not natural to me. It's what this place has done to me."[5]

The Op's personal immersion in violence reaches its climax in a drunken party with Dinah Brand. Trying to escape the emotional tension between his hatred of Personville and his doubts about the bloodlust into which his personal crusade to clean up the city has fallen, the Op gets drunker and drunker. Finally, he asks Dinah for a drink of laudanum and falls into a nightmarish semiconsciousness in which he dreams that he is hunting through a strange city for a man he hates. When he finds the man, he is on the roof of a tall building. The ending of the dream symbolizes the Op's own destruction in the violence he has sought.

> His shoulder slid out of my fingers. My hand knocked his sombrero off, and closed on his head. It was a smooth hard round head no larger than a large egg. My fingers went all the way around it. Squeezing his head in one hand, I tried to bring the knife out of my pocket with the other—and realized that I had gone off the edge of the roof with him. We dropped giddily down toward the millions of upturned faces in the plaza, miles down.[6]

When the Op awakes in the morning, he finds that he is holding an ice pick in his right hand and that the pick's "six-inch needle-sharp blade" is thrust into Dinah Brand's breast. But, instead of being devastated by the realization that he has killed a woman for whom he had begun to feel a real comradeship and affection, the Op becomes once again the detached and cynical professional with a job to do.

> I knelt beside the dead girl and used my handkerchief to wipe the ice pick handle clean of any prints my fingers had left on it. I did the same to glasses, bottles, doors, light buttons, and the pieces of furniture I touched or was likely to have touched.
>
> Then I washed my hands, examined my clothes for blood, made sure I was leaving none of my property behind, and went to the front door. I opened it, wiped the inner knob, closed it behind me, wiped the outer knob, and went away.[7]

At this point in the story, Hammett shifts the narrative focus from the Op as hunter to the Op as hunted. Instead of manipulator of forces and puppet-master of violence, the Op himself becomes a wanted man as the town explodes into a final chaos of violence. Such a shift is necessary to resolve the moral ambiguities of the Op's role without directly confronting the meaning of violence in such a way as to take *Red Harvest* out of the moral fantasy of heroic adventure and make it a mimetic action. To remain within the limitations of the hardboiled formula, Hammett must somehow pull his hero out of the moral dilemma created by his immersion in violence, thus freeing him from the devastating awareness of personal guilt. He does this by a device that has been well prepared for in the course of the novel and, as we saw in a previous chapter, became one of the foundations of the hard-boiled detective formula: the violence and corruption are finally attributed to the city itself, to Poisonville. Through this means, the Op is exonerated, his causal role in so many murders being legitimated as an act of purification. Finally, the Op tracks down the one surviving gang leader, now mortally wounded. This gangster makes a dying confession to the murder of Dinah Brand. With the elimination of the underworld elite and a final clean-up by the National Guard, the Op is able to leave the devastated city. "Personville, under martial law, was developing into a sweet-smelling and thornless bed of roses."[8]

Though he finally brings about the exoneration of his hero and the legitimation of his role as an agent of destruction and purifying violence, Hammett ironically undercuts this resolution in several ways. All the murder and destruction accomplish very little. As the Op himself realizes, the eventual result of his terrible crusade to purify Poisonville is that the city will be handed back to Elihu Willsson, "all nice and clean and ready to go to the dogs again." Purification through violence only prepares the way for another "red harvest." Moreover, as the orgy of murder reaches its climax, even the Op loses control over the process and the National Guard has to be called in to stand watch over the shambles of a city. This final scene brings to mind the conclusion of Akira Kurosawa's movie "Yojimbo," a Japanese analogue of *Red Harvest*. In the film's last scene, the samurai hero stands among the smoking ruins and scattered bodies of the town he has cleaned up. Turning to the old man who had originally begged him to break the power of the town's rival gangs, he says with bitter irony, "Well, old man. You'll have lots of peace and quiet now." Though the Op does finally discover that Dinah Brand was murdered by the gangster Reno Starkey, his essential guilt can hardly be escaped. Not only did his determination to purify Poisonville by setting the rival gangs against each other establish the motive for Dinah's murder, his own actions directly caused the killing. As Starkey tells the Op, he had come to Dinah's house the night of the murder in order to trap "Whisper" Thaler, but was suspicious that the trap might be for himself:

> "I'm leary that I've walked into something, knowing her. I think I'll take hold of her and slap the truth out of her. I try it, and she grabs the pick and screams. When she squawks, I heard man's feet hitting the floor. The trap's sprung, I think. . . . I don't mean to be the only one that's hurt. I twist the pick out of her hand and stick it in her. You gallop out, coked to the edges, charging at the whole world with both eyes shut. She tumbles into you. You go down, roll around till your hand hits the butt of the pick. Holding on to that, you go to sleep, peaceful as she is."[9]

Though he may not literally have struck the blow, the Op's hand held the weapon. Like Sam Spade in *The Maltese Falcon*, the conclusion of the Op's case requires the destruction of a woman who has offered him a wider range of emotion and fulfillment than the bleak and rigid rituals of the job. And the final irony is that there is not much sense of heroic completion to the Op's crusade. The final curtain of *Red Harvest* comes down to the tune of the Op's boss roasting him for his illegal tactics in Personville: "I might just as well have saved the labor and sweat I had put into trying to make my reports harmless. They didn't fool the Old Man. He gave me merry hell."[10]

In Hammett's hands what later became the hard-boiled story was a bitter and ironic parable of universal corruption and irrational violence. *Red Harvest* might be interpreted as a political parable—Personville being a symbol of the exploitative capitalistic society that has reached the point where its internal contradictions keep it in a state of perpetual corruption and chaos. Such a reading might fit the details of the novel and our knowledge of Hammett's personal ideological commitments, but it seems basically irrelevant to *Red Harvest*. Instead, the book suggests that underneath his radicalism Hammett was a bleak and stoical pessimist with no more real faith in a revolutionary utopia to come than in existing societies. Though *Red Harvest* distantly resembles other "proletarian" novels in which the clash of capital and labor in a gang-ridden company town leads to violence, there is no surge of optimistic hope for the future at the end. Proletarian novels usually ended with the conversion of the protagonist to a vision of the proletariat on the march, but *Red Harvest* leaves us with a bitter, fat, aging, and tired detective who has survived the holocaust only because he is harder and tougher and doesn't ask much out of life. The enemy that Hammett's bitter fictions found beneath the decadent facade of twentieth-century capitalist society was the universe itself. More than any other hard-boiled writer, Hammett's work reflects the vision of a godless naturalistic cosmos ruled by chance, violence, and death that dominates such major twentieth-century writers as Conrad, Crane, and Hemingway. Though his work is shaped by the formulaic imperatives of mystery, suspense, and the victorious protagonist, Hammett's stories have a philosophical power and seriousness beyond most other writers of hard-boiled detective stories. Like the greater works of Conrad, Crane, and Hemingway, his stories are essentially about the discovery that the comforting pieties of the past—belief in a benevolent universe, in progress, in romantic love—are illusions and that man is alone in a meaningless universe. [U of Chicago P, 1976: 168-173]

NOTES

1. Dashiell Hammett, *Red Harvest* (New York: Perma Books, 1956) 6-7.
2. Ibid, 96.
3. Ibid, 127.
4. Ibid, 130.
5. Ibid, 135.
6. Ibid, 136-37.
7. Ibid, 179.
8. Ibid, 178.
9. Ibid, 179.
10. Ibid, 179.

Forms of Labor in Dashiell Hammett's
Red Harvest

Carl Freedman and Christopher Kendrick

What kind of work does a detective do when he detects? Dashiell Hammett's most complex novel, *Red Harvest*, suggests some interesting answers. Originally published in book form in 1929, it counts as one of the first attempts—and perhaps still the greatest attempt—to forge a type of detective fiction that contrasts sharply with the classic deductive tradition most centrally identified with Sherlock Holmes. The new variety has been generally associated with the adjective *hard-boiled* and, especially during the 1920s and 1930s, with the American magazine *Black Mask*.[1] Perhaps its most obvious innovation was the abandonment of the intellectual-puzzle formula as the basis of narrative construction. Although *Red Harvest* is not without puzzles, its main interest lies elsewhere, and one can adequately summarize the text without even mentioning a "problem" of the Sherlockian type.

Red Harvest is set in Personville, also known as Poisonville, a small industrial city in the western United States. The workers at the Personville Mining Corporation, owned by Elihu Willsson, had been represented by the IWW, but the union local was crushed during a strike and the tough Wobbly leader, Bill Quint, was defeated. To beat the union, however, Elihu Willsson had enlisted the help of several gangster leaders and their thugs, and since their victory they have refused to leave and have insisted on taking a share in running the town. As the novel opens, an operative of the Continental Detective Agency has been summoned by Donald Willsson, Elihu's son and Personville's reform-minded newspaper editor. When Donald is killed before meeting with the Continental Op, Elihu himself hires the detective to "clean up" the town, that is, to remove the gangsters who have usurped much of Elihu's power and profit. The main action of the novel concerns the Op's successful efforts to carry out his charge. He consults with Bill Quint, forms a useful friendship with the community's leading courtesan, Dinah Brand, and, in general, acquires pertinent information about the structures and personalities of the town. Working his way into the highest levels of the gangster establishment, he eventually succeeds in setting the different gangs (one of which is technically the local police force) murderously against one another, with the result that the major gangster leaders are killed and their hold on the town destroyed.

Our detailed reading of *Red Harvest* centers on the term of our opening question, namely, work or labor. We argue that the narrative structure is based on several forms of labor, each autonomous and yet complexly interrelated with the others. Our greatest stress is on the linguistic or dialogic work of the Op and on the decentering symbolic impersonality of dialogue itself. We conclude by considering not only the generic composition of the novel but also its political resonances and implications. Work in the normative capitalist sense of productive wage-labor—that is to say, economic labor—is in fact absent from the manifest text of *Red Harvest*. But its absence is strongly determinate, conditioning—while contrasting with—three other forms of labor: the political, the linguistic, and the sexual. Economic labor that is normative under capitalism may be considered a determinate absence in two different ways. In the first place, the labor of the Continental Op himself is a paradigm of the "liberated" activity that constitutes an important part of detective fiction. For detective work might almost be called a bohemian kind of labor: as work that frees the worker from the homogenized space-time of most capitalist labor and that in so doing brings the powers of the "whole man" at least potentially into play, detective work is a peculiarly nonalienated variety of labor. And it is precisely because of the atypical, nonalienated character of this labor that normative, exploited, alienated wage-labor is largely displaced by the other forms of labor that the novel's world comprises. Second, and on the level of plot, economic labor, while invisible, remains the first and most fundamental term of the novel's chain of events. The gangster establishment of Poisonville depends, after all, on the breaking of the Wobbly-led strike, and the strike itself is a consequence of the intensely alienated and exploited labor performed at the Personville Mining Corporation.[2] The nameless miners are in a certain sense the collective protagonist of the novel, but their labor is never explicitly shown—we do not even know what they mine—and, after the first chapter, is never so much as mentioned.

What *is* shown—and indeed foregrounded, since it provides much of the novel's subject matter—is what we call political labor: the various practices of administration and violence established by the uneasy coalition among the capitalist Elihu Willsson, the gangsters hired to suppress the strike, and the gangsterlike local police. This political labor is, however, itself economic, not only because it ultimately owes its being—or, at least, its municipal hegemony—to the conditions of economic production at the Personville Mining Corporation but because it is immediately based on a (mostly illegal) service economy: bootlegging, gambling, smuggling, and the loan and bail-bond business. The gangster power structure, as it quickly moves into the center of the novel, cancels the vision of class struggle conveyed by Bill Quint and replaces it with a strictly intraclass politics whose forms of power are at once more monolithic and more individualistic than those of Quint's socialism. For though the novel describes the course of a prolonged conflict between Elihu and the gangsters (between "legitimate" and "illegitimate" capitalism) in which Elihu is the ultimate victor, for the greater part of the book the gangsters and Elihu appear to be parts of a single, monolithic power bloc that is dominated and defined by the gangsters. The gangsters' murderous activities generally appear to constitute the sole form of real political power, and Elihu usually seems to be just another gangster. At the same time, however, the gangsters' political structure is also radically individualist: their leaders must operate without the formal sanction of the state, and to retain command each must rely on the undependable personal loyalty of his own band of thugs. Hence even specifically gangster economics (e.g., bootlegging) are subordinated, in the telling, to gangster politics (e.g., gang warfare). The individualism of the gangster power structure makes for a permanent state of anarchic emergency that renders the gangsters vulnerable in a way that Elihu's capitalism never is. Whereas the position of the Personville Mining Corporation could be assaulted—and unsuccessfully at that—only by the collective action of the militantly organized working class, the actual defeat of the gangsters is triggered by the lone, chubby figure of the Continental Op (who is officially employed, not accidentally, by Elihu Willsson). His own labor, though directly political and thus indirectly economic, is in itself primarily linguistic.

For the Op's modus operandi, in *Red Harvest* as in many of Hammett's other fictions, is mainly dialogic: he "stirs things up" (in his own phrase) by making false suggestions, dispensing carefully calibrated doses of true information, and extracting verbal promises and commitments; most important, he subtly insinuates himself, primarily through his verbal style, into the criminal-political milieu of Personville as one thoroughly at home with its workings and hence capable of being a formidable ally or opponent. Thus, while the Continental Op, as the first major character in the *Black Mask* school of hard-boiled detective fiction, may be considered a paradigm of American macho, it is macho defined less as physical toughness (though he is physically tough) than as the ability to construct an authoritative rhetorical ethos—a point emphasized by his unprepossessing appearance: he stands five feet six and weighs 180 to 190 pounds.

The Op's emphatically rhetorical labor fits well with the gangster polity that he combats. His work, like the gangsters', is on the one hand apparently monolithic—inasmuch as discourse in this first-person novel presents itself as a total pregiven system—and on the other hand individualistic, inasmuch as discourse reflects the resource of the particular speaker and readily bears the stamp of the individual stylist. Hence, although political labor and linguistic labor may seem to exist on different planes, they are homologous; and this homology is a condition for the confrontation between them that forms the novel's main conflict—that is, the Op's war against the gangsters. In addition, however, that war, and indeed the Op's very work of detecting, can be seen to mask a deeper conflict between two modes of explanation (which are two worldviews), as both political and linguistic forms of labor are revealed to serve a common repressive function. Just as the vision of gangster politics displaces the vision of class struggle glimpsed in Bill Quint's story, so the Op's rhetoric, though in fact at the service of Elihu Willsson's capitalism, appears self-subsistent and thus also effaces the socioeconomic realities of class and production. Linguistic labor is also repressive in a more obvious and direct way. If the workers at the Personville Mining Corporation are the primary economic presence in the novel, then Dinah Brand is the primary sexual presence, and sexual labor on her part bears roughly the same relation to the Op's linguistic labor that the miners' economic labor does to the gangsters' political labor. For Dinah's sexual activity and desirability largely determine the Op's procedures, since only through sex does she obtain the information and personal contacts of which the Op makes crucial (and primarily linguistic) use. Yet the reader sees no more of Dinah copulating than of the miners mining, and the Op himself has as little to do with sexuality as the gangsters do with economic production. The Op—like every male, apparently—perceives Dinah's attractions, yet sex is emphatically repressed in favor of language: they just talk.

Each of these four forms of labor, however, animates each of the other three in ways still more complex than we have thus far suggested. We can consider some of these further complexities most conveniently by examining the novel's character structure. We may begin with those characters identified primarily with labor in its economic form—Bill Quint and Elihu Willsson. Neither Quint nor Elihu, however, directly represents economic labor in its classically capitalist sense, despite the fact that they "stand for" Labor and Capital, respectively. Even Quint, the character most able to speak of and for the wage-laborers (not one of whom ever makes even a walk-on appearance), is not actually a wage-laborer himself but, evidently, a full-time official of the IWW. He arrives on the scene (from Chicago, the traditional center of American working-class militancy) when Personville is on the verge of becoming Poisonville, that is, when the municipal economy has been plunged into crisis by Elihu's reneging on his agreements with the IWW local representing the miners—in other words, when the economic is presenting itself in a transparently political form. He is thus a political laborer from the start, and so he has something in common with the main politicians of the book, the gangsters, in one of whose speakeasies he explains, for the Op and for the reader, the primarily economic matrix of the gangsters' ascension to power. And, indeed, despite the relative lucidity of his class analysis, what he describes is also the matrix of his own local position, which he views, to some extent, in rather gangsterlike terms of personal patronage and dependency: "Hell with Chi!" he tells the Op, "I run 'em here" (8). The novel also implicitly links him to the gangsters by way of his previous sexual relationship with their playmate, Dinah. Dinah, the great instrumentalist of sexual labor, uses him just as she does the gangster Whisper Thaler, for her own economic gain; finding that advance knowledge of strike activity or inactivity can be useful in planning her investments, she in effect reduces this proletarian militant to a stockbroker.

It is indeed through Dinah, who functions as sexual "filter," that Quint is also thrown into comparison with his archenemy and opposite number in the class struggle, Elihu Willsson. Elihu's apparent gangster status (his lack of direct, unshared political control) is nowhere more neatly symbolized than in his clandestine "affair" with Dinah. With Elihu as with Quint, sex (which means Dinah) works to efface economic realities, at least symbolically, and to recast primarily economic figures in political terms. But Elihu, again like Quint, is a political worker in a more literal sense also. A legitimate capitalist who has been wont simply to "own" politicians ("a United States senator, a couple of representatives, the governor, the mayor, and most of the state legislature" [9]), he has been forced by the economic crisis in Personville to join forces with the gangster politicians in order to maintain his economic position, thus subjecting himself to their political modes and ideologies. These amount to a series of weighty but unreliable "covenants" of personal fidelity that are supported by violence and the threat of violence.

In establishing and entering the gangster polity, Elihu strips himself of much of his real political power, not only because, lacking a personal band of thugs, he is ill equipped for violence but also because the gangster covenants compromise his legitimacy. He temporarily loses the possibility of legal redress against the gangsters, since any such action would expose his own illegal complicity with them. His strictly political position is thus weak out of all proportion to his economic power, and this weakness is figured linguistically.

The two aspects of his political weakness correspond to two ways in which he is mastered by language. On the one hand, his vulnerability to gangster violence is signified by the vehement, disconnected shouting that seems to be his normal mode of oral discourse and that is also, as the Continental Op clearly discerns, a sign of physical terror. On the other hand, his legal vulnerability is signified by his relation to the various scripts and documents that appear throughout the novel: the most obviously dangerous are the records that Dinah obtains for Donald Willsson and that he has with him when he is killed, though they are useless for Donald's reforming purposes since they incriminate his father as well as the gangsters. More important, the contract that the terrified Elihu makes with the Op (and puts in writing at the Op's insistence) licenses the Op to clean up Personville by any means and thus pins Elihu to his character as legitimate capitalist, much to his own peril and against his later wishes.

Elihu, indeed, might be called a figure of the letter. Whether he is shouting stock orders and threats or signing certified checks, he is controlled by, and at the mercy of—in fact his character is projected or figured by—linguistic repositories of one kind or another, standard forms of discourse. Even his sex life enters by way of the letter. His relationship with Dinah is revealed only when his love letters to her surface in a blackmail attempt against him. Since the novel offers no other manifestation of the feeble and elderly Elihu's sexuality, sex and the letter are virtually one for him, and his sexual weakness is figured linguistically in much the same way as is his political insecurity: in sex as in politics his "legitimacy" commits and shackles him to the letter, to which he is therefore vulnerable.

Elihu, accordingly, occupies an extremely complex position regarding the various modes of labor under discussion. Linguistic labor (the form that might seem furthest removed from the economic labor that ultimately defines his place) absorbs the other three types and comes to serve as a multivalent code sending forth economic, political, and sexual messages simultaneously. But the overdeterminacy of the presiding (linguistic) code for Elihu is only a particularly telling manifestation of a system of mutual intercoding that informs character presentation in other aspects as well.

For example, intercoding makes for a curiously abstract symbolism that finds its clearest expression in the character of Dinah Brand, whose primary work is sexual. Her sexuality projects more as aura than as activity, and Dinah's defining work involves the production of sexual charisma or appeal. This appeal is conveyed not by movie-star beauty but by the apparent spontaneity of her actions or, more inclusively, by the general ambience of unrepressed openness that she makes her medium. This quality is most neatly figured by the small but blatant disorders that the Op keeps noticing in her apparel—runs in stockings, tears in dresses, and the like. Her slovenliness signifies an overabundant energy that the social forms of the gangster world cannot thoroughly contain or structure—witness the Op's remark, after Dinah's hose have run yet another time: "[Y]our legs are too big, they put too much strain on the material" (79). Dinah's runs and tears, however, not only represent her patent sensuality but also suggest (in the abstract form of surplus energy) the direct economic activity that sexual labor functions to distance and repress, to "filter" into its own terms. For Dinah's sexual labor is itself directly economic—she is after all a high-class whore—and so may be seen as a distortion of normative, productive economic labor. Hence Dinah's eruptions onto the political and linguistic scenes appear, in part, as the return of the repressed, of direct economic production. If we consider, too, that the entire gangster polity is characterized by a principle of plenitude analogous to Dinah's surplus energy, then Dinah's runs take on a further, allegorical significance: in this light, they figure the crucial weaknesses in the gangster polity (the excess of material over structure) on which the Op founds his strategy. Dinah's disarrangements are thus so many symbolic "clues," for the Op and for the reader, to the gangsters' world.

This world is, like Dinah herself, a body of vibrant energy unsanctioned by the official guarantor of bourgeois legitimacy—that is, by the letter of the law which (thanks to the Op's linguistic machinations) eventually sweeps away the gangster polity and, with it, the opportunity for the kind of sex Dinah had practiced. But whereas the central physical activity of Dinah's sexual labor (copulation) is, like the miners' mining, never explicitly shown, the central physical activity of the gangsters' political labor (violence) is shown again and again. *Red Harvest* is, as the title suggests, an extraordinarily bloody book (the Op on one occasion is dizzied in tallying the murders that have taken place since his arrival), and this stress on violence—that is, on the political—is crucial to the novel's social vision. Since, after all, capitalism ultimately determines bourgeois legality, what could an "illegitimate" capitalism be?

Hammett at one point seems to draw a parallel between fascist Italy and gangster-dominated Personville, but the novel is not exactly "about" fascism, except in the allegorical sense we consider later. While its concrete terms may not be irrelevant to the formulation of an adequate theory of fascism, what they actually suggest is the feudalization of illicit power. The relative absence of strong, central, universalizing state power; the prominence of private and semiprivate armies; the corresponding importance of personal loyalty between master and dependent; and, above all, the way in which this highly visible, dynamic polity can overshadow economy (the reader in fact sees very little bootlegging, gambling, and the like), as the fully bourgeois politicians owned by the "real" capitalist Elihu Willsson can never overshadow him—these features of the gangster polity are all precapitalist and classically feudal. Removed from capitalist law, the gangsters temporarily appear all the stronger—is not their capacity for illicit violence a manifest sign of strength?—and they are, indeed, strong enough to rescue and then to dominate Elihu Willsson. But such dominance is unstable, because in the larger society beyond Personville full-fledged capitalism is still unchallenged and the letter of the law still operates.

One index of the gangsters' apparent strength is a mastery of discourse: contrast Max Thaler's ominous, effective whispering or Noonan's fluent Irish-cop ·heartiness with Elihu's wearisome vehemence. Finally, however, the gangsters are far less linguistically capable than Elihu; in other words, their political weakness as "feudalists," as less than full-fledged capitalists, is determined in part linguistically. For the kind of legal documentation to which Elihu is partially and temporarily vulnerable is ultimately fatal to them. Decisively outside the letter of the law, they are decisively vulnerable to it (though it must not be forgotten that the letter of the law itself ultimately means a capacity for greater violence—in this case, the intervention of the National Guard). Indeed, this disparity in linguistic power partly explains why the Op, the linguistic laborer, can demolish the gangsters but makes no serious attempt to overthrow Elihu, whom he seems to find equally detestable.

In fact, the Op, for all his mastery of discourse, is strictly limited by two closely related laws. First, the economic law of profit requires that the Continental Detective Agency act in the interests of its clients (and the Op, surely enough, does a good job for Elihu, returning him to undisputed control of Personville). Second, an even more striking restriction obliges the Op to operate in alliance with (if not necessarily within) the letter of bourgeois legality; thus he acts decisively only against those who have placed themselves irrevocably outside the law. This alliance points to a crucial ambiguity in the very identity of the private detective. Though he is on one level independent of the police—and hence free of certain statist constraints on the individualist or "whole man"—his entire position as a respectable entrepreneur (or an entrepreneur's loyal employee) ties him to the state and makes him function, in the last analysis, as an adjunct to the official forces of law and order. The appealing personal hostility that a Sam Spade or a Philip Marlowe displays toward the cops is thus mainly gestural. The Continental Op himself (whose own designation phonetically suggests the word *cop*) tends, in most of Hammett's fictions, to eschew even such gestures, maintaining a cautious but usually cordial relationship with the police. In *Red Harvest*, however, there is admittedly a partial vacuum where the official forces of bourgeois legality ought to be: Noonan's police are really just another private gangster army—at one point the thugs loyal to the bootlegger Pete the Finn are sworn in as new members of the force—and the Op's ultimate alliance with the National Guard is presented in extremely abstract form. Nonetheless, the Op's actions remain largely determined by his fundamental allegiance to the letter of the law.

Still, the private detective's nonofficial status does partly condition the relative autonomy that the Op enjoys vis-à-vis the written law, an autonomy expressed, symbolically and actually, by his relying more on the spoken than on the written word. The novel is in one respect almost a Platonic fable on the superiority of dialogue to document.[3] Document "doesn't know how to address the right people, and not address the wrong. And when it is ill-treated and unfairly abused it always needs its parent to come to its help, being unable to defend or help itself." The dialectician of dialogue, in contrast, deals in "words which can defend both themselves and him who planted them, words which instead of remaining barren contain a seed whence new words grow up in new characters" (Plato 521-22).

The relative defenselessness of the written word that Socrates notes in the *Phaedrus* is well illustrated by the haplessness of the newspaper editor Donald Willsson, who, with his trust in documentation, is, so to speak, the "official" reformer—or would-be reformer—of Personville. Shortly before his death, however, as if unconsciously grasping the Socratic point, he summons the help of a truly dialogic dialectician, the Continental Op. While not entirely forgoing legal and quasi-legal documentation (and, in fact, ultimately tied to it, as we have indicated), the detective realizes the need for a more supple and dialogic sort of linguistic labor. (Such is the relative absence of documentation from his world that, until the dialogic labors are complete, the Op deliberately neglects—and orders his subordinates Dick Foley and Mickey Linehan to neglect—the written reports required by their boss, the Old Man.) What he calls his "experiment" with the Cooper-Bush fight is designed in part to provide the reader with a sample of the Op's dialogic prowess. By spreading a hot tip through the town's gambling population and by a short conversation with Ike Bush, he constructs a situation in which four apparently meaningless words—"Back to Philly, Al"—can unfix a fixed boxing match and result in a man's death. The great bulk of the Op's crucial work amounts to one or another variation on "Back to Philly, Al." His dialogic achievement climaxes in the amazing "peace conference" scene, where the Op talks face-to-face with, and more adroitly than, all the gang leaders; one seed planted there, that of Noonan's death, blossoms within minutes. It is not only the substance of the

Op's speech—the precisely measured bits of true and false information—that does the trick but the style as well. Much of his leverage, at the peace conference and in Poisonville generally, results from his insinuating himself into the highest levels of the gangster polity as a potentially formidable friend or foe; he is depended on, at different times, by Noonan, Thaler, and Reno, and he owes this stature not to his physical prowess but to the good impression he makes, mainly because his mastery of gangster idiom—informal, laconic, understated, oblique, amoral, enriched by an occasional striking metaphor—is superior to that of any of the actual gangsters. All this has little to do with formal structures of documentation, with letter and law, which plainly have determining power at the beginning and the end of the novel but effectively disappear through most of it, as the novel becomes absorbed in the Op's rhetorical ethos. (Indeed, the Op explicitly recognizes this disappearance when he tells his two assistants that since the gangsters "own the courts, and, besides, the courts are too slow for us now," he plans to use other, speedier methods that will result in the gangsters' having "their knives in each other's backs, doing our work for us" [110].) One might say that the Op's dialogue becomes not only the medium in which he and (less successfully) most of the other characters live but a determining structure that lives them. While the letter of the law is suspended, dialogue is a world unto itself. And it is a world that, extending beyond the matter placed between quotation marks, encompasses the entirety of this first-person, eminently spoken novel.

The construction of this dialogic world, the detachment of the spoken word from its alliance with the letter into an autonomy that constitutes, as it were, the detective's proper homeland—this is a central accomplishment of the novel and a major end of the Op's work of detection, even though it is an end apparently only incidental to his stated goal of solving crimes or, rather, of eliminating a criminal situation. The Op's low-key version of detective macho precludes his visibly drawing any aesthetic satisfaction from the dialogic free play structuring his world and thus prevents the emergence of that aestheticist vein which typifies, for example, many of Raymond Chandler's Marlowe stories (an aestheticism, one suspects, that largely explains the professional literati's preference for Chandler over Hammett).[4] Yet a different sort of aesthetic component figures quite prominently in *Red Harvest* as a function of the Op's work of detecting, of his linguistic mastery: in a sense, indeed, that work is akin to artistic creation as classically defined, for it takes the Op into a realm of freedom and play in which the activity of detection appears to constitute an end in itself. The definitive entrance into this realm, and with it the surcharging of the Op's activity with immanent aesthetic value, occurs at the point where the initial puzzle (who killed Donald Willsson?) is solved and the novel opens out onto the gangster "pastoral" promised by the title. Here the contract between Elihu and the Op sets the Op down naked, as it were, in Poisonville, with $10,000 and his personal resourcefulness but with only a general goal to work toward—the destruction of the gangster polity—and, correlatively, with no specific devices at hand to implement his ends. This apparent freedom and open-endedness give the Op's detective operations their aesthetic character of play. Put another way, the reorientation and generalization of the Op's aims in the context of the entire gangster polity determine the aestheticization of detective work by bringing dialogue to the fore as both tool and medium, as both a means of achieving the Op's goal and as an end in itself, as a climate in which the Op feels truly at home.

This dual function of dialogue plays a crucial role: it marks the place where the chief contradiction in the Op's work—that between his alliance with the normative capitalist order and his apparent independence from it, between the social function and the individualist character of his activities—achieves a highly ideological resolution. For the duality of dialogue effectively resolves the split between the Op as instrument and as individualist, by absorbing it into a strictly technical unity of means and ends. Dialogue as "climate," as apparent end in itself, not only makes the Op comfortable and furnishes him with his proper habitat but also, as we have explained, empowers him in his professional capacities. It is by establishing a plausibly stable dialogic style that the Op makes things happen; dialogue as medium is a generalized tool, working in the long term to disrupt the already unstable gangster polity but serving immediate ends that are often unforeseen by the Op and the reader alike. But whether the Op is planting his effects with precision (as when he sets up Noonan during the gangster convocation) or whether, as is more often the case, he is playing things by ear, fishing for effects, he gives the impression of having a quasi-sympathetic knowledge of how his actions will affect the intricacies of the gangster establishment. So it is that this generalization of the instrumental character of the Op's labor, this foregrounding of dialogue as medium, fuses the Op's means and ends and in so doing assimilates him to the gangster world.

For the world of dialogue in which the Op is at home is virtually one with the gangster world, though the Op lives in that world with a difference. The gangster polity, structured by a tacit division of labor and by ties of personal dependence, is in effect a world of the word—of unwritten agreements—backed by violence. To preserve their hegemony, the gangsters must attempt to fix the series of agreements regulating their actions. To remain at least apparently as good as his word, each gangster chief must not only keep up his retinue of thugs but also set out for himself a dialogic terrain or register, maintaining the dialogic style that signifies self-control and power. Gangster laconicism in its various modes (as used by Whisper or Reno or even by a relative nonentity like O'Mara) acquires a ceremonial significance: it represents the ritual that symbolizes and fixes gangster relations of exchange. But this style also fixes the code of violence that is built into these relations; in gangster understatement, the more that is meant than meets the ear amounts to murderous force. Thus laconicism crystallizes within itself the tendency of the gangster kingdom to self-destruction, and the decentering effect of dialogue as medium and climate, as structural determinant of gangster activity, can only accentuate this tendency.

The scene in which Reno Starkey, at the end of the novel, literally holds himself together and talks himself to death well illustrates the function of gangster style and of dialogic necessity:

> I knew he would go on talking as soon as he got himself in hand. He meant to die as he had lived, inside the same tough shell. Talking could be torture, but he wouldn't stop on that account, not while anybody was there to see him. . . . [S]itting there listening to and watching him talk himself to death wasn't pleasant. (197-98)

This last, anticlimactic interview has a medicinal effect on the Op, not only because he learns that he himself is definitely not Dinah's murderer but also because the episode, as a kind of spectacle, satiates his will to comprehend gangsterism and allows him to distance himself from the gangster community and its ethos. The spectacle thus helps him control the unnatural bloodlust and fear that the violence in Poisonville and, more important, his own participation in it inspired in him. His violent mood—his "fever," as he calls it—reaches its crest, and indeed goes out of control, in the scenes that take place in Dinah's apartment just after the "peace conference": before drugging himself into a helpless though a not necessarily harmless state, the Op informs Dinah that the whole convocation and all the resulting violence were unnecessary, since he could at this point have enlisted Elihu's aid "to swing the play [against the gangsters] legally." He has done otherwise, he explains, because "it's easier to have them killed off, easier and surer, and, now that I'm feeling this way, more satisfying" (145). Here, in the fever that threatens to assimilate him ever more deeply to gangsterism, the Op seems on the verge of losing his all-important self-control and dialogic mastery, as he unwittingly terrifies Dinah and then allows her to give him the incapacitating laudanum. The chapter that follows, in which the Op awakens from his dreams and finds himself beside Dinah's corpse, goes further toward investing him (symbolically) in gangster guise. His near unity with the gangster world is at this point so close and intense that it threatens to throw him off balance and thus to co-opt his labor. Here, then, we discover a further dimension of the ideological resolution in dialogue of the contradiction between the social function and the individualistic character of the Op's work. This resolution—that is, the Op's construction of a dialogic world that completes and overloads the gangster world—effectively replaces the conflict between the Op's freedom and the capitalist order with the more immediate conflict between the Op and the gangster polity: it is the gangster polity in its totality, as fixed and over-loaded by dialogue, that threatens to take over and reinstrumentalize the Op's "unalienated" labor by destroying his freedom to make conscious play with the flexibility of dialogue.

But dialogue as medium is dangerous to the Op in what we might call its symbolic impersonality as well as in its potential for confining him to the fixity and violence of the gangster code.[5] For dialogue, as we have argued, constitutes a force in itself, a force whose effects can be seen in the gestures, the stylistic signatures, of the various characters (Elihu's vehemence, Max's ominous whisper, Dinah's casual openness). Dialogue as a massively informing and decentering structure thus appears to write the characters' lines for them and, paradoxically, almost to take on itself the attributes of the letter, of the written line, while the characters, in turn, seem to be functions of the dialogic world. (This "literal" quality of dialogue amounts to a subterranean return of the letter of the law in highly mediated form.) The Op, then, must finally guard himself against the splintering, depersonalizing tendency inherent in the dialogic world as abstract structure and symbolic Other, as well as against the violence fetish of the gangsters. At this strictly linguistic level, the Op's labors consist in maintaining a proper relation to dialogue, to the symbolic function. He prevents the linguistic alienation of his powers not by attempting directly to control dialogic free play, for there can be no question of that, but rather by rolling with the flow of dialogue, by ambiguously complying with dialogue so that it can fulfill its dual function as means and end.

Accordingly, although dialogue as structure and medium endangers the Op's equilibrium, the free play of dialogue is what preserves the unalienated and aestheticized form of his work. The Op labors, for the most part, by tapping the various energies harbored within dialogue and (through dialogue) within the gangster polity, whose structural disunity makes it susceptible to the Op's dialogic maneuvering. His modus operandi, then, is a new kind of detective procedure: it involves not the decoding of a discrete series of facts but, rather, an encoding process that activates the surplus energy inherent in his world, not deduction or ratiocination but an attempt at totalizing comprehension. This process, in which relations are to be grasped between foregrounded details and an entire social structure, defines itself against the detective process in the classic, or Sherlockian, tradition, where clues are set off from the social totality and where reason tends to be instrumentalized. The Op's detective work is hardly a "reasonable" process of that sort. It requires instead the apparently spontaneous capacity both to activate the energies present in the dialogic world and to weather the anarchic psychological and social effects that are thus set in motion: "Plans are all right sometimes," the Op explains to Dinah. "And sometimes just stirring things up is all right—if you're tough enough to survive, and keep your eyes open so you'll see what you want when it comes to the top" (79). Accordingly, the detective must live and move in the dialogic world without being subsumed by it, without losing his labor's freedom vis-à-vis the forces in this world. The Op, one might say, must consciously live his own decenteredness.

We may conclude, then, that the Op's situation typifies the limits of individualism in both form and content: not only is the Op's dialogic freedom qualified by dialogue itself as a medium and informing symbolic structure, it is also, though less urgently, compromised by the Op's ultimate political and economic ties to bourgeois legitimacy, to the letter of the law. But if the Op cannot finally be read as occupying a critical or negative position toward the normative capitalist order, the same finding is not necessarily valid for the novel as a whole, despite the natural temptation to identify the book with the character who speaks or quotes nearly its entire semantic content.

The title *Red Harvest* (perhaps the only line of the novel that is clearly not spoken by the Continental Op) is a pun: the harvest is both a bloodbath and the culmination of a chain of events launched by proletarian militancy. In this regard, we are bound to notice that the novel does contain an antifascist allegory of fascism,[6] if we agree to define fascism as the domination of the working class through open physical terror imposed by "respectable," though unusually reactionary, capital. Indeed, the novel can almost be read as a prophecy of the popular front (to which Hammett did adhere), for the final defeat of gangsterism ushers in the restoration of Elihu's "normal" exploitation, which is sanctioned by the liberal-democratic state. Whatever degree of radicalism one may grant to popular frontism, however, it is also true that the political vision that the novel foregrounds is not antifascist or popular-frontist or leftist in any way but, rather, anarchic and Hobbesian.[7]

In the world through which the Op moves—the "local color," as it were, of the novel—proletarian solidarity counts for little (it has, after all, been defeated before the novel begins), competition is merciless and frequently deadly, and one may constantly be thrown back exclusively on one's own resources. The prevailing lack of social trust enables the Op to set the gangsters at one another's throats and so to defeat them; but, once again, this world is to a large extent the Op's as well, and the same distrust exists between the Op and his own client, Elihu; between the Op and his own boss, the Old Man; and between the Op and his own assistant Dick (he has *some* trust in his other assistant, Mickey). In a sense, the fissure in the novel between antifascism and anarchic Hobbesian-ism is a matter of point of view. If one looks at the gangster polity from the outside (as Bill Quint does), it appears to be an analogue or figure of fascist power that is explicable in Marxist terms. Seen from the inside (the perspective of the Op and virtually all the other characters), the gangsters' world seems a savage, inescapable place where dog-eat-dog individualism is the only philosophy that makes sense.

The antifascist allegory of fascism is not, however, the only or the most pervasive way that *Red Harvest* stands critically opposed to capitalism. The book may be read more generally, in its formal substance, as an attack on socioeconomic relations, on the quality of social life, in the United States at the time of writing—that is, during the transitional period in which monopoly capital was beginning to be the dominant form of capital in America. The growth of monopoly capital (and of its necessary social and political concomitants, such as advertising and direct state intervention in the economic sphere) accelerates the rate at which the commodity structure penetrates into all levels of social life, into lived experience itself; and thus the reification that informs social activity and social relations is intensified and deepened in all its aspects.[8] In this light, the local-color component of the novel, the "authentic" gangster milieu, possesses a kind of conservative-radical value and takes on the poignance that is always a defining quality of local color. For what the homogenizing commodity world eradicates, as it increasingly encroaches on all areas and levels of society, are precisely the conditions of possibility—the traditional differences—that local color celebrates (it might be noted that the relative backwardness of capitalism in the western United States partly determines Hammett's use of this literary mode).

But the gangster world of *Red Harvest* may also be read as an even more direct protest against the reification imposed by the commodity world—a protest lodged through the generic slippage by which "local color" becomes "allegory of fascism," by which the gangster world, instead of remaining simply a particular local community, attains figurative status as a world unto itself. It is in this generic slippage, which is at one with the creation of the gangster world, that gangster "pastoral" comes to bear, in its essence, something like the negative imprint of the commodity world itself, inasmuch as the autonomization (and subsequent interrelation) of the various forms of labor that constitute the novel's modus operandi—the central principle of its composition—is itself previously determined by the extension of the capitalist commodity world, which, as the result of the reification and instrumentalization of social relations, is characterized by an autonomy of its various constituent activities. So it is that monopoly capitalism provides Hammett's local color with its ideological raw content, in the guise of the four discrete forms of labor that define the Op's milieu. The construction of this milieu, then, may be understood as an attack on the instrumentalization of labor enforced by the commodity structure, as an attempt to undermine reification by transforming capitalism's abstract labor into sensuously immediate activity, into activity whose relations with the total social context can be felt as if from the inside. The interdetermination of the four forms of labor (which we discussed, for instance, in connection with Elihu, whose political weakness is figured sexually and linguistically) contributes to the inherent relatedness of all activity within the gangster polity—and to the concomitant sense of it feeling "at home" with one's surroundings, however murderous.

In this way, the gangster polity comes to function as a quasi-utopian figure. But it is an impossible figure from its very emergence, since the gangster world is posited precisely through the operation of the reified categories that it attempts to undermine; thus it is both a product of reification and an attack on it. (The very transformation of *Person*ville into *Poison*ville is after all a symbolically paradigmatic process of reification—one that is introduced in the novel's opening sentences and that, as the Op explains, cannot be reduced to the phonetics of gangster dialect.) This aspect of the book's utopian component is expressed, in its very impossibility, through the form taken by the elegiac-pastoral strain (alluded to in the title), which does not appear in particular passages but, rather, attaches to the entire gangster polity and thus communicates against the grain of the writing. The impossibility of this figurative utopia comes out more concretely, however, in the pastoral theme itself, the motif of abundance and plenitude. It is at this point that the attack on reification shades into the merely aesthetic, into a mute glorification of the surplus energies released by the reification of activity; and it is here, of course, that the gangster polity reveals its central weakness. It is, after all, precisely by manipulating the disunity of the gangster world, by activating the untapped and as-if-unstructured energies within it, that the Continental Op manages his work of detection and destruction. The utopian plenitude and connectedness of the gangster domain would seem, then, to confess their illusory quality as the detective work proceeds, and as it does so the essential reification of the various forms of labor in the Op's world becomes more transparent.

Thus nothing finally succeeds as a critique of the capitalist order—not the Op himself, or the antifascist allegory, or the protest against reification contained in the local-color utopia of the gangster polity. We may conclude, however, by considering the novel's actual generic composition in the same light and in a more systematic way than we have yet done. For *Red Harvest* is not only a new kind of detective novel. It contains, as it were, three novels, each a different response to the reified raw material provided by American capitalism. There is, first of all, an (unwritten) proletarian novel—more precisely, a strike novel (Bill Quint, probably, is its protagonist) dealing with the struggles of the workers of the Personville Mining Corporation. This strike novel, we may infer, attempts a radical, perhaps even a revolutionary, attack on the exploitation of labor and the consequent all-pervasive reification of life. Though it could not be written because the strike failed, it remains a strongly determinate absence, generating the also radical but more abstract allegory of fascism; formally, that is, the failure of the strike "demotes" overt textual radicalism from novel proper to subnovelistic allegory. Accordingly, in the novel proper an important generic shift is marked in the speakeasy scene of the first chapter. There Bill Quint, as the protagonist of the strike novel, gives us a précis of that narrative and hands over to his drinking companion, the Continental Op, the role of protagonist in the novel now about to begin in earnest—namely, the *mystery* novel, the novel whose title might be "Who Killed Donald Willsson?" Here, as in any classic mystery tale, the project is to grasp and reveal a reified social totality by focusing attention on a series of discrete clues comprehensible to the superlative intelligence of the master detective. The Op, who is in fact qualified to be a Sherlockian detective, notices, for instance, as surely as Holmes or Lord Peter Wimsey or Hercule Poirot would, that a .32 is the kind of gun likely to be available to a bank clerk. Yet, as we have pointed out, *Red Harvest* is more concerned with clues of a different sort—a sort calling for construction or encoding rather than for deduction or decoding. Thus, judged by the standards of its genre, this mystery novel is both too successful and not successful enough. It is too successful because it ends prematurely; the book is little more than a quarter done when the puzzle is solved and Robert Albury is arrested for the murder of Donald Willsson. (Although the mystery novel does have a kind of afterlife in such subsequent puzzles as, Who killed Tim Noonan? and, Who killed Dinah Brand? they are not the main focus of the novel's interest, and Dinah's murder marks a particularly savage swerve from the classic mystery pattern, since the detective must number himself among the suspects.) The mystery novel is not successful enough, however, in that the confession and arrest of Albury contribute nothing to the Op's main goal, the destruction of the gangster polity. In formal terms, the book is by this point overloaded with reified clues and resonance—such as Dinah's runs and tears—that are not at all susceptible to merely deductive work.

With Albury's arrest, then, the book's generic structure again shifts, and the third and main novel of *Red Harvest* blossoms out—the adventure or gangster novel. Now the Op as decentered linguistic laborer truly comes into his own. He remains the protagonist but becomes far more a hard-boiled detective than a classic one. It is no accident that it is shortly after the arrest of Albury that he tries the Cooper-Bush experiment, his first major venture into the linguistic work of encoding and overloading the polity of Poisonville. Now he confronts the reified gangster totality through the dualities that determine his identity as a private detective—sympathetic knowledge of gangsterism and professional distance from it, bohemian individualism and ultimate bourgeois accountability. It is also at this point, as the Op becomes more and more assimilated to the gangster polity he is fighting, that the local color of *Red Harvest* comes into its own and successfully competes for our attention on the subnovelistic level, quite overshadowing the antifascist allegory. But the matter is not quite so simple. For, if the unwritten strike novel, incapable of resolving the reification of its raw material, gives way to the mystery novel, and the mystery novel, likewise incapable, gives way to the adventure novel, then how shall the adventure novel—and the whole book—end? Of course, the Op does defeat the gangsters, and by the close of the book all adventure is over, all puzzles solved. But it is just here that the strike novel and its allegorical ghost, the story of fascism now defeated by legitimate capitalism, again make themselves felt. "Go to hell!" (188) are the Op's final words to the client whom he has returned to unshared exploitative control of Personville, which, as the Op later notes with bitter sarcasm, is now "developing into a sweet-smelling thornless bed of roses" (199).

In other words, the problem of exploitation remains, and the Continental Op's dissatisfaction at the end suggests an awareness that his own labor has inevitably been reified into an instrument wielded for the benefit of the despicable capitalist boss Elihu; indeed, Elihu's relation to the (still invisible) miners is parodically mirrored by the Op's troubles with the Old Man, which are in the book's final sentence "He gave me merry hell" (199). *Red Harvest* has left things as it found them before the strike novel, and all three novels may now be seen as moments in a larger crisis novel, which, attempting to resolve the reification, twists itself this way and that through different genres and finally must admit defeat. Reification remains, and there is no question of its resolution.

But few novels—and certainly very few novels originating in the subliterary ghetto to which detective fiction has often been consigned—have made so serious and powerful an attempt to comprehend reification. Trying to comprehend reification: that is the kind of work a detective does when he detects. [*PMLA* 106 (1991): 209-21]

NOTES

1. Most detective-fiction criticism has concerned the deductive, Sherlockian line, but there is some work on the hard-boiled variety, especially in contrast to the older type. Perhaps the single most important statement in this regard remains Raymond Chandler's great manifesto-like "The Simple Art of Murder: An Essay" (1-21). In "The Hippocratic Smile: John le Carré and the Tradition of the Detective Novel," Glenn W. Most offers some interesting and less polemical reflections on the contrast (Most and Stowe, esp. 342-53). Ken Worpole provides an excellent and more sociologically oriented account of the same matter, especially in his second chapter, "The American Connection: The Masculine Style in Popular Fiction" (29-48).

2. See Dennis Porter on Poisonville as "the typical environment of an unregulated industrial capitalism, which acknowledges no limits to the pursuit of private wealth" (197).

3. Throughout, we use the categories of dialogue and the dialogic simply to refer to spoken as opposed to written discourse; we do not intend their somewhat more technical (and currently influential) Bakhtinian sense. Though there are some affinities between Bakhtin's concepts and our more colloquial usage, particularly in the context of the novel (see, e.g., Bakhtin 259-422), they can hardly be detailed here.

4. See Fredric Jameson's important account of Chandler as an aesthetically self-conscious stylist. Worpole usefully comments, "Chandler's own writing, based as it was originally on a total admiration for the styles of Hammett and Hemingway, often specifically mentioned, became increasingly sophisticated and moved away from the popular and demotic. The descriptions of the settings became longer, although they were always characterized by a mordant and acerbic irony. The similes piled on top of each other, the dialogue became more consciously dry-witted and more often self-consciously studded with intellectual and literary allusions, the perorations on human weakness, civic corruption and sexual infidelity became longer. The cost of refining the genre was that it began to look towards a different readership for approval as it became more self-consciously literary and settled back again into conventional narrative forms" (44-45). Stephen Knight suggests an additional but related reason for the highbrow tendency to prefer Chandler to Hammett: for all his apparent gritty realism, Chandler, unlike Hammett, always preserves a full-blooded romantic individualism (138).

5. Though it is not our purpose here to explicate the "symbolic order" as it figures in Lacanian psychoanalysis, our general debt to Lacan will be evident to anyone familiar with his work (see, e.g., Lacan 30-113).

6. The most explicit formulation in this regard occurs in the Op's retelling of Bill Quint's narrative: "But, said Quint, old Elihu didn't know his Italian history. He won the strike, but he lost his hold on the city and the state. To beat the miners he had to let his hired thugs run wild. When the fight was over he couldn't get rid of them . . ." (9).

Though the passage could easily refer to a commonplace situation in Renaissance Italy, it also accurately describes the relation that obtained between big capital in Italy and Mussolini's government after the defeat of the Italian labor and socialist movements. The Fascist party, however, was officially organized in 1919, and Mussolini seized state power three years later; since these events were relatively recent when *Red Harvest* was written, the term *history* in the above passage may seem curious. Yet, to the historically minded, like Hammett, even recent history is history, and in view of his general political formation, it is difficult to believe that he was not consciously thinking of fascism. Of course, the allegory of fascism works whether or not the author explicitly meant to signal it.

7. Stephen Marcus makes this point well in one of the most insightful essays on Hammett to date. He describes the world through which the Op moves as one "of universal warfare, the war of each against all, and of all against all. The only thing that prevents the criminal ascendancy from turning into permanent tyranny is that the crooks who take over society cannot cooperate with one another, repeatedly fall out with each other, and return to the Hobbesian anarchy out of which they have momentarily arisen" (xxiii-xxiv). Though Marcus's concern is more with Hammett's short stories about the Continental Op than with *Red Harvest*, this passage is a fine account of the novel.

8. Throughout, we use the category "reification" in the classically Lukácsian sense; see Lukács 83-222.

WORKS CITED

Bakhtin, M.M. *The Dialogic Imagination*. Trans. Caryl Emerson and Michael Holquist. Ed. Michael Holquist. Austin: U of Texas P, 1981.

Chandler, Raymond. *The Simple Art of Murder*. New York: Ballantine, 1972.

Hammett, Dashiell. *Red Harvest*. New York: Random, 1972.

Jameson, Fredric. "On Raymond Chandler." *Southern Review* 6 (1970): 624-50.

Knight, Stephen. *Form and Ideology in Crime Fiction*. Bloomington: Indiana UP, 1980.

Lacan, Jacques. *Ecrits: A Selection*. Trans. Alan Sheridan. New York: Norton, 1977.

Lukács, Georg. *History and Class Consciousness: Studies in Marxist Dialetics*. Trans. Rodney Livingstone. Cambridge: MIT P, 1971.

Marcus, Stephen. Introduction. *The Continental Op*. By Dashiell Hammett. New York: Random, 1975.

Most, Glenn W., and William W. Stowe, eds. *The Poetics of Murder: Detective Fiction and Literary Theory*. New York: Harcourt, 1983.

Plato. *Phaedrus. The Collected Dialogues of Plato*. Ed. Edith Hamilton and Huntington Cairns. Princeton: Princeton UP, 1961.

Porter, Dennis. *The Pursuit of Crime: Art and Ideology in Detective Fiction*. New Haven: Yale UP. 1981.

Worpole, Ken. *Dockers and Detectives*. London: Verso, 1983.

The Dain Curse

Reviews

Here is a story which opens mildly enough with the theft of eight small diamonds worth all together somewhere in the neighborhood of a thousand dollars, a crime too utterly trivial to engage the attention of a writer of detective stories. But any reader who stops at the end of the first chapter will miss a lot of perfectly gorgeous murders. The theft of the diamonds is a mere preliminary and has very little to do with the rest of the story except to introduce the detective who tells it and who is in the thick of the stirring events that follow. The book is in three parts. In the first part there are four or five murders, and that section of the book ends with the mystery apparently solved, although the detective has his doubts, which are subsequently proved to have been well founded. In the second part there are more murders (one loses count of the actual number) and there is another solution, no more satisfactory to the detective than the first. The third part, with still more murders, ends with a solution which satisfies the detective, although the reader may have just cause to complain that it is a bit illogical. The best feature of the book is the racy narrative style of the author's detective mouthpiece. [Bruce Rae, *New York Times Book Review* 18 August 1929: 16]

We want to say right here that Mr. Hammett is our favorite writer. He thrills, scares, amuses and delights us, all at once—and at the same time makes us respect his knowledge of the ways of criminals and detectives, which has quite obviously not been gained by reading the detective stories of other writers. His detective is neither an artificial pseudo-sophisticate nor a combination of encyclopedia and adding machine. He is simply a hard-boiled human with a better-than-the-average brain and a good deal of presence of mind, who succeeds as most of us do—if we do—by the method of trial and error. We admire him more because we understand him, and his solution of the curse which seemed to hang over pretty Gabrielle Leggett, and the means by which he hunted down the murderer of her father, her husband, and several other people connected with her, is both ingenious and exciting. We can think of only one story of the kind better than this second book of Mr. Hammett's, and that is his first book. [Walter Brooks, *Outlook and Independent* 31 July 1929: 552]

Try this one if life seems dull and colorless. Every move a corpse, but so cleverly managed that the story takes on the fascination of an authentic newspaper account. Starting with a fair to middling diamond robbery, Mr. Hammett adds a suicide (or is it murder?) and another fatality in a San Francisco suburb, then moves on to strange doings in the temple of a sinister cult and adds more dirty work at Quesada, with hard-boiled detectives, dope, abductions, minor crimes and young love in the picture and that horrid past bobbing up at every turn. Keep your eye on Gabrielle Leggett, a young woman with Lombrosian stigmata, assorted neuroses, deplorable habits generally and a pistol. Gabrielle is thought to suffer from the curse of the mad Dains, and her activities go far to confirm the report. This speedy tale is more than competently narrated by a cop with a picturesque line of vernacular and professional lingo. Recommended for its weird characters and really astonishing speed. The author is an ex-Pinkerton operative. [Will Cuppy, *New York Herald Tribune* 11 August 1929: 11]

Few detective stories manage to differ greatly from the general patterns. What is interesting in this story of Gabrielle Leggett is that the author does invoke a sense of genuine mystery and the feeling that a real curse hangs over the girl. . . . More than once a less clever detective would have felt that the case was finished. Mr. Hammett's detective hangs on, however, and the more he hangs on the more mystery follows Gabrielle. It is not until he has gone through the horror of her dope-cure that the end appears in sight. The solution is unexpected because the criminal who is discovered is unusual among the criminals of fiction. [*Boston Evening Transcript* 4 September 1929: 2]

From *Dashiell Hammett: A Casebook*

William F. Nolan

The Dain Curse (written for *Black Mask* as separate novelets to please [Joseph T.] Shaw, who disliked using serials) suffers in its adaptation to book form. Lacking the cohesive element of a single locale, this story jumps from seacoast to city to country, while the reader is forced to cope with over thirty characters . . . That [Hammett] could bring the story off at all is to his credit—and there are few writers who could have unified the narrative's disparate parts as well as he—yet to some extent one could agree with Hammett himself who later called it "a silly story." *The Dain Curse* marked a plateau, not an upward step, in his career. [McNally and Loftin 1969: 51]

From *California Writers*

Stoddard Martin

There is a degree of "goofiness" throughout *The Dain Curse* that makes its creator seem confused at times, silly at others. Patches of evocation are brilliant: the picture of California cultism at this early stage in the Haldorn's phony cult of the Holy Grail, which lures the already effete of the Golden State and prefigures a motif that would become standard by the time of *Farewell, My Lovely*. Often, however, the Gothic ornamentation seems extrinsic: the Devil's Island escape story and French aristocratic history of Gabrielle's father, which intrude from the realm of decadent literature to which Hammett felt such an attraction-repulsion. Personal disquiet with the book may be indicated by the fact that the author makes a writer the evil genius behind Gabrielle's "possession." [St. Martin's Press 1983: 136-137]

From "The Hardboiled Dicks"

Donald Westlake

Several years ago, a movie producer approached me to write a screenplay of *The Dain Curse* and I re-read it for the first time in several years, making notes on how a lot of that underbrush could be cleared away and simplified, to make something of movie-size. When I got to the end, I discovered that the one character I had definitely eliminated as extraneous was the murderer. There was also no way to turn that book into a movie, which I told the producer, suggesting he make a movie out of a Hammett short story called "The Gutting of Couffignal" instead. He did even better; he got out of the movie business and didn't make any picture at all. [*Armchair Detective* 17 (Winter 1984): 10-11]

The Dain Curse: The Epistemology of the Detective Story

Sinda Gregory

"That's the kind of story it is. I warned you there was no sense to it."
—the Op, in *The Dain Curse*

Although the Continental Op appears again as the main character and narrator of Dashiell Hammett's second novel, *The Dain Curse* (1929), there are surprisingly few similarities in Hammett's first two novels. The tough, corrupt atmosphere of Personville with its gangsters, bootleg whiskey, colorful language, and crooked politicians is replaced in *The Dain Curse* by a shifting series of settings and ambiences that range from urbane, continental intrigue to small-town melodrama. Murder and violence are still very much present, but the book's highly stylized action and selfconscious artifice invest its unfolding with a playful quality that was lacking in *Red Harvest*. In his second novel, Hammett uses the elements of various mystery genres—the classical mystery story, the gothic thriller, the small-town potboiler—to build a work which directly explores the fiction-making process. Indeed, on one level the novel is an exercise book in "types" of mystery fiction. Yet despite its qualities of artifice and fancifulness, *The Dain Curse* is not a "light" novel. Hammett may play with the form and style of the detective novel, but his intent is not primarily parodic; rather, *The Dain Curse* is a novel about how we impose a fictional sense of order in our lives and in our literature. As he willfully emphasizes the artifice of his own writing, he also suggests that what we see, what we believe, and what we think is what we have created ourselves.

Not only does the tone of *The Dain Curse* differ from Hammett's first novel, but the Op is presented in a significantly different manner. He is physically the same, of course—"a middle-aged fat man" (p. 112) who remains unnamed—but his personal code, a major issue in *Red Harvest*, receives little attention in *The Dain Curse*.[1] In addition, the Op has changed from instigator to interpreter; that is, whereas in *Red Harvest* the Op actively participates in the murders and mayhem, in *The Dain Curse* his presence usually makes no difference in the unfolding of the sequence of violence. The Op struggles throughout the novel to illuminate and interpret the bizarre events surrounding his client, yet, at the same time, he emphasizes that any order is likely to be suspect and that even the most probable solution is only one rendering of the "reality" of the case. The role of the Op, therefore, becomes complex and ambiguous in a different manner than appeared previously: though Hammett allows him to act out a series of "character roles" that could be seen as a survey of detective types, the Op himself constantly undercuts these roles by frequently suggesting that he is well aware that these roles are, in fact, only *imitations,* for he is very uncertain whether or not the detective—or anyone—can ever uncover any final solutions to life's mysteries. Stepping out of his detective roles occasionally, he analyzes the elements in the case with his novelist friend, Owen Fitzstephan (who turns out to be the murderer himself), and debates the very issues which are the basis of detective fiction; these discussions generate a self-reflexive, metafictional thrust to the novel and, in a large sense, allow Hammett to develop a sophisticated inquiry into the basis of how we arrive at what we know.[2]

Whereas Hammett uses the plot in *Red Harvest* primarily to focus our attention on the Op, he employs the complex configurations of events in *The Dain Curse* for more abstract purposes—largely, to develop his metafictional and epistemological concerns and to illustrate the difficulties of arriving at Truth. The plot structure of this book does resemble *Red Harvest* in that both reveal the answers to puzzles before the final conclusion, rather than waiting for the end of the book as in most detective stories. Yet, while in the first book the answers to the mysteries at least remained stable, in *The Dain Curse* these answers are constantly shifting. Hammett divides and labels his second book into three parts—"The Dains," "The Temple," and "Quesada." Each part ends its section with a solution which, in turn, changes the answer to the preceding puzzle. To illustrate this process, we might imagine children playing with a small set of Lincoln logs. With rather limited material, they build a simple cabin using all of the pieces at their disposal; later they are given additional material and begin to restructure the cabin, using the larger quantity of logs, until the cabin is now a ranch house, complete with fence. Now they are given a final set of materials, and in order to use all of the pieces, they are forced to start once again, restructuring and yet still using past materials, as well as the new ones. The final result is a complex system of buildings and corrals—all of which are built out of the same basic material with which they began. This method of using ever-increasing amounts of material is central to *The Dain Curse*'s development. Because of this approach, plot plays a more central role here than in *Red Harvest* since its structure actually illustrates the central theme in an isomorphic manner: from the structure of the plot we learn that we can only make sense of things from what we know—and what we know will always be limited.

Like most novels of this form, however, *The Dain Curse* begins with an apparently simple crime: the Op answers a routine call to investigate the theft of a few small diamonds from the home of Edgar Leggett, a mysterious yet locally respectable scientist who works out of a laboratory in his own residence. In the process of "Part One: The Dains," the Op discovers that this theft is only a minor incident in a case that involves multiple murders and spans twenty-five years and three continents. As the Byzantine history of the case is gradually revealed during the course of the Op's investigation, we learn that Leggett, a young Frenchman studying art in Paris, was trapped into matrimony by Lily Dain, the impoverished daughter of a British naval officer; shortly after their marriage, she had a child, Gabrielle. Alice, the sister of Lily, was intensely jealous of the marriage and wanted Leggett for herself—not out of love for Leggett but because she and Lily "were true sisters, inseparable, hating one another poisonously" (p. 56). To acquire Leggett, she planned the murder of her sister. The details of the murder are left in doubt, but she purposefully involved her niece, Gabrielle, by training her to play a game with guns. Alice's claim that Gabrielle actually shot her mother is later questioned by the Op, but Leggett was convinced by it at the time and took the blame for the murder in order to protect his daughter. He was tried, sentenced to Devil's Island, escaped from there to South America, and, after a further series of murders and intrigues, managed to settle in the United States without being detected. Years later, Alice and Gabrielle found him there, living in San Francisco, and Alice married him. Within a few years, however, men appear who know the history of the family, including the violent period Leggett spent in South America, and they attempt to blackmail Alice Dain. She pays one of the men in the diamonds that were reported stolen and thus begins the whole chain of events that lead to the Op's involvement in the case. At the end of this section, following a climactic scene in which the details of this history are brought out, Alice is killed, but not before she pronounces the "curse" of the Dains to her niece. "'You're her daughter,' she cried, 'and you're cursed with the same black soul and rotten blood that she and I and all the Dains have had; and you're cursed with your mother's blood on your hands in babyhood; and with the twisted mind and the need for drugs that are my gifts to you; and your life will be black as your mother's and mine were black; and the lives of those you touch will be black as Maurice's was black'" (p. 58).

The setting of this first section is an interesting contrast to the other two parts of the novel and to *Red Harvest*, as well. The action takes place in San Francisco, but the city itself is not important to the plot's development; unlike the poisonous, corrupting urban monster that was depicted in Hammett's first novel, San Francisco is neutral and unobtrusive. References to streets and locales carry no thematic or symbolic weight. In his next two novels—*The Maltese Falcon* and *The Glass Key*—the notion of urban decay and corruption will once more serve to emphasize setting, but here the city is simply not a factor in the book's development. Indeed, the more significant aspect of setting in this section is the Leggett home. As is so frequently the case in classical detective fiction, the most dramatic moments of action in *The Dain Curse*—many of the crimes, the confrontation with the villain, the revelation of "truth"—all take place in a single, secluded residence. The Leggett house would be appropriate in a classical detective story for obvious reasons: it is tastefully wealthy, with antique oriental rugs, handcrafted walnut furniture, and valuable Japanese prints. There is a sitting room with brocaded chairs, a study, and a laboratory on the second floor—exactly the sort of setting found so often in works by G. K. Chesterton, Agatha Christie, and many other classical detective writers.

In addition to the physical setting, other elements add to this classical detective atmosphere. The history behind the Leggett/Dain family has a distinct quality of old-world decadence that we rarely find in a hard-boiled novel—the subtly incestuous love triangle in Paris, fratricide, the escape from Devil's Island. There is even a servant to be suspected and a wide-eyed fiancé (a male ingénue figure named Eric Collinson) who is said to be "young, blonde, tall, broad, sunburned, and dressy, with the good-looking unintelligent face of one who would know everything about polo, or shooting, or flying, or something of that sort" (p. 13). The description of Leggett by Fitzstephan is, in itself, highly suggestive of the Sherlock Holmes/Auguste Dupin type of classical detective. "There's something obscure in him, something dark and inviting. He is, for instance, physically ascetic—neither smoking nor drinking, eating meagerly, sleeping, I'm told, only three or four hours a night—but mentally, or spiritually, sensual—does that mean anything to you?—to the point of decadence. You used to think I had an abnormal appetite for the fantastic. You should know him" (p. 20).

In this atmosphere so like that of the classical detective story, the Op remains essentially the hard-nosed private eye, responding, for example, to Collinson's sarcastic comment about the dangers he has put Gabrielle through ("I hope you're satisfied with the way your work got done") with the terse reply, "It got done" (p. 60). But in the climatic scene of part 1, the Op quickly assumes the role of the classical detective. Here all the prime suspects are gathered in the study (a traditional setting for murder and denouement in classical detective stories), clustered around the body of Leggett which lies slumped over his desk. This scene clearly imitates the tone and construction of a classical work as the Op recognizes, through logically analyzing clues, that the note assumed to be a suicide message is, instead, a letter the man intended to leave behind after his escape. In the exchanges between the Op and the other people in the study, there is even a prolonging of suspense, which is very uncharacteristic of Hammett's usual style.

> "Did he leave any messages besides the one I read?"
> "None that's been found," O'Gar said. "Why?"
> "Any that you know of, Mrs. Leggett?" I asked.
> She shook her head.
> "Why?" O'Gar asked again.
> "He didn't commit suicide," I said. "He was murdered."
> Gabrielle Leggett screamed shrilly and sprung out of her chair, pointing a sharp-nailed white finger at Mrs. Leggett. (P. 52)

During this scene, the Op is highly conscious of the effect of his presence on the suspect, and like any good actor, he adjusts the tone of his voice to match his role.

> I filled my lungs and went on, not exactly bellowing, but getting plenty of noise out. (P. 53)

> I didn't give her a chance to answer any of these questions but sailed ahead, turning my voice loose. (P. 54)

> "*You,*" I thundered, my voice in fine form by now. (P. 54)

When the conventional moment arrives when the Op must make his formal accusation (in this case, of Alice Dain Leggett), he slips into the role of the supremely confident, all-knowing private detective, complete with rhetorical flourishes. "'He shielded you. He had always shielded you. *You,*' I thundered, my voice in fine form by now, 'killed your sister Lily, his first wife, and let her take the fall for you. *You* went to London with him after that. Would you have gone with your sister's murderer if you had been innocent? *You* had him traced here, and *you* came here after him and you married him. You were the one who decided he had married the wrong sister, and you killed her'" (pp. 54-55).

There is a considerable amount of humor and irony in the Op's posturing in this role, but there is also a more subtle irony at work that assumes greater significance as the novel progresses: despite his authoritative, persuasive tone and his carefully analyzed explanation of motive and method, the Op's solution here is wrong, and as we discover somewhat later, the Op is well aware of the fact that his explanation may be incorrect (as he tells Fitzstephan his view of the case, the Op admits, "One guess at the truth is about as good as another" [p. 62]). But only the Op and, of course, the murderer realize that his explanation is insufficient and that he is merely playing a role in his dramatic confrontation scene; like the characters in any classical story (and its readers), all the other people involved in the case accept the Op's constructed theory because it seems to obey the rules of logic and causality and because, more simply, his "fiction" provides a satisfactory system which explains away the mystery. In this scene the Op, like the classical detective, *seems* to define the "reality" of the Leggett case, and because the reality he creates out of the events appears logical, he is convincing. We are also given, however, the Op's later conversation with Fitzstephan in which he admits that other explanations would also fit the facts.

The second section of *The Dain Curse*, "The Temple," offers a distinctly different ambience and a distinctly different role for the Op. Although the temple of the chapter's title is located in San Francisco,[3] almost everything about the setting is highly reminiscent of a gothic thriller.[4] Inside the temple where Hammett focuses most of the chapter's action, there is a strange exotic cult that claims to be a reincarnation of a Gallic church, dating from the period of King Arthur. Members of this cult, the Temple of the Holy Grail, experience bizarre, religious "visions" and worship at a marble altar of "brilliant white, crystal, and silver" (p. 80) in the cult's main chamber—a surreal, inner courtyard whose walls, rising six stories to an open roof, are completely white and smooth except for a single door. The leaders of the cult, Aaronia and Joseph Haldorn, are a strikingly dramatic couple, and as described by the Op, their dark inscrutability and otherworldly appearance seem perfectly in keeping with the gothic atmosphere of their temple.

> I saw her eyes [Aaronia Haldorn's] first. They were enormous, almost black, warm, and heavily fringed with almost black lashes. They were the only live, human, real things in her face. There was warmth and there was beauty in her oval, olive-skinned face, but, except for the eyes, it was warmth and beauty that didn't seem to have anything to do with reality. It was as if her face were not a face, but a mask that she had worn until it had almost become a face. Even her mouth, which was a mouth to talk about, looked not so much like flesh as like a too perfect imitation of flesh, softer and redder and maybe warmer than genuine flesh, but not genuine flesh. Above this face, or mask, uncut black hair was tied close to her head, parted in the middle, and drawn across temples and upper ears to end in a knot on the nape of her neck. Her neck was long, strong, slender; her body tall, fully fleshed, supple; her clothes dark and silky, part of her body. (P. 39)

Joseph Haldorn was tall, built like a statue, and wore a black silk robe. His hair was thick, long, white, and glossy. His thick beard, trimmed round, was white and glossy. . . . His face, healthily pink, was without line or wrinkle. It was a tranquil face, especially the clear brown eyes, somehow making you feel at peace with the world. (P. 72)

When the second section opens, Gabrielle Leggett has gone to the temple to recover from the emotional stress caused by having witnessed the death of her parents. Hired by the family lawyer, who is suspicious of the Haldorns, the Op moves into a room across the hall from Gabrielle. During the Op's first night there, events prove the lawyer's fears to be well-founded: Joseph Haldorn has gone mad, and as part of his insanity, he has become obsessed with Gabrielle. In the Op's struggles to protect his client, he faces dangers that a hero in a gothic melodrama might encounter. For example, he meets a monstrous "ghost" with whom he struggles and barely subdues. "Not more than three feet away, there in the black room, a pale bright thing like a body, but not like flesh, stood writhing before me" (p. 87). Next, while groping his way through a labyrinth of darkened rooms and halls, the Op discovers the body of Gabrielle's doctor lying on the steps of the altar as if he had been made a sacrificial victim. When the Op finds Gabrielle, she appears like a sensationalized Lady Macbeth.

Gabrielle Leggett came around a corner just ahead of us. She was barefooted. Her only clothing was a yellow silk nightgown that was splashed with dark stains. In both hands, held out in front of her as she walked, she carried a large dagger, almost a sword. It was red and wet. Her hands and bare arms were red and wet. There was a dab of blood on one of her cheeks. Her eyes were clear, bright, and calm. Her small forehead was smooth, her mouth and chin firmly set. (P. 79)

Such parodic excesses also invest the scene in which the Op must fight with mad Joseph, who, believing himself to be God, is able to struggle with supernatural strength.

I yelled, "Stop," at him. He wouldn't stop. I was afraid. I fired. The bullet hit his cheek. I saw the hole it made. No muscle twitched in his face; not even his eyes blinked. He walked deliberately, not hurrying, towards me.

I worked the automatic's trigger, pumping six more bullets into his face and body. I saw them go in. And he came on steadily, showing in no way that he was conscious of them. His eyes and face were stern, but not angry. When he was close to me the knife in his hand went up high above his head. That's no way to fight with a knife; but he wasn't fighting; he was bringing retribution to me, and he paid as little attention to my attempts to stop him as a parent does to those of a small child he's punishing.

I was fighting. When the knife, shining over our heads, started down I went in under it, bending my right forearm against his knife-arm, driving the dagger in my left hand at his throat. I drove the heavy blade into his throat, until the hilt's cross stopped it. Then I was through. (P. 95)

When the gory violence and melodramatic action are over, the Op has successfully fulfilled part of his role as gothic hero: he has rescued the helpless heroine and destroyed the "supernatural" opponent. But the hero in a gothic melodrama is also expected to separate appearances from reality in the story and, ultimately, to vanquish the supernatural by bringing order and reason to the mysterious events. Just as he did in the first section, however, Hammett makes it impossible for the Op to fulfill his role by subtly undermining the Op's ability to see beneath the surface of things and to dissipate the final mystery. The motif, then, of delusion and false appearances runs throughout the section, including the discussions between the Op and Fitzstephan, which act as a kind of self-referential, running commentary on the Op's role in the case. For instance, the outward appearance of the temple's building certainly provides no clues about what it contains: the exotic Temple of the Holy Grail (which itself turns out to be a phony fraud scheme) is located in "a six-story yellow brick apartment building" (p. 37). Similarly, the external appearance of Joseph Haldorn belies his madness and violence and provides the Op with a very mistaken sense of comfort and serenity.

> It was a tranquil face, especially the clear brown eyes, somehow making you feel at peace with the world. The same soothing quality was in his baritone voice:
> He said: "We are happy to have you here."
> The words were merely polite, meaningless, yet, as he said them, I actually believed that for some reason he was happy. Now I understood Gabrielle Leggett's desire to come to this place. I said that I, too, was happy to be there, and while I was saying it I actually thought I was. (Pp. 72-73)

Throughout this section the Op is repeatedly misled in this manner, for external signs are consistently ambiguous or deceiving. Indeed, on several occasions the Op is unable to distinguish illusion from reality. When he confronts the ghost in Minnie Hershey's room, his struggles enact, in miniature, his relationship to the shifting, deceptive elements of the Dain case.

> It was tall, yet not so tall as it seemed. . . . Its feet—it had feet, but I don't know what their shape was. They had no shape, just as the thing's legs and torso, arms and hands, head and face, had no shape, no fixed form. . . . No feature or member ever stopped twisting, quivering, writhing long enough for its average outline, its proper shape, to be seen. . . . I knew then that I was off-balance from breathing the dead-flower stuff, but I couldn't—though I tried to—tell myself that I did not see this thing. It was there. It was there within reach of my hand if I leaned forward, shivering, writhing, between me and the door. I didn't believe in the supernatural—but what of that? The thing was there. It was there and it was not, I knew, a trick of luminous paint, a man with a sheet over him. (Pp. 87-88)

Like the ghost confronting the Op, nothing in the Dain case will stop "twisting, quivering, writhing long enough for its average outline, its proper shape, to be seen," and the Op's efforts to determine the shape are made all the more difficult because he can trust none of his senses. Thus the Op's ability to *see*, to understand, and to bring things into focus is constantly thwarted, as in the following scene:

> I was half-way between the second and the first floors when I saw something move below—or, rather, saw the movement of something without actually seeing it. It moved from the direction of the streetdoor towards the interior of the house. I was looking towards the elevator at the time as I walked down the stairs. The banister shut off my view of the street-door. What I saw was a flash of movement across half a dozen of the spaces between the banister's uprights. By the time I had brought my eyes into focus there, there was nothing to see. I thought I had seen a face, but that's what anybody would have thought in my position, and all I had actually seen was the movement of something pale. (P. 77)

By the end of part 2, the Op does manage to rescue Gabrielle and to explain some of the mystery surrounding the peculiar elements in the case (he discovers that the ghost was only a technological gimmick and that Gabrielle had been tricked into believing she had murdered Riese), but even at the section's conclusion, while he explains the meaning of the events to Fitzstephan, the Op acknowledges his inability to provide any *final* answers. After he suggests to Fitzstephan that Joseph Haldorn had tried to murder his wife, the Op replies to Fitzstephan's incredulity by saying:

> "Yeah, but what difference does that make? It might as well have been anybody else for all the sense it makes. I hope you're not trying to keep this nonsense straight in your mind. You know damned well this didn't happen."
> "Then what," he asked, looking puzzled, "did happen?"
> "I don't know. I don't think anybody knows. I'm telling you what I saw plus the part of what Aaronia Haldorn told me which fits in with what I saw. To fit in with what I saw, most of it must have happened pretty nearly as I've told you. If you want to believe it did, all right. I don't. I'd rather believe I saw things that weren't there." (P. 103)

Coming as these remarks do after the conventional "solution" has been supplied and all the loose ends tied together, the Op's admission undercuts our expectations: the detective is supposed to reassure us through confident claims to accuracy and not, as the Op does here, to suggest the arbitrary basis of final truths. Although an explanation has been provided which fits the facts, the real mystery remains intact since, as the Op suggests, there are many other theories which would serve as well.

In the third section of *The Dain Curse* there is another change of setting and of detective story "types." According to the Op's description, Quesada, where much of the action in this setting occurs, is a typical coastal small town. "Quesada was a one-hotel town pasted on the rocky side of a young mountain that sloped into the Pacific Ocean some eighty miles from San Francisco. Quesada's beach was much too hard and jagged for bathing, so Quesada had never got much summer-resort money. For a while it had been a hustling rum-running port, but that racket was dead now: bootleggers had learned there was more profit and less worry in handling domestic hootch than imported. Quesada had gone back to sleep" (p. 110). Thus the continental atmosphere of the first section and the gothic atmosphere of the second are here replaced by a rural ambience that provides the Op with a new role: the romantic, protective hero. Quesada is the sort of community where a person has not "a chance in the world of getting anything to eat . . . before seven o'clock" (p. 111), where it is difficult to find your way "unless you knew the country" (p. 111), and where the law enforcement officers have common, folksy names like Dick Cotton and Ben Rolly. When the Op is looking for Rolly (the deputy sheriff), he encounters a citizenry which is "countrified" both in language and in custom, despite its proximity to San Francisco.

> I went back to Quesada . . . and asked the clerk—a dapper boy, this one—who was responsible for law and order there.
>
> "The marshall's Dick Cotton," he told me; "but he went up to the city last night. Ben Rolly's deputy sheriff. You can likely find him over at his old man's office."
>
> "Where's that?"
>
> "Next door to the garage."
>
> I found it, a one-story red brick building with wide glass windows labeled *J. King Rolly, Real Estate, Mortgages, Loans, Stocks and Bonds, Insurance, Notes, Employment Agency, Notary Public, Moving and Storage* and a lot more that I've forgotten.
>
> Two men were inside, sitting with their feet on a battered desk behind a battered counter. One man was a man of fifty and with hair, eyes, and skin of indefinite, washed-out shades—an amiable, aimless-looking man in shabby clothes. The other was twenty years younger and in twenty years would look just like him.
>
> "I'm hunting," I said, "for the deputy sheriff."
>
> "Me," the younger man said, easing his feet from desk to floor. He didn't get up. Instead, he put a foot out, hooked a chair by its rounds, pulled it from the wall, and returned his feet to the desk-top. "Set down. This is Pa," wiggling a thumb at the other man. "You don't have to mind him." (P. 115)

Hammett creates several other scenes which also illustrate country etiquette and vividly contrast city and country ways. A scene such as the following seems drawn right out of a comedy of manners:

> "Howdy, Mary," Rolly greeted her. "Why ain't you over to the Carters'?"
> "I'm sick, Mr. Rolly." She spoke without accent. "Chills—so I just stayed

home today."

"Tch, tch, tch. That's too bad. Have you had the doc?"

She said she hadn't. Rolly said she ought to. She said she didn't need him: she had chills often. Rolly said that might be so, but that was all the more reason for having him: it was best to play safe and have things like that looked after. She said yes but doctors took so much money, and it was bad enough being sick without having to pay for it. He said in the long run it was likely to cost folks more not having a doctor than having him. I had begun to think they were going to keep it up all day when Rolly finally brought the talk around to the Carters again, asking the woman about her work there. (P. 122)

Appropriately enough, this change in setting also signals a further transformation of the Op's role; having already adopted the roles of classical detective and gothic hero, he now seems to become the gentlemanly, romantic hero of a domestic melodrama. His new persona is a complex, multileveled blend of tough-guy, psychologist, homespun philosopher, and gentleman protector. He remains, of course, the sleuth who solves the mystery, but this effort appears largely subordinate to his personal ministrations to Gabrielle, whom he protects and cures of her morphine habit. Not only does he watch out for her physical well-being, the Op also generally reestablishes her sense of worth. Thus the Op functions as a kind of father figure who advises Gabrielle where to stay, hires a nurse to watch out for her, and even tells her when she should get under the bed covers (p. 157). Gabrielle places herself totally in his hands, and like the most old-fashioned of heroes, the Op takes care of her without any attempt to compromise her virtue. At one point, he even pretends to Gabrielle that his tough-guy professionalism is merely a disguise that masks a sentimental heart.

"I'm twice your age, sister; an old man. I'm damned if I'll make a chump of myself by telling you why I did it [helped her], why it was neither revolting nor disgusting, why I'd do it again and be glad of the chance."

She jumped out of her chair, her eyes round and dark, her mouth trembling. "You mean—? "

"I don't mean anything that I'll admit," I said; "and if you're going to parade around with that robe hanging open you're going to get yourself some bronchitis. You ex-hop heads have to be careful about catching cold." (P. 199)

Despite the Op's ability to project himself into these various roles, Gabrielle Leggett eventually sees through his masks and indicates that she understands the nature of his multileveled persona. In a revealing scene which follows the one in which the Op implies that he might love her, Gabrielle confronts him with his deception. "You sat there this noon and deliberately tried to make me think you were in love with me. . . . I honestly believed you all afternoon—and it *did* help. I believed you until you came in just now, and then I saw—. . . A monster. A nice one, an especially nice one to have around when you're in trouble, but a monster just the same, without any human foolishness like love in him" (p. 204). Although, as we have seen, this issue of the Op's absolute allegiance to his job at the expense of human involvement recedes in importance in *The Dain Curse*, it occasionally does resurface in scenes such as this one. Certainly here, as in *Red Harvest*, the Op's professionalism seems genuine enough; in trying to solve the Dain case as efficiently as possible, his helpfulness and seeming concern towards Gabrielle are perfectly in keeping with that end. Her accusation that he is a "monster" and her earlier observation that "there's no personal relationship with you. It's professional with you—your work" (p. 168) indicate that she finally sees him for what he is.

In addition to providing such insight into the Op's character, Gabrielle Leggett helps unify the widely varying sections of the novel. While the nature of the Op's role changes in each of the three sections, her character remains constant: she is the stereotypical female victim. Whether she is the heroine of a classical story, a gothic thriller, or a country romance, she is passive and helpless to the point of catatonia, unable to control or interpret anything that happens around her, and constantly needing men to rescue her from other men. Indeed, the whole saga of Gabrielle Leggett is so outrageous and excessive that it could be read as a darkly humorous parody of the trials and tribulations genre of popular fiction and films. At the age of five she is involved in the murder of her mother (perhaps even having pulled the trigger herself and certainly having witnessed it), and thereafter she is raised by her mad, murderous aunt. As an adult, she witnesses the murders of several people (her father is murdered as well as her stepmother, her husband, and her doctor); she is kidnapped; she attempts suicide; she is molested by every family member mentioned in the book; and she is also addicted to morphine, mentally unstable, and sexually frigid. As the Op sums things up, "All the calamities known to man have been piled up on you" (p. 167).

The villain of the case likewise ends his career in a manner so excessive that it is more whimsical and parodic than realistic. Unlike the typical murderer in most hard-boiled fiction who is dispatched in a hail of bullets or who dies in a dramatic showdown with the detective or who is prosaically executed by the state, Fitzstephan meets with a truly extraordinary fate. Although he is almost literally blown in two, losing his right arm, right leg, and the right side of his face, he eventually recovers to explain his own involvement in the case to the Op. After being found insane at the trial, he is sent to a mental institution for a year and is then released into the custody of Joseph Haldorn's widow—a woman he himself once tried to murder—who whisks him away to an island off Puget Sound.

Although this final twist in the case—the murderer disappearing to a western isle with one of his intended victims—is bizarre, it is an appropriate end to *The Dain Curse*. Just as in *Red Harvest*, where personal relationships were twisted and corrupt, the traditional alliances of people—husband/wife, lovers, parent/child, friends—are characterized by strange, unaccountable, often destructive emotions. Most of the rules governing relationships have been broken down along with the traditional view that love unifies, heals, and makes life cohere. If the final assessment of relationships is less bleak here than in Hammett's first novel (at the novel's conclusion, Gabrielle has been taken in by her in-laws and seems happy with them), this is due more to tone than to content, for the samples we see of human relations here range from the distasteful and unethical attempts at seduction by the family lawyer to the pathetic infidelities of Mrs. Cotton. Many of these relationships start with and end in violence: one of the sisters murders another and then raises her niece only to have the power to force the girl's father to marry her; Joseph Haldorn tries to murder his wife because of his love for Gabrielle—and does so right before the eyes of his son; in Quesada a husband murders his wife because she has been unfaithful. In *The Dain Curse* relationships are so twisted and intensely passionate that people's behavior becomes virtually inexplicable by normal standards. For example, Alice Dain hates her sister so much that she skillfully plays the part of the loving aunt for years. "There was nothing her Aunt Alice wouldn't do for her dear niece; because her preferring me infuriated Lily, not that Lily herself loved the child so much, but that we were sisters; and whatever one wanted the other wanted, not to share, but exclusively" (p. 57). Even Aaronia Haldorn, who appears to be relatively sane, has an attachment for Fitzstephan that is irrational and mad; despite the fact that he has tried to kill her, she is willing to take him, a hopeless cripple, away after he is released from the mental institution. Fitzstephan is himself the clearest, most extreme example of these grotesque relationships. The primary impetus for much of the violence and horror in the novel is his alleged love for Gabrielle, a woman he views as his rightful property, "bought with the deaths he has caused" (p. 209). In developing these emotional excesses, wild extremes of passion and hatred, and unpredictable responses to events, Hammett is not only presenting a commentary on the precarious, unstable nature of human emotions and personality. Just as importantly, Hammett uses these unfathomable extremes to justify a manipulation of the plot elements, deepening the mystery and making it virtually impossible for us—or for the Op—to put the pieces of the case into a coherent whole. As we shall see, the labyrinthine nature of the plot is an important aspect of Hammett's self-conscious, metafictional intent in the novel.

Although the three sections of *The Dain Curse* are separate and closed installments with differences of excess in each, the overall effect of the plot is unified because each section reinforces Hammett's central intent in the novel—to explore the knowing process by an examination of the formal properties of fiction in general and of detective fiction in particular. Thus, each of the three sections can be viewed, on one level, as Hammett's effort to examine the way that different mystery genres operate, to see how they relate to one another and what their form implies. But Hammett does not just develop these "types" in a straightforward fashion; rather, his manipulations are so obviously excessive, often almost parodically so, that a playful self-consciousness is present in *The Dain Curse* that was utterly absent in *Red Harvest*. Certainly readers familiar with the genres Hammett was mimicking in the three sections would find his manipulations often amusing or at least technically interesting and would thus be distanced from the action of the book in a way uncharacteristic of most detective fiction. Indeed, the story is too fantastic for the issue of credibility or realism to ever really arise. By making the plot so outlandish and by providing a series of contradictory denouements, Hammett forces us to see the absurdity of one of the principal assumptions of the detective genre: that a single truth exists somewhere that accounts for mystery, whether it be the mystery of a crime or the mystery of why people feel and act as they do. Hammett's intent to examine how we arrive at such truths—truths which he reveals to be "fictions"—is evident not only in his manipulations of plot but also in the way he develops the key relationship between the Op and Fitzstephan, detective and murderer.

As we have seen, each section of *The Dain Curse* concludes with the Op arriving at an explanation of what has happened and who the guilty parties are, based on the evidence at his disposal. Each denouement satisfies our expectations of the genre: puzzling clues are clarified, missing pieces supplied, guilt assigned, and loose ends worked into a coherent system. Each conventional conclusion, however, is undermined by the action of the next section which introduces matters that make the previous solution inadequate. What happens on the level of plot, of course, is that *new* puzzling events occur, evidently related to the earlier events; new clues and information are supplied which place previous action in a totally new light. Obviously, such a system of plot development undercuts the usual epistemological assumptions of detective fiction. . . . [T]he detective's main duty, either in the classical or hard-boiled story, is to separate illusion from reality and to arrive eventually, by use of reason and logic, at a final answer which dispels the mystery in the case. In *The Dain Curse*, however, Hammett ironically creates a detective who believes that final solutions are merely fictional projections of our need to impose order on an inexplicable and fundamentally mysterious universe. The Op's views about his own personal role in interpreting these mysteries will be examined more fully when we turn to his relationship with Fitzstephan, but these attitudes suggest that, even on the level of the novel's action, he is not a trustworthy perceiver. It is not that he has some particular bias that distorts his perception; it is simply the partial nature of all perception. Again and again, the Op is placed in circumstances where he realizes that what he sees is likely to be deceptive. Certainly the woman who appeared on the Leggett porch at the beginning of the novel (Alice Leggett) whom the Op describes as "about my age, forty, with darkish blond hair, a pleasant plump face, and dimpled pink cheeks" with "a lavender-flowered white housedress" (p. 5) does not *look* like the vicious murderer of her sister and several others, just as the ghost the Op fights in the temple *looks* real enough at that time. With our senses so patently unreliable, our ability to reason inductively and to draw conclusions from our experiences becomes suspect. Indeed, the fact that our hold on reality is so tenuous and our methods of arriving at truth are so haphazard makes us cling to our illusions of order ever the more tightly. In one of the novel's key passages, the Op explains to Gabrielle his recognition of how unreliable our mechanisms for arriving at truth are.

> "Nobody thinks clearly, no matter what they pretend. Thinking's a dizzy business, a matter of catching as many of those foggy glimpses as you can and fitting them together the best way you can. That's why people hang on so tight to their beliefs and opinions, because, compared to the haphazard way in which they're arrived at, even the goofiest opinion seems wonderfully clear, sane, and self-evident. And if you let it get away from you, then you've got to dive back into that foggy muddle to wrangle yourself out another to take its place." (P. 166)

The Op ultimately fails at the "dizzy business" of fitting these "foggy glimpses" together perfectly. He is correct in identifying Owen Fitzstephan as the murderer and is able to deduce the course of his crimes,[5] but he overlooks the most portentous clue of all: Fitzstephan is a Dain and, as such, is susceptible to the "Dain Curse." When Owen tells him this fact, the detective—the man who supposedly has everything under control by the end of the story—can only respond, "I'll be damned" (p. 202). This detail of Owen's ancestry may have no bearing on the mechanics of the crimes themselves, and the Op is able to figure out Owen's guilt without this knowledge, but it is an added element that emphasizes Hammett's central point all the more strongly: that we can never know *enough*, either about others or ourselves, to comprehend life. As the Op puts it at one point, "Evidence of goofiness is easily found: the more you dig into yourself, the more you turn up" (p. 166), and because we cannot know enough, we should hesitate about making moral judgments, which is one reason why the Op avoids self-righteous denunciations of the chief villains in both *Red Harvest* and *The Dain Curse*. At the conclusion of the novel, Owen's insanity is viewed by the courts and public as the key to his crimes and the ultimate explanation for his behavior. But the Op is well aware that, while such designations as "insanity" conveniently label or categorize actions, they do not explain them. To call a man insane does not explain his behavior any more fully than to claim it results from a family curse. Throughout the novel, the Op rejects the validity of all systems that classify. For instance, when Fitzstephan tries to explain the fact that his friend Ralph Coleman "always had the most consistently logical and credible reasons for having done the most idiotic things" by labeling him "an advertising man," the Op disdainfully comments, "as if that explained it" (p. 100). Likewise, the Op tells Ben Rolly that he mistrusts the theory of the curse. "The trouble with it is it's worked out too well, too regularly. It's the first one I ever ran across that did." Rolly agrees with him but adds that in this kind of world anything is possible. "Still and all, you do hear of them working out. There's things that happen that make a fellow think there's things in the world—in life—that he don't know much about. . . . It's inscrutable" (p. 117). Certainly the Op is unwilling to use a label like insanity to dismiss the ambiguities of events because he fully realizes the inexplicable nature of nearly all people and events; as he tells Gabrielle, "anybody who started hunting for evidence of insanity in himself would certainly find plenty, because all but stupid minds were jumbled affairs" (p. 172). As will be seen, this skepticism of the ability of any humanly devised system, no matter how complex, to provide final solutions is also crucial for the metafictional concerns of *The Dain Curse.*

If the plot of *The Dain Curse*, with its successive, contradictory revelations, serves to undermine the usual authority of the detective-as-reasoner, so, too, do the debates between Fitzstephan and the Op develop these same epistemological notions. Introducing the series of conversations between the murderer and the detective in which both men analyze the meaning of the case and debate various issues concerning literature and reason is probably Hammett's most brilliant strategic success in the novel, for these discussions allow him to create a complex and playful ironic commentary on the action in the novel *and* on the fictional strategy he himself employs in its presentation. More specifically, these running conversations serve at least five interconnected functions in the novel: (1) they allow the Op to bring together all the clues before us and to announce his analysis of them; (2) they *further* the mystery (rather than clarifying it) since Fitzstephan constantly tries to confuse the issues and throw the Op off the track; (3) they generate a metafictional commentary on the assumptions underlying traditional fiction in general and detective fiction in particular; (4) they comment upon Hammett's own approach to detective writing; and (5) they focus the central epistemological issues of the book by demonstrating how closely related the concept of "fiction making" is for the novelist, for the detective, and for the ordinary person.

When the name Owen Fitzstephan is casually introduced in connection with the Leggett case (chapter 1), the Op recalls that they had been "fairly chummy for a month or two" (p. 18) when they had first met on a case in New York, and he decides to look him up to obtain some inside information about the Leggett household. The two key facts that we must always keep in mind while trying to analyze Fitzstephan's role in the novel are that he is a professional novelist and that he is the villain, the man responsible for most of the murders and therefore anxious to keep the Op off the scent of his trail. Because Owen is the murderer, we must always view his remarks with suspicion—and Hammett has a considerable amount of fun in presenting Owen's comments in the context of an elaborate game of wits between these two unlikely adversaries. But it is also no accident that Fitzstephan is given the profession of a novelist, for this allows Hammett to create an intricate interplay between Fitzstephan—a kind of traditional novelist figure—and the Op—who becomes the embodiment of the spokesman for Hammett's own theory of fiction writing.

When the Op first calls on Fitzstephan, we are told of the writer that he is "a man who pretended to be lazier than he was, would rather talk than do anything else, and had a lot of what seemed to be accurate information and original ideas on any subject that happened to come up, as long as it was a little out of the ordinary" (p. 18). This description might well apply to many eccentric fictional detectives, from Dupin to Holmes to Philo Vance, and as it turns out, Fitzstephan is eager to play amateur detective by "assisting" the Op in unraveling the case. Throughout the novel the two men spend considerable time together going over the case's facts, analyzing new evidence, and developing potential solutions. On a very simple level, Owen plays a kind of straight man, a conventional role often found in detective fiction: like that of Watson in the Sherlock Holmes series, Fitzstephan's presence provides an excuse for the Op to lay out the elements of the complicated case, explain his reasoning about the connection of the clues, and discuss alternative solutions. Fitzstephan assists this process in the conventional manner by raising important issues, questioning the detective about unclear elements, and providing possible alternative answers. Naturally, however, the fact that Owen is the actual murderer makes all his remarks and observations highly ironic; he is anxious to assist the Op in creating an inductively developed premise or final solution, but only so long as it never implicates *him* in the case. Thus he not only deliberately obscures elements that are crucial to the case, but he also constantly reinforces the Op's conclusions when they are leading in the wrong direction.

Having the detective analyze the case with the murderer creates a series of amusing and dramatically effective incidents.[6] But there are also serious issues Hammett can present by using this approach. Not only does Fitzstephan play the role of murderer trying to disguise his involvement in the crimes, but he can also be shown to approach the entire case much as a *novelist* would—with a novelist's strong sense of proper narrative structure, the tendency to rely on psychological systems to explain character motivation, the delight in colorful, vivid details, and the desire for absolute answers that will produce a pleasing, aesthetic whole. Obviously, each of the "novelistic biases" is very useful to Fitz-stephan, for if the Op were to try to solve the Dain case as if it were a case in a traditional novel, he would probably fail; life, Hammett always implies, simply does not supply the kind of ready answers that most novelists are so anxious to provide. Fitzstephan embodies exactly the kind of novelistic stance that Hammett personally despised and which he was reacting against in his own work. The Op, on the other hand, represents Hammett's disdain for theatrics and simplistic solutions and a distrust of easy psychological explanations for complex human behavior; like Hammett the Op is well aware that most fiction—and especially detective fiction (including the "fictional presentations" of newspaper reporting)[7]—is too quick to assume there are absolute answers and too ready to take what is colorful and aesthetically correct as true, hence missing life as it really is—dull, trivial, and often utterly ambiguous and inscrutable, even to the trained detective's eye. Thus as we watch the Op grappling with the bizarre complexities of the Dain case, we should gradually realize that neither he nor Hammett is going to be able to supply the kind of well-rounded whole that we expect in a novel; it is in this way that Hammett's personal and metafictional themes can be seen to subtly intersect and support each other.

From their first encounter onward, the contrast between the Op' pragmatic, cautious method of handling the Dain case and Fitzstephan's more flamboyant, "novelistic" approach is clearly evident. One of Owen's first remarks to the Op—"Don't try to be subtle with me, my son; that's not your style at all" (p. 20)—indicates his awareness of the Op's straightforward approach to detection (these remarks are also a good example of many similar passages where Hammett may be playfully calling attention to his own literary strategies). This approach distrusts any efforts to dramatize or embellish a case—efforts that are, however, crucial for a good novelist. When Fitzstephan demands a quick evaluation of "what Leggett's been up to" the Op explains one of the key differences between their respective ways of handling their "material." "We don't do it that way. . . . You're a storywriter. I can't trust you not to build up on what I tell you. I'll save mine till after you've spoken your piece, so yours won't be twisted to fit mine" (p. 20).[8] As the exchange continues and Owen displays his novelistic tendencies by creating a neatly detailed psychological profile (a profile as noted earlier that evokes the Holmes/Dupin figure), the Op is quick to undercut what he sees as fabrication.

> "He's [Leggett] always interested me. There's something obscure in him, something dark and inviting. He is, for instance, physically ascetic—neither smoking or drinking, eating meagerly, sleeping, I'm told, only three or four hours a night—but mentally, or spiritually, sensual—does that mean anything to you?—to the point of decadence. You used to think I had an abnormal appetite for the fantastic. You should know him. His friends—no, he hasn't any—his choice companions are those who have the most outlandish ideas to offer: Marquard and his insane figures that aren't figures; Denbar Curt and his algebraism; the Haldorns and their Holy Grail sect; crazy Laura Joines; Farnham—:
>
> "And you," I put in, "with explanations and descriptions that explain and describe nothing. I hope you don't think any of what you've said means anything to me." (P. 20)

In a scene such as this one, it is obvious where Hammett's sympathies lie. The essence of the difference between the Op and Fitzstephan is not that Owen is a creative thinker and the Op a hardnosed pragmatist; it is rather that Owen consistently demands a single system to produce a single answer, while the Op knows that such systems evolve from *aesthetic* attitudes and our desire for order and clarity and that they simply are not adequate in the real world. In one of their crucial confrontations, the Op arrives at Owen's house to find "the novelist in Fitzstephan . . . busy trying to find what he called Mrs. Leggett's psychological basis" (p. 60-61). The rest of their conversation is a good example of the complex interplay that is present in all their encounters.

> "The killing of her sister is plain enough, knowing her character as we do

now," he said, "and so are the killing of her husband, her attempt to ruin her niece's life when she was exposed, and even her determination to kill herself on the stairs rather than be caught. But the quiet years in between—where do they fit in?"

"It's Leggett's murder that doesn't fit in," I argued. "The rest is all one piece. . . . She was simply a woman who wanted what she wanted and was willing to go to any length to get it. Look how patiently, and for how many years, she hid her hatred from the girl. And her wants weren't even very extravagant. You won't find the key to her in any complicated derangements. She was simple as an animal, with an animal's simple ignorance of right and wrong, dislike for being thwarted, and spitefulness when trapped."

Fitzstephan drank beer and asked:

"You'd reduce the Dain curse, then, to a primitive strain in the blood?"

"To less than that, to words in an angry woman's mouth."

"It's fellows like you that take all the color out of life. . . . Doesn't Gabrielle being made the tool of her mother's murder convince you of the necessity—at least the poetic necessity—of the curse?"

"Not even if she *was* the tool, and that's something I wouldn't bet on. . . . Gabrielle had been brought up to believe her father the murderer—so we can believe that. . . . But, from that point on, one guess at the truth is about as good as another. . . ."

"You jump around so," Fitzstephan complained. . . . "Why don't you stick to your answer? . . ."

"That was good enough to say then," I admitted; "but not now, in cold blood, with more facts to fit in." (Pp. 61-62).

Owen's desire for a simple, straightforward explanation is obviously motivated by his desire to keep the Op away from the complex realities of the case, but his comments here are also perfectly in keeping with the aesthetic impulse of his art, which relies on causal explanations and character motivation that readers can easily follow. In virtually all novels, no matter how intricately developed, there must finally be a "solution" provided, whereby the reader can solve the mystery of the plot by having paid careful attention to the "clues" planted by the author.[9] Owen obviously would like the Op to believe that the world operates on this same principle; consequently, he is constantly deriding the Op's qualified explanations and his tiresome attention to trivial details as being aesthetically uninteresting. "You've got it all certainly as tangled and confused as possible," he tells the Op, to which the Op replies, "It'll get worse before it's better" (p. 32); later Owen disgustedly comments: "Aw, shut up. You're never satisfied until you've got two buts and an if attached to everything. . . . Always belittling. You need more beer to expand your soul" (p. 63); and, similarly, after the Op begins another recital of the alternative explanations: "Not now. Later, after you've finished the story, you can attach your ifs and buts to it, distorting and twisting it, making it as cloudy and confusing and generally hopeless as you like" (pp. 103-4). But perhaps his strongest indictment occurs when he tells the Op: "Nobody's mysteries ought to be as tiresome as you're making this one. . . . *I* like the Nick Carter school better" (p. 154)—a remark which, again, calls our attention to Hammett's own self-reflexive interests.

For his part, the Op largely dismisses Fitzstephan's charges as being naïve and too "literary." When Owen calls him about a puzzling phone call that he has received, the Op is quick to deride his tendency to storify events. "Spring the puzzle. Don't be too literary with me, building up to climaxes and the like. I'm too crude for that—it'd only give me a bellyache" (p. 131). "Crude" or not, the Op has his own method of proceeding in a case, a method which is unglamorous, painfully slow, and realistic about its limitations. Despite Dupin and Holmes, the detective does not catch criminals because he has a superior artistic imagination. Thus, when Fitzstephan asks whether or not the criminal in this case may be too wily for him and has outwitted him, the Op says: "You've got a flighty mind. That's no good in this business. You don't catch murderers by amusing yourself with interesting thoughts. You've got to sit down to all the facts you can get and turn them over and over till they click" (p. 153). The Op echoes this summary of his own approach to his work in two other passages.

> I spent most of the afternoon putting my findings and guesses on paper and trying to fit them together in some sort of order. (P. 33)

> I piled up the facts I had, put some guesses on them, and took a jump from the top of the heap into space. (P. 190)

As all three passages pointedly suggest, the Op hardly views himself as the embodiment of reason who can put the pieces of reality's mystery back into a coherent whole. Quite the contrary, he views the operations of the mind with considerable distrust, fully aware of the arbitrary nature of putting the pieces into any particular formation that seems to work. "Nobody thinks clearly," he says and later adds that all beliefs and opinions are derived in a "haphazard way" (p. 166). With such a skeptical outlook, it is not surprising that he never claims to have discovered any final solutions; as is appropriate in a novel plotted to continually add new information, the Op's "solutions" are always presented as temporary, convenient guesses which somehow manage to account for the evidence.[10]

The end products of people's criminal actions, then, are definable (theft, rape, murder), but the *human reality* that underlies these actions (motivation, passion, emotion, personality) can never be fully understood or conveniently explained. The question asked by Fitzstephan, "What happened after that?"—the classic response of the listener to the storyteller—and the Op's answer, "Nothing. . . .That's the kind of story it is. I warned you there was no sense to it" (p. 105), reverberate far beyond Gabrielle Leggett and her troubles. For Dashiell Hammett the "truth" is always elusive and any pattern that claims total validity is merely "a matter of catching as many of those foggy glimpses as you can and fitting them together the best you can" (p. 166). The Op interrupts a traditional denouement to ask Fitzstephan, "You actually believe what I've told you so far?" and when the answer is yes, he continues: "What a childish mind you've got. . . . Let me tell you the story about the wolf that went to the little girl's grandmother's house and—" (p. 104). Because the world, as Hammett sees it, is irrational and random, we can best interpret it and live in it if we are aware of the dangers of absolutes—a theme he develops more fully in *The Maltese Falcon.* [Southern Illinois UP, 1985: 61-87]

NOTES

1. This is not to suggest, however, that the issue of the Op's job does not appear at all in this novel. There are several instances where the Op's insistence on job—and his lack of human emotion—appears in *The Dain Curse*, as well. For several examples where the Op seems to respond coldly to the human reality of the case while rationalizing his lack of emotion as being "job-oriented," see pp. 43, 60, 135, and 168.

2. This interest in epistemology is, for the most part, missing in *Red Harvest*, and since most critics regard Hammett's second novel as merely a sequel to the first, very little attention has been paid to the issue. There are no critical articles that deal solely with *The Dain Curse*, but the most valuable general discussion is Steven Marcus's introduction to *The Continental Op*. Although the discussion does not pertain specifically to either *Red Harvest* or *The Dain Curse*, it does provide an insightful analysis of the metaphysical impulse in Hammett's work. Marcus focuses on how Hammett integrates his metaphysical/metafictional interests with the detective novel format. As Marcus details the usual pattern of the Op's cases, the Op is typically called to the scene of a crime or a potential crime where he is met by conflicting stories, motives, and accusations. Different versions of "reality" have been constructed by different characters—some with the clear intention of creating confusion, some merely the result of ignorance or prejudice—and as detective, the Op's job is "to deconstruct, decompose, deplot and defictionalize that 'reality' and to construct or reconstruct out of it a true fiction, i.e., an account of what 'really' happened" (New York: Vintage, 1975), p. xix. Marcus goes on to point out, however, that this process does not lead to the omnipotent unveiling of a final truth, as ordinarily happens in other hardboiled detective fiction, but to the replacing of myriad illusions of reality with a single vision—the Op's.

> What happens in Hammett is that what is revealed as "reality" is a still further fiction-making activity—in the first place the Op's, and behind that yet another, the consciousness present in many of the Op stories and all the novels that Dashiell Hammett, the writer, is continually doing the same thing as the Op and all the other characters in the fiction he is creating. That is to say, he is making a fiction (in writing) in the real world; and this fiction, like the real world itself, is coherent but not necessarily rational. What one both begins and ends with, then, is a story, a narrative, a coherent yet questionable account of the world. (Marcus, p. xxii)

3. Hammett also gains a certain amount of verisimilitude by setting this section in San Francisco, for he undoubtedly relied on the fact that most of his readers would feel California was the most likely place for a cult such as this one to take root (the Jim Jones tragedy of 1978 only reinforces this conviction). Within the novel itself, there are two

specific references to this popular association of California and "kooky cults": at one point Collinson comments of the Temple of the Holy Grail that "it's the fashionable one just now. You know how they come and go in California" (p. 36); later the Op agrees with this assessment. "They brought their cult to California because everybody does, and picked San Francisco because it held less competition than Los Angeles" (p. 97).

4. Although few hard-boiled detective novels carry the gothic atmosphere as far as does *The Dain Curse*, it is important to note that these gothic elements exist in other forms in the genre. There has always been an obvious connection between classical detective fiction and the gothic thriller, beginning with Poe and Doyle (especially *The Hound of the Baskervilles*) but with hard-boiled fiction, these gothic elements are transformed by an urban twentieth century sensibility. The mysterious, all-powerful villain who controls those around him from his solitary country estate becomes a czar of organized crime who lives in the city he rules. The monster often becomes the city itself, uncontrollable and threatening. But in almost all hard-boiled fiction, these gothic elements are rendered as inconspicuously as possible; Hammett, however, blatantly exploits them. And in that exploitation, he insists once more on the artifice of his own fiction.

5. Hammett skillfully leaves even the Op's final solution open to question; a reader may well wonder if there might not be *some* elements of truth in Gabrielle Leggett's "confession"—she claims *she* is the real murderer and supplies a surprisingly coherent explanation of all that has happened considering the fact that she is in the throes of morphine withdrawal symptoms (pp. 196-97). It would be easy enough, if we took her story seriously, to disregard Owen Fitzstephan's confession since it is just possible that he is in love with her; horribly mutilated by the bomb blast, Owen might well have decided to take a chance by confessing to the crime himself, especially since he felt he had an excellent chance to "beat the rap" (which he basically does, by reason of insanity).

6. This method is fairly common and has been employed with great success on the television series "Columbo," although there the tables are turned since the detective—and the viewers—know who is guilty, while the criminal is not aware of this.

7. Hammett makes fun of newspapers' tendency to fictionalize events for mere sensation's sake throughout his fiction. In this novel, Fitzstephan comments, for example, that he needs "direct" news of events, "instead of having to depend on what I can get out of you [the Op] and what the newspapers imagine their readers would like to think had happened" (p. 96).

8. The Op makes another disparaging comment about Owen's tendency to romanticize people and events when he says: "So you read newspapers? What do you think he is? King of the bootleggers? Chief of an international crime syndicate? A white-slave magnate? Head of a dope ring? Or queen of the counterfeiters in disguise?" (p. 21).

9. For a complete treatment of this analogy between readers of traditional fiction and detectives, see William Spanos's "The Detective and the Boundary: Some Notes on the Postmodern Literary Imagination," *boundary 2* 1 (Fall 1972): 147-68.

10. The Op also has no illusions about the role of "truth" in our court systems. When Gabrielle's lawyer, Madison, asks the Op at one point if he thinks Gabrielle actually believes one of his hypotheses, the Op snaps: "Who said anybody believes it? I'm just telling you what we'll go into court with. You know there's not necessarily any connection between what's true and what you go into court with" (p. 188).

WORKS CITED

Hammett, Dashiell. *The Dain Curse*. New York: Vintage, 1972.
Marcus, Steven. "Introduction." In *The Continental Op*, by Dashiell Hammett. New York: Vintage, 1975.

"A Long and Laughable Story": Hammett's *The Dain Curse* and the Postmodern Condition

Bruce Gatenby

> There was no way of really knowing anything, not even that there was no way of really knowing anything.
> —Joseph Heller, *Catch 22*

> I'm a detective. I know everything.
> —Dashiell Hammett, "Dead Yellow Women"

The detective genre is a supreme example of what Lyotard, in *The Postmodern Condition*, has termed "metanarratives of legitimation." These grand narratives "have the goal of legitimating social and political institutions and practices, laws, ethics, ways of thinking" (18). As a metanarrative, the detective genre is caught up in the modernist concern with the legitimacy of knowledge, a legitimacy that is realized in the truthful solution of a crime. According to Wlad Godzich:

> We should bear in mind that the issue of the legitimacy of knowledge is the underlying problem of modernity in as much as the latter cut itself off from the divine guarantees of knowledge, so that the problem that haunts all modern thinkers from Descartes, Locke, and Kant onwards, is that of ensuring the reliability of knowledge (i.e., its legitimacy) and of all forms of individual and collective action that rest on it. (114)

The detective genre, then, is deeply rooted in Kantian reason, in analysis by the senses as the legitimator of knowledge. Reliable knowledge is linked to the transcendental as a guarantor of legitimacy.

In the work of Dashiell Hammett, there is a loss of faith in the metanarrative of the detective genre. Especially in *The Dain Curse*, Hammett engages in a paralogical investigation of the rules of the genre itself;[1] thus, the application of a given category (the rules that govern the detective genre) cannot be an adequate judge or interpretation of this novel. It cannot be judged by the application of the very rules that it is displacing.

The Dain Curse has often been criticized as one of Hammett's weaker efforts, a collection of *Black Mask* novellas conveniently strung together for book publication. But it is this very quality of fragmentation that I find to be the book's greatest strength. As a novel, *The Dain Curse* is a collection of "little narratives," supplementary in nature, which never really add up to a metanarrative of legitimation. This lack of absoluteness disrupts traditional literary notions of completeness, of a revelatory interpretive truth or final solution. *The Dain Curse*, then, not only investigates the conventions of detective fiction but the conventions of literature as well.[2]

As a writer of detective fiction, Hammett questions not only the *disdain* for supposed genre fiction and its lack of literary value (its "curse") but the notion of literary value itself, with its supposed ability to interpret and reveal a transcendental truth about human nature (its "curse"). In doing so, Hammett's concerns are decidedly *postmodern*, in Lyotard's sense of the word: the postmodern being not what merely comes after modernism (which would make it the new modernism) but something which precedes and constitutes modernism, an other which always contains the possibility of a radical revision of modernism. According to Fredric Jameson, this revisionary function is the fundamental feature of postmodernism:

> Namely, the effacement in [the work] of the older (essentially high-modernist) frontier between high culture and so-called mass or commercial culture, and the emergence of new kinds of texts infused with the forms, categories, and contents of that very culture industry so passionately denounced by all the ideologues of the modern . . . (296)

In *The Dain Curse*, Hammett pits his postmodern detective, the Continental Op, against the modern psychological novelist, Fitzstephan, in a battle of competing "truths," a mixing of the categories of high and low culture which reveals not only the inability of analysis to reveal the "truth," but the "hocus pocus" of the modernist belief in interpretation—what Hammett calls "the literary grift." For Hammett, literature constitutes a game—a con game.

Sinda Gregory has already addressed Hammett's questioning of the ability of the detective to arrive at the truth, to discover what Anne Riordan, in Chandler's *Farewell, My Lovely*, sarcastically calls "the great solution."[3] In "*The Dain Curse*: The Epistemology of the Detective Story" (from her *Private Investigations: The Novels of Dashiell Hammett*), Gregory writes:

> Hammett may play with the form and style of the detective novel, but his intent is not primarily parodic; rather, *The Dain Curse* is a novel about how we impose

> a fictional sense of order in our lives and in our literature. As he willfully
> emphasizes the artifice of his own writing, he also suggests that what we see,
> what we believe, and what we think is what we have created ourselves. (61-62)

Gregory's point is that the Op's solutions throughout the novel are wrong
because he can never really know enough to arrive at the truth or a final
solution[4]: "Hammett forces us to see the absurdity of one of the principal
assumptions of the detective genre: that a single truth exists somewhere that
accounts for mystery . . . Hammett's intent [is] to examine how we arrive at
such truths which he reveals to be 'fictions'" (77).

And yet Gregory herself comments that the Op "is correct in identifying
Owen Fitzstephan as the murderer and is able to deduce the course of his
crimes" (79). However, if identifying Fitzstephan as the murderer is the
"correct" solution, then why would Hammett's "intent" be to show us that the
Op's truths are "fictions"? Wouldn't the Fitzstephan solution be merely one
more fiction that the Op creates and imposes on reality? If all truths are fictional
creations how can the "truth" about Fitzstephan be the "correct" one? In the
end, Gregory's analysis is contradictory because it is caught up in the same
modernist concerns that Hammett himself is questioning. She interprets *The
Dain Curse* using the terms of modernist critique (artifice, ambiguity,
complexity, parody, genre types) to arrive at the supreme modernist perspective:
the subjective truth of fiction. "Final solutions," Gregory writes, "are merely
fictional projections of our need to impose order on an inexplicable and
fundamentally mysterious universe" (78).[5] Modernism, while questioning the
nature of absolutes, insists ultimately on *subjective* truth, on the "truth" of the
subjective creation (or imposition) of order. And thus Gregory, in believing in
a correct solution, has imposed order on an inexplicable and fundamentally
mysterious novel.

For critics like Gregory, then, the detective becomes an embodiment of the
modernist belief in an *a priori* subject which reads; according to Lyotard, this
modernist subject is constituted by reading in such a way that the belief in an *a
priori* subject is induced. The detective's subjectivity, however, from a
postmodern rather than a modernist perspective, is constituted by the crime he
"reads"—there is no autonomous subjecty *prior* to the text of the crime. It is the
text of the crime which constitutes the subject of the detective and induces the
very belief in an *a priori* subject capable of reading and interpreting a legitimate
solution. To solve the crime is to posit the existence of a transcendental self
capable of solving the crime.

If it is not possible for a detective, as *a priori* subject, to interpret "truth,"
then does this mean we should abandon the concept of truth, that truth is
something incapable of being discovered? According to Richard Rorty, in
Contingency, Irony, and Solidarity:

> To say that we should drop the idea of truth as out there waiting to be discovered

is not to say that we have discovered that, out there, there is no truth. It is to say that our purposes would be served best by ceasing to see truth as deep matter, as a topic of philosophical interest, or 'true' as a term which repays 'analysis'. (8)

This abandonment of the belief in the legitimacy of knowledge (such as categories and genres) is the primary difference between the modern and postmodern perspective. According to Lyotard, in *The Postmodern Explained*,

The postmodern artist or writer is in the position of a philosopher: the text he writes or the work he creates is not in principle governed by preestablished rules and cannot be judged according to a determinant judgment, by the application of given categories to this text or work, such rules and categories are what the work or text is investigating. (15)

Hammett's paralogical text neither validates objective nor subjective representations of truth. According to Bill Readings, "postmodern art does not seek a truth at all but seeks to testify to an event to which no truth can be assigned, that cannot be made the object of a conceptual representation" (74). For me, Readings definition of postmodern art best describes Hammett's approach in *The Dain Curse*. Ultimately, even the Op's final solution of Fitzstephan as the mastermind behind the Dain curse must be questioned; the curse itself is an event which resists truth, resists representation. The detective becomes what Nietzsche, in *Beyond Good and Evil*, calls a philosopher "of the dangerous 'maybe'" (11).

Hammett's point is that, once we move away from interpretation, meaning can be defined as multiplicity rather than unity. The existence of multiple meanings displaces the very notion of an interpretive truth. According to Derrida, in *Spurs: Nietzsche's Styles*:

The hermeneutic project which postulates a true sense of the text is disqualified under this regime [of multiple meanings]. Reading is freed from the horizon of meaning or truth of being, liberated from the values of the product's production or the present's presence. (107)

The Dain Curse is structured around not one, but multiple solutions to the mysterious "curse" that seems to be attached to Gabrielle Dain Leggett. In the first section of the novel, the Op arrives at a solution through old-fashioned analysis of the facts; in the second section he arrives at another solution through hard-boiled violence; in the third, it is the police who arrive at yet another solution; and in the fourth and final section it is the Op along with the authority of the courts who arrives at the great solution. These solutions are counterpointed throughout with confessions, both written and verbal, from various characters; and in the end, even Fitzstephan's confession as the insane criminal mastermind becomes as suspect as all the other ones in the novel.

Instead of unity, truth, seriousness, literature, we are presented with fragments, play, laughter, and, as we shall see, the abyss of untruth.

The novel opens with an image of infinite, eternal value: a diamond, one of eight stolen from Edgar Leggett's laboratory. Eight is the symbol for infinity and becomes symbolic in the novel of the transcendental truth that literature holds out as its great promise to its readers. However, these diamonds are flawed, are only an illusion of eternal value. Leggett had developed a process of coloring glass that he'd been trying to apply to flawed diamonds, to make them appear more valuable than they really are. For Hammett, this is what literary techniques and values do: they make works of art appear more valuable and eternal than they really are. From the opening image of the novel, he is undercutting the supposed values of literature over genre fiction.[6]

This attack continues with the character of Owen Fitzstephan, a writer, a practitioner of "the literary grift." Literature, according to Fitzstephan, is something not to be understood but worshipped as an eternal creation, subtle in its revelation of truth. Directly opposed to this idea is the Op, with his direct and sarcastic style. According to the Op, literature is composed of "explanations and descriptions that explain and describe nothing" (156). To which Fitzstephan responds, "tell me what's up while I find one-syllable words for you" (156).

When discussing the case with the Op, Fitzstephan relates it to Dumas, then accuses the Op of merely relating it as "a piece of gimcrackery out of O. Henry" (156). According to Fitzstephan, a novelist works with "souls and what goes on in them" (157), the abstract and eternal, while a writer of genre fiction deals only with the physical. But when Fitzstephan offers his views of the case, the Op responds: "there's no sense to that . . . you're just being literary" (158). There is a continual interplay in the novel between these categories of (low) genre and (high) literature, which results in the displacement of the values of both.

So Hammett is also effacing the traditional structures of the detective genre as well. The detective's loyal confident and sidekick in this story turns out to be the supposed criminal mastermind behind the curse. The traditional gathering of everyone into a room for the revelation of the truth happens in the first quarter of the novel. And in this "revelation" scene it is not the Op who reveals the "solution," but Leggett's written confession, which challenges the Op's authority through writing, a representation of the dead man's voice. But this confession misleads, misrepresents, is incapable of revealing the truth.[7] It is only by pointing out the inconsistencies in Leggett's letter and accusing Mrs. Leggett of stealing the diamonds and committing the murders that the Op is able to assert, if not the truth, then at least his authority. The scene ends with three competing versions of the truth: Leggett's written "confession," the Op's analysis of the facts, and Alice Leggett's confession. Hammett does not offer a legitimate solution but a multiplicity of little narratives.

While Alice Leggett defines the Dain curse as "the same black soul and rotten blood that [Gabrielle] and I and all the Dains have had" (183), the Op reduces it to merely "words in an angry woman's mouth" (185). Fitzstephan argues for the "poetic necessity" of the curse if there is to be an explanation for what happened. The Op, summing up Hammett's attitude, responds, "one guess at the truth is about as good as another" (185). He realizes his explanation in the laboratory is a fabrication, only one version of many possible versions. While the case seems to be solved after the first section of the novel, the Op remains in doubt—doubt not only about his explanation but about the concept of a stable truth itself. Fitzstephan critiques the Op's uncertainty by telling him that "you're never satisfied until you've got two buts and an if attached to everything" (186). Fitzstephan's critique implies that the Op's postmodern method of the dangerous maybe only insures that no unifying solution will ever be arrived at.

According to Sinda Gregory, however, Gabrielle herself serves as the unifying force of the novel, constant, stereotypical:

> Gabrielle Leggett helps unify the widely varying sections of the novel. While the Op's role changes in each of the three sections, her character remains constant: she is the stereotypical female victim . . . passive and helpless to the point of catatonia, unable to control or interpret anything that happens around her. (75)

Using Nietzsche's metaphor in the preface to *Beyond Good and Evil* equating woman with truth,[8] however, we can see that Gabrielle's function is not to unify the novel's little narratives, nor to be a stereotypical victim. The ability to solve the essence of the curse would be the ability to solve the essence of truth itself. It is women who continually present the Op with the opportunity to solve the mystery of the curse; and yet he is never able to do so because through their confessions of the "truth" they continually deflect him away from the concept of a stable truth. This is because the element of woman's power is *distance*. According to Derrida:

> There is no such thing as the essence of woman because woman averts, she is averted of herself. Out of the depths, endless and unfathomable, she engulfs and distorts all vestige of essentiality, of identity, of property. And the philosophical discourse, blinded, founders on these shoals and is hurled down these depthless depths to its ruin. There is no such thing as the truth of woman, but it is because of that abyssal divergence of the truth, because that untruth is "truth." Woman is but one name for that untruth of truth. (51)

In *The Dain Curse*, philosophical discourse is not the only discourse hurled down to its ruin. Each woman's confession only reveals the untruth of truth. While it is the crimes of the Dain curse which constitute the Op's subjectivity as detective, ironically it is Gabrielle herself who averts the Op's masculine analytic ability as capable of solving these crimes. In trying to discover the essence or truth of Gabrielle, the Op's abilities will only be effaced by the very lack of truth which she embodies. This is why he turns to Fitzstephan, and their masculine discourse, in order to put together the "truth." In the presence of the feminine, the concept of truth is not verified but continually averted. The Op, ironically, seeks the truth in the very abyss where truth becomes the "divergence of the truth."[9]

The Op's doubts about his first solution to the curse are confirmed as he is pulled back into the case when Gabrielle returns to the Temple of the Holy Grail to recover from her parents' deaths. The Temple is a parody of the temple of high literature—traditional, white, and pure, but full of charlatans, hocus-pocus, quackery—a cult. At its center is the ghost the Op "sees," the transcendental spirit of the temple:

> The thing was a thing like a man who floated above the floor, with a horrible grimacing greenish face and pale flesh that was not flesh, that was visible in the dark, and that was as fluid and as unresting and as transparent as tidal water. (203)

Fleeing the ghost, the Op stumbles into Joseph Haldorn, about to sacrifice his wife, with Gabrielle standing by. The Op shoots and stabs him to death and reveals the Temple, its founders and its spirit as a sham. But Gabrielle remains a mystery, mocking and teasing the Op, who has had to resort to hard-boiled, masculine violence in order to affirm his power as detective.

Once again, with high literary values shown to be merely a cult, a scam, and as the Op and Fitzstephan have dinner, the case seems to be solved once more: this time through hard-boiled violence rather than old-fashioned analysis. Fitzstephan complains of not having witnessed the affair first hand, of having to rely on the Op's subjective version of what happened. During their conversation, the Op shows he has begun to reject the value of analysis:

> "I hope you're not trying to keep this nonsense straight in your mind. You know damned well all this didn't happen."
> "Then, what" [Fitzstephan] asked, looking puzzled, "did happen?"
> "I don't know. I don't think anybody knows." (214)

Repeating himself, Fitzstephan comments that the Op's method is "to attach your ifs and buts to it, distorting and twisting it, making it as cloudy and confusing and generally hopeless as you like" (214). Even the Op admits his explanation, the great solution, is merely a fairy tale, like Little Red Riding Hood. There is no great solution. "Indeed," writes Derrida, "there is no such thing as a truth in itself. But only a surfeit of it. Even if it should be for me, about me, truth is plural" (103).

And this is what the Op is beginning to find out. For, while the case is supposedly solved a second time, the Op is dragged back into the affairs of Gabrielle Dain Leggett a third time by Eric Collinson, who is now her husband, and whom the Op discovers dead when he arrives in Quesada. Both the evidence and the authorities point to Gabrielle as the murderer. However, Fitzstephan receives a phone call and a letter claiming Gabrielle's been kidnapped, and the

Op, having exhausted the possibilities of factual analysis and hard-boiled violence, is content to sit back and watch as the country bumpkins of the local law put together an outrageous story from the facts and various local jealousies. Marshall Cotton attempts to set up his rival Harvey Whidden as the kidnapper because Whidden is having an affair with his wife. After Mrs. Cotton is killed, her written "confession" is discovered, confirming Whidden as the kidnapper and thus confirming the "official" version of the truth.

This scene parallels the scene in the laboratory where both Edgar Leggett's and Alice Dain Leggett's "confessions" supposedly solved the case of the Dain curse, so by now we are suspicious of writing's ability to solve the mystery. Confessions in this novel displace the value of the written word. It is ironic that women offer up most of the confessions here in order to give the Op his "truth," "because if woman *is* truth, *she* at least knows that there is no truth, that truth has no place here and that no one has a place for truth" (Derrida, *Spurs*, 53). Even though the Op and company find Gabrielle, come to the conclusions that Whidden is the kidnapper and Marshall Cotton the murderer of his wife, the Op still feels the case isn't officially over. The official version of the truth becomes just one more version competing for legitimacy. Rather than accept any version so far offered, whether confessional or otherwise, the Op, even though confronted with evidence of the plurality of truth, leans once more on the concept of analysis: "you've got to sit down to all the facts you can get and turn them over and over till they click" (249).

The problem, as Gregory has pointed out, is that more and more facts continue to pile up. Tom Fink, one of the special effects men behind the Temple's charades, arrives with even more new information for the Op. A bomb goes off, blowing up the Op's room and mangling Fitzstephan, the novelist who wanted a first hand taste of things. With Fitzstephan in the hospital, the Op decides to cure Gabrielle of her curse and her morphine addiction. In the throes of withdrawal, Gabrielle confesses to all the murders that have occurred, but her confession is just as suspect as all the others in the novel, since she'll say anything to get morphine. Confronted with yet another of the multiple solutions offered in the case, the Op finally concedes that factual analysis, interpretation, cannot discover truth: "I piled what facts I had, put some guesses on them, and took a jump from the top of the heap into space" (276).

The Op's leap lands him firmly onto Fitzstephan, the only character who fits the Op's new theory that there must be a connection between all the murders in the case, a criminal mastermind behind it all. And yet, is this the "correct" solution, as Gregory maintains? When the Op accuses him, Fitzstephan's defense is, ironically, the Dain curse, as he claims to be a Dain (a cousin of Alice) and only a lunatic could have committed so many crimes. However, the feminine curse's function of aversion does not work for *men*. This time, through gender transformation, it appears that the Op is able to solve the essence of the curse and arrive at the truth. As long as the curse is embodied in women, he is unable to do this. It is only when the curse becomes *masculine* that the masculine faculty of reason and analysis is able to function. Thus the Op never really succeeds in discovering the essence of Gabrielle or the curse itself. His fingering of Fitzstephan as the criminal mastermind becomes only one more little narrative in a series of little narratives which never add up to a metanarrative of legitimation.

As the Op spins the latest of these great solutions, even he admits that Fitzstephan is legally entitled to beat the rap, especially given all he's been through. Fitzstephan, who has claimed the insanity defense, replies, "but damn it, that spoils it . . . it's no fun if I'm really cracked" (285). So, is Fitzstephan insane, or is he only pretending to be insane? Is he the guilty criminal mastermind or isn't he? Because the Dain curse is now masculine, interpretation appears to function in its quest to freeze, to solidify a single meaning, a final solution. The novel ends with a supposedly objective narrative summary by the Op (similar to Faulkner's strategy in the fourth part of *The Sound and the Fury*)[10] of Fitzstephan's role in the crimes, supported by the authority of a court judgment, but in the end, Fitzstephan's confession, insane or not, is just as suspect as Edgar Leggett's, Alice Leggett's, Mrs. Cotton's and Gabrielle's. The Op summarizes Fitzstephan's confession as "the story with which this crazy man, thinking himself sane, tried to establish his insanity, and succeeded" (290). We would be hard pressed to find a more confused example of "logical" thinking. As the Op commented earlier in the novel:

> Thinking's a dizzy business, a matter of catching as many of those foggy glimpses as you can and fitting them together the best way you can. That's why people hang on so tight to their beliefs and opinions; because, compared to the haphazard way in which they're arrived at, even the goofiest opinion seems wonderfully clear, sane, and self-evident. (258)

Multiple confessions, theories, facts, alibis and cons embody a plurality which can never add up to the great solution. There is no metanarrative of legitimation, only a mysterious curse that defies representation and classification as "truth." The Op's comment on a story Mickey Linehan tells earlier in the novel summarizes Hammett's postmodern approach to both *The Dain Curse* and the metanarrative of the detective genre: "he made a long and laughable story of it. Maybe some of it was the truth" (268). [This essay was written specifically for this volume]

NOTES

1. The paralogism is Lyotard's term for what defines the postmodern function of art as opposed to the innovative function of modernist art. According to Bill Reading, "paralogism seeks the move that will displace the rules of the game, the 'impossible' or unforeseeable move. Innovation refines the efficiency of the system, whereas the paralogical move changes the rules in the pragmatics of knowledge" (*Introducing*

Lyotard: Art and Politics [London: Routledge, 1991], p. 73).

2. In the history of Western metaphysics, literature has always been subordinated to the philosophical concept of truth and popular, or genre, fiction to the "truth" of literature. This subordination has been accomplished by "the closed philosophical structure that comprehends or includes its own outside" (Peggy Kamuf, *The Derrida Reader: Between the Blinds*, ed. Peggy Kamuf [New York: Columbia Univ. Press, 1991], p. 146). Philosophy can determine its other only through concepts that are already philosophical in nature—just as literature can determine what is literary only by using concepts that are already defined as literary. See Derrida's "Tympan," where he investigates how to break free from the closure of the logocentric model of philosophical discourse "according to a movement unheard of, by philosophy, an other which is no longer *its other*" (Jacques Derrida, "Tympan," in *Margins of Philosophy*, trans. Alan Bass [Chicago: Univ. of Chicago Press, 1982, pp. ix-xxix], p. xiv.); in this case, the intrusion of literature into philosophy: "one would have to displace philosophy's alignment of its own types. To write otherwise. To delimit the space of a closure no longer analogous to what philosophy can represent for itself under this name, according to a straight or circular line enclosing a homogenous space" (p. xxiv). My argument is that Hammett accomplishes this displacement not only with the concept of "truth" but with the concepts of "literature" and "genre" as well.

3. The questioning of the detective as a traditional figure of reliability and authority has become almost as traditional as the detective genre itself. A recent example is the quirky hit television show "Twin Peaks," where David Lynch questions this role as FBI Agent Dale Cooper solves the mystery of Laura Palmer's death not through an analysis of the facts, but through Cooper's quest for knowledge through play. Cooper's method, described by Martha Nochimson as "an exercise that pointedly avoids the routine detective apparati of logic, clues, or muscle" ("Desire Under the Douglas Firs: Entering the Body of Reality in 'Twin Peaks,'" *Film Quarterly*, Vol. 46, Number 2 [Winter 1992-93, pp. 22-33], p. 25), involves such playful acts as throwing rocks at a bottle as each suspect's name is read. This is a far cry from Joe Friday's signature "nothing but the facts, ma'am."

4. An interesting parallel with this idea can be found in Paul Verhoeven's film, "Total Recall," where, through the concept of memory implants, Verhoeven is showing that absolute knowledge, or "total recall" about any situation is impossible; there is never an ultimate figure of authority who can verify if something is "real" or an "implanted" memory. Each source of information is displaced by another source which reveals the incomplete knowledge of the previous source, in an endless series of disruptions without resolution.

5. See Wallace Stevens' "The Idea of Order at Key West": "And when she sang, the sea,/whatever self it had, became the self/That was her song." This "blessed rage for order" is also evident in Lawrence Durrell's *The Alexandria Quartet*, where Darley concludes: "There *was* no answer to the questions I had raised in very truth. [Pursewarden] had been quite right. Blind as a mole, I had been digging about in the graveyard of relative fact piling up data, more information, and completely missing the mythopoetic reference which underlies fact. I had called this searching for truth! . . . I began to see that the real 'fiction' lay neither in Arnauti's pages nor Pursewarden's—nor even my own. It was life itself that was a fiction—we were all saying it in our different ways, each understanding it according to his nature and gift" (*Clea* [New York: Washington Square Press, 1978], pp. 167-68).

6. Hammett's influence continues to be felt, especially in film. For example, the Coen Brothers' reworking of *Glass Key* in "Miller's Crossing" and Quentin Tarentino's "Reservoir Dogs" (which seems to be a scaled-down version of Hammett's "The Big Knockover"). Indeed, the opening of *The Dain Curse* is reflected in "Reservoir Dogs," which is about a diamond heist by eight hoods gone awry, with the eight hoods fragmented into a fractured, fighting group of paranoids. Rather than the diamonds themselves being flawed, here it is the criminals themselves (including one who turns out to be an undercover cop).

7. The mistrust of writing is ingrained in the Western system of metaphysics. In the *Phaedrus*, Plato claims that writing is not only removed from truth, living knowledge, memory, but from the prime origin itself. In other words, writing has too little connection to *anamnesis*, the process of half-forgetting/half-remembering of truths that living knowledge can cause the soul to remember. Speech, as opposed to writing, is a living organism, with a connection to the prime origin, "a living father . . . a father *present, standing* near it, behind it, within it, sustaining it with his rectitude, attending it in person in his own name" (*Phaedrus and Letters VII and VIII*, trans. Walter Hamilton [New York, Penguin, 1973], p. 77). Writing, for Plato, is a *pharmakon*, a poison. Derrida has criticized this attitude as the metaphysics of presence and has claimed that writing functions as a "dangerous supplement" (see his "Plato's Pharmacy" in *Dissemination*, trans. Barbara Johnson [Chicago: Univ. of Chicago Press, 1978] for a discussion of this).

8. "Supposing truth is a woman," Nietzsche writes, using this metaphor to critique the "gruesome seriousness, the clumsy obtrusiveness with which [philosophers] have usually approached the truth" (*Beyond Good and Evil*, p. 1). Philosophers, according to Nietzsche, have been awkward and inexpert about winning a woman's heart. The same cannot be said about the Op's deliberately malicious method of "curing" Gabrielle.

9. The Op's identity as truth seeker is simultaneously constituted and disrupted by the very person in which he seeks the truth. Hammett makes this point clear in "Flypaper," where the mystery of Sue Hambleton's death, which allows the Op to function as a detective, is not solved but displaced onto a variety of solutions. The Op ultimately abandons his own "suicide hypothesis" for the Old Man's reading of the crime, via *The Count of Monte Cristo*. Once again, literary values take precedence over the values of the detective genre.

10. The fourth section of *The Sound and the Fury* is no more of a "truthful" account of the Compson's story than the preceeding three sections of the novel. In this way, Hammett's various "solutions" to the Dain curse reflect a similar narrative strategy to that of Faulkner's. As Quentin remarks in *Absalom, Absalom!*, *"maybe nothing ever happens once and is finished"* (emphasis Faulkner's; *Absalom, Absalom!* [New York: Vintage, 1972], p. 261).

WORKS CITED

Chandler, Raymond. *Farewell, My Lovely*. New York: Vintage, 1988.

Derrida, Jacques. *Dissemination*. Trans. Barbara Johnson. Chicago: Univ. of Chicago Press, 1978.

_____. *Margins of Philosophy*. Trans. Alan Bass. Chicago: Univ. of Chicago Press, 1982.

_____. *Spurs: Nietzsche's Styles*. Trans. Barbara Harlow. Chicago: Univ. of Chicago Press, 1979.

Durrell, Lawrence. *Clea*. New York: Washington Square Press, 1978.

Faulkner, William. *Absalom, Absalom!*. New York: Vintage, 1972.

Godzich, Wlad. "Afterword: Reading Against Literacy." *The Postmodern Explained*. Jean-François Lyotard. Trans. Ed. Julian Pefanis and Morgan Thomas. Minneapolis: Univ. of Minnesota Press, 1993.

Gregory, Sinda. *Private Investigations: The Novels of Dashiell Hammett*. Carbondale: Southern Illinois Univ. Press, 1985.

Hammett, Dashiell. *The Dain Curse*. *Dashiell Hammett: Five Novels*. New York: Avenel Books, 1980. 143-292.

Jameson, Fredric. *Postmodernism, or the Cultural Logic of Late Capitalism*. Durham: Duke Univ. Press, 1991.

Kamuf, Peggy, ed. *A Derrida Reader: Between the Blinds*. New York: Columbia Univ, Press, 1991.

Lyotard, Jean-François. *The Postmodern Condition: A Report on Knowledge*. Trans. Geoff Bennington and Brian Massumi. Minneapolis: Univ. of Minnesota Press, 1984.

_____. *The Postmodern Explained*. Trans. Ed. Julian Pefanis and Morgan Thomas. Minneapolis: Univ. of Minnesota Press, 1993.

Nietzsche, Friedrich. *Beyond Good and Evil: Prelude to a Philosophy of the Future*. Trans, Walter Kaufmann. New York: Vintage, 1989.

Nochimson, Martha. "Desire Under the Douglas Firs: Entering the Body of Reality in 'Twin Peaks.'" *Film Quarterly*. Vol. 46, Number 2 (Winter 1992-93). 22-33.

Plato. *Phaedrus and Letters VII and VIII*. Trans. Walter Hamilton. New York: Penguin, 1973.

Readings, Bill. *Introducing Lyotard: Art and Politics*. London: Routledge, 1991.

Rorty, Richard. *Contingency, Irony and Solidarity*. Cambridge: Harvard Univ. Press, 1989.

The Maltese Falcon

Reviews

In the effort to guide your eager feet through the ghastly bloodstained maze of recent crime literature, we have for the past week been reading far into the nights, and we shall indicate below a few of the most gruesome by-paths. First and foremost among the new thrillers comes Dashiell Hammett's *The Maltese Falcon*. It stands out among the rest like a .45 among a flock of cap pistols. It's about a detective, Sam Spade, whose partner is murdered while shadowing a man for a client. In finding the murderer, Spade runs afoul of the police, as well as of several sets of people who are all after a mysterious statuette. The story has plenty of action, a good plot, excellent characterization, and a startling denouement. Also, Mr. Hammett knows all about detective work, and the authors who really know that can be counted on the thumbs of one hand. This is not only probably the best detective story we have ever read, it is an exceedingly well written novel. There are few of Mr. Hammett's contemporaries who can write prose as clean-cut, vivid and realistic. [Walter Brooks, *Outlook and Independent* 26 February 1930: 350]

Let's get down to brass knuckles and argue that no one has any business reading detective stories because they're read by tired presidents, or because they teach coppers how to have and hold a crook. In real life, the important thing is to catch the murderer in the quickest round-up. In fiction, the important thing is not to catch the murderer for two hundred pages. And if in real life, our jaded presidents and unemployed wives find "escape" in detective fiction, then so do all readers of Norse myths and the Scotch ballads and the exploits of romantic cowboys. The real, right detective story is and should be a myth wherein the demigod (disguised as a superman) pursues the demon-crook through the tangled maze of heart-shuddering adventure. For "real" murders, you have the dullness of courtroom scenes and the dull evidence given by two-fisted dicks.

Until the coming of Mr. Dashiell Hammett in *Red Harvest* and now in *The Maltese Falcon*, the memorable detectives were gentlemen. The ever-delightful M. Lecoq and his copy, Mr. Sherlock Holmes, are fair gods against the gnomes. Their only worthy successor, Father Brown, is a priest. Scratch every other detective and you'll find a M. Lecoq. Now comes Mr. Hammett's tough guy in *Red Harvest* and his Sam Spade in *The Maltese Falcon* and you find the Pinkerton operative as a scoundrel without pity or remorse, taking his whiffs of drink and his casual amours between catching crooks, treating the police with a cynical contempt, always getting his crook by foul and fearless means, above the law like a satyr—and Mr. Hammett describing his deeds in a glistening and fascinating prose as "American" as Lardner's, and every bit as original in musical rhythm and bawdy humor.

There is nothing like these books in the whole range of detective fiction. The plots don't matter so much. The art does; and there is an absolute distinction of real art. It is (in its small way) like Wagner writing about the gnomes in *Rheingold*. The gnomes have an eloquence of speech and a fascinating mystery of disclosure. Don't get me wrong, bo. It's not the tawdry gum-shoeing of the ten-cent magazine. It is the genuine presence of the myth. The events of *The Maltese Falcon* may have happened that way in "real" life. No one save Mr. Hammett could have woven them to such a silver-steely mesh. [Donald Douglas, "Not One Hoot for The Law," *New Republic* 9 April 1930: 226]

From the Introduction to *The Maltese Falcon*

Dashiell Hammett

Spade had no original. He is a dream man in the sense that he is what most of the private detectives I worked with would like to have been and what quite a few of them in their cockier moments thought they approached. For your private detective does not—or did not ten years ago when he was my close colleague—want to be an erudite solver of riddles in the Sherlock Holmes manner; he wants to be a hard and shifty fellow, able to take care of himself in any situation, able to get the best of anybody he comes in contact with, whether criminal, innocent by-stander or client. [Modern Library Edition 1934]

From "Why Do People Read Detective Stories?"

Edmund Wilson

Still fearing that I might be unjust to a department of literature [the detective story] that seemed to be found so absorbing by many, I went back and read *The Maltese Falcon*, which I assumed to be a classic in the field, since it had been called by Alexander Wollcott "the best detective story America has ever produced" and since, at the time of the its publication, it had immediately caused Dashiell Hammett to become—in Jimmy Durante's phrase, referring to himself—"duh toast of duh intellectuals." But it was difficult for me to understand what they thought—in 1930—they were toasting. Mr. Hammett did have the advantage of real experience as a Pinkerton detective, and he infused the old formula of Sherlock Holmes with a certain cold underworld brutality which gave readers a new shudder in the days when it was fashionable to be interested in gangsters; but beyond this, he lacked the ability to bring the story to imaginative life. As a writer, he is surely almost as far below the rank of Rex Stout as Rex Stout is below that of James Cain. *The Maltese Falcon* today seems not much above those newspaper picture-strips in which you follow from day to day the ups and downs of a strong-jawed hero and a hardboiled but beautiful adventuress. [*The New Yorker* 14 October 1944: 57]

From *Heroes and Highbrows and the Popular Mind*

Leo Gurko

The center of [the hard-boiled detective's] existence is the I, bristling with defenses and traps for the enemy. . . . Its central figure, Sam Spade, is a characteristic specimen. When his partner in the detective agency is murdered while on assignment, he is upset not because of any love for the dead man but because if he does not bestir himself to catch the killer, it would be bad for business. Later, he has an affair with a beautiful client, but when he discovers that she is the murderess, he unhesitatingly turns her over to the police. Not because of any love of the police. Or out of a desire to see justice done. Or to avenge his slain partner. But simply to save his own skin. . . . [In fact] Everyone in the story, regardless of affiliation, is in eternal pursuit of a "fall guy," a victim who can be tossed to the police if they get too close. This sacrificial offering . . . is accepted procedure which adds no end to the rat race of the hard-boiled detective thriller, and gives to the egotism of its participants an even more knifelike and carnivorous edge. . . . [In the end] The hard-boiled detective story becomes a capsuled version not so much of reality as of Darwinism carried to its ferociously logical extreme. [Bobbs-Merrill, 1953: 188-89]

From "*The Maltese Falcon*: The Emergency of the Hero"

George J. Thompson

That critics see such apparently diverse qualities in Sam Spade may suggest that *The Maltese Falcon* is a flawed work or that Hammett's underlying conception has not been clearly discerned. I wish to offer a hypothesis that the novel has a very particular plot—a renunciation plot—and that the effect achieved is one of admiration. Hammett subjects his protagonist to severe moral temptations, and shows that he contains the potentiality for falling to the numerous lures presented in the novel if he so chooses. Brigid is, of course, the greatest temptation, and the power of the plot derives from his vulnerability to her. His renunciation of her proposal at the end is shown to be extremely difficult for him, and it is because Hammett shows it to be so that we can rightly measure Spade's moral strength and courage in saying no. [*Armchair Detective* 7 (1973): 179]

From *Saint With a Gun*

William Ruehlman

Irving Malin has shown how Spade resorts to the certainty of ceremony—the ritualized rolling of cigarettes, the measured shaking of hands. It is the refuge of a man who, as close friend Lillian Hellman said of Hammett himself, "made up his mind that there was no certainty in any form anywhere." Spade's adherence to the ceremonial extends to his adoption of a behavioral code that is really inverted chivalry: never perform out of sentiment, be a sucker for nobody . . . Hammett's book is not a novel in praise of that code; it is an examination of its consequences for a man who has nothing else. [NYU Press, 1974: 75]

From *Dashiell Hammett*

Julian Symons

Today the name of Sam Spade has become synonymous with that of a tough hero, but one of the attractions in reading the book is our uncertainty about his honesty. There comes a point—perhaps for most readers near the end, in Chapter Nineteen, when Spade refuses to let Cairo walk out on Gutman, Brigid and himself, saying irritably: "Good God! Is this the first time you stole anything?"—when we are almost convinced that he is as crooked as the rest of them. Nor are these doubts dissipated when Brigid asks what he would have done if the falcon had been real, and he replies that it makes no difference now, adding: "A lot of money would have been at least one more item on the other side of the scales." . . . . The lasting ambiguity of the character makes Spade a much richer, more complex figure than Chandler's Marlowe or Ross Macdonald's Lew Archer. [Harcourt Brace Jovanovich, 1985: 63]

Focus on *The Maltese Falcon*:
The Metaphysical Falcon

Irving Malin

Dashiell Hammett is usually praised for his effective "clipped dialogue," "brutal characters," and "violent action"—I am quoting from the publisher's blurb in the Vintage *Maltese Falcon*—but he is more than a simple-minded, tough novelist. He refuses to give us easy documentaries of crime; he presents, instead, unsettling and inverted ceremonies. He is "metaphysical," not merely "physical."

In the first chapter of *The Maltese Falcon* many physical details—Spade's face, Miss Wonderly's clothing, cigarette ashes which dot the desk—are described at length. We assume that they are superficial, that they can be quickly observed and understood. But Hammett disturbs us. He makes them mysterious (or sees their mystery). He tells us, for example, that Spade's face makes him look "rather pleasantly like a blond Satan"; he insists that Miss Wonderly's eyes are "both shy and probing"; he notes the "twisting" and "crawling" ashes as the wind blows them. The solid details become deceptive, fluid, nonsubstantial.

The mystery is intensified throughout the novel. Not only does Spade have to explore the significance of the objects—statuettes, guns, newspapers—he must come to terms with underlying *motives*. Miss Wonderly changes her identity, becoming Miss Leblanc and Miss O'Shaughnessy. (The latter is her real name, but it reveals little about her personality.) Joel Cairo acts so "queerly" that he cannot be trusted to sit still. Iva Archer calls at unpredictable times. The police try to frustrate Spade when he least expects it. In the middle of his quest, Spade relates an anecdote (or it is a parable?) of Flitcraft, the man who suddenly left his family and then turned up years later with another family. What caused his transformation? It seems that he ran away because a falling beam almost killed him. "He knew then that men died at haphazard like that, and lived only while blind chance spared them. . . . What disturbed him was the discovery that in sensibly ordering his affairs he had got out of step, and not in step, with life." He decided to end his unnatural life; *he became someone else*. Spade is obviously fascinated by this parable; it incarnates the lives he and all "detectives" live every day.

Ironies multiply. Spade plays the cosmic game, as Flitcraft did, by trying to outwit it. He lies, cheats, and masquerades. He becomes others; he wears them (as they wear him). He agrees, for example, with Dundy that he "really" did kill Archer. He informs Gutman that he will deliver the falcon. He goes along with Miss O'Shaughnessy. He masters life (or yields to its playful, haphazard rhythm?) by tricking it—at least for a while.

Thus Spade is our "hero." He understands that he is alone (his partner is killed in the second chapter) and that he can never depend on anyone. His secretary, who seems helpful and knowing, is fooled by Miss O'Shaughnessy. She admits this gullibility finally by saying, "I know—I know you're right. You're right. But don't touch me now—not now." Spade cannot even trust himself, especially with women who are always "beyond" him. Although he apparently has a definite, strong identity (it resembles the physical details I have mentioned), we and he know that he is shadowy, wavering, and changeable. Perhaps he can be himself only when he participates in the various ceremonies he invents.

Spade is always ceremonial. After he learns about Archer's murder—the phone rings in darkness; a man's voice speaks from "nowhere"—he makes a cigarette.

> Spade's thick fingers made a cigarette with deliberate care, sifting a measured quantity of tan flakes down into curved paper, spreading the flakes so that they lay equal at the ends with a slight depression in the middle, thumbs rolling the paper's inner edge down and up under the outer edge as forefingers pressed it over, thumbs and fingers sliding to the paper cylinder's ends to hold it even while tongue licked the flap, left forefinger and thumb pinching their end while right forefinger and thumb smoothed the damp seam, right forefinger and thumb twisting their end and lifting the other to Spade's mouth.

This elaborate ceremony reminds us of Nick Adams' in "Big, Two-Hearted River." But Spade does not avoid "the swamp"; on the contrary, he dives into it. He continually lives by his low "religion." Miss O'Shaughnessy may tempt him to convert—she sees no need to go to jail as a murderess, especially because she loves the detective. But Spade holds fast. He methodically offers six or seven reasons for turning her over to the police, hoping thereby to keep himself intact. He is miraculously complete (or empty?) when he functions, not when he thinks.

Spade eludes us—as he eludes his other selves. He shares the archetypal qualities of such mythic heroes as Odysseus, Samuel, and Jesus in a peculiarly contemporary way. He is as resourceful as Odysseus, but he believes in playful chance as *the deity, not as one divine attribute.* San Francisco is his kingdom—one he must win or lose daily. His first name, Samuel, suggests his biblical namesake who can identify the first Hebrew ruler. Perhaps he is also prophetic in his uncanny ability to see through the details to the mysteries within. Spade as Jesus? Yet he is ready to sacrifice himself for the truths (or are they lies?) he embraces ironically. He is the man between thieves and police, unsure of his mission, but foolish or wise enough to die for it. Hammett is able to undercut traditional values of heroism, quest, and romance by disguising idealism a cynicism, prophecy as sham, serious play as "sport." He resembles Spade: Hammett too eludes us as we try to determine the underlying motives for his curious, new mythology.

The falcon is the deity of the mysterious world I have suggested. Joel Cairo is the first to describe it as a "statuette," the "black figure of a bird." But it is as paradoxical as Spade's face or Miss Wonderly's eyes. The more we learn about it, the more "metaphysical" it becomes. This is the secret—the falcon changes. It is at times great wealth for Gutman, Cairo and all the thieves who want to possess it; it is also haphazard justice (the oxymoron is at the heart of the novel) for Sam Spade. Although it has a long history (it was "worshipped" in the Middle Ages), it has somehow transcended time. *It is a changing symbol of change itself.* It can never really be grasped; it vanishes triumphantly.

In the chapter of revelation all the "detectives" discover that they have been deceived. The statuette which Gutman as black priest finally uncovers is a *fake*.

> Gutman turned the bird upside-down and scraped an edge of its base with his knife. Black enamel came off in tiny curls, exposing blackened metal beneath. Gutman's knife-blade bit into the metal, turning back a thin curved shaving. The inside of the shaving, and the narrow plane its removal had left, had the soft grey sheen of lead.
>
> Gutman's breath hissed between his teeth. His face became turgid with hot blood. He twisted the bird around and hacked at its head. There too the edge of his knife bared lead. He let knife and bird hang down on the table while he wheeled to confront Spade. "It's a fake," he said hoarsely.

Because the falcon *is* fake, it divinely judges their own deception. How fitting that they "die" for untruth! Gutman and Cairo may think that they can get the original statuette back from the Russian who tricked them with this hoax, but we are made to believe that the original, if it can be found, is also fake.

I have stressed the metaphysical currents of *The Maltese Falcon* because they are often slighted. Most critics tend to discuss technique—if only in clichés about toughness and Americanism—without realizing that it is symbolic. Hammett tries to be flat and impersonal when he describes the "surface," but he suggests that it contains deep truth. Consider this lengthy, representative example. After Spade learns of Archer's death, he walks to the scene.

> Spade crossed the sidewalk between iron-railed hatchways that opened above bare ugly stairs, went to the parapet, and, resting his hands on the damp coping, looked down into Stockton Street.
>
> An automobile popped out of the tunnel beneath him with a roaring swish, as if it had been blown out, and ran away. Not far from the tunnel's mouth a man was hunkered on his heels before a billboard that held advertisements of a

moving picture and a gasoline across the front of a gap between two
store-buildings. The hunkered man's head was bent almost to the sidewalk so that
he could look under the billboard. A hand flat on the paving, a hand clenched on
the billboard's green frame, held him in this grotesque position. Two other men
stood awkwardly together at one end of the billboard, peeping through the few
inches of space between it and the building at the end. The building at the other
end had a black grey sidewall that looked down on the lot behind the billboard.
Lights flickered on the sidewall, and the shadows of men moving among lights.

Spade turned from the parapet and walked up Bush Street to the alley where
men were grouped. A uniformed policeman chewing gum under an enameled
sign that said Burritt St. in white against dark blue put out an arm and asked:
"What do you want here?"

"I'm Sam Spade. Tom Polhaus phoned me."

"Sure you are." The policeman's arm went down. "I didn't know you at
first."

The first impression is that Hammett is simply giving us "what happened." Here
are many details—the noise of the car, the "blank grey" wall of the building, the
gum of the policeman—which suggest that Spade is committed to physical
reality. Notice, however, that he is the "private eye" somewhat removed from
the scene. He must identify himself to the policeman. (Throughout the novel
identity is questioned, as in Miss Wonderly's changing names, Flitcraft's
disappearance, the bird itself.) He must master the movement and the fog which
distort safe, static evaluations. The movement itself—the lights flickering, the
car roaring, the arm extending—mirrors the violent processes Spade confronts.
He is, continually, the running man who must keep up with or "outrun" events.
He cannot sit still, waiting for things to happen. The foggy darkness is a
symbolic condition—the latter is especially noticeable in the drug-induced sleep
of Spade and Gutman's daughter.

This lengthy passage, therefore, effectively demonstrates Hammett's
descriptive power. Because he can fuse "blank" reality and teasing symbol, he
is philosophically agile. Although there are many other strong
descriptions—Gutman cutting the bird is probably the most violent, beautiful
passage—the novel consists largely of devious "interviews" in which the
dialogue is as flat and complex as the descriptions. There are quick movements
again; sentences begin and end abruptly as the characters hide or disclose their
motives. Communication is difficult. In the first chapter Miss Wonderly speaks
"indistinctly"—the adverb can modify all the interviews, because words and
motives are separate. I don't want to imply that Hammett employs the "absurd"
dialogue of Beckett or Pinter, but he does stress the *nonbelief of conversation.*
Even his characters do. Miss Wonderly says, "He wouldn't tell me anything,
except that she was well and happy. But how can I believe that? This is what he
would tell me anyhow, isn't it." Spade agrees, "Sure . . . but it might be true."
Unanswered questions and curious hints abound. Cairo screams for help, at one
point, while the police are visiting Spade, but he and the detective claim it is all

a joke. Gutman deliberately avoids "crude" statements. No wonder that Spade often flees from the elliptical, suggestive, and social uses of language into the ceremonies I have discussed. These ceremonies are silent, comforting, and true—until they are interrupted by other unrelenting interviews.

Hammett's "clipped dialogue," "violent action," and "brutal characters" are not employed for mere sensationalism and toughness but, rather, for metaphysical subtleties. In its many symbolic, odd descriptions and conversations *The Maltese Falcon* transcends the hard-boiled school of detective writing. It is a special "case"—one that we "detectives" will not easily solve. [*Tough Guy Writers of the Thirties*. Ed. David Madden. Southern Illinois U P, 1968: 104-109]

Jameson, Genre, and Gumshoes: *The Maltese Falcon* as Inverted Romance

Jasmine Yong Hall

Of all detective stories, *The Maltese Falcon* (1930) has some of the most direct connections to the romance. Like the Grail Quest, it is a story of adventurers in search of a mystical object—"a glorious golden falcon encrusted from head to foot with the finest jewels" (Hammett 128) whose origins can be traced to a romantic period of knights, crusades, kings, and pirates. All detective stories, however, have a central, structural connection to the romance, for like the romance, the detective story highlights the division between word and world, matter and meaning. D.W. Robertson, Eugene Vinaver, and Northrop Frye have all described romance in terms of an external world of adventures, and a sacred truth which must be discovered in that external world. Tzvetan Todorov sees the structure of romance as composed of two different kinds of narrative:

> One unfolds on a horizontal line: we want to know what each event provokes, what it does. The other represents a series of variations which stack up along a vertical line: what we look for in each event is what it is. (*Poetics* 135)

Todorov goes on to point out that this opposition between actions in the world and their interpretation also lies at the heart of the detective story—where crime is the absent "real" event which must be represented by the investigation. Both the detective story and romance, then, are structurally divided into a narrative of action (the crime, the adventure), and the narrative which "reads" that action, giving it meaning and significance.

Frye does not make as concise a connection between the detective story and romance, but his frequent allusions to detective stories in *The Secular Scripture* make it clear that he considers the detective story a type of romance. Frye's description of romance, in fact, provides the best point of comparison with *The Maltese Falcon*, but before proceeding further let me point to a problem in this comparison which Frye does not articulate. Frye shows that movement between an external, material world, and a meaningful world form the structure of romance; he sees the ending of romance in an ascent to the meaningful—in which the word and world become one. But whether "the marriage of matter and meaning" (Vinaver 23) ever takes place in *The Maltese Falcon* is questionable. In *The Maltese Falcon,* there is a much stronger emphasis on the story as story, rather than on the story as revelation of truth.

The reason that this gap between sense and matter is harder to bridge in *The Maltese Falcon* lies in historical differences between the world of romance and the world of the detective story. Todorov points out that the passage from matter to meaning is made possible in the Grail Quest by the existence of a code, "a divine language" (*Poetics* 129); this code "is not the personal invention of the author of *The Quest for the Holy Grail*, it is common to all the works of the period" (125), but it is not a code available to the author of *The Maltese Falcon*. This text presents us with a secular world—a world in which religion does not provide a medium by which the material world can be translated into meaningful signs. If there is a transcendent power in *The Maltese Falcon*, it is the power of money, not of God. As Caspar Gutman's valuation of the Falcon suggests, it is money which defies description:

> The maximum? . . . I refuse to guess. You'd think me crazy. I don't know. There's no telling how high it could go, sir, and that's the one and the only truth about it. (135)

If one ascends to a higher world here—a world in which one can finally get the "truth about it"—it is not heaven, but a world in which untold riches will finally be able to be told.

How can one analyze the implications of placing money rather than religion at the transcendent center of this novel? Frye's approach to genre criticism does not offer a methodology for dealing with this important difference between a medieval romance and the modern detective story; however, a more fruitful approach is developed by Fredric Jameson in his chapter on "Magical Narratives" in *The Political Unconscious*. Jameson shows that, by finding the same patterns in romance from the earliest myths to present day works of popular culture, Frye "aims at reinforcing our sense of the affinity between the cultural present of capitalism and the distant mythical past of tribal societies. . . ." Frye's approach is ahistorical—a "'positive hermeneutic,' which tends to filter out historical difference and the radical discontinuity of modes of production and of their cultural expressions." Jameson suggests instead the use of a "negative hermeneutic" which

> would on the contrary wish to use the narrative raw material shared by myth and "historical" literatures to sharpen our sense of historical difference, and to stimulate an increasingly vivid apprehension of what happens when plot falls into history, so to speak, and enters the force fields of the modern societies. (130)

The difference between the two approaches, then, is that Frye categorizes an individual text according to a generic definition, while Jameson examines the way in which an individual text deviates from its inherited generic structure. Following Jameson's lead, I will be looking at *The Maltese Falcon* through the filter of romance in order to highlight the historical differences between the romance structure which originates in a Christian, feudal society, and the novel which is produced in a capitalist, monied one.

Frye's definition of romance structure divides into two main subcategories: the quest romance, and the social romance. The quest romance centers on a hero whose purpose is to find a sacred object, while the social romance centers on a heroine whose purpose is to recover her social position/identity and to marry. The two types have a very similar structure: there is a break of consciousness at the beginning followed by a descent to a lower world. The lower world is a world in which external, physical reality is radically divorced from meaning. It is usually ruled over by a monstrous figure—a dragon, a giant, or in more displaced romances a giant man, like Front de Boef in *Ivanhoe;* the protagonist's contact with this monstrous figure represents over-involvement with the physical and abandonment of the search for this world's truth. This over-involvement in the physical continues as the protagonist becomes trapped—in prisons, labyrinths, and finally within his/her own body. Through amnesia, loss of consciousness, or the presence of doubles, the protagonist is confined within the body without a clear sense of identity—of personal meaning. Underlying these stories of imprisonment is the fear that one is trapped within the body by death, the final loss of identity. The ending of the romance serves to defuse this threat through the protagonist's ascent to a higher, more meaningful plane—either in heaven, or through marriage.

The movement of ascent from the lower world is signalled by an escape, return of memory/consciousness, and/or a discovery of the protagonist's real identity. Usually these events are associated with the recovery of a talisman or precious object which comes out of the sea, and with this recovery the romance reaches its conclusion, one which serves to combine the two worlds of matter and meaning. In the social romance, the physical world is given social meaning through marriage: physical desire becomes socially sanctioned. In the quest romance, the recovery of the precious object, by fulfilling the language of prophecy, shows that there is a connection between language and the world. With the recovery of the talisman the divine language is shown to stand behind the events of the world, and the hero can ascend to the source of that language in heaven (Frye 65-157). In examining *The Maltese Falcon*, I will make use of elements from both quest romance and social romance; however, the critical question to be addressed is whether *The Maltese Falcon* ever achieves the successful combination of meaning and matter which ends the romance.

At the outset, *The Maltese Falcon* looks very much like a romance, with the same loss of identity and proliferation of doubles. There are two detectives, Spade and Archer, and two damsels in distress, Miss Wonderly and her sister, who has been seduced by Floyd Thursby. The two detectives are reduced to one when Archer is killed, but Spade's identity becomes confused with the killer's: Did he kill Archer? Or did he kill Thursby, who presumably killed Archer?

The two sisters resolve into one woman when we discover that Miss Wonderly's sister was merely a fabrication of Miss Wonderly's, a lure to get the detective to tail Thursby. However, Miss Wonderly herself also disappears, resurfacing as "Miss LeBlanc," who then tells Spade that her *real* name is Brigid O'Shaugnessy. Her identities proliferate at a rapid rate at the beginning of the novel: as Spade remarks to Effie, his secretary, "She's got too many names" (43).

In many ways, Brigid hearkens back to the romance heroine who must constantly rely on disguises, tricks, and lying. Like Rosalind in *As You Like It*, her motto might be "I shall devise something, but I pray you commend my counterfeiting to him" (IV.iii.181-82). An important difference, though, is that unlike the romance heroine, Brigid uses tricks and ploys to protect not her virginity, but her identity as murderer. In fact, she uses her sexuality to protect that secret: she seduces Spade halfway through the novel to end his interrogation of her, which is leading closer and closer to revelation. I will discuss this difference more thoroughly in describing the ending of the novel; however, I want to point to the fact that Brigid, far from preserving her virginity, uses her body to try to obscure her connection with that other body—the corpse. In romance, the important body is the virgin's; the integrity of this body allows the revelation of the woman's identity at the end of the story. But in *The Maltese Falcon* the important body is a corpse, which is uncovered with the revelation of the woman's identity as murderer.

Brigid's most impressive skill, though, is not her sexual allure; her abilities as a story-teller are far more impressive. Caught in one lie by Spade, she will quickly manufacture a new one out of the threads of the old. Spade's habitual reply to her lies—"You're good, you're very good" (36, 58)—is both ironic and admiring, for Spade shares the ability to construct a story quickly. Spade's ability to switch from one interpretation of events to another is the source of his power over the other characters. This is especially evident in his dealings with Joel Cairo and Wilmer, neither of whom have the verbal dexterity of Spade or

Brigid. Cairo, for example, complains after he, and not Spade, has had to spend the evening being interrogated by the police because of a rather unbelievable story Spade tells them. Spade comes up with yet another story to explain to Cairo why he told the police what he did. Cairo replies a bit "dubiously," "You have always, I must say, a smooth explanation ready," to which Spade answers: "What do you want me to do? Learn to stutter?" (100).

Wilmer, who does stutter, as well as grunt and whimper at various points in the novel, is disarmed by Spade both physically and verbally. Having stripped him of his weapons, Spade further humiliates him in front of his boss, Caspar Gutman, by telling Gutman that the guns were taken by "A crippled newsie, . . . but I made him give them back" (216). Wilmer is the most frequent object of Spade's verbal ridicule because he can't speak well. While often reduced to non-verbal communication, Wilmer also reveals his inability to use language through his use of clichèd expressions. He threatens Spade in phrases limited by the role he plays:

> "Keep on riding me and you're going to be picking iron out of your navel."
> Spade chuckled. "The cheaper the crook, the gaudier the patter," he said cheerfully. (125)

Spade triumphs over Wilmer not only (or even primarily) through physical force, but through superior verbal skills. He can beat Wilmer because he can "type" him according to the kind of language Wilmer uses. Spade also correctly identifies Brigid by her use of language. After hearing several versions of her involvement with the Falcon, he exclaims, "You *are* a liar" (192). This ability to name his opponents correctly is one that Spade shares, not with the hero of romance, but the romance's seer or sage figure. Like all detectives he plays a double role: he is both the adventurer doing battle with the forces of evil in the lower world, and the sage who reads the truth of this lower world through his interpretation of clues, or his discovery of "real" identities. However, Spade's interest in the truth becomes less clear as he descends further into this lower world. When he talks to Cairo, for instance, he does not refer to the truth to justify his stories; instead he refers to his own verbal "smoothness," the fact that he doesn't stutter, as justification for being a story-teller.

The story which Cairo complains of, the story which sends him off with the police, even more clearly illustrates the continuing division between world and word in Spade's language. In the chapter entitled "Horse Feathers," first Brigid, then Cairo, and finally Spade tell the police different versions of the events that have just transpired. Spade's version is actually farthest removed from the truth, and draws the description of "Horse feathers" (82) from Lt. Dundy. The fantastic nature of this story leads not to belief, but to Spade's control of the situation. In Spade's version of events everything which has just taken place has been faked in order to play a joke on the police. Spade's story discounts "reality" in two ways: it is a lie, and it is a lie which claims that the real is a fraud, a fiction. The two policemen, Dundy and Polhaus, find themselves unable to cope with this story. Spade's control of the police and the two criminals in this scene shows that his power originates not in reconstructions of the real events, but in reconstructions which purposely maintain their distance from the real.

Dundy's final reaction, which is to hit Spade, does not represent the policeman's physical triumph but his verbal defeat—a defeat which leaves Spade free from police-questioning so that he can pursue the case on his own. However, the division between matter and meaning continues here, because Spade does not use his time to pursue the case, but to pursue Brigid and the Falcon. As he descends into the lower world he loses his identity as detective not only in being accused of the two murders, but also in seeming to lose interest in discovering Archer's murderer—in discovering the truth hidden by the corpse and by the seductive female body. The proliferation of stories, then, does not represent a search for truth, but the distance from truth; one story must quickly follow another, as Cairo's follows Brigid's, and Spade's follows Cairo's, because no transcendent true story ends the chain from signifier to signifier.

Spade's most important verbal confrontations in the lower world are with Caspar Gutman. Gutman embodies the two defining and divided aspects of that world: materiality, and the language which continually fails to explain that materiality. Like Brigid and Spade, he is an adept liar, and his gigantic size symbolizes his obsession with the material world. The narrator describes him as a man composed of a vast quantity of flesh and more body parts than are considered standard equipment:

A fat man came to meet him. The fat man was flabbily fat with bulbous pink cheeks and lips and chins and neck with a great soft egg of a belly that was all his torso, and pendant cones for arms and legs. As he advanced to meet Spade all his bulbs rose and shook and fell separately with each step in the manner of clustered soap bubbles not yet released from the pipe through which they had been blown. His eyes made small by fat puffs around them, were dark and sleek. (108)

Like Front de Boef, Gutman is the monstrous figure which the hero must vanquish in order to escape the lower world. But unlike Front de Boef and Ivanhoe's, Gutman and Spade's battle is a battle of words. Gutman is a man who "likes talking to a man that likes to talk" (110). Gutman is therefore quite pleased when Spade tells him that he is a man who likes to talk; however, in their first two encounters Spade is not given much of a chance to exhibit his skills. In talking about the "Black Bird" (110), Gutman is able to overwhelm Spade with the story of "The Emperor's Gift" (title of Chapter 13). As Gutman gets closer and closer to revealing the value of the bird, a value which he emphasizes is impossible to name, Spade loses consciousness. He has been drugged by Gutman, but his loss of consciousness seems more directly related to the story Gutman is telling; it is when Spade tries to ask about the highest price the Falcon might bring that the drug begins to affect him: "'The—the minimum, huh? And the maximum?' An unmistakable sh followed the x in maximum as he said it" (135).

The story which Spade is attempting to follow does not lead upward toward a revelation of truth; instead it sends Spade further into the lower physical world where he begins to lose the verbal skills necessary to complete the investigation. The hardboiled detective's "x's" become soft "sh's" as he loses consciousness, losing his identity and becoming only his physical body. Spade descends into this world because the story he listens to is not a sacred one, though it does have its roots in the crusades; it is, instead, a story of money. This story of money, as Gutman tells it, seems to embody world history. The Falcon originates as a tribute paid by the Knights of Rhodes to the Emperor Charles V. On its way to the Emperor it is stolen by the pirate, Khaired-Din, who takes it to Algiers where it stays for a hundred years. It is next recorded in the possession of Sir Francis Verney who takes it to Sicily, and there it becomes the possession of Victor Armadeus II. The story continues on like this for several pages, with remarkable details and references to obscure historical texts. It is interesting to note that it is much easier to give the history of the fetishized object than it is to discover the history of any of the characters in the novel. Just as the Falcon does not inherently belong any of the people through whose hands it passes, it seems to rob those people of any inherent identity. They are merely ciphers who acquire value and meaning momentarily with the ownership of the precious object. But as there are no "right[s] of possession" (132) in this object, these characters have only a transitory identity as owners. The humanist ideal of individual rights breaks down in this story of money, as does the ideal of individual identity itself, and this breakdown of identity continues with Spade's loss of consciousness.

Gutman's story of money also secularizes the past, revealing that the crusades themselves were not religious quests, for as he tells Spade, "We all know that the Holy Wars . . . were largely a matter of loot" (128). In this secularization, the material world is not raised to the level of meaning; rather, meaning is constantly referred back to the material world—meaning equals price. And, as we have seen above, when meaning becomes price, and identity becomes ownership, meaning and identity no longer present themselves as unified, transcendent concepts.

Some remnants of the romantic tradition seem to remain in the Black Bird, however, for with its recovery from the ship *La Paloma*, Spade begins his ascent out of this meaningless world. The possession of the Falcon gives Spade power over Gutman in their final confrontation, a power which expresses itself in Spade's taking over again as story-teller. He demands that a plausible story be put together for the benefit of the police, a story that will involve pinning the murders on either Wilmer or Brigid (who are in fact the murderers). Even though Spade's identification of the murderers is couched in terms of coming up with a good story, this story does, in fact, reveal the truth. Here Spade begins to reassert his identity. He will not be the criminal: as he states to Effie at the end of the novel, "Your Sam's a detective" (229). And in the detective's role as sage, Spade finally gives the correct interpretation to the violent actions of the novel: Wilmer has killed Thursby and Captain Jacoby; Brigid killed Miles Archer.

Does the correct identification of the killers, and the return to the detective's role, lead to the marriage of meaning and matter in a rejuvenated world such as we find at the end of romance? Looking first through the filter of quest romance, we see that an important difference emerges. The Falcon turns out to be not the precious and meaningful object of a quest romance, but a fake—a black enamelled lead paper weight. When the Grail is found it fulfills God's word in a material object, but when the Falcon is found it fails to live up to the words Gutman used to describe it. From pricelessness it declines to worthlessness.

Even before the Falcon is revealed as a fake, its value takes a radical turn downward. Gutman has promised Spade half-a-million for his part in obtaining the bird, but once Spade fulfills his part of the bargain, he is given only ten thousand:

> "We were talking about more money than this."
> "Yes, sir, we were," Gutman agreed, "but we were talking then. This is actual money, genuine coin of the realm, sir. With a dollar of this you can buy more than ten dollars of talk." (183)

Actual value is contrasted here with the value of "talk." As in the expression "talk is cheap," language and the material world are divided, not connected. At this point, though, Gutman still anachronistically clings to a belief in the inherent value of money by describing it as "genuine coin of the realm." But "genuine coin of the realm," like "ten dollars of talk," is fictional money; in fact, it is a romance version of money. Gutman alludes to a feudal monetary system in which meaning and material were the same; gold both stands for value, and is in itself valuable, while the dollar only stands for value. Once the Falcon is in Gutman's possession, however, he finds that it has more in common with the dollar than with "genuine coin." Thus matter and meaning remain divided. Furthermore, the Falcon's worthlessness as a possession demonstrates what happens when value is abstracted into exchange value in a capitalist economy. Like money, the Falcon is only valuable as it passes from hand to hand; once possessed it is found to have no use value. The Falcon is an exemplum of the fetishized commodity.

Brigid O'Shaugnessy goes through a similar devaluation. In the opening of the novel she is Miss Wonderly, the romantic embodiment of femininity, "tall and pliantly slender, without angularity anywhere" (14). But by the end of the novel she is Brigid O'Shaugnessy, the murderer who is nothing *but* angles. Comparing the ending of Brigid's story with that of the heroine of social romance reveals other interesting reversals. When Gutman gives Spade the ten thousand dollars in the final confrontation scene, Spade discovers that one thousand dollars is missing, and Gutman implies that Brigid may have it. Throughout the novel, Spade has had the ability to "read" her correctly, to tell magically when she is lying. Here, however, Spade forces Brigid to undress in full sight of the others, and then searches her. Instead of ascending to a world where meaning becomes apparent, we are descending back to a world whose focus is on the physical. This accounts for Effie's reaction when Spade turns Brigid in. Even though Brigid killed one of her bosses, Effie is horrified that Spade has given Brigid over to the police, and she responds to his embrace with physical aversion. She has been expecting the more traditional social romance ending of marriage, but *The Maltese Falcon* ends with the lover's incarceration. In the traditional social romance, the revelation of the heroine's identity leads to a marriage which gives social meaning to physical desire. But *The Maltese Falcon* does not end on a higher, social plane. It descends back to the physical: the revelation of identity is pictured as a rape; and the heroine is decisively returned to a constricting physical world.

An earlier incident in the novel serves as a summary of this theme. When Rhea Gutman is drugged, she scratches her stomach with a pin to keep herself awake—she tries to avoid unconsciousness by writing on herself. Stories in *The Maltese Falcon*, like these scratch-marks, are ways to avoid entrapment in the physical body—to avoid death. But they are written over the body itself. Stories of adventure in a traditional romance end in a higher social or religious truth, but stories in *The Maltese Falcon* always return to the body—Rhea's body, Brigid's body, and finally Miles Archer's body. Stories, here, do not lead out of the lower world's threat of death, they return to it.

Perhaps the final place to look for meaningful conclusion to the novel would be in the punishment of Archer's killer, Brigid. Two of Spade's justifications for turning in Brigid should point to the significance of this final act in the novel: first, he won't behave as Miles Archer did—he won't "play the sap" (224, 225) for her; and second, he won't let her go because "all of me wants to" (227). I will deal with these justifications in reverse order. First, Spade says he must give Brigid up, just because he doesn't want to. *The Maltese Falcon* presents a world that is the very opposite of the wish-fulfillment world of romance; one can never have "Miss Wonderly." At the end of the traditional social romance the individual's desires and society's laws combine in marriage, but in *The Maltese Falcon*, Spade's public role as law-enforcer is directly at odds with his feelings. *The Maltese Falcon* ends not with the reintegration of the personal and the social, but with the alienation of the individual from the world at large.

Spade refuses to "play the sap" for Brigid; however, by the end of the novel he is turning into "the sap," Miles Archer. In the very last scene of the novel, Miles Archer's wife Iva is waiting for Spade in the outer office. Iva is an aging version of Brigid, and while Spade cannot have Miss Wonderly, or even Brigid, he can have Iva (whose very name suggests possession—"I've a"). She is, however, a possession that he has been trying to avoid since the beginning of the novel. At the time of Miles's death, it becomes clear that Spade had been having an affair with Iva. When Miles is killed, Iva wants Spade to become Miles's replacement—an assignment Spade does not seem to relish. Spade successfully avoids Iva as long as he is involved with the story of the Falcon, but at the end of the novel he directs Effie, with a "shiver" (229) in his voice, to send her in. He reacts to Iva with the same physical aversion that Effie displays to him.

Like the final possession of the Falcon, possession of the woman is presented in a strongly negative light. Iva is not romantically described, as is Miss Wonderly. Instead she is "sturdy," with a "facial prettiness [which] was perhaps five years past its best moment" (185). Iva's description allies her with the physical world: like Gutman, she is too fleshy, and like any other object in the physical world, she is subject to the forces of decay—her face has already passed its "best moment." She represents Spade's return to a decaying, material world. In embracing her, he also seems to be embracing Miles's fate (death).

Finally, it would seem that the detective story still finds its meaning in Spade's identification of Archer's killer. However, here too there is a problem. Spade says that he knew who the killer was as soon as he saw the body, an event which took place in Chapter 2. The size of the bullet hole showed that the killer had to stand close to Archer, and Brigid, Spade explains, is the only one who could have stood that close. Spade has known the identity of the killer virtually from the beginning of the novel. The whole plot, then, the detective story itself, is a meaningless delay between Archer's murder and Spade's exposure of Brigid as his killer.

The detective story—which in its conventional form promises both to reveal the truth about the world and return that world to order—becomes, in *The Maltese Falcon*, an arbitrary ellipsis framed by a corpse, a physical world devoid of meaning or order. In the middle of the novel, Spade tells Brigid a story which encapsulates this vision of the world, and demonstrates his knowledge that what he does as a detective is always meaningless. Spade had been hired to find a missing person named Flitcraft by Flitcraft's wife. Flitcraft is difficult to trace because there seems to be no motive for his disappearance; however, Spade eventually finds him and hears the story behind that disappearance. Flitcraft had led a very ordinary life: he was a real-estate agent with a wife and two kids who lived in a suburb of Tacoma. One day, though, he was almost hit by a beam falling off a construction site, and this near fatal accident revealed to him that people have no necessary or determined relationship with the material world. A falling beam could come out of the sky and hit you for no reason, not because you are good or evil, but just by chance. After this accident, Flitcraft abandoned his settled and ordered life and drifted from one place to another. He finally settled in Spokane, where Spade finds him leading pretty much the same life he had lived before the accident—now he is an automobile salesman, with a wife and baby living in a Spokane suburb. This is the part of the story which Spade enjoys the most: "He adjusted himself to beams falling, and then no more of them fell, and he adjusted himself to them not falling" (167). Flitcraft organized his life around a story in which he played the main role as father and breadwinner. The physical world intruded and showed him the meaninglessness of that organization. Yet he returns, in the end, to another version of that same story. Similarly Spade plays his role in the detective story only to confront the meaningless physical world represented by the Falcon, by Iva's presence, and by Archer's body. Yet he, too, returns to his role in the story; he continues to play the detective, an identity as meaningless as being the Falcon's owner.

Jameson notes that in studying the history of romance as a mode it is important to discover what takes the place of religion or magic in the modern work (113). In *The Maltese Falcon*, money takes the place of any other system of belief. As Spade says of Brigid's initial presentation, "We didn't exactly believe your story. . . . We believed your two hundred dollars" (133). But money does not present a transcendent value system as religion or magic do. It is inherently valueless. It must, itself, be connected to the material world in order to have meaning. This connection is not a necessary one, as people discovered in the 1929 Crash and the Depression that followed. If there is nothing behind these pieces of paper they are worthless; we can continue to exchange them but we cannot reach a stopping-point. Similarly *The Maltese Falcon*, initially published at the same time as the stock-market crash, offers no final resting place of meaning. In *The Maltese Falcon* people like Flitcraft move from one version of story to another; money as the arbiter of meaning causes endless exchange of stories—stories are passed back and forth like worthless stocks. There is no ascent to the upper world here, only the discovery of a radical division between meaning and the material world—a division revealed by the falling beam, or the corpse. The ending of stories is presented not as transcendence, but as alienation—alienation which can only be escaped by a return to story.

Jameson describes writers such as Kafka and Cortazar as "the last unrecognizable avatars of romance." In the works of these writers, the structure of romance is used to show the "absence at the heart of the secular world" (Jameson 135)—to show that there is nothing to take the place of religion or magic. *The Maltese Falcon*, I would suggest, goes one step further. Here, the structure of romance reveals that in a capitalist, monied society, money and exchange value take the place of religion and magic. The hardboiled detective novel, with its origins in Depression-era America, demystifies its romance background by showing that romantic tales are frauds—like the Falcon, like the histories of the Holy Wars, and even like the detective plot of the novel itself. Placing money at the heart of the romance inverts the structure of romance; as Philip Marlowe remarks in *The Big Sleep*, "Knights had no meaning in this game. It wasn't a game for knights" (Chandler 95). We end the social romance not with marriage, but with incarceration. We end the quest romance not with the precious talisman, but with the corpse. Finally we end not with transcendence and wish-fulfillment, but with the separation of private and public, of desire and possession, of matter and meaning, which is at the heart of the capitalist society. [*The Cunning Craft: Original Essays on Detective Fiction*. Ed. Ronald G. Walker. Western Illinois UP, 1990: 109-19]

WORKS CITED

Chandler, Raymond. *The Big Sleep*. New York: Random House, 1988.

Frye, Northrop. *The Secular Scripture: A Study of the Structure of Romance*. Cambridge: Harvard UP, 1976.

Hammett, Dashiell. *The Maltese Falcon*. New York: Random House, 1929.

Jameson, Fredric. *The Political Unconscious: Narrative as a Socially Symbolic Act*. Ithaca: Cornell UP, 1981.

Todorov, Tzvetan. *The Poetics of Prose*. Trans. Richard Howard. Ithaca: Cornell UP, 1977.

Vinaver, Eugene. *The Rise of Romance*. New York: Oxford UP, 1977.

Dashiell Hammett and the Challenge of New Individualism: Rereading *Red Harvest* and *The Maltese Falcon*

Christopher Metress

In this present reconstructive era of American literary history, Dashiell Hammett's fiction has played an invaluable role in breaking down canonical barriers and empowering marginalized popular fictions with newly recognized importance. With the publication of his stories and novels in the late 1920s and early 1930s, many critics praised Hammett's linguistic, structural, and thematic innovations, insisting, for example, that "Hammett has something quite as definite to say, quite as decided an impetus to give the course of newness in the American tongue, as any man now writing."[1] Along with this laudatory critical reception, Hammett captured wide readership as well. Thus, Hammett long remained on the threshold between what are often considered two antithetical positions in American letters—accepted literary artist and popular storyteller.

When questions of canon formation and the politics of literary history became central to the focus of many critics, Hammett emerged as a seminal figure in the reconstruction of American literary studies. Today, his place in American literature is secure, and the critical accessibility of his art has for years now encouraged perceptive reevaluations of his literary progeny in both detective and hard-boiled fictions.

But security by no means suggests consensus, and Hammett's works have engendered diverse readings. Most often, Hammett is read in light of his contributions to the detective and hard-boiled genres. Even here, though commentators agree that Hammett fathered the American detective novel and laid the foundations for hard-boiled fiction, they disagree as to exactly what it is he fathered and whether or not his offspring misread him. Recently, however, critics have been willing to consider Hammett as more than simply a master of generic formulas and a constructor of heroic archetypes. Fortunately, they have resisted Leonard Moss's 1966 plea that Hammett "cannot through any generosity be considered a complex author. It would be fatuous to search for profound ethical, sociological, or psychological implication."[2] Instead, citics have done exactly that; they have read Hammett with an eye for the very complexities that make his fiction, unlike so much else that has won popular approval, so richly rewarding.

Perhaps the most misunderstood dimension of Hammett's work is his position on individualism. We expect Hammett to be an unabashed proponent of rugged individualism, for are not the descendants of Hammett's heroes such representative individualists as Chandler's Philip Marlowe, Spillane's Mike Hammer, Ross Macdonald's Lew Archer, and John D. MacDonald's Travis McGee? Critics have long noted how the hard-boiled detective of the twentieth century is merely an urban reincarnation of the nineteenth century apotheosis of American individualism—the cowboy. Understanding the American detective as the distinct progeny of the American cowboy (in the words of Leslie Fiedler, the modern detective is "the cowboy adapted to life on the city streets"),[3] too many critics, however, thoughtlessly embrace the notion that writers of American detective fiction are unequivocal advocates of nineteenth century-styled American individualism. As founder of this fiction, so the logic goes, Hammett must also be such an advocate: "If there is any Romantic element in Hammett's worldview," insists H. H. Morris, "it is the glorification of every individual, the passionate commitment to personal freedom that underlies the American myth of the frontier."[4] In her recent study of Western and hard-boiled novels, Cynthia S. Hamilton maintains that both genres "are built around the testing and confirmation of key American values, especially individualism" and that the "theme which permeates every aspect of the master formula [supporting both Western and hard-boiled fictions] is the primacy of the individual; he is seen to be the key unit of society."[5]

Fortunately, several readers have refused to see Hammett's fiction as a glorification of this inherited frontier individualism. While it is true that

Chandler, Spillane, Macdonald and others influenced by Hammett have each embraced to some extent an ethos of rugged individualism, Hammett's fiction does not support such a doctrine. David Geherin justly asserts that "the conception of the private eye as a knight figure would be effectively developed by many later writers (notably Raymond Chandler) but it appears that Hammett wanted no part of it."[6] David Glover concurs with Geherin's view that the individualism of Hammett's heroes is markedly different from his successors:

> What is interesting in the Hammett novels is the way in which . . . individualism is tempered by a kind of job-consciousness; so that although their violence is sensationalized and given a sadistic attractiveness it is never pushed completely into the world of fantasy in the way we find in, for example, the James Bonds books. For the individualism of action and decision is not used to ground an illusion of total freedom—it is only relative to the job or work that the detective performs.[7]

In his seminal essay on the poetics of the private-eye, Robert Edenbaum proclaims that Hammett's novels not only temper individualism but also "present a 'critique' of the tough guy's freedom as well: the price he pays for his power is to be cut off behind his own self-imposed masks, in an isolation that no criminal, in a community of crime, has to face."[8] Sinda Gregory goes one step further in asserting Hammett's critique of individualism by insisting that a novel like *Red Harvest* "examines the failure of both the community and the individual to maintain justice, order, and human rights."[9] In a 1985 study, Robert Shulman offers a more complex understanding of Hammett's position on individualism when he suggests that in *Red Harvest*, *The Maltese Falcon*, and *The Glass Key*, rather than blindly promoting a frontier brand individualism, Hammett "brings alive the conflicting versions of individualism that society emphasizes."[10]

My focus on the problem of American individualism in Hammett's fiction is markedly different from previous critics because it depends heavily on understanding the socio-cultural debates over the nature and direction of individualism that dominated the first three decades of this century. If Hammett's work "brings alive conflicting versions of individualism that society emphasizes" then we had better take a closer look at what those conflicting versions of individualism were before we reevaluate Hammett's own critique of individualism. What will arise from this discussion is the concept of a "new individualism" that called for a complex submission and/or allegiance of the individual's desires to those of a larger, less traditionally individualistic collective body. Like his contemporaries, Hammett struggled to reconceive the nature of American individualism, to explore the possibility of redirecting the insalubrious elements of an inherited frontier ethic into a more socially responsible new individualism. Hammett's two most important and influential novels, *Red Harvest* (1929) and *The Maltese Falcon* (1930), enact this exploration, for in them Hammett investigates the antagonistic relationship between residual nineteenth-century traditions of self-centered individualism and emerging twentieth-century calls for social collectivism.

I

Perhaps the best place to begin our discussion of this new individualism in the twentieth century is with Herbert Croly's *The Promise of American Life* (1909). Rejecting the great tradition of American individualism proclaimed by Crèvecouer, Jefferson, and Emerson, Croly expressed a central ethos of his time: "The Promise of American life is to be fulfilled—not merely by a maximum amount of economic freedom, but by a certain measure of discipline; not merely by the abundant satisfaction of individual desires, but by a large measure of individual subordination and self-denial."[11] Croly felt, as did most of his post *fin-de-siècle* generation, that "the traditional American system was breaking down" and that a twentieth century faith in social planning needed to usurp a nineteenth century faith in "chaotic individualism": "The experience of the last generation plainly shows that the American economic and social system cannot be allowed to take care of itself, and that the automatic harmony of the individual and the public interest, which is the essence of the Jeffersonian democratic creed, has proved to be an illusion."[12]

Croly's call for "individual subordination and self-denial" in shaping America's future continued to influence American social and political thought well into the 1910s and 1920s. Whereas in 1893 Frederick Jackson Turner could assert that frontier individualism, though it had "from the beginning promoted democracy," had "its dangers as well as its benefits,"[13] by 1917 Van Wyck Brooks could highlight only the insalubrious: "Our ancestral faith in the individual and what he is able to accomplish . . . as the measure of all things has despoiled us of the instinctive human reverence for those divine resources of collective experience, religion, science, art, philosophy, the self-subordinating service of which is almost the measure of the highest happiness. In consequence of this our natural capacities have been dissipated . . ."[14] Though rejecting the "aberrant individualism" of such "preëminent cranks" as Henry David Thoreau and Henry George, Brooks did not reject outright the concept of individualism; instead he sought a redefinition of individualism "totally different in content from the individualism of the past." For Brooks, the "old spiritual individualism" was "essentially competitive" and "gave birth to the crank, the shrill, the high-strung propounder of strange religions, the self-important monopolist of truth." The new individualism, however, had "no desire to vaunt itself . . . it is not combative, it is coöperative, not opinionative but groping, not sectarian but filled with an intense, confused eagerness to identify itself with the life of the whole people."[15]

Croly, Brooks, and other political and social Progressives were seeking a balance between individual assertion and collective needs, and since the old individualism of the nineteenth century had created vast economic imbalances and had stratified social classes, a new type of individualism was sought, one which would be more amenable to collective change. Even such an "unashamed individualist" as Herbert Hoover tempered his nineteenth-century faith in individualism with a twentieth century desire for collective social change. At the conclusion of his appropriately entitled *American Individualism* (1923), Hoover called for an adherence to individualism which seemed untouched by the Progressivist dialogue:

> Humanity has a long road to perfection, but we of America can make sure progress if we preserve our individualism, if we will preserve and stimulate the initiative of our people. . . . Progress will march if we hold an abiding faith in the intelligence, the initiative, the character, the courage, and the divine touch in the individual. . . .We can make a social system as perfect as our generation merits and one that will be received in gratitude by our children.[16]

All this seems a far cry from Croly's proclamation a decade earlier that reformers should "understand that there must be vigorous and conscious assertion of the public as opposed to private and special interests, and that the American people must to a greater extent than they have in the past subordinate the latter to the former."[17] Throughout Hoover's book, however, we sense, as we do with Croly and Brooks, that the individualism here championed is once again being redefined, that a "new individualism" is being offered in place of an old, outdated, and inherently destructive individualism: "Salvation will not come to us out of the wreckage of individualism. What we need is steady devotion to a better, brighter, broader individualism—an individualism that carries increasing responsibility and service to our fellows. Our need is not for a way out but a way forward."[18]

A way out of individualism is exactly what many political and social philosophers of the 1920s desired. Led by Communist thinkers such as Michael Gold, many intellectuals took the Progressivist call for a new individualism of subordination and discipline one step further and demanded that Americans reject all individualism, whether old or new. By the end of the decade, the nature and role of individualism in the collective effort to reshape society was at best precarious, and individualism, however it was defined, became the central focus of many texts. The calls for self-denial and discipline in reshaping American individualism seemed to have failed, and an emerging political and social radicalism increasingly threatened to throw individualism into violent conflict with the demands of social reform. In *Individualism Old and New* (1930), John Dewey noted "a submergence of the individual," proclaimed that "individuals are confused and bewildered," and, more than a decade after Brooks, offered his own ideas "Toward a New Individualism."[19] Horace M. Kallen, in *Individualism: An American Way of Life* (1933), lamented that "Individualism [not just "rugged individualism"] is in eclipse."[20] In *The Conflict of the Individual and the Mass in the Modern World* (1932), Everett Dean

Martin insisted that recent attempts to subordinate individual needs for the collective good had not created a new individual at all: "In practice the submergence of the individual in the mass, as the mass is organized to-day, divides the individual against himself. He is no longer a whole person, he counts only as he is part of some public. It is as producer, consumer, voter, subscriber—not as a person that he is of public interest."[21]

But these voices met with resistance. Many intellectuals still claimed that individualism, modified or not, continued to be a powerful and unhealthy influence in American culture. In *A Planned Society* (1932), George Soule urged that "Today more than ever we need synthesis, coördination, rational control . . . [We are] thwarted by the dogma of absolute Liberty, by the chaos of indeterminateness, which is the natural accompaniment of planless 'freedom.' We are concerned . . . with freedom from the blind compulsions of a disorganized and unreasoned society."[22] In a 1931 editorial, *The New Republic* warned its readership that "the old recipes of 'rugged individualism' and uncontrolled competition are seen on every hand to be insufficient. Our mechanized civilization has advanced to a point where it cries out for planning and control in the interests of all—a sort of planning and control which cannot possibly be executed without encroaching on vested [individual] interests. . . ."[23]

Amidst all of this dialogue on individualism in the late 1920s and early 1930s, perhaps Dewey best expressed the importance of the issue: "The problem of constructing a new individuality consonant with the objective conditions under which we live is the deepest problem of our time. . . . So regarded, the problem is seen to be essentially that of creation of a new individualism as significant for modern conditions as the old individualism at its best was for its day and place."[24]

Red Harvest and *The Maltese Falcon* can be understood as explorations of this call for a new individualism. Each novel examines the possibility of refashioning the inherited impulses of nineteenth-century individualism into a "better, brighter, broader individualism" which seeks, either through allegiance and/or willing submission, to promote collective rather than individual needs. In *Red Harvest*, Hammett's hero initially seems to have transcended the impulses of rugged individualism, and through allegiance to the Agency he appears to have submitted his own desires to those of a collective body. The novel enacts the Op's struggle to resist the impulses of aberrant individualism and to maintain his new individualism of collective identification. In *The Maltese Falcon*, Sam Spade begins as one immersed in competitive, self-centered individualism, for he is both unwilling and unable to act out of interests other than his own. His struggle is the reverse of the Op's: he must find a way out of a maddening and destructive individualism towards a new individualism which, through "control" and "self-sacrifice," will allow him allegiance to something beyond the self. Seen as such, *Red Harvest* and *The Maltese Falcon* embody what Dewey considered the "deepest problem" of Hammett's time.

II

Hammett locates his first novel in the aptly named town of Personville, Montana, a place victimized by nineteenth-century individualism run amok. As the name suggests, Personville is indeed a town of persons rather than a community, and each citizen seeks above all else to protect his or her own interests.[25] Dominating the politics and economics of Personville, Old Elihu Willsson embodies the most unhealthy results of these unrestrained vested interests.

> For forty years old Elihu Willsson . . . had owned Personville, heart, soul, skin, and guts. He was president and majority stockholder of the Personville Mining Corporation, ditto of the First National Bank, owner of the *Morning Herald* and *Evening Herald*, the city's only newspapers, and at least part owner of nearly every other enterprise of any importance. Along with these pieces of property he owned a United States senator, a couple of representatives, the governor, the mayor, and most of the state legislature. Elihu Willsson was Personville, and he was almost the whole state.[26]

Eventually challenged by the labor advances of the IWW, Willsson unmercifully squashes any threat of collective reforms: "Old Elihu hired gunmen, strike-breakers, national guardsmen and even parts of the regular army. . . . When the last skull had been cracked, the last rib kicked in, organized labor in Personville was a used firecracker" (7). In silencing this collective unrest, however, he surrenders most of his local control to the thugs he hired to protect his interests. As a result, Personville is ruled by four gangs that form a violent criminal network where, as critic Peter Wolfe suggests, "self-reliance knows no bounds."[27] The town's one voice of social reform, Willsson's son Donald, is murdered before he appears in the text. A nightmare landscape of brutal self-interest, Personville is the twentieth-century apotheosis of nearly every evil associated with America's old, opportunistic individualism (note that Old Elihu's domination of Personville reaches back forty years, clearly identifying him and the town with the previous century). Perhaps Dinah Brand, Personville's beleaguered Siren, best articulates the town's attitude when she insists that "If a girl's got something that's worth something to somebody, she's a boob if she doesn't collect" (24).

It is down these mean streets that the Continental Op must go. Seeking the murderer of his would-be client, the Op demands that Personville "talk sense for a change" (12) and insists that "things have got to be explained" (17). As efficient as Hammett's hard-boiled prose, the Op moves about Personville with very little wasted effort, successfully pumping everyone he meets for information. Even before he solves Donald Willsson's murder, others note his skillful management and efficiency. Soon, Old Elihu wants to hire him to "clean this pig-sty of Poisonville . . . to smoke out the rats, little and big" (29). When the

Op asks for a ten thousand dollar retainer Old Elihu at first refuses to give so much money to a "man who's done nothing I know of but talk" (30). The Op's response, however, indicates how well he, unlike the citizens of Personville, has merged his own individuality with a larger collective body, suggesting that he has perhaps become what so many social and political philosophers of the times desired—a "new individual" seeking not self-assertion but loyalty to interests beyond his own: "When I say *me*, I mean the Continental" (30).[28] Only a short while later the Op will again assert this collective loyalty as he rejects a bribe: "The Continental's got rules against taking bonuses or rewards" (43).

Yet the Op's subordination to the rules of the Agency is not nearly as inviolate as the early sections of this novel lead us believe. When the chief of police betrays the Op and tries to have him killed, the Op loses his professional detachment. The self-denial he must maintain to perform effectively within the rules of the Agency gives way to vested self-interest. The efficient reformer can no longer subordinate his own desires and place them second to those of the Agency. After the attempt on his life, the Op no longer desires collective justice but personal revenge: "Your fat chief of police tried to assassinate me last night. I don't like that. I'm just mean enough to want to ruin him for it. Now I'm going to have my fun. I've got ten thousand dollars of your money to play with. I'm going to use it opening Poisonville up from Adam's apple to ankles" (43).[29] So much for reform.

The rest of the novel records the Op's "red harvest" of bloody revenge. The values of rational planning and cool efficiency asserted at the beginning of the novel collapse as the Op turns inward to fulfill his own violent form of frontier self-interest. We are witnessing a transformation in the Op's allegiances. The new individual who once equated his self with his Agency now reverts to the ethics of old individualism. Certainly, as Wolfe has suggested, "Responsibility to the Continental should have stopped [the Op] from playing the footloose justicer of cowboy fiction who cleans up a troubled town."[30] Unfortunately, the impulse to act from self-interest is too strong and the more independent the Op becomes from the regulations of the Agency the more he begins to assume the guise of the cowboy justicer, except that unlike the heroic cowboy the Op "rejects his professionalism not to become the white knight who will liberate the countryside from evil and corruption but to get even."[31]

The Op's plans, once so effective, soon begin to go awry. Trying to antagonize the crime bosses, the Op "refixes" a fixed fight and, against plan, one of the fighters is murdered.[32] Soon, the Op confesses that "Plans are all right sometimes . . . And sometimes just stirring things up is all right—if you're tough enough to survive, and keep your eyes open so you'll see what you want when it comes to the top" (57). His loyalties altered by his lust for personal revenge, the Op no longer desires to "clean" Personville. Pursuing his self-interests, he has turned Personville into a battleground, in the process losing his social consciousness:

> Off to the north some guns popped.
>
> A group of three men passed me, shifty-eyed, walking pigeon-toed.
>
> A little farther along, another man moved all the way over to the curb to give me plenty of room to pass. I didn't know him and didn't suppose he knew me.
>
> A lone shot sounded not far away.
>
> As I reached the hotel, a battered black touring car went down the street, hitting at least fifty, crammed to the curtains with men.
>
> I grinned after it. Poisonville was beginning to boil out under the lid, and I felt so much like a native that even the memory of my very un-nice part in the boiling didn't keep me from getting twelve solid end-to-end hours of sleep. (77)

Finally, like the native he has become, the Op rejects the demands of the Agency in favor of his own criteria: "It's right enough for the Agency to have rules and regulations, but when you're out on a job you've got to do it the best way you can" (78). When he tells two fellow operatives "don't kid yourselves that there's any law in Poisonville except what you make for yourself" (79), we can see the Op participating fully in Personville's powerful ideology of vested self-interests.[33]

Instead of being the town's efficient reformer, the Op admits that he has been "juggl[ing] death and destruction" (103). Rather than self-discipline, he must confess to having taken a less noble path: "[I could have played] legally. I could have done that. But it's easier to have them killed off, easier and surer, and, now that I'm feeling this way, more satisfying" (104). Unable to rationalize his actions, the Op confesses to Dinah that he is "going blood-simple" (104). Two surrealistic dreams preface the final movements of this otherwise intensely realistic narrative, further highlighting the irrationality which has slowly come to define the Op's experience. By the end of the novel, the reformer needs reforming. The "new individual" we saw at the beginning, the one who had merged his needs and allegiances with those of the Agency, we now find fixing up his reports "so that they would not read as if I broken as many Agency rules, state laws and human bones as I had" (142).

The Op has become, as it were, a modern day Ahab, juggling death and destruction to satisfy the most irrational of self-centered desires—personal revenge. And, just as Ahab represented nineteenth-century individualism in destructive excess, so too does the Op represent the corruption of twentieth-century individualism, for as John Whitley proclaims, "Little in [the Op's] behavior suggests loyalty to ideals, human relations, or even abstract concepts of the law. He believes only in himself in the narrowest possible sense."[34] Fused momentarily to the reformative desires of a social agency, the Op succumbs to chaotic individualism and thus undermines the efficacy of collective action. In the end, Personville, the horrific landscape of American individualism, corrupts the Op, for "despite his code and despite being an indirect representative of law as an operative of the Continental Agency [he] becomes as lawless as the gangsters and crooked politicians."[35] As Dennis Dooley maintains, we, and perhaps the Op himself, have "glimpsed a frightful truth: that in the end evil springs not merely from greed or organized crime . . . [but] from the eternal willingness of human beings to compromise their ideals and betray their nobler impulses to satisfy their baser needs."[36]

III

In *The Maltese Falcon* Hammett further explores the destructive pull of old individualism. In *Red Harvest* Hammett moves the Op from a stance of willing subordination to a posture of aberrant self-interest, and in doing so he undercuts the Op's position as the hero of the novel, a position the Op claims throughout the early chapters. The Op's failure to remain a "hero" is intimately related to his failure to resist an unhealthy individualism. The destructive threats of self-centered individualism are an even greater danger to Sam Spade. Whereas Hammett successfully suppressed two key elements of the Op's individuality—his name and specific physical description—he now positions these two elements at the very beginning of The Maltese Falcon:[37]

> Samuel Spade's jaw was long and bony, his chin a jutting v under the more flexible v of his mouth. His nostrils curved back to make another, smaller, v. His yellow-grey eyes were horizontal. The v motif was picked up again by thickish brows rising outward from twin creases above a hooked nose, and his pale brown hair grew down—from high flat temples—in a point on his forehead. He looked rather pleasantly like a blond satan. (295)

Compare this opening paragraph to that of *Red Harvest*:

> I first heard Personville called Poisonville by a red-haired mucker named Hickey Dewey in the Big Ship in Butte. He also called his shirt a shoit. I didn't think anything of what he had done to the city's name. Later I heard men who manage their r's give it the same pronunciation. I still didn't see anything in it but the meaningless sort of humor that used to make richardsnary the thieve's word for dictionary. A few years later I went to Personville and learned better. (3)

In *Red Harvest*, the focus rests on the community and we eventually see how this community of perverted self-interests manages to "poison" the reformative desires of the hero. In *The Maltese Falcon*, however, the focus begins with the individual and the "poison" exists within him, for he is "a blond satan." If the Op moves from hero to anti-hero as he succumbs to the poison of a selfish individualism, then Sam Spade, already poisoned, begins as an anti-hero.[38] Hammett's description of Spade in the introduction to the 1934 Modern Library edition of the novel attests to Spade's unhealthy self-focus: "he wants to be a hard and shifty fellow, able to take care of himself in any situation, able to get the best of anybody he comes in contact with, whether criminal, innocent by-stander or client."[39] The Op's challenge is to resist participating in the destructive individualism of Personville and to maintain his professional allegiance to the Agency. Certainly, the Op fails. Spade's challenge is to overcome his own destructive embracing of self-interest and to seek a greater collective identity.

The early chapters of *The Maltese Falcon* attest to Spade's anti-heroic posture of privileged individualism. Recall how in the opening chapters of *Red Harvest* the Op assumes an admirable stance, and, via his client Donald Willsson, is closely allied with social reform. The Op's early concerns for efficiency and justice position him well in our hearts. Not so for Spade. Whereas the Op has a client, someone he works for, Spade has a "customer" (295). Whereas the Op insists that Personville "talk sense for a change," Spade speaks "in a tone that was utterly meaningless" (304). Nearly all of Spade's early actions are self-centered, having less to do with advancing justice than with satisfying his own personal needs (recall his unwillingness to speak to Iva after Archer's murder). His secretary, Effie Perine, warns him of the dangers of his ways, but in response Spade only reasserts his individualism:

> "You worry me," she said, seriousness returning to her face as she talked. "You always think you know what you're doing, but you're too slick for your own good, and some day you're going to find it out."
>
> He sighed mockingly and rubbed his cheek against her arm. "That's what Dundy says, but you keep Iva away from me, sweet, and I'll manage to survive the rest of my troubles." He stood up and put on his hat. "Have the *Spade & Archer* taken off the door and *Samuel Spade* put on. I'll be back in an hour, or phone you." (312-13)

Spade's individualism is explained in his story about Flitcraft, a man whom Spade, at the time working in Seattle, was once hired to track down. Spade tells us that "Flitcraft had been a good citizen and a good husband and father, not by any outer compulsion, but simply because he was a man who was most comfortable in step with his surroundings" (335-36). One day, however, when a falling beam at a construction site nearly kills him, Flitcraft learns that he, "the good citizen-husband-father, could be wiped out between office and restaurant by the accident of a falling beam. He knew then that men died at haphazard like that, and lived only while blind chance spared them" (336). This experience gives Flitcraft a "new glimpse of life," one which leads him to the "discovery that in sensibly ordering his affairs he had gone out of step, and not into step, with life" (336). Flitcraft deserts his family and job in Tacoma, rejecting the social roles of citizen-husband-father, and, confronting absurdity for the first time, he embraces a meandering, uncommitted individualism: "He went to Seattle that afternoon . . . and from there by boat to San Francisco. For a couple of years he wandered around and then drifted back to the Northwest . . ." (336). The individualism Flitcraft embraces, however, does not endure, for soon after his drifting he settles down in Spokane and remarries. What fascinates

Spade is Flitcraft's seemingly easy return to the "ordering of his affairs" after having rejected all such ordering as absurd. As Spade puts it, "He adjusted himself to beams falling, and when no more of them fell, and he adjusted himself to them not falling" (336).

Flitcraft's story serves to complement Spade's current position. Flitcraft's life before the beams begin falling is completely unlike Spade's present life: Flitcraft participates in society as citizen-husband-father, all roles that called for the subordination of self-interest to the larger collective interests of society and family. Spade has rejected all such roles, and goes so far as to mock the role of husband by committing adultery. When the beams begin to fall, Flitcraft adjusts to his new glimpse of life. Convinced of "blind chance" and life's "haphazard" nature, Flitcraft makes a path for San Francisco via Seattle, a path symbolizing a rejection of his social roles in favor of a more self-centered individualism. Flitcraft, once so unlike Spade in his acceptance of social roles, is now very much like Spade. Note that Spade too moves to San Francisco from Seattle and that doing so suggests a rejection of a collective role for a more individual stance. In 1927 Spade was "with one of those big detective agencies in Seattle" (335); he is now, of course, on his own, first with *Spade & Archer*, and then with *Samuel Spade*. Flitcraft's movement away from a collective identity to a purely individual one comes full circle when he repositions himself into his social role through remarriage. Spade, however, has yet to make such a return; in fact, Spade seems to be moving further and further into pure individualism (i.e., *Spade & Archer* to *Samuel Spade*). Thus his fascination with Flitcraft's ability to "settle back naturally into the same groove he had jumped out of" (336) is in part a fascination with one man's ability to reassume social roles and obligations after experiencing a period of uncommitted individualism. Spade still feels what Flitcraft felt that day the beam fell. For Spade life is irrational, governed by blind chance, haphazard at best. Thus he believes in the one thing he can control and promote: his own self-interest. Faced with absurdity and chaos, Spade rejects social obligations and seeks stability by asserting his own desires and independence.

In pursuing the Maltese Falcon, Spade must confront the unhealthy effects of his rugged individualism when it is embraced by others. It is easy for Spade to promote his own self-interests while he able to disassociate himself from others: it takes only a new paint job to remake the office door and simply a quick phone call to Effie to ward off the claims of Iva. Soon, however, Spade finds himself caught in a community where disassociation is not so easy and where self-interest is the supreme motivation of all. The world of Gutman, Brigid, Cairo and the ever-elusive falcon represents, as does Personville in *Red Harvest*, a community of aberrant individualists embracing an unhealthy doctrine of self-interests over the needs of others. When Gutman asks Spade whom he represents in this case and Spade indicates himself, Gutman articulates the philosophy of the micro-community to which Spade is now bound:

"That's wonderful. I do like a man that tells you right out he's looking out for himself. Don't we all? I don't trust a man that says he's not. And the man that's telling the truth when he says he's not I distrust most of all, because he's an ass and an ass that's going contrary to the laws of nature." (365)

What Gutman here embraces, the social and economic reformers of the early twentieth century rejected outright, and the "new individual" of Croly, Brooks, Soule, and Dewey is in Gutman's world an "ass."

Supposed hero of the novel, Spade is as guilty as any in this circle of falcon-seekers. Gutman's exhortations could well be Spade's, for the detective has yet to act in any way which might indicate he thinks otherwise about "the laws of nature." At this point, the true "quest" of the novel emerges. Certainly Spade and the others seek the falcon, but, as the novel will soon bear out, that search proves to be an illusion. The real quest, the truly elusive (but not illusory) search, belongs to Spade. Repeatedly immersed in his own self-centered desires, Spade must somehow differentiate himself from his criminal associates and become the "hero" of the text. To do this, he must reshape his desires according to the demands of some system or code greater than himself. In other words, Spade must make the first move toward a "new individualism," that is, begin to merge his own identity with a larger movement or collective body. Such a move calls for self-discipline and willing subordination, two traits Spade has heretofore lacked. Spade's final confrontation with Brigid enacts his struggle to overcome the insane individualism which has dominated this novel, an insanity in which he has fully participated.

When Spade tells Brigid that he knows she killed Archer, he also tells her that he will turn her over to the police. His motivations again appear to be fully shaped by self-interest: "You're taking the fall. One of us has got to take it, after the talking those birds [Gutman and Cairo] will do. They'd hang me sure. You're likely to get a better break" (436). Here, however, we can excuse Spade's "selfishness"—the self-centeredness at this moment does not resemble his brush offs of Iva or his willingness to auction off his services to the highest bidder—because Brigid does indeed deserve to be turned over. In turn, Brigid demands to know why Spade must do this to her, for, as she tells him, "Surely Mr. Archer wasn't as much to you as [I was]" (438). Spade's litany of reasons, tripartite in structure, is quite telling and deserves careful reading.[40]

In his first attempt to explain his motivations, Spade calls on the code of the detective. The reasons are worth quoting in full:

"When a man's partner is killed he's supposed to do something about it. It doesn't make any difference what you thought of him. He was your partner and you're supposed to do something about it. Then it happens we were in the detective business. Well, when one of your organization gets killed it's bad business to let the killer get away with it. It's bad all around—bad for that one organization, bad for every detective everywhere. Third, I'm a detective and expecting me to run criminals down and then let them go free is like asking a dog to catch a rabbit and let it go. It can be done, all right, and sometimes it is done, but it's not natural." (438)

Embracing the discipline of the detective code, Spade willingly subordinates his own needs to the needs of "every detective everywhere." What is "natural" here is not Gutman's insistence that all men look out for themselves; instead, professional demands and allegiances dominate any self-interests. Most critics consider these allegiances to be Spade's true motivation throughout the novel; they are thus able to excuse Spade's inexplicable moments of self-centeredness.

Should we believe, however, that Spade has been acting within this code all along?[41] If he has been, then Spade is indeed an heroic "new individual," acting always of out interests beyond his own in hopes of servicing justice. But, as Sinda Gregory notes of Spade's other actions throughout the novel, "Since the reader constantly sees Spade adopting whatever role seems most expedient, it becomes impossible for us to be certain of any of his intentions."[42] The same is true here. We would, I believe, like to think that Spade's actions have been intentionally serving a larger, collective good. Perhaps they have been, but then again, perhaps not. At best, we might be able to explain some, but not all, of Spade's actions as stemming from this collective code. The uncertainty confronting the reader here is not a fault in the novel. Instead, Hammett forces the reader to reconsider Spade's motivations and to reposition Spade's possible allegiances. We must listen further, for we feel at this moment as does Brigid: we do not fully believe that the code encompasses all of Spade's actions. His exhortation of the detective code may well be just another one of his well-devised deceptions.

Spade's second attempt to explain himself reveals a different set of motivations. Again, it is worth quoting in full:

> "Fourth, no matter what I wanted to do now it would be absolutely impossible for me to let you go without having myself dragged to the gallows with the others. Next, I've no reason in God's world to think I can trust you and if I did this and got away with it you'd have something on me that you could use whenever you happened to want to. That's five reasons. The sixth would be that since I've also got something on you, I couldn't be sure you wouldn't decide to shoot a hole in *me* some day. Seventh, I don't even like the idea of thinking that there might be one chance in a hundred that you'd played me for a sucker." (438)

Most critics privilege Spade's first three reasons (all having to do with loyalty to the code) and largely ignore reasons four through seven. We should consider, however, that both sets of motivations compel Spade (whether one or the other is *more* compelling is difficult to say at this point, though the novel would seem to bear out the primacy of individual desires over professional codes).[43] In this way, Spade enacts an important tension of his generation, for he desires affiliation with a collective body while still refusing to repress the importance of his own needs. His first three reasons submerge his own individual demands; the next four reasons assert them. Spade seems split between two allegiances: the collective good and individual self-interest.

Spade's third and final explanation receives little attention but it is perhaps the most important in his development:[44] "If [all of my reasons don't] mean anything to you forget it and we'll make it this: I won't [let you go] because all of me wants to—wants to say to hell with the consequences and do it—and because—God damn you—you've counted on that with me the same as you counted on that with the others" (439). Not wanting "to play the sap," Spade discovers a way out of the insane individualism of the Gutman-Cairo-Brigid trio: self-denial. Spade knows that Brigid has been counting on him to act in his own self-interests and to cover up for the lady he loves. Spade wants to let her go and a great deal in this final scene suggests that he may indeed love her. But he will not act upon his own desires exactly because they are his own desires.

If we recall Hammett's original description of Spade looking "rather pleasantly like a blond satan," then this moment of self-imposed self-denial astounds us. Certainly this initial image of Spade as a pleasant satan conjures up for us the image of another pleasant satan, that of Milton's in the early books of *Paradise Lost*. Like Milton's Satan, Spade and his defiant individualism initially attract our sympathies. But as their narratives mature, we perceive the divisive ramifications of such myopic stances. Spade finally sees the implications as well and thus embraces not self-assertion but self-denial as his final posture. He is, as it were, no longer shaking his defiant fist against the heavens and fate but against himself.

At the end of *The Maltese Falcon* we know that Spade is doing the right thing and that the right thing involves a curious calculation of allegiances to both personal and professional codes. Ultimately, however, the sum of these calculations adds up to self-denial. Via this self-denial Spade begins to reshape his individualism, recalling for us the words of Herbert Croly quoted earlier in this essay: "The Promise of American life is to be fulfilled—not merely by a maximum amount of economic freedom, but by a certain measure of discipline; not merely by the abundant satisfaction of individual desires, but by a large measure of individual subordination and self-denial." Spade's decision to surrender Brigid stands as a moment of discipline for a man repeatedly described in terms suggesting not discipline but bestial ("wolfish") need for satisfaction.[45] Spade's dilemma at the conclusion of the novel enacts a dilemma of his entire generation: in moments of crisis, where do we put our allegiances, how do we protect our own self-interests without violating the demands of a larger community, how do we fuse our own needs with the needs of society and still retain our inherent American desire for self-promoting individualism?

In *Red Harvest* and *The Maltese Falcon* we witness Hammett struggling with his generation's reconception of American individualism. Just as intellectuals were calling for the refashioning of nineteenth-century individualism through efficient planning, social control, and self-denial, Hammett was investigating the possibilities of achieving and maintaining this new individualism. These investigations, however, do not supply easy answers. In *Red Harvest* Hammett portrays the failure of new individualism, for the Op and all his allegiances to the Agency cannot withstand the pull of an old, self-seeking individualism. The lesson here seems to be that the inherited self-interest of the American landscape remains too powerful for the new allegiances to overcome. And yet in *The Maltese Falcon* Hammett reverses this movement and takes his hero from a self-indulgent individualism to a new individualism which seeks to wed collective and personal interests via self-denial. But, as John Patterson properly maintains, this movement towards a new individualism is far from triumphant: "Returned to his desk in the final scene of his career, [Spade] is in fact a bleak, lonely, and unhappy figure, without home, without love, without community, conscious perhaps that his victory is far from final and that it may have cost him far too much."[46]

The pull of old and new individualism is not resolved in these two novels, only highlighted. Hammett neither assures us of the possibility of achieving a new individualism nor does he maintain the necessary and inevitable victory of the old individualism. It has been said of detective stories that they are "wish-fulfillment fantasies designed to produce certain agreeable sensations in the reader, to foist upon him illusions he wants to entertain and which he goes to this literature to find."[47] If so, then Hammett has successfully transcended the genre, for his novels offer us profound complexities in the place of wish-fulfillments, irreconcilable realities instead of entertaining illusions. If we approach *Red Harvest* and *The Maltese Falcon* as complementary explorations of a similar dilemma, then we must face the disagreeable sensations produced by these texts when read in tandem: that is, that the refashioning of American individualism towards a more collective identity, as desirable and as necessary as it may be for the promise of American life, has been, and will always be, a painful and a precarious process. [*Essays in Literature* 17 (Fall 1990): 242-60]

NOTES

1. William Curtis, "Some Recent Books," *Town and Country*, February 15, 1930 cited in Richard Layman, *Shadow Man: The Life of Dashiell Hammett* (New York: Harcourt, 1981) 113.

2. Leonard Moss, "Hammett's Heroic Operative," *New Republic* 154 (January 8, 1966) 34.

3. Leslie Fiedler, *Love and Death in the American Novel* (New York: Criterion Books, 1960) 476.

4. H. H. Morris, "Dashiell Hammett in the Wasteland," *Midwest Quarterly* 19 (Winter 1978): 200-01.

5. Cynthia S. Hamilton, *Western and Hard-Boiled Detective Fiction in America: From High Noon to Midnight* (Iowa City: U of Iowa P, 1987) 1 and 2. To her credit, Hamilton grants Hammett a high level of sophistication on the problem of individualism

in his work. Of Hammett's novels, she writes, "Hammett appears to be caught in a philosophical 'Catch—22': competitive individualism is bad because it is divisive, but collective action is impossible because individuals are competitive. Hammett cannot get past the basic ideological assumption of the primacy of the individual, and can pose no alternative. In this respect, the later condemnation of Hammett's work as subversive must be considered wryly ironic" (32). Like Hamilton's, my focus is on Hammett's handling of complicated issues of individualism. But whereas Hamilton insists that Hammett "cannot get past the basic ideological assumption of the primacy of the individual" I would argue that Hammett is not trying to "get past" individualism but is exploring competing versions of individualism and their respective attractions and shortcomings. Any "alternative" which Hammett might pose would thus not be something outside of individualism but would be a different type of individualism.

6. David Geherin, *The American Private Eye: The Image in Fiction* (New York: Ungar, 1985) 21-22.

7. D. Glover, "Sociology and the Thriller: The Case of Dashiell Hammett," *Sociological Review* 27 (February 1979): 26.

8. Robert Edenbaum, "The Poetics of the Private-Eye: The Novels of Dashiell Hammett" in *Tough-Guy Writers of the 1930s*, ed. David Madden (Carbondale: Southern Illinois UP, 1968) 81.

9. Sinda Gregory, *Private Investigations: The Novels of Dashiell Hammett* (Carbondale: Southern Illinois UP, 1985) 29. Compare Gregory's statement to Hamilton's claim that in Hammett's novels the "need for self-reliance is emphasized . . . [and thus] The individual is shown to be the only source of positive social action" (31).

10. Robert Shulman, "Dashiell Hammett's Social Vision," *Centennial Review* 29 (Fall 1985): 400. Shulman opposes the individualism of the Continental Op, Sam Spade, and Ned Beaumont (a type of individualism Shulman often refers to as merely "different") to the "competitive individualism" of those whom they must confront. Though I agree with Shulman's observation that a novel like *The Maltese Falcon* "brings to a suggestive focus [Hammett's] concern with American individualism," I would suggest that the conflicting versions of individualism in such novels as *Red Harvest* and *The Maltese Falcon* are most often played out within the hero rather than between the hero and his competitive society. Such a reading reveals not only Hammett's critique of an acquisitive capitalist culture, which most readings of his work manifest, but also emphasizes Hammett's critique of his heroes as well.

11. Herbert Croly, *Promise of American Life* (New York: Macmillian, 1909) 22.

12. Croly 25, 23, 152.

13. Frederick Jackson Turner cited in *Individualism and Conformity in the American Character*, ed. Richard Rapson (Boston: Heath, 1967) 26.

14. Van Wyck Brooks, "Toward a National Culture" in *Van Wyck Brooks: The Early Years*, ed. Claire Sprague (New York: Harper, 1968) 185.

15. Brooks 186, 190, 190, 190.

16. Herbert Hoover, *American Individualism* (Garden City: Doubleday, 1922) 71-72.

17. Croly 153.

18. Hoover 66.

19. John Dewey, *Individualism Old and New* (New York: Capricorn Books, 1930) 51 and 52. For the chapter "Toward a New Individualism" see 74-100.

20. Horace M. Kallan, *Individualism: An American Way of Life* (New York: Liveright, 1933) 20.

21. Everett Dean Martin, *The Conflict of the Individual and the Mass in the Modern World* (New York: Holt, 1932) 33.

22. George Soule, *A Planned Society* (New York: Macmillan, 1932) 91-92.

23. Cited in Richard H. Pells, *Radical Visions and American Dreams: Culture and Social Thought in the Depression Years* (Middletown: Wesleyan UP, 1984) 50.

24. Dewey 31-32.

25. The town's geographical location also holds symbolic resonance. Gregory writes that Personville's "pollution, in both a physical and spiritual sense, is even more dramatic because of its geographical position; by placing the city in the West, Hammett suggests a sort of ultimate corruption: the West—the promised land whose expanse offers freedom, escape, and the realization of America's promise of opportunity and unlimited possibility—has become as 'dirtied up' as the rest of the country" (31).

26. Dashiell Hammett, *The Complete Novels of Dashiell Hammett* (New York: Knopf, 1965) 7. All further references are to this edition and are cited in parenthesis.

27. Peter Wolfe, *Beams Falling: The Art of Dashiell Hammett* (Bowling Green: Bowling Green U Popular Press, 1980) 90.

28. Gregory astutely observes the importance of the Op's allegiance to the Agency: "Unlike almost all of the hard-boiled detectives who work from a small one-man office and who pride themselves on their independence (Philip Marlowe, Mike Hammer, Race Williams), the Op is part of an organization. Thus he is not a renegade maverick at odds with the police. . . . The Continental Detective Agency is, in fact, a business that approaches crime and violence with no moralistic or evangelical zeal. The Op's anonymity is reinforced by his position in such an agency" (44). This description of the Op's unusual position in hard-boiled fiction will serve as an interesting contrast to Hammett's next creation, Sam Spade.

29. Discussing the importance of this moment, Glover observes: "It is this stubbornness which mitigates against seeing the Continental Op solely as the organization man he is and which limits the strong tendency for the detective to be reduced solely to his occupational function. Furthermore it is this irrepressible egoism which shifts the narrative towards the timeless realm of fantasy where the individual is totally superordinate and autonomous. The antinomies which the text invokes—between individual and occupation, realism and fantasy—are never ultimately resolved but provide for different modes of exposition and emphasis as the plot unfolds" (25-26).

30. Wolfe 87.

31. Gregory 50. George J. Thompson notes the Op's vengeful motives but argues differently: "The harvest of revenge promises to be red. Nowhere does the Op talk about law or justice in this vow; the matter is partly a personal one. The detective seems to represent himself more than his client, and yet his personal stand implies a social, even moral, perspective as well. The Op's emphasis is on a cleaning up, a harvesting of rottenness and corruption. The harvest image suggests a natural, if not moral, necessity for action" ("The Problem of Moral Vision in Dashiell Hammett's Detective Novels, Part II: *Red Harvest* 'The Pragmatic and Moral Dilemma,'" *Armchair Detective* 6 (4) 1972, 217).

32. Seeking to vindicate the Op's actions, Thompson insists the following: "Stirring things up and trying to stay tough enough to survive prove to be the Op's method throughout *Red Harvest*. In this initial case [of the fixed fight], his method is tried out: it's a pragmatic experiment, one which get results even though a man is killed in the process. . . . we are not morally upset that Kid Cooper gets killed. He is not innocent,

and his death is seen, though as non-legal, as poetic justice" ("The Problem of Moral Vision in Dashiell Hammett's Detective Novels, Part II: *Red Harvest* 'The Pragmatic and Moral Dilemma,'" 218).

33. In his study of popular genres, John G. Cawelti insists that "to preserve his integrity [the hard-boiled hero] must reject the public ideals and values of the society and seek to create his own personal code of ethics and his own set of values" (*Adventure, Mystery, and Romance: Formula Stories as Art and Popular Culture* [Chicago: U of Chicago P, 1976] 161). Certainly this is true of many hard-boiled heroes, but in the case of the Op it is not so. When the Op chooses to begin his vendetta against Personville he is embracing, not rejecting, the public ideals and values of the society. Also, when the Op seeks to fashion his own personal code and set of values (codes and values free of Agency constraints) we see the dissolution of integrity, not the preservation of it, as the Op descends into the ethics of revenge. Perhaps the harshest criticism of the Op's "personal code of ethics" comes from Christopher Bentley: "Apart from his narrow and sometimes questionable professionalism, it is hard to see that the Op has any ethical code, or that his violence is any more meaningful than that it serves to keep him alive and to kill people whom he wishes to see dead" ("Radical Anger: Dashiell Hammett's *Red Harvest*" in *American Crime Fiction: Studies in the Genre*, ed. Brian Docherty [New York: St. Martin's Press, 1988] 64).

34. John S. Whitley, "Stirring Things Up: Dashiell Hammett's Continental Op," *Journal of American Studies* 14 (Dec 1980): 449.

35. Gregory 57.

36. Dennis Dooley, *Dashiell Hammett* (New York: Ungar, 1984) 85.

37. Dooley writes: "How fitting, after six years of stories and novels featuring a nameless hero, that the first words of Hammett's new book should be the name of his detective" (99).

38. As William Ruehlman notes, "When Spade is compared to a 'blond satan' in the first paragraph, Hammett is deliberately setting him forth as a character who is a long way from being a hero" (*Saint With a Gun: The Unlawful American Private Eye* [New York: New York U P, 1974] 73).

39. Cited in Layman 106.

40. Thompson gives the most thorough reading of this confrontation, placing, as I do, great importance on all of Spade's reasons for surrendering Brigid ("The Problem of Moral Vision in Dashiell Hammett's Detective Novels, Part IV: *The Maltese Falcon* 'The Emergency of the Hero,'" *Armchair Detective* 7 (May 1974) 189). Though Thompson is not concerned as I am with Spade's struggle with competing versions of individualism, he recognizes, as many critics fail to do, that Spade's reasons "bridge moral and professional and personal concerns" (189). In contrast to most critics, William Kenney fails to discern the indispensable importance of the Spade-Brigid confrontation to the meaning of the novel. Kenney sees the confrontation as an "afterthought" because the main action of the novel, the quest for the falcon, ends with the discovery of the fake ("The Dashiell Hammett Tradition and the Modern Detective Novel," *Dissertation*, Michigan 1964, 110 cited in Thompson, 'The Problem of Moral Vision in Dashiell Hammett's Detective Novels, Part IV: *The Maltese Falcon* 'The Emergency of the Hero,'" 179).

41. Many critics do, though I believe unjustly so. For instance, William F. Nolan believes that in this scene Spade "reveals the emotions of a man whose heart is with the woman, but whose code forbids his accepting her" (*Hammett: A Life at the Edge* [New

York: Congdon and Weed, 1983] 61). Edward Margolies insists that Spade "can surrender Brigid to the police because, even though he loves her, his code comes first" (*Which Way Did He Go?: The Private Eye in Dashiell Hammett, Raymond Chandler, Chester Himes, and Ross Macdonald* [New York: Holmes and Meier, 1982] 30). William Marling asserts that Spade is "more perfectly than the Op a knight of the detective code" (*Dashiell Hammett* [Boston: Twayne, 1983] 76). Walter Blair concurs with the primacy of Spade's code in controlling his behavior throughout the novel: "Through his reading of much of the book the reader is kept in the dark as to what makes Spade tick. But as the story concludes, Spade's actions make clear that he is the only character who has integrity, who obeys a code" ("Dashiell Hammett: Themes and Techniques," in *Essays on American Literature in Honor of Jay Hubbell*, ed. Clarence Gohdes [Durham: Duke U P, 1967] 306). My inclinations are more in sympathy with Hamilton, who acknowledges that "we are never told [Spade's] thoughts, only given his words and actions. Spade may have involved himself with Brigid, Gutman, and Cairo in order to solve the murders, recover the falcon and prosecute the thieves; or he may be an opportunist who finds he must turn everything over to the police in order to save himself. Some understanding of Spade is possible because the vision underlying the book is his vision, but this does not help us to interpret his actions or to place moral value on them" (132). I feel it is not necessary to accept that Spade believes in a code; what is more important is that Spade desires to be affiliated with such a code, that he seeks, rather than believes in, allegiance to that code.

42. Gregory 105. It is interesting to note here that although Gregory suggests the impossibility of discovering Spade's intentions, she is willing to believe in Spade's professionalism: "Despite all his personal complexities and idiosyncracies, Sam Spade is, above all, a very efficient private investigator, a man who has a shrewd business sense and loyalty to and respect for his profession" (94).

43. Perhaps John Paterson is correct in asserting "that when a man has so many reasons to advance he is not really sure of any of them" ("A Cosmic View of the Private Eye," *Saturday Review* 65, 22 August 1953, 32). Again, however, what remains important is not that we ascertain Spade's true allegiances but that we note Spade's struggle to articulate those allegiances.

44. I obviously disagree with Thompson, who feels that at this moment "Spade's diction—'If that doesn't mean anything to you forget it and we'll make it this'—certainly implies he is over-simplifying his complex reasons because he realizes all too well her inability to understand their meaning" ("The Problem of Moral Vision in Dashiell Hammett's Detective Novels, Part IV: *The Maltese Falcon* 'The Emergency of the Hero,'" 189). Spade is not over-simplifying his motivations at this moment so that Brigid may understand him; instead, he is asserting, in a crystallized not an over-simplified form, his newly discovered virtue of renunciation.

45. Dooley writes: "As the novel nears its conclusion, we glimpse the animal in Spade again, looking 'hungrily from her hair to her feet and up to her eyes again.' But he denies his hunger, knowing that to satisfy it would be his undoing" (108).

46. Patterson 32.

47. William Aydelotte, "The Detective Story as Historical Source," in *Dimensions of Detective Fiction*, ed. Larry Landrum (Bowling Green: Popular P, 1976) 69.

The Glass Key

Reviews

Another of Dashiell Hammett's grand detective stories is out. In *The Glass Key*, Ned Beaumont, gambler and political hanger-on, tries to protect his friend, Madvig, a political boss, from a murder charge that is hanging over him. The suave and deadly opposition boss, Shad O'Rory, Senator Henry and his daughter Janet, Madvig's daughter, Opal, the killer, Jeff, and the various other guerrillas, gangsters, politicians and their women, stand out clearly and sharply, softened by no romantic haze. Mr. Hammett does not show you their thoughts, only their actions, and the story is amazingly swift, harsh and thrilling. Be you high, low, or middle-brow, don't miss this item by a man who has now written the three best detective stories ever published. [Walter Brooks, *Outlook and Independent* 29 April 1931: 601]

Get your copy of *The Glass Key*, the best of the spring mysteries by quite some margin. This department believes and can prove that Mr. Hammett's new volume is about twice as good as his *The Maltese Falcon*, hitherto regarded by the better fans as about the last word in hard-boiled detectivism. Since you'll have to take sides in this argument, don't delay learning about the strange, brutal and fairly enigmatic career of Ned Beaumont, his gambling luck, his doings in dirty civic politics, his solution of a murder and maybe his great love for Janet Henry, daughter of Senator Ralph Bancroft Henry, and sister of the corpse.

It seems that Ned is lieutenant and buddy to Paul Madvig, a city boss, who is trying to elect Senator Henry and wipe out Shad O'Rory, another boss, when somebody up and murders the senator's son on China Street—it might have been Paul Madvig, some of Shad's anthropoid gangsters, or a lot of other people. The secret is well kept and expertly spilled at the proper second. More and greater mysteries reside in the mental and emotional make-up of Mr. Hammett's characters, who provide fascinating problems in all directions. What one reader wants to know, just out of idle curiosity, is this: Are there people like that? And if so, can any thing be done? Meanwhile you get a story positively without rubber stamps, a brilliant study in the ugly and abysmal which should be read by authors of all kinds and distributed as tracts to the mystery mongers.

Mr. Hammett's is plain, blunt writing and it is most effective. "The Kid yelped and fell down on the hallway floor," says he, when he wishes to indicate that the Kid yelped and fell down on the hallway floor, and the occasional lapses with dictionary words needn't be worried about. Moreover, he belongs to the "he said" and "she said" school of dialogue—instead of "he jibbed" and "she guzzled"— and that, too, is effective, if it doesn't absorb all your attention with its simplicity. In other words, *The Glass Key* is a whiz of an opus. [Will Cuppy, *New York Herald Tribune* 26 April 1931: 13]

There can be no doubt of Mr. Hammett's gifts in this special field, and there can be no question of the success of his latest book. Municipal politics at its lowest is his theme and he has done the subject justice with a score of convincing underworld characters and their satellites. Senator Ralph Bancroft Henry is up for re-election, with the backing of the unsavory Paul Madvig, when the Senator's son, Taylor Henry, is murdered. Ned Beaumont, Madvig's lieutenant, apparently knows something about the crime, and so do half a dozen others, including a gambler's girl and a couple of gunmen. The Senator has a daughter, of course, and Beaumont, who strikes one as a cheap honky tonker, falls in love. Plenty of authentic and coarse dialogue gives realism to the story. Mr. Hammett's new book is bound to find favor, although probably not as much as was accorded his earlier work, *The Maltese Falcon*. [Bruce Rae, *New York Times Book Review* 3 May 1931: 23]

From "Oh, Look—Two Good Books!"

Dorothy Parker

[Dashiell Hammett's] new book, *The Glass Key*, seems to me nowhere to touch its predecessor. . . . For I thought that in *The Glass Key* Mr. Hammett seemed a little weary, a little short of spontaneous, a little dogged about his simplicity of style, a little determined to make startling the ordering of his brief sentences, a little concerned with having his conclusion approach the toughness of the superb last scene of *The Maltese Falcon*. But all that is not to say that *The Glass Key* is not a good book and an enthralling one, and the best you have read since *The Maltese Falcon*. [*New Yorker* 25 April 1931: 83-84]

A Letter to the Editor of *Writer's Digest*

Joseph T. Shaw

Dear Editor:

. . . . as far as I have any knowledge, *Black Mask* has published only one story in which the gangster was in any sense the "hero," and that story is the great novel by Dashiell Hammett, which recently was published under the title of *The Glass Key*. This was a story of modern gangsters, a seriously written and highly dramatic presentation of the present day alliance between corrupt politicians and public officials and organized crime—which alliance is the sole reason for the profitableness of crime as a profession.

Even in this story, virtue comes out on top—the crook who has ruled a city is defeated, his gang is broken up, the corrupt politicians who have made his career possible are swept out of office by the voters. This novel, incidentally, will be published in book form by Alfred Knopf this Fall, as have all of Mr. Hammett's novels. If you have read this story, or will read it, you will agree with me. I am sure, that publication of it, and of stories like it, is a public service. Not until the general public realizes that modern crime, modern gangs, cannot exist without the collusion of corrupt and equally criminal police and public officials, will it be possible to cure what is undoubtedly one of the most serious illnesses, to put it mildly, that our body politic has ever suffered from.

Black Mask never has and never will make money or attempt to make money by appealing to the appetite for stories which present crime and criminals in a prepossessing and alluring light: our policy is and always will be the exact opposite—to appeal to those who hate crime and criminals and who get pleasure from reading stories in which they can identify themselves with the detective or other officers who are solving crimes and capturing criminals. [*Writer's Digest* September 1930: 7-8]

On *The Glass Key*

Rex Stout

Hammett's *The Glass Key* is a more pointed and profound, a deeper commentary on certain aspects of the behavior of the human male, than anything Hemingway ever wrote. The things that were bothering Hammett's heroes were exactly the same things that bothered Ernie all his life. And I think Dash did a better job of dealing with them. But it will never be considered such, because his book is a mystery. [from "Who's Afraid of Nero Wolfe?: An Interview with Rex Stout" by Richard S. Lochte. *The Armchair Detective* 3 (June 1970): 213]

From *Mortal Consequences*

Julian Symons

The Glass Key is the peak of Hammett's achievement, which is to say the peak of the crime writer's art in the twentieth century. Constant rereading of it offers fresh revelations of the way in which a crime writer with sufficient skill and tact can use violent events to comment by indirection on life, art, society, and at the same time compose a novel admirable in the carpentry of its structure and delicately intelligent in its suggestions of truths about human relationships. As a novel *The Glass Key* is remarkable, as a crime novel unique. [Schocken Books, 1973: 139-40]

On *The Glass Key*

James M. Cain

Question: To many persons, "hardboiled fiction" in America means you, Horace McCoy, Hammett, and Chandler. Do you feel the affinity?

Cain: No. To tell you the truth, I never read but ten pages of Chandler's books, if that. I never read one word of Horace McCoy. I read twenty pages of Hammett in Greenwich, Connecticut, when I worked for *The New Yorker* in 1931. I was managing editor and had to go there every Sunday to the printer and put the magazine to bed. Lying around there was this book, *The Glass Key*. I would pick the thing up and try to read it and, at the end of four or five Sundays, when I'd read only about twenty pages, I said forget this goddamn book. And that's my total knowledge of Hammett. [From "Tough Guy: An Interview" by Peter Burnette and Gerald Perry. *Film Comment* (May-June 1976): 50]

From *The New Wild West: The Urban Mysteries of Dashiell Hammett and Raymond Chandler*

Paul Skenazy

A violent, even sadistic book, *The Glass Key* was Hammett's personal favorite among his works. In its way, it is a remarkable novel, close to total denotation in its language. It opens with a gambling table, with a magnified vision of the dots on a die, and it maintains the magnification of a world of chance throughout. It prefigures the experiments with point of view, objectivity, and materialism as method and meaning that were to come in the French New Novel. [Boise State UP, 1982: 25]

From "Setting the Record Straight on *Dashiell Hammett: A Life*"

William F. Nolan

[In *Dashiell Hammett: A Life*, Diane Johnson's] portrait of Ned Beaumont . . . is superficial and wrong-headed. She calls him Hammett's "most plausible and fallible hero" and claims that "his heroes were getting to be more and more like himself." She adds that Beaumont "searches for value in values, for merit in authority." Well, first of all, Ned Beaumont is no hero; he is an outright crook, a politician's hanger on, and a moral sellout. He values his gambler's luck above all else, and sees no merit whatever in authority. And although Hammett gave Beaumont his own physical characteristics, this character is totally *unlike* his creator. Hammett never "sold out" to anybody. Johnson totally misses the whole point to Beaumont—that *he's* the broken "glass key," the hollow man. Hammett is not creating a hero; he's drawing a portrait of a moral failure. [*The Armchair Detective* 17 (Winter 1984): 38]

The Riddle of the Key

Will Murray

Probably the most intriguing icon in all the history of detective literature is the legendary Maltese Falcon—even though the "Black Bird" itself never appeared in Dashiell Hammett's classic novel of the same name. Almost as intriguing is the title object of another Hammett novel, *The Glass Key*. It, too, was absent from the novel named after it. But where the Maltese Falcon was simply missing in *The Maltese Falcon*, the glass key of *The Glass Key* was not a physical object, but a metaphysical one. There was no glass key. It was simply an element in a dream, and one that had no palpable impact on the story or its characters.

Despite, or perhaps because of, that fact, students of Dashiell Hammett's work have attempted to interpret the significance of the glass key. In two of the three Hammett biographies published in the last five years, the biographer takes a stab at interpreting the meaning of the glass key, and each arrives at a different conclusion.

According to William F. Nolan, in his *Hammett: A Life at the Edge:*

> The novel's title seems overly symbolic. Most critics have assumed that it refers to a dream of Janet Henry's. In the dream, as she relates it, Janet and Ned are together, and very hungry. They reach a house with food inside, but the door is locked. They have a glass key to open the door with, but if they use it they will release the snakes writhing on the floor. In her first recounting of the dream, Janet lies to Beaumont, telling him that they were able to eat the food and escape the snakes. He does not believe this. When they are about to go away together at the end, Janet admits the truth: that the glass key shattered, and "we couldn't lock the snakes in . . . they came out all over us."
>
> Hammett is telling us that the lovers are due for a bad time, that they should not feed their hunger for one another, because the snakes will, in turn, devour them. . . .
>
> Ned's luck has gone bad again. . . . In winning . . . Ned has actually lost again, matching the constant pattern of his life. Hammett obviously means to tell us that he will lose again in New York with Janet.
>
> Ned Beaumont himself is the key of glass, fragile in character and, at the end, broken.

Richard Layman, author of *Shadow Man: The Life of Dashiell Hammett*, sees it differently:

> Freudian-symbol hunters have distorted this passage as a clue to Beaumont's impotence and to his and Janet Henry's guilt-ridden sexuality. Even with Hammett's interest in psychology, that is unlikely. The glass key is symbolic of the action in the novel, but in a more artistic way. It represents the various kinds of knowledge Ned Beaumont and other characters gain during the course of the novel. Once a door is opened and you learn what is on the other side, you must live with all that is found there, not simply the best of it, and what is found there can never be unlearned. A glass key works only once, to unlock a door. The metaphor applies to Senator Henry, who learns the extent to which he has been consumed by his lust for political power; to Paul Madvig, who is unable to undo his foolishness in attempting to cover up the senator's crime; to Janet Henry, who learns for the first time the extent of her father's corruption; and to Ned Beaumont, who ironically must break with his friend Paul Madvig to save his friend's life.

Diane Johnson, in her *Dashiell Hammett: A Life*, prudently does not address the question, except to note that Hammett's hardcover publisher, Knopf, was unhappy with the book's title, having "heard a lot of unfavorable opinion about Hammett's titles not having enough to do with the book."

Only Hammett himself could comment authoritatively on which of these two interpretations—if either—is accurate. Literary speculation is a dicey occupation and often doesn't take into account the practical working methods of an author or the exigencies of modern publishing.

This may be the case with *The Glass Key*.

I have the following story from Charles Spain Verral, a contemporary of Hammett's. During the 1930's, Verral was perhaps best known for the lead novels he wrote for Street and Smith's *Bill Barnes, Air Adventurer* magazine, under the house name of "George L. Eaton," for editor F. Orlin Tremaine. Verral did not know Hammett personally, but knew several of his fellow *Black Mask* writers. As Verral recalls it, it was during a writers' gathering in the '30s that he and his wife Jean (past editor of a pulp titled *Underworld Romances*) first heard this explanation given for the glass key:

> The incident of the glass key came about when Jeanie and I were with a bunch of detective writers, and probably some *Black Mask* people, and we were talking about Dashiell Hammett. And we were also talking about, I think, the advances I used to ask from Street and Smith. Orlin would say, "Okay, give me a title." And I'd give him a title and the check would be in the next mail. It came out that Hammett was facing the same situation, and he was asked for a title for, I guess, *Black Mask*. Thinking of a tricky title, he said "The Glass Key." And then, when he had to write the thing, he couldn't figure out how to get the glass key in the title into the story. And he had his character have a dream. And of course when the key went into a lock, it shattered.

Verral does not recall exactly who told the story to him. "It was just conversation," he says, but "it may have been Fred Nebel who told me that." Nebel, of course, would have gotten it from Hammett himself, or at worst from Hammett's editor at *Black Mask*, Joe Shaw. Nebel knew Hammett and wrote for *Black Mask*.

This kind of advance was a common practice among established writers and editors in the pulp publishing world. Verral himself resorted to it often. So it is a plausible story. But is it likely?

Circumstantially, it fits the scenario in which *The Glass Key* was written. The novel was initially serialized in *Black Mask,* beginning in the March 1930 issue and concluding in the June issue. According to Diane Johnson, *The Glass Key* was written in a violent rush, the last third of it in a thirty-hour marathon early in February 1930—the same month the March *Black Mask* would have appeared on newsstands. This means that the first installment, entitled "The Glass Key," had been announced in the previous issue, thus committing Hammett to his "tricky title" before he had even finished the story. It is especially significant that the glass key dream is not mentioned until near the end of the story. If, as the anecdote goes, Hammett had simply given Shaw a title off the top of his head, he must have been chagrined to find himself stuck with that title from the first installment, and he had no choice but to introduce a glass key—any glass key—somewhere along the line. Hammett's need to complete the novel virtually overnight may have been a consequence of losing valuable writing time attempting to solve that technical problem. If so, it had an unfortunate career consequence: Hammett later ascribed his failure to finish any novel after his next one, *The Thin Man*, to his inability to duplicate this creative splurge.

This was not the only instance of Hammett's "tendency to live on books not yet finished," as Diane Johnson phrases it. Hammett did much the same thing with *The Thin Man*, in that instance requesting a number of advance payments against unearned royalties from Knopf.

If it is true the choice of title for *The Glass Key* was nothing more significant than an author's device to chisel some fast money out of a friendly editor, that necessity need not cancel out the validity of a textual interpretation of the meaning of the glass key. But from a realistic—not interpretive—point of view, most pulp writers, working against crushing deadlines, did not take the time to insert meaning or metaphysics into their fiction. And it certainly seems unlikely that Hammett would have put a lot of thought into an element that appeared in the one section of the novel he wrote virtually overnight. But, under the eyes of readers and critics, fiction sometimes assumes a kind of life beyond an author's actual intentions—even if the "interpretations" of those intentions prove to be as fragile as, well, a key of glass. [*The Armchair Detective* 22 (Summer 1989): 290-95]

Dashiell Hammett's Hard-Boiled Modernism

Jon Thompson

The division between the personal and the class individual, the accidental nature of the conditions of life for the individual, appears only with the emergence of the class which itself is the product of the bourgeoisie. This accidental character is only engendered and developed by competition and the struggle of individuals among themselves. Thus, in imagination, individuals seem freer under the dominance of the bourgeoisie than before, because their conditions of life seem accidental; in reality, of course, they are less free, because they are more subjected to the violence of things.

—Karl Marx, *The German Ideology*

Cities of Blood

Dashiell Hammett's fiction has always occupied an uncertain position within the literary canon. Although his work has generally been relegated to a kind of second-tier status thought to be appropriate to "genre" fiction, because of its stylistic sophistication and existential atmosphere it has also attracted its share of literary admirers. Critics often praise Hammett's spare, chiseled prose for its stylistic similarity to Hemingway's minimalist fiction. It would be misleading, however, to read Hammett's fiction as a pale reflection of high modernism. Hammett's modernism, and the modernism of the hard-boiled school, is based not on a repudiation of mass culture, but instead on an embracing of its possibilities. The distinctiveness of Hammett's fiction consists of its recuperation of modernist themes and techniques in a predominantly realist form that Hammett made contemporary through his command of American English. In the process Hammett virtually produced the distinctively American hard-boiled detective genre.[1]

Hammett's modernism is thus different from the European modernism rooted in the avant-garde, but, as Ken Worpole notes, it is a modernism rooted in similar responses to the modern urban world of the early twentieth century: "The jungle of the cities which Brecht wanted to portray to European theatre audiences, Hammett had already fictionalized for his dime magazine readers" (*Dockers and Detectives*, 43). But unlike many avant-garde movements in Europe, Hammett did not reject the artistic forms of the past; instead, he transformed a seemingly exhausted form into a distinctively new genre, a genre with its own distinctive language and worldview. As Raymond Chandler testified in his famous essay "The Simple Art of Murder," Hammett "gave murder back to the kind of people that commit it for reasons, not just to provide a corpse; and with the means at hand, not with hand-wrought dueling pistols, curare, and tropical fish. He put these people down on paper as they are, and he made them talk and think in the language they customarily used for those purposes" (Howard Haycraft, ed, *The Art of the Mystery Story*, 234). Though Chandler plays down Hammett's stylization of ordinary language, his comments do suggest the transformations Hammett made in the detective-story genre. It is thus ironic that although Hammett's fiction was not regarded as serious in his own time, it succeeded in reaching the mass audience that the European avant-garde coveted but could never reach.[2]

Although Hammett was a modernist in his response to the post-world-war society he observed and criticized, he was, characteristically, a modernist on his own terms, albeit an unorthodox modernist writing for pulp magazines. In what follows, I will explore the ways in which the combination of a number of ideological elements—Hammett's individualism, his skepticism toward bourgeois law and order, his philosophical and ideological relativism, the contradictory sexual politics of his fiction, and his rejection of rationality—produced the hard-boiled modernism found in *The Glass Key* and Hammett's other fiction.

If crime fiction partly exists as a response to the anxieties produced by modern, industrialized, urban environments, it attempts, and not always successfully, to mediate that anxiety by producing consoling versions of society. Poe sought to resolve his distaste for a democratic, industrialized America by creating a detective figure whose independence, superiority, and omniscience ensure his freedom from the demands of any kind of affective community. Dupin is thus outside society, but capable of resolving its most perplexing mysteries. Sherlock Holmes represents another version of the empowered detective figure, but one whose function resides in affirming, not rejecting, the industrial society for which the labyrinthine complexity of London is the most obvious symbol. Christie's work, like Poe's, expresses a desire to eliminate the modern landscape, but unlike Poe's, her protagonists are not alienated from society but are its staunch members, guardians almost of its order and propriety. Hammett's protagonists—the Continental Op, Sam Spade, Ned Beaumont et al.—generally exist on the margins of society, and although they are for the most part isolated and estranged from it, and its value and political systems, their interest as characters derives from their connection, antagonistic as it may be, with the bourgeois society. Unlike Poe, Conan Doyle, and Christie, Hammett tends to offer critical, rather than consoling, images of society. Thus the principle of equivalence between the underworld and the bourgeois society proper that produces an essentially anarchistic vision of society in *The Secret Agent* finds resonances in the violent, mayhem-filled cities described in Hammett's fiction. Indeed, for Hammett, as for Marx, the "violence of things" is due to class and the kinds of conflicts it engenders.

Hammett's fiction thus is part of the tradition of crime fiction that grew out of and responded to the urban, industrial moment of modern history. Part of a general culture of modernism that has its most recognized representatives in the work of high modernism, Hammett's detective fiction similarly explores what it means to be modern. Unlike many high-modernist novelists, however, Hammett does not try to convey the meaning of this experience by accentuating subjective consciousness, but instead evaluates the social and political forms modernity took in the early decades of the twentieth century. In *Red Harvest* he analyzes the gangland violence that consumes the industrial town of Personville, otherwise known as "Poisonville," a town that as its name suggests, is supposed to be representative of any middle-American town. The urban blight of Personville objectifies the diseased social relations of the town: "The city wasn't pretty. Most of its builders had gone in for gaudiness. Maybe they hadn't been successful at first. Since then the smelters whose brick stack stuck up tall against a gloomy mountain had yellow-smoked everything into uniform dinginess. The result was an ugly city of forty thousand people, set in an ugly notch between two ugly mountains that had been dirtied up by mining. Spread over this was a grimy sky that looked as if it had come out of the smelters' stacks" (3). The rest of the novel is essentially an elaboration of the political corruption that led to the disfigured landscape of Poisonville. This sense of political decay pervades Hammett's fiction: In *The Maltese Falcon* deceit and mistrust erode all social relations, even relatively nonpolitical ones like the one between Sam Spade and Brigid O'Shaughnessy, come under intense scrutiny.

Similarly, in *The Glass Key* official politics have become indistinguishable from the actions of gangsters; Senator Henry, it transpires, is responsible for the murder of his own son. As Steven Marcus has noted, Hammett's fiction calls into question some of the most fundamental distinctions by which bourgeois society operates: "The respectability of respectable America is as much a fiction and a fraud as the phony respectable society fabricated by the criminals. Indeed, he unwaveringly represents the world of crime as a reproduction in both structure and detail of modern capitalist society that it depends on, preys off, and is part of" (*The Continental Op*, xxiv). After Hammett, this skepticism toward the self-representations of the powerful, and toward their claim to respectability, becomes a convention of the hard-boiled poetic found in Raymond Chandler, James M. Cain, Ross Macdonald, and more recent practitioners of the genre, such as Chester Himes and Sarah Paretsky.

Thus, although in one sense Hammett's protagonists are as alienated from modern urban "civilization" as are D.H. Lawrence's, in another sense they are deeply identified—and identify themselves—with it. It is almost impossible to imagine Sam Spade or the Continental Op working outside the city. For the Continental Op the city is the locus of corruption and vice, just as it is for Sam Spade and Ned Beaumont. And while all of these protagonists feel they have a duty to rectify these ills, all of them, to a man, feel the attraction of the criminal life, not merely because of the lifestyle that the dirty money supports, but because they have grasped, as Marcus notes, that the facade of respectability that legitimate society puts up is also essentially a fiction. This is why all of these detectives adhere so tightly to their own personal codes of behavior. In a world in which order and integrity inevitably give way to disorder and corruption, it becomes all the more necessary to have a stable personal code by which to operate. As the Continental Op confesses to Dinah Brand in *Red Harvest*:

> This damned burg is getting me. If I don't get away soon I'll be going blood simple like the natives. . . . I've arranged a killing or two in my time, when they were necessary. But this is the first time I've ever got the fever. It's this damned burg. You can't go straight here. I got myself tangled at the beginning. When old Elihu ran out on me there was nothing I could do but try to set the boys against each other. I had to swing the job the best way I could. How could I help it that the best way was bound to lead to a lot of killing? (102)

For Hammett, unlike Poe, the possibility of mastering the city by means of a superior intelligence no longer exists; the city has now become dominant, and threatens to crush the detective.

At first glance, the dominance-of-the-city motif seems to signal the similarity of Hammett's fiction to naturalism. Ultimately, however, Hammett's detective fiction cannot itself be considered naturalistic inasmuch as a certain degree of human agency must be accorded to the detective figure in order for him to perform his job. The hard-boiled detective can never be entirely defeated by his environment, for that would result in his abdication of his role as problem solver; moreover, one of the most basic conventions of the hard-boiled genre is an active, physically vigorous protagonist who can give a punch as well as take one. Hammett's "naturalism" is tempered by a full-blooded individualism; more specifically, there is an unreconciled tension in his fiction between two ideologies, one stressing the efficacy of human effort, the other asserting its ultimate futility. This ambiguity concerning the effectiveness of human agency, this uncertainty about the potency of human effort in the face of what appears to be an increasingly dominant and determinative social reality—a determinacy represented in modern literature by its obsession with the metropolis as the preeminent locus of modern life in which everything is in a constant state of becoming and flux, propelled forward by the dynamic energies of capitalism—is but another sign of the modernism of Hammett's fiction.

Codes and Questions: The Style of Hard-Boiled Fiction

The detective figure's personal code, therefore, is as much a means of survival as it is an alternate mode of behavior, often almost indistinguishable from the less savory forms of behavior that the detective investigates. Ultimately the Continental Op and Sam Spade owe their highest allegiance to a workmanlike devotion to a sense of doing a job well; Ned Beaumont's allegiance, on the other hand, is based solely on his sense of personal loyalty to friends, particularly to Paul Madvig, one of the city's big political bosses. In this sense, the personal codes that structure the behavior of Hammett's detectives are as much a sign of the entropy that has overtaken the urban landscape of his novels as are the corruption and deceit that they are paid to undo, for the circumscribed, violent, almost emotionless lives these protagonists lead assert the ascendancy of the city over the individual. The Continental Op can work effectively in the war-torn city of Personville, but he cannot afford to have any kind of affective life, for this would leave him too vulnerable to danger. This is why he resists the blandishments of Dinah Brand, and partially why Sam Spade resists the pleas of Brigid O'Shaughnessy at the end of *The Maltese Falcon*. For the Continental Op, as for so many other heroes of American literature, the only solution—even it is unsatisfactory—is for him is to flee the civilization represented by Personville.

In his essay on Hammett, Steven Marcus calls attention to another modernist trait in Hammett's work, "the ethical irrationality of existence, the ethical unintelligibility of the world" (xvii). It could be argued that Hammett made this an intrinsic aspect of hard-boiled fiction in that he created a genre that registers this sense of irrationality and unintelligibility in details that emphasize the disordered, contingent, almost hallucinatory quality of reality—a mode of writing most famously associated with Kafka and Joyce. This sense of irrationality and unintelligibility is also conveyed by Hammett's creation of narratives that are committed to the posing of questions. Like many high modernist heroes (and antiheroes), Hammett's detective figures are obsessed with questions, ones that have to do with the fundamental contradictions of modernity. *The Glass Key* is thus a representative text for any case focusing on a popular form of modernism inasmuch as it is evaluative, committed to exploring institutionalized corruption as social and political forces in American society. Hammett's exploration of the role of the individual in this society is enabled by his choice of protagonist. Ned Beaumont is the lieutenant of the political boss, Paul Madvig. As such, he participates in the manipulation of big-city politics that the Continental Op, for example, attempts to end in *Red Harvest*.

Indeed, like *Red Harvest*, *The Glass Key* foregrounds the connection between the novel of big-city politics and hard-boiled fiction. Undergirding a number of seeming unrelated subplots in the novel is the political career of Senator Henry, who at the start of the novel is running for reelection. Paul Madvig supports the candidacy of Senator Henry; in return, Madvig hopes to marry the senator's daughter, Janet Henry. Madvig's power and ascendancy are due in large part to the political acumen of his right-hand man, Ned Beaumont. When Senator Henry's son, Taylor Henry, is murdered, political tensions in the city escalate. While the senator's opponents see in the murder an opportunity to discredit the incumbent, some of Madvig's henchmen begin to betray their leader because they think that Madvig is the murderer. Madvig's troubles are compounded further when a rival gangster (and ward boss) makes a bid to challenge Madvig's ascendancy. Beaumont is made special investigator by the district attorney's office to get to the bottom of Taylor Henry's murder. In the end, surprisingly, Madvig admits to the murder but Ned doesn't believe him. Deducing that Madvig is only protecting someone else, Ned then accuses the senator of murdering his son. After trying to shift the blame to Madvig, Senator Henry admits that he killed his son accidentally, in a fit of range. The novel ends with the departure of Ned Beaumont and Janet Henry, and the poignant acceptance of this relationship by Madvig, who remains loyal to Beaumont despite the fact that Beaumont is leaving with the woman Madvig loves.

Within hard-boiled detective fiction Beaumont is thus a non-unusual protagonist—an amateur detective who sanctions political corruption at the same time that he uncovers more virulent forms than his own morality allows him to condone. In creating an obviously flawed detective figure in Beaumont, and in placing him in a situation that calls attention to a compromised social and political order, Hammett is able to question some of the most basic conceptions of morality while at the same time destabilizing some basic conventions of detective fiction. Hammett's fiction doesn't offer any answers to the questions it raises, but in one sense that doesn't matter: as Sinda Gregory notes, "Hammett's plots, then, and the overall structure of his novels satisfy genre conventions by answering the questions that must, by definition of the form, be raised (who is the murderer? how was it done? how was the solution found?) while at the same time they nullify through irony and paradox the validity of those answers" (*Private Investigations*, 14). It is partly this open-ended quality of his fiction, its refusal to yield to pat answers and easy solutions, that marks its affiliation with one ideology of modernism. Hammett brought detective fiction into the modern world, not merely by seeming to be more realistic, as Chandler believed, but also by introducing this ideology into the genre. In part, he achieved this by undermining some of the oppositions typical of detective fiction. Hammett not only brought detective fiction to a new level of technical and artistic achievement, he also inaugurated the antidetective novel by dissipating the binary oppositions of detective/villain, good/evil, and order/disorder that characterized the rational moralism of the formal English novel of detection.[3] The textual ideology of much of Hammett's fiction is relativistic inasmuch as it does not subscribe to any absolute worldview (excepts its own, another characteristic of modernism), but it is not relative in regard to the social reality it evaluates. In this matter, hard-boiled detective fiction as a genre is critical of civilization, of bourgeois law and property, and ultimately of the ideologies that assert an absolute distinction between the criminal and the law-abiding citizen. Much of the critical edge of this fiction is due to its incorporation of representations of the "lower classes," whether they are the working classes or simply the disenfranchised and criminal classes. In any event, this incorporation of disenfranchised experience, and its worldview, throws into question assumptions of justice, orderliness, and naturalness by which predominantly bourgeois societies typically justify and legitimate their existence.

Like any other fiction, hard-boiled fiction mediates this evaluation through language; like the classic English novel of detection, it lays claim to being referential. Yet both are fictions of crime, regulated by the demands of their subgenres; both are conventional (although they adhere to different conventions); both represent stylized versions of ordinary speech. Hammett's fiction purports to use more ordinary English—and indeed one finds registers of English in his works that one doesn't find sympathetically represented in Christie's novels—but these registers have been reworked and tailored into a stylized version of lower-class speech. The tough-guy speech in hard-boiled fiction, like the genteel diction of the classic English detective story, is thus a literary representation of a speech type, but there is nothing natural about it. Take, for example, the famous first line of *Red Harvest*: "I first heard Personville called Poisonville by a red-haired mucker named Hickey Dewey in the Big Ship in Butte" (3). Few tough guys, or, for that matter, novelists, have the sense of pace, slang, alliteration, and syntactic control displayed in Hammett's style. Hammett was responsible for refining a style that was to become famous in modernist and postmodernist fiction. As Key Worpole observes in *Dockers and Detectives*:

> The narrative styles of Hemingway and Hammett are clear examples of this renunciation of all detail other than the action, the dialogue and the minimal description of the setting. No characters ever have their thoughts articulated; what we know about their inner lives has to be inferred from their speech and their behavior. The omnipotent, all-seeing narrator of conventional narrative discourse has been dispensed with, and one can argue that the "dime novel" arrived at this position several decades ahead of the "nouveau roman." (40)

Although Hammett's style gives his fiction the spareness characteristic of this kind of experimental writing, his style is also oriented "outward," toward an assessment or evaluation of society.[4] It is this role of language in his fiction that I now want to examine more closely.

Evaluative Modernism

Unlike the nineteenth-century classic realist novel, Hammett's fiction contains very little description of external reality. Most of his fiction consists of dialogue, and it is through dialogue that Hammett establishes the worldview of his protagonists and, ultimately, the novel itself. The element of social evaluation in his fiction is thus mediated through the language of his protagonists. The judgments are never direct; they remain implicit, typically made in terms of the individual. Hammett's fiction exists as a literary response to the moment of modernity in the twentieth century defined by the Depression-era, labor-capital conflicts of urban capitalism; and though it is ideologically modernist, by availing itself of the negative capability of evaluative realism, his fiction is able to critique the dislocations of modernity. Hammett's fiction remains intellectually and emotionally compelling, however, because that critique is made "in terms of the qualities of persons" (Raymond Williams, *The Long Revolution*, 278) and is not imposed as an abstract, tendentious schema on the narrative; on the contrary, the critique arises out of the tensions within the narrative. As an example, then, of what might be called Hammett's evaluative modernism, consider the following passage from *The Glass Key*, a heated exchange between Janet Henry and Ned Beaumont near the end of the novel:

> She asked: "Why don't you like Father?"
> "Because," he said hotly, "I don't like pimps."
> Her face became red, her eyes abashed. She asked in a dry constricted voice: "and you don't like me because—?"
> He did not say anything.
> She bit her lip and cried: "Answer me!"
> "You're all right," he said, "only you're not all right for Paul, not the way you've been playing him. Neither of you were anything but poison for him. I tried to tell him that. I tried to tell him you both considered him a lower form of animal life and fair game for any kind of treatment. I tried to tell him your father was a man all his life used to winning without much trouble and that in a hole he'd either lose his head or turn wolf. Well, he was in love with you, so—"
> He snapped his teeth together and walked over to the piano.
> "You despise me," she said in a low hard voice. "You think I'm a whore."
> "I don't despise you," he said irritably, not turning to face her. "Whatever you've done you've paid for and been paid for and that goes for all of us." (585)

This passage represents both the emotional climax of the novel and the culmination of its social evaluation. Most obviously, the scene discloses the rising sexual tension between Ned Beaumont and Janet Henry. This disclosure, interestingly, occurs at the same time that the reader learns the full extent of the corruption of city politics and its morally debilitating effects on the citizens, particularly Senator Henry. The senator, the civic leader of the community, turns out to be the most ethically base, for not only is he responsible for the murder of his own son, but he was also willing to kill Paul Madvig in order to protect his secret and his career. Thus the emotional denouement and the moment of sharpest social criticism coincide in *The Glass Key* and are dependent on one another. Without the social criticism implicit in Beaumont's comments, the sexual confrontation would not be so charged, insofar as the criticism lends the scene an emotional energy, one rooted in Janet Henry's realization of the various forms of betrayal in her life: Senator Henry has betrayed his son by killing him; he has also betrayed his daughter by using her as bait for Madvig; conversely, Janet has betrayed Madvig and her own integrity by colluding in her father's plans. Janet's anger and frustration reach their peak when she realizes the cost of these betrayals in terms of her own lost integrity and that of her father. Similarly, without the emotional impact of the confrontation between Ned and Janet, the political critique would be arid and abstract.

Sexual Politics of Hard-Boiled Fiction

The encounter between Janet Henry and Ned Beaumont also foregrounds the sexual politics of *The Glass Key* and illustrates those of hard-boiled fiction in general. One crucial difference between the English gentleman-detective and the American hard-boiled detective is that the latter's presence usually marks the recognition of the crime; indeed, frequently he himself is deeply implicated in the crime. By contrast, the gentleman-detective—Hercule Poirot or Peter Wimsey, for example—usually arrives at the scene of the crime long after the crime has been committed and sets to work solving it, secure in the knowledge that ultimately intellect will triumph over evil (typically, evil is seen in moral rather than social terms). Rarely does his mere presence initiate a murder or set in motion a chain of effects resulting in the crime that the novel will untangle. Even rarer is the gentleman-detective's sexual involvement with another character. Yet casual liaisons of this sort are quite common in hard-boiled detective fiction—although Sam Spade may not think it is good business practice to let Brigid O'Shaughnessy off the hook, he is not above sleeping with her. This might lead one to conclude that the sexual politics of the hard-boiled school diverge radically from those of the classic English detective story, and in many senses this is true. But there are, however, startling similarities. One of the most striking of these is the empowered position of men in detective fiction.

With the exception of Nora Charles in *The Thin Man*, all of Hammett's detectives are men. They are all astute, physically able, and tough (as well as sentimental). Some of them, like Ned Beaumont and Sam Spade, are both intellectually and sexually vigorous. Their superiority does not arise primarily from mere strength or cleverness, although they are that, too; rather, it arises from the fact that they have grasped fundamental truths about society that few other people understand. Other people often know at least as much about this or that murder as the detective, but he alone sees the corpse as the signifying presence of institutionalized social corruption. He sees the crime not as a localized incident, but as a social phenomenon, implicating and involving every level of society. In short, hard-boiled detectives see ideology as myth.

However, in hard-boiled fiction, when women are not sultry seductresses, they are supplicants, most often supplicants after knowledge. Hammett thus most frequently figures women as intellectually inferior—and this has become a common topos in hard-boiled fiction. As Hélène Cixous has noted, this kind of superior/inferior opposition is an all-too-common way of representing women: "Organization by hierarchy makes all conceptual organization subject to man. Male privilege, shown in the opposition between *activity* and *passivity*, which he uses to sustain himself. Traditionally, the question of sexual difference is treated by coupling it with the opposition: activity/passivity" (*The Newly Born Woman*, 64).[5] As the supplicant after knowledge, Janet Henry is represented as intellectually passive, as intellectually inferior to Ned Beaumont. Beaumont tells her the identity of the murderer, but more important than that is the fact that Janet seeks a more comprehensive knowledge of her situation and her relations with others. Significantly, it is to Beaumont that she turns. At one level, then, this ending to the novel reaffirms a cultural stereotype—that men are sexually and intellectually superior to women. In terms of its sexual politics, then, Hammett's fiction may be read as conservative, even reactionary. Although his fiction is radically antibourgeois in that it affirms the corruption at the heart of bourgeois society, and society's complicity in producing that corruption, the sexual politics of his fiction undercut this radicalism by maintaining the essential superiority of men. Indeed, the sexual politics of much of the hard-boiled genre in general undermine the genre's political radicalism by affirming the hierarchies and relations between the sexes sanctioned by bourgeois society.

At the same time, though, Ned Beaumont rejects the easy suggestion that Janet Henry is a whore, and to this rather limited extent he rejects the virgin/whore opposition that informs much hard-boiled fiction (and much fiction in general). Although this is hardly emancipatory, it does suggest a movement away from some of the distorting stereotypes of women that *The Glass Key* otherwise uncritically accepts. Janet may be culpable, but in this society, everyone else is, too. Nor does Beaumont presume to judge Janet; he rejects the ubiquitous cultural assumption that a man has a right and a duty to pass judgment on the moral character of women. The sexual politics of the novel are thus contradictory, containing elements that range from the culturally stereotypical to the atypical. If the ending of *The Glass Key* is a reprise of the famous ending of *The Maltese Falcon*, it is clear that in the later novel Hammett has not entirely rejected his earlier stereotypical representations of women as treacherous seductresses; nor has his fiction initiated a radically different exploration of the relationships between women and men (or indeed between women and society). However, the sexual politics of *The Glass Key* suggest the contradiction involved in embodying a radical critique of society while implicitly affirming some of that society's most reactionary and repressive relations. To this extent, ironically, the hard-boiled detective supports the status quo about which he is so scathing. Something of the inverse situation obtains in the formal English novel of detection, which often features a conservative ideology and female detective figures. Here too the sexual politics of the novel often contest the textual ideology by suggesting the capability of the female detective, a capability that is often at odds with the restrictive gender roles sanctioned by a hierarchical, patriarchal society. In both subgenres, then, sexual politics call into question some of the novel's dominant ideological assumptions.[6]

Class Politics, or the Fiction of Crime

The exchange between Janet Henry and Ned Beaumont also effectively demonstrates that Hammett achieves his evaluation of the "quality of a whole way of life" (Williams, *The Long Revolution*, 278) by suggesting in fictional terms the way in which the political has perverted the personal. Part of this evaluation consists of a criticism of class relations, relations that during the Depression assumed a more prominent character as divergences in wealth and class became more pronounced. Much of Beaumont's criticism of the Henrys is rooted in his belief that they assumed an attitude of class superiority to Paul Madvig because he came from a lower class. As he says bitterly to Janet: "I tried to tell him you both considered him a lower form of animal life and fair game for any kind of treatment" (585). It is significant that part of the criticism of city politics and urban life in general in *The Glass Key* is made against the pretensions that are enabled by, and thrive in, a class-based society. This is significant because the criticism is made by a character who has wittingly participated in the manipulation of the political system, and who therefore cannot claim moral ascendancy over anyone. In this sense, crime as such is not criticized. For Hammett, crime is in one sense democratic and entrepreneurial: it has the potential of making those excluded by class society financially and politically as powerful as those who have benefited by class division. Moreover, Hammett's antibourgeois social vision also grants criminals a kind of integrity: they may be criminals, but they don't pretend to adhere to ethical standards they can't maintain. They thus lack the hypocrisy found in legitimate society, which condemns criminals and yet sanctions and participates in illegal activities ranging from the relatively minor (bootlegging) to the very serious—the manipulation of the political system by the business community, the underworld, the politicians, and the police. As Ken Worpole notes: "In Hammett's hands, especially, the detective novel became an important vehicle for radical social criticism, without reading like a polemical text. The assumption which informs all Hammett's work is that the police, politicians and big business combine together to run the city administration in their own interests, even though this often involves murder, gang-slayings, bribery and perjury" (*Dockers and Detectives*, 43).

Hard-boiled fiction represents America as an empire, but it is an empire in decline, built on the legality of a class system and the illegality of corruption. By Hammett's standards, class society is both hypocritical and covertly criminal; however, unlike the underworld, it is not susceptible to change by the criminal-entrepreneur but maintains its identity and power by seeing itself as morally superior, even while it punctiliously supports an inherently biased social order. Senator Henry thus stands as the most egregious example of this middle-class hypocrisy. In *The Glass Key*, as in Hammett's other fiction, the detective figure navigates in this seedy, morally skewed environment. In hard-boiled fiction, the decaying urban landscape articulates a set of moral equivalences that are the inverse of normative bourgeois values: the city may be the locus of crime, and may be run-down and shabby, but it is no more or less corrupt than the well-kept houses of the well-to-do, as the famous opening description of the Sternwood mansion in Raymond Chandler's *The Big Sleep* attests. Hard-boiled fiction starts from the assumption that everyone's point of view is a fiction or an ideology, and the genre is particularly suspicious of bourgeois claims to represent a morally transparent order that the reader can take straight without having to read it as a fiction.

Hard-boiled fiction, that is, revels in its negative capacity, in its ability to evaluate the post-World War I urban American experience of modernity. Although it does not have any pretensions toward documentary truth, it is oriented toward an evaluation of this reality, and this suggests that Hammett's fiction does not see itself as a self-reflexive, autonomous work or art, detached from the time and place of its production, but instead sees itself as engaged with contemporary society, as a part of it. By incorporating slang, wisecracks, and more colloquial, vernacular registers of English, Hammett not only enlarges the creative possibilities of detective fiction, but also explores the possibilities for writing in a modernist mode using the language of the streets. In so doing, the language of Hammett's fiction asserts the dialogic nature of his fiction, its relations to society. Hammett's hard-boiled fiction indicates the linguistic resources available in colloquial speech. Even the colloquial language in Ned Beaumont's speech—for example, "I don't like pimps" and "only you're not all right for Paul, not the way you've been playing with him"—asserts a kind of connection with ordinary life. Indeed, this connection with lower- and working-class life, as well as with the criminal underworld, expressed in a stylized version of those discourses, is used to make a political point. Tough-guy speech shows irreverence for authority and establishes the hero's disdain for bourgeois norms. So when Ned labels Janet's father a "pimp," Hammett is establishing, among other things, Ned's perception of his individualism: he seems himself as both uninhibited and independent in relation to authority. Hammett's use of language thus contains a class element that is used to criticize class society. Hammett uses the language of the hard-boiled world's lower-class criminals to impugn the pretensions of legitimacy, morality, and ethical behavior that characterize middle-class characters in his novels. Thus, the colloquial language within Hammett's fiction exists as a marker between "less hypocritical" crooks—the class defined as criminal by bourgeois law—and "dishonest" crooks, which for Hammett include virtually all of the middle classes.[7]

Unlike Poe's, however, Hammett's language does not affirm a positive vision of knowledge. There is for him no master epistemology such as rationalism that will allow him to solve the dilemmas he is presented with, partly because the problems he engages are not limited to the solving of a whodunit: a crime in hard-boiled fiction always signifies the presence of a wider social or political malaise of which the corpse is merely the signifier. Ultimately, there can be no solution to a crime, because crime is not extrinsic to the system but intrinsic, part of it. Even if the detective discovers the identity of the murderer, the implications of the crime extend far beyond the matter of a mere corpse and are so endemic that they are, finally, intractable. If in the formal English novel of detection the resolution of the crime seeks—unsuccessfully, I would argue—to exonerate society, the ending in a hard-boiled novel almost invariably suggests the wholesale corruption of society. Individuals may be exempt, but the social order stands condemned. In *The Glass Key*, as in most hard-boiled fiction, society itself is essential unknowable. Nothing is what it seems (in this narrow sense the formal English novel of detection and the hard-boiled novel are alike); everyone and everything is tainted in some way; every institution is compromised. Ned Beaumont's statement that "whatever you've done you've paid for and been paid for and that goes for all of us" (585) is the acknowledgement of this ineluctable fact of life in hard-boiled fiction. This is why the endings of Hammett's fiction often describe the departure of the detective figure from the city he has investigated. The only thing the hard-boiled dick knows for sure is that you can run but you can't hide.

NOTES

An altered version of parts of this chapter appeared in my essay "Realisms and Modernisms: Raymond Williams and Popular Fiction," in *Views Beyond the Border Country: Raymond Williams and Cultural Politics*, ed. Dennis L. Dworkin and Leslie G. Roman (London: Routledge, 1993).

1. The best elaboration of this argument is David I. Grossvogel's "Agatha Christie: Containment of the Unknown," excerpted in *The Poetics of Murder*, 252-65.
2. For more on the failure of the European avant-garde to achieve any connection with a genuinely mass audience, see Andreas Huyssen's *After the Great Divide: Modernism, Mass Culture, Postmodernism*.
3. I am paraphrasing Sinda Gregory's argument that Hammett is the inaugurator of the antidetective novel. This argument is elaborated in greater detail in *Private Investigations: The Novels of Dashiell Hammett*, especially page 13.
4. See, for example, Dennis Porter's *The Pursuit of Crime: Art and Ideology in Detective Fiction*, especially chapter 7.
5. For more on the ways in which the feminine is inscribed, or significantly absent, in twentieth-century literature and theory, see Alice Jardine's impressive study *Gynesis: Configurations of Woman and Modernity*.
6. It should be noted that this neat mirroring of the disruptive effects of sexual politics in each form of detective fiction is disturbed by the emergence of a relatively new subgenre, the feminist hard-boiled detective novel, which brings together the critical ideology of hard-boiled fiction and the intellectual capability of the female detective figures of the formal English novel of detection, although many of them are more active physically than their Edwardian antecedents.
7. On the subject of Hammett's use of colloquial speech I am indebted to LeRoy L. Panek's essay "The Naked Truth: The Origins of the Hard-Boiled School," in *The Armchair Detective*.

WORKS CITED

Hammett, Dashiell. *Five Complete Novels*. New York: Avenel Books, 1980.

Haycraft, Howard, ed. *The Art of the Mystery Story: A Collection of Critical Essays*. New York: Simon and Schuster, 1946.

Marcus, Steven. Introduction. *The Continental Op* by Dashiell Hammett. New York: Vintage, 1975. vii-xxix.

Williams, Raymond. *The Long Revolution*. New York: Columbia University Press, 1961.

Worpole, Ken. *Dockers and Detectives*. London: Verso, 1983.

The Thin Man

Reviews

In my somewhat limited experience of English detective stories, far too many murdered men are discovered in the panelled libraries of ancestral country houses near Sevenoaks, and far too many detectives, detectives' amateur aides, suspects and the suspected accomplices of suspects, speak in what is vaguely but euphemistically termed a "public school accent." Gentlemanliness haunts the scene of the crime; though the criminals themselves—Chinamen, Bolsheviks, international dope-peddlars and the like—may resort to such desperate and ungentlemanly methods of procedure as plunging their victims, still alive, into baths of bubbling and seething acid, the meteoric appearance of Bulldog Drummond, magnificent with wavy brilliantined locks and something that resembles an old-Etonian tie, turns our thoughts to the Motherland at her brightest and best. Behind Drummond are the misty elm-rows of an English playing field; in front of him is the aureate image of a "nice girl."

There no trimmings of this kind to Dashiell Hammett. We have all heard—many of us a trifle impatiently—the admiration expressed by bishops, statesmen, scientists and distinguished litterateurs for works by the modern detective school; but, among exponents of that art, Dashiell Hammett is almost alone in being praised by writers as a serious writer and by good novelists as a master of their business. Hemingway and Sinclair Lewis combine to admire him. From internal evidence, I should imagine that Dashiell Hammett also admired Hemingway; for his new novel, *The Thin Man*, is not only an absorbing and extremely ingenious "thriller," but contains portraits, snatches of dialogue—written in a terse colloquial vein—and lurid glimpses of New York drinking society, that Hemingway himself could not have improved on. His characters exist apart from the drama; while reading the conventional detective story, it is necessary to bear in mind a certain number of names and titles, attached to fictitious personages who are distinguished from one another by various rudimentary and easily remembered personal traits, but who have no intrinsic claim to our attention. Mr. Hammett's characters are completely unorthodox. What will the British public say of a detective—now happily married—who has once had "immoral relations" with the woman he suspects of having murdered her divorce husband's mistress and confidante?—whose first thought, when he wakes up in the middle of the night, is to ask his wife to pour him a whisky and soda?

Beside this gregarious modern sleuth, the morphinomaniac solitary beast of Baker Street, brooding like Paganini over his violin, shrinks away into jaundiced insignificance. For *The Thin Man* introduces us to real characters; Mimi Jorgensen, a "dizzy blonde" now considerably past her prime; Dorothy Wynant, her daughter, whom Nick Charles describes—briefly and expressively—as "cute but cuckoo"; and Gilbert, her studious, neurotic son. Suspense is maintained to the final page. Mr. Hammett adheres to the recognized and well-tried formula that responsibility for a crime should eventually be brought home where it is least expected; but, during the course of the story, suspicion is distributed with such a clear, yet such a casual and rapidly moving, hand, that the most practised reader may be forgiven if he loses the trail. *The Thin Man*—unusually brilliant read as a detective-story—has every right to consideration on its literary merits.
[Peter Quennell, *New Statesman and Nation* 26 May 1934: 801]

Now that Dashiell Hammett is beginning to be taken seriously by the highbrows, my first enthusiasm for him is beginning to cool a little. Not that *The Thin Man* is not a first-rate murder story, and one that only Dashiell Hammett could have written. But, perhaps because he has turned the trick so easily before that he is now getting a little tired of it, perhaps because we are beginning to notice that he sometimes repeats his effects, *The Thin Man* seems a less excitingly fresh performance than, say, *The Maltese Falcon*. It is still head-and-shoulders above any other murder story published since his last one. His hero this time is Nick Charles, a retired detective, whose holiday in New York with his rich young wife is threatened by the disappearance of Clyde Winant [sic], an eccentric inventor, an old client of Nick's—in Nick's own words, "a good guy, but screwy." When it comes to that, the whole Winant [sic] family are pretty screwy, and Nick quite pardonably wants to have nothing to do with the case. He gets dragged in, willy-nilly, however, and in spite of his apparent laziness and an obvious addiction to liquor in a harsh and frequent form (his first remark to his wife in the mornings is usually a request for a drink "to cut the phlegm"), he bestirs himself sufficiently to get his man.

One reason why Hammett's books have been so outstanding, aside from the naturalism of his style, the careless humanity of his characters, is that his murders are gangster-political affairs, they come naturally out of his tough backgrounds instead of being the kind of academic and farfetched bridge problems in a vacuum of the ordinary detective-story writer. In *The Thin Man*, though his New York setting is authentic, and contains some very lifelike policemen, speakeasy proprietors and "rats," the crime and the criminal are in the orthodox tradition. Perhaps Mr. Hammett is coasting, or perhaps a little blue eagle has whispered something in his ear. [T.S. Matthews, "Mr. Hammett Goes Coasting," *New Republic* 24 January 1934: 316]

Detective stories do not often make their way into this department, but the Landscaper would be failing in his duty if he did not report that one of the recent books that gave him the greatest amount of pleasure was Dashiell Hammett's *The Thin Man* (Knopf, $2), Mr. Hammett being the distinguished author of *The Maltese Falcon*, among other books, and generally recognized as the top of the heap in his field. *The Maltese Falcon*, by the way, is now available in the Modern Library edition, a recognition it heartily deserves, since it is one of the finest thrillers ever to be put between covers.

The Thin Man is a murder-mystery, cut more or less according to pattern, with the difference that the detective seems entirely credible and all the people talk and act as if they had wandered in off the streets, or right out of the first pages of your favorite newspaper. They are a mad lot, most of them, but real. And the punch of Mr. Hammett's stream-lined dialogue, which is like nobody else's, never fails. There is a good deal more to be said on this subject, as the author in question is unique in his field, but other books are waiting, and the Landscaper closes the matter by recommending *The Thin Man* as ace writing, much too good to be missed, whether you ordinarily like detective stories or not. [Herschel Brickell, *North American Review* March 1934: 283]

From an advertisement, *The New York Times*
January 30, 1934

Alfred Knopf

I don't believe the question ["didn't you have an erection?"] on page 192 of Dashiell Hammett's *The Thin Man* has had the slightest influence upon the sale of the book. It takes more than that to make a best seller these days. Twenty thousand people don't buy a book within three weeks to read a five word question.

From *Shadow Man: The Life of Dashiell Hammett*

Richard Layman

Though *The Thin Man* is the weakest of Hammett's novels, measured against any standard except his own work, it is better than average. Nick and Nora Charles are Hammett's most charming characters, and Hammett capitalized on the strength of Nick's characterization by having the story told in the first person by him. The Charles's opulent, carefree life in 1932, a year before the repeal of prohibition, and in the month when the nation was suffering its gravest economic crisis of the Great Depression, was glamorously attractive to an audience that thrived on fantasies of wealth and leisure. [Harcourt Brace Jovanovich, 1981: 142]

From *Private Investigations: The Novels of*
Dashiell Hammett

Sinda Gregory

While Hammett's last novel, *The Thin Man*, is viewed by some as a retreat from such "serious" considerations, it may well be his most subtle and, in certain ways, his most controlled work. . . . [It] is a stylish, urbane novel that deals more blithely than usual in hard-boiled detective fiction with the grubbier aspects of crime, but as with all of Hammett's books, this outward appearance belies what lies beneath—a stark and stubborn insistence on the human capacity for cruelty and "cannibalism." The book works successfully on a lighter level, and we can be amused by the eccentricities of the Wynant family and the social lives of the wealthy, yet if we step back we see something else at work that is not amusing and not so light. The first of these perspectives exists exclusive of the second—Hammett never insists that his reader must look beyond the obvious meanings of his novels. But the second perspective—not only is the world neither charming nor gay, it is painful, destructive, and personally divisive—depends upon the first, for the reverberations between the outward cheerfulness and the inner chill give an unexpected edge to the entire novel. [Southern Illinois UP, 1985: 177-78]

The Thin Man: The End Game

George J. Thompson

With the exception of one or two commentators, Dashiell Hammett's fifth and last novel, *The Thin Man* (1934), has earned very few admirers. Peter Quennell in a review of the novel in 1934 was one of those few. He admired several achievements of the work:

. . . it contains portraits, snatches of dialogue—written in colloquial vein—and lurid glimpses of New York drinking society, that Hemingway himself could not have improved upon.[1]

Many critics who otherwise find little to say about the novel that is positive would agree that it contains several good individual scenes,[2] but few would go as far as Joseph T. Shaw in proclaiming that both Nick Charles and Philip Marlowe (hero of Raymond Chandler's novels) are three-dimensional characters, and that in both novels (Shaw uses *The Big Sleep* as an example of Chandler's work) character conflicts are set up, and

> The main crime and its victims are off-stage, and, while the solution of the crime is woven into the pattern of each story, it by no means constitutes the essence of the story.[3]

These lines suggest that Shaw believes *The Thin Man* to possess not only depth but resonance as well, a view that runs counter to most critical opinion. Presumably, from Shaw's point of view the novel is more than the sum of its parts because the action radiates meaning above and beyond the solution of the mystery. Walter Blair argues a very similar point when he says:

> Nick is very different from the Continental Op: he is attractive, sophisticated and witty. He resembles the earlier narrator in being cynical and worldly and in being unrevealing about his emotional and intellectual responses to most people and events. In the final novel as in the first, the author therefore utilizes a fictional point of view that is well adapted to the genre which he is writing—one productive of mystery and suspense.[4]

Unfortunately Blair does not go into detail in an effort to define that fictional point of view or to show how the action in *The Thin Man* is handled artistically.

By and large, critics have been rather silent on *The Thin Man*. There are numerous short and pithy pronouncements on the novel's worth, but almost no close analysis of its plot action or its meaning. To my knowledge, for example, George Grella, one of the most interesting and provocative interpreters of the *Black Mask* school of writing and the hardboiled novel in general, ignores the novel almost entirely in three of his best works on the subject.[5] David Bazelon is content to say simply that the novel is weak because Nick Charles' "Weakness is the weakness of deliberate unconsciousness,"[6] an understandable comment from someone who believes that Hammett's art is wholly concerned with the work ethic. Ben Ray Redman sees *The Thin Man* as an illustration of sadism and heroic drinking,[7] and Philip Durham brushes aside serious consideration of the work by remarking that it was obviously "written under Hollywood influence."[8]

Two critics who expend useful critical energy on *The Thin Man* are William Kenney and Robert I. Edenbaum. Kenney calls it a novel of parts, not a successful whole, and points to the marvelously comic scenes in the Pigiron

Club, the handling of the audacious Mimi Wynant-Jorgensen, and the fascination of Nora in her husband's underworld connections to support his point.[9] He argues that one of the major flaws of the novel is its plot: "The plot seems too often merely a pretext for cleverly executed but unfocused individual scenes and character touches."[10] Further, characterization is another major problem of the novel because the murderer, Herbert Macauley, is "the most weakly drawn character in the novel."[11] Once again we are faced with the problem we had with Fitzstephan in *The Dain Curse*, Brigid in *The Maltese Falcon*, and even Madvig and the Senator in *The Glass Key*: the artist cannot allow us to get inside the guilty minds if mystification is to be sustained.[12] Kenney is certainly accurate in arguing that Macauley is an unmemorable figure. Hammett managed with some skill to make Fitzstephan, Brigid, and Madvig interesting and memorable in their own right despite the limitations of his genre but Macauley has even less personality than a man we never do meet in the novel: Clyde Wynant, the thin man of the title.

Kenney cannot find an organizing principle to the novel and, except to say that it resembles the preceding novels in its emphasis on the loss of love between men and women and the corruption of the family unit,[13] he finds little or no development of ideas or innovation in form in it which might distinguish it from the earlier works.

Robert Edenbaum argues that Nick Charles is the logical extension of Jack Rumsen in *The Glass Key*:

> That modification of the private-eye character in the direction of the cynicism and timidity of self-interest prepares the way for Hammett's last novel, *The Thin Man* . . . Nick Charles and his boozing is what happens to the Op/Spade when he gives up his role as ascetic demi-god to become husband, man of leisure, investor in futures on the stock market.[14]

In short, Edenbaum suggests the tough guy has disappeared from Hammett's pages:

> The martini-for-breakfast cracking wise of William Powell and Myrna Loy more than anything else accounts for the popularity of *The Thin Man*. Despite Nick Charles' tough manner, Hammett's tough guy has been retired for good before this book appeared.[15]

Like Kenney, Edenbaum believes *The Thin Man* lacks substantiality because it is superficial and without visionary force and, presumably, because it does not do what the preceding novels did. But suppose Hammett has different intentions in this last novel? What bothers me about most of the negative criticism on *The Thin Man* is that it originates from questions about what the novel is not, rather than what the novel is. Edenbaum suggests that Hammett's power is weakened considerably by the absence of an authentic tough guy in this last novel, implying that Hammett should have kept doing what he had been doing. I think a fairer approach would be to ask why Hammett might have chosen to alter the character of this protagonist and whether the new figure makes any significant difference in our understanding of Hammett's developing moral and social vision.

I think it does, and I argue further that if we approach *The Thin Man* from this perspective we see that it is not an anomaly in Hammett's work but rather a continuation and a logical extension of the themes and concerns of the preceding novels. [In an earlier article I] noted that *The Glass Key* portrayed the destruction of Beaumont's relationship with Madvig and ended with him estranged from all that he had previously found meaningful. In his book *The Uncommitted*, Kenneth Keniston argues that the concept of alienation implies that "a positive relationship has ceased to exist" and that in many cases "alienation merely implies lack of any relationship at all—detachment and indifference."[16] *The Thin Man* captures this sense; without job or interest, Nick Charles is an apt post-Beaumont character. Hammett's social and moral vision has grown bleaker and bleaker as he has moved from *The Dain Curse* and *The Maltese Falcon* to *The Glass Key*. This last novel, *The Thin Man*, in one sense then, is the darkest of all because it suggests the almost total alienation of modern man. If I am right, it cannot then be an anomaly in Hammett's fiction.

Because the critics have been more interested in determining what the novel is not rather than what it is, they have isolated weaknesses that should more properly be seen as strengths, strengths that are intrinsically connected with Hammett's intention to render a dark vision. For example, it is accurate to call Herbert Macauley the weakest villain Hammett ever created. Like Fitzstephan and Madvig who are friends of the protagonist, Macauley is a friend of the ex-detective Charles, but unlike the Op-Fitzstephan and Beaumont-Madvig relationships, the Charles-Macauley connection is static and undeveloped. But is this necessarily a weakness in Hammett's conception? Is it not possible that Hammett intends us to notice this stasis? Similarly, should we not ask the same questions concerning the Nick and Nora relationship? It, too, seems relatively devoid of feeling and development. William Kenney comments that

> This brittle, harddrinking, wisecracking couple seem almost as a matter of principle to avoid any direct expression of feeling for each other.[17]

Kenney apparently takes this to be a criticism of their relationship, but is it necessarily so? Can we be so very sure that a lack of direct expression of feeling is evidence that no feeling exists whatsoever? Even if the answer to these questions is affirmative, does that necessarily mean the novel is flawed? I think such questions need asking, and I believe that the answers will show us that *The Thin Man* deserves a far better reputation as a work of art than has hitherto been conceded.

I have argued that in the earlier novels detection and human relationships have had an organic connection. Spade's detection of Brigid's guilt affects his relationship with her, and Beaumont's discovery of Madvig's complicity in Taylor Henry's murder affects his relationship with him. But we notice that in *The Thin Man* though relationships are stated, they are never allowed to develop. The discovery that Macauley is the murderer affects neither Charles' sense of personal relationships nor his sense of himself. His detective work, unlike Spade's or Beaumont's, leads to no discovery beyond the answer to a riddle. What are we to make of this? Ought we to see this as a weakness? I think not. Surely Hammett's point is that the quest for truth no longer carries any inherent meaning. Answers may be found, but nothing changes, and this suggests that what was once a meaningful human activity is no longer so.

Robert Edenbaum implies that Nick Charles is a tough guy *manqué* and William Kenney argues that Nick "is distinguished only by a certain ironic detachment from his aimless and amoral friends."[18] Both seem to agree that Nick is a failed creation, but I could not think it is this simple. Previously, Hammett has successfully indicated the absence of all values in society by locating all existing ones within his protagonists, but here in *The Thin Man* there is little or no emphasis on values of any kind. The Op/Spade/Beaumont code has all but shrivelled up; Nick's articulation of a code can only be seen as a hollow echo of the former stances. In Chapter Nine, for example, as Nick sees he is being forced into the Wynant case, he says:

> "I want to see the Jorgensen's together at home, I want to see Macauley, and I want to see Studey Burke. I've been pushed around too much. I've got to see about things."[19]

And a page later:

> "I don't see what I'm going to do because I don't know what's being done to me. I've got to find out in my own way." (614)

Despite these declamations of determination and individualism, however, Nick continues to resist being drawn into the case, and he never again mentions his desire to know or to do anything. In fact, later in the novel he is to say:

> "Things . . . riddles, lies, and I'm too old and too tired for them to be any fun. Let's go back to San Francisco." (690)

No comment better serves to reflect his emotional and mental state throughout the novel. Where the earlier heroes have worked to keep themselves true to their personal visions of reality and their identity, have, like Sisyphus, continued to push their own thing, Nick Charles has given up. The fact that Hammett's characters become mutilated in their struggle to *become* (like Beaumont) or to preserve what they are (like Spade) is in itself a kind of existential exaltation.

But with Nick Charles the struggle has ceased, and with its cessation, Hammett implies, the dignity that was once man's.

A careful examination of the novel goes a long way towards confirming such a point of view. For the first time values are almost nowhere apparent. In marked contrast to the earlier works, *The Thin Man* fails to suggest the viability of any truth or value. Hammett uses one third of his novel showing Nick resisting Nora's interest in the Wynant affair, yet Nick's reasons are never made clear. In *The Dain Curse* the Op is pulled into the proliferating cases by a desire to finish a job and exact personal satisfaction, and in *Red Harvest*, by a desire to find the answers to what seem three separate cases. Spade in *The Maltese Falcon* is drawn into the falcon affair by his desire to help Brigid and his continuing desire to find the murderer of his partner. Beaumont enters the Henry affair initially out of loyalty to Paul, and he stays with it for the same reason. But Nick's disinterest is repeatedly stressed. Sometimes it seems to stem from laziness, sometimes from tiredness, and sometimes from indifference, but Hammett consistently suggests that detective work no longer holds much value for Charles. What conclusion can we draw from this portrayal?

There is surely one. Like Beaumont, Charles is not a detective; he is only an ex-detective, now retired and living on his wife's money and stock securities. Hammett's last protagonist is no longer a member of that special species of men who choose to stand midway between criminality and the law. Rather, he chooses not to; to a great extent, he is an establishment man, with the slick manners, disinterested attitude, and the bank-roll of that group. The quasi-proletarian hero—Op, Spade, Beaumont—is replaced by an ex-white collar worker whose interest in work has evaporated with his good fortune. When his wife makes repeated efforts to get him interested in Dorothy Wynant's case, he resists:

> "Anyway, it's nothing in my life . . . But besides I haven't time: I'm too busy to see that you don't lose any of the money I married you for." (598)

This is partly tongue in cheek, a characteristic aspect of his sardonic humor, but how much so we cannot be sure. Humor or not, Nick's point is always the same: "Let the Charleses stick to the Charleses' troubles and the Wynants stick to the Wynants'" (599). Such a statement has for the 1970's reader a wonderfully "relevant" sound to it: it's the uncommitted declaration which to so many of us seems partially responsible for the social failure of our time. We know that Hammett himself believed that man ought to be committed to something, not simply a hanger-on, and it is hard to see how he would find Charles a positive figure.

Hammett goes out of his way to emphasize just how difficult it is to involve Charles in the action. He creates a series of episodes that function, in one way or another, to pull Nick in against his will. First there is Dorothy's plea for help, followed closely by her mother's: "Won't you help me, Nick? We used to be friends" (604). Nick's response, "For Christ sake, Mimi . . . there's a thousand detectives in New York. Hire one of them. I'm not working at it any more" (604), clearly reveals his disinterest. If words won't move him, actions get a better result. The gangster Morelli comes to his apartment to proclaim his innocence of Julia Wolf's murder and he is not convinced by Nick's argument that he is no longer a detective. The police unexpectedly show up and Morelli panics, shooting Nick and wounding him slightly. Nick finds himself caught up in a web of chance and accident. Morelli had come to Nick because of his reputation for being an on-the-level detective, and the police had staked out his apartment because Nora's intense interest in the Wynant-Wolf affair had led her to encourage the Jorgensen family to spend a lot of time at her apartment. Trapped by circumstances, Nick gives us his "I've got to see about things" speech.

Yet even now he is not committed. When a telegram is received, supposedly from Clyde Wynant, and he is asked to enter the case, he simply sends it on to the police, paying no more attention to it. The police even request his aid in the investigation and he denies he's working for Wynant, saying: "If people keep on pushing me into it, I don't know how far they'll carry me" (623). He has no inner response to these repeated calls for help except exasperation. His diction conveys, at best, his intention to remain a passive figure, pushed along only by the interest of others.

In some ways Hammett's exposition seems to be working very traditionally—that is, the hero's importance and stature is stressed by the fact of everyone else's need to turn to him for help. But Hammett is using this traditional form ironically. Nick Charles is more the anti-hero, resisting the call. The impotence of modern society is suggested by showing that the police need Nick's help, and Nick's lack of commitment suggests the death of the last stronghold of justice: the private eye. Hammett has commented that the society that has need of a private detective lives by questionable values,[20] but how much bleaker must it be if the need is there but there is no one who cares any longer to do the job. If Archie Jones is correct in arguing that the private eye was created to replace the cowboy myth, to perform "the ritual cleansing of the new stables" and "to reassure the people that the lonely individual could still triumph,"[21] then Hammett's novel must, to a considerable extent, be seen as a shattering of that myth. As presented, although Nick finally ferrets out the truth, his entire demeanor exudes an absence of personal commitment or satisfaction in the deed. He is much more the armchair detective, remote and alienated from the world he so unwillingly serves. Charles' hardboiled exterior covers only emptiness; he seems quite representative of the kind of figure Sheldon Grebstein describes in some of Hemingway's novels:

> This bleakness and despair, this exacerbated awareness of the betrayal of what had once been a precious innocence, and the grimly distrustful and corrosively ironic response which follow inevitably from the betrayal, compose the nucleus

of the tough *Weltanschauunq.*[22]

Though we are not given much information about Nick's past, a reader of Hammett's novels can sense that the betrayal which befalls Beaumont in *The Glass Key* provides the Hammett perspective for this his last major fictive hero. From this point of view, Nick is really the only possible creation left for Hammett.

A reading such as this presupposes the kind of moral and social vision I have been arguing for. If indeed *Red Harvest* is Hammett's initial and unsuccessful search for a hero and dynamic form, and if indeed *The Dain Curse* represents Hammett's redefinition of that hero and a new direction in form, and if indeed *The Maltese Falcon* and *The Glass Key* represent Hammett's formulated vision of the dilemmas of a moral protagonist in a world devoid of values, then *The Thin Man* represents Hammett's pessimistic recognition that such men are no longer of this world. The hardboiled skin survives, but its reason for existing is gone.

Seen from this perspective, the so-called weakness of the novel in Edenbaum's and Kenney's analyses must be seen as strengths. We can now see that *The Thin Man*, though it seems considerably different in style and form from its predecessors, has its place in the total spectrum of Hammett's work. It is the novel of the end: it evacuates from the hardboiled hero precisely those qualities the other four novels tried so subtly to render. The relationship between Charles and Macauley is devoid of meaning because both are indifferent or incapable of dynamic relationships. The code is dissipated in Charles because he has nothing within him to make it a meaningful stimulus for action. The earlier heroes had direction and purpose, or found it, but Charles has nothing to hold on to except perhaps Nora and his wry disinterest in the world around him. The static world of the novel is best described by Nick himself at the very end. In response to Nora's question concerning what the end result will be of all that has taken place, he answers:

"Nothing new. They'll go on being Mimi and Dorothy and Gilbert just as you and I will go on being us and the Quinns will go on being the Quinns. Murder doesn't round out anybody's life except the murdered's and sometimes the murderer's." (726)

For the first time in Hammett's work, detection fails to become a metaphor for existence. Not only is there no education in moral terms, there is no change at all. Previously, detective work had, like a pebble dropped into a stagnant pool, created ripples of significance and meaning. In *The Thin Man* the pebble is dropped—the truth is discovered—but the stagnant waters are too turgid to respond. The tendency of the earlier novels was to suggest that very few, perhaps only the detective, learned from experience. This novel makes it categorical.

In short, the purported weaknesses of the novel—the lack of characterization, the superficiality of the hero, and the lack of resonances—become emblems of Hammett's dark vision of America's loss of a hero. *The Thin Man* illustrates the loss of self in modern times perhaps more completely than any other detective novel in the 1920's-1930's. Perhaps it is this recognition which prompts Ross Macdonald to say:

> Hammett was the first American writer to use the detective-story for the purpose of a major novelist, to present a vision, blazing if disenchanted, of our lives.[23]

Hammett creates a protagonist who lacks even the impulse to dream a better world. Though Nick is convinced of the unreality of the world around him, he feels no pain as a result of this perception. It may be that we are to interpret his obsessive drinking and hedonistic urges as a sign of his inner need to numb his sensibilities, but we cannot be sure. It may be that it would be more fitting to read his indulgences in drink and wit as the Hammett hero's last attempt to keep his distance from the corruption surrounding him.

The other characters in the novel express a negation of life through their actions, but Nick and Nora seem somehow different. Judged from conventional standards, their relationship seems superficial, but in the context of the novel their relationship seems the best possible. In a world where everyone else takes themselves so terribly seriously, often at the expense of others, Nick and Nora's ability to laugh at each other and themselves seems very healthy and refreshing. Their inability to communicate on a direct emotional level shows them to be creatures of Hammett's dark new world, but they seem free of the worst of that world. Their relationship seems to have its own rules and game theory; less a traditional marriage and more an understanding, they remind a reader of Lillian Hellman's description of her relationship with Hammett:

> We never again spoke of that night because, I think, he was ashamed of the angry gesture that made him once again the winner in the game that men and women play against each other, and I was ashamed that I caused myself to lose so often.[24]

Hammett and Hellman fought hard, drank hard, and laughed hard together, and Nick and Nora do the same. In comparison with the other marriages in the novel, Nick and Nora have something going for them. They understand one another and they interact. Where the others have surely lost connection, they seem right for one another in regard to their tastes and level of wit.

In fact, much of *The Thin Man* evinces a serious authorial concern for the way people relate. Hammett narrows and compresses his social vision markedly. His focus is on the disintegration of the family unit.[25]

The usual Hammett theme of deception is almost entirely illustrated through the portrayals of the various families in the novel. Such compression of focus suggests Hammett's overriding concern with the most corrosive of forces in modern America: family breakdown. Edenbaum remarks that

> *The Thin Man* is perhaps less concerned with murder and the private-eye than with the people around the murder—with a wide range of social types spiritually sibling to the Alfred C. Packer of the long entry Gilbert Wynant reads in *Celebrated Criminal Cases of America.* The man-eaters Mimi, Dorothy, and Gilbert Wynant; Christian Jorgensen, Herbert Macauley, the Quinns, the Edges; as well as underworld characters like Shep Morelli and Julia Wolf are little less cannibalistic than Packer . . .[26]

Edenbaum is quite right. *The Thin Man* is the least hero-centered novel of the group. It is most like *Red Harvest* in its social emphasis. Everyone in the novel exerts a negative influence on a family, and Hammett's intention is to explore and expose the hollowness of modern society.

Edenbaum is right to argue that man's cannibalism is the major theme in *The Thin Man.* The "true" Packer case reflects on the fiction just as the fiction reflects on life in modern America as Hammett sees it. The theme of the Packer story is similar to that of Goldings' *Lord of the Flies* or Robert Ardrey's *African Genesis*: in a state of isolation man will revert back to his innate primitive nature. Packer, with his five companions in the wilds of the Colorado mountains, are joined together by the common desire for gold. As Packer tells the story, when the group finds starvation imminent, it agrees to a survival compact, a family agreement to eat the fleshiest members first. When only Packer and a man named Bell are left, they enter "into a solemn compact that as we were the only ones left we would stand by each other whatever befell, rather than harm each other we would die of starvation" (638). As Packer tells it, Bell breaks the compact and tries to kill him, thus forcing him to kill Bell first and to use him for food. Of course, this family compact turns out to be a fabrication. Under the pretense of human concern, Packer attempts to save his own neck. The truth is, he killed all five, obviously in hopes of keeping all the expected treasure for himself, and ate their flesh to sustain himself.

The Packer story reflects in a variety of ways the main action of the novel. The "truth" as Packer tells it turns out to be a tissue of lies just as the "truth" as articulated by Mimi, Dorothy, Gilbert and Macauley turns out to be webs of deception. Further, the Packer story functions as a paradigm of all the family relationships pictured in the novel. What we see in the Wynant family, the Quinn family, the Edge family, and the Nunheim family is cannibalism masquerading behind the illusion of the family compact. In each case, the motivation for their vicious behavior is a combination of greed and a feeling of the necessity of self-survival, precisely the ingredients of the Packer story.

The novel opens, in fact, with Dorothy's description of her broken family and her hatred of her mother, her father, and her brother (596). As the novel develops, we see the mutual hatred, mistrust, and greed which motivates the

Wynant-Jorgensen family. Dorothy is repeatedly beaten by Mimi (613, 677, 688), and Hammett's diction suggests the viciousness underlying the act: "Mimi slashed Dorothy across the mouth with the back of her hand" (677). Dorothy tells us that her step-father Christian intends to stay married to Mimi only so long as her money holds out (616) and that he married her only for her alimony-rich bank account (702-3). Jorgensen, it turns out, not only violates the marriage compact by committing adultery with Olga Fenton (646) but has violated it from the beginning by being a bigamist.

Jorgensen's ruthless approach to marriage is mirrored point by point by Mimi's behavior. Suspecting that her husband, who has just been discovered to be her former husband's business rival, Rosewater, married her solely to revenge himself on Clyde, she is more than willing to frame him for Julia Wolf's murder:

> "That son of a bitch made a fool of me, Nick, an out and out fool, and now he's
> in trouble and expects me to help him . . . The police, they don't believe me.
> How can I make them believe that he's lying, that I know nothing more than I've
> told them about the murder?" (678)

Initially out of revenge and monetary gain against Clyde (whose watch chain she found in Julia's room the day she was murdered), now, out of spite for having been played a fool by Jorgensen, Mimi is willing to send him to the gas chamber by holding back evidence against Clyde. She follows her most primitive instincts, wanting to strike back at the man who has hurt her. All pretense of a civilized relationship is dropped.

Affection is never given freely in the Wynant family. Gilbert, feeling his position as Dorothy's knight threatened by Nick, purposely lies to her about having seen her father and knowing who killed Julia in order to gain respect in her eyes. He lies out of hate and jealousy of Nick:

> "I was . . . I suppose it was jealousy really . . . You see, Dorry used to look up
> to me and think I knew more than anybody else about everything . . . and . . .
> when she got to seeing you, it was different. She looked up to you and respected
> you more." (708-9)

As Nick himself describes the Wynants:

> "There doesn't seem to be a single one of them in the family—now that Mimi's
> turned against her Chris—who has even the slightest reasonably friendly feeling
> for any of the others, and yet there's something very alike in all of them." (662)

The similarity is their equal lack of human feeling for any one other than themselves; ironically, Hammett suggests that intense self-interest only reveals the hollowness that lies within. Gilbert is only able to measure his identity by an external pecking order; his actions reveal his recognition that there exists no sound basis for a relationship between himself and his sister. He confuses affection with worship. Mimi's sole desire is to sell herself to the highest bidder, and Hammett illustrates the absurdity of this motive for living when he shows her unwittingly cheating herself by agreeing to Macauley's proposal toward the end of the novel.

The other families in this novel are likewise shattered by distrust and greed. Harrison Quinn, we are told, lusts after Dorothy and hopes to divorce his wife and marry her. Alice Quinn, his wife, remembers when "he had muscles" (665), probably her equivalent of manhood, and later admits to Nick and Nora that she only stays with him "for his money" (665). The last we hear of their relationship is that Harrison has disappeared from home.

The Alice-Harrison Quinn marriage is mirrored by the Nunheim-Miriam marriage. Nunheim, too, is unfaithful to his wife, and neither has any respect for the other. As she puts it,

> "I don't like crooks, and even if I did, I wouldn't like crooks that are stool-pigeons, and if I liked crooks that are stool-pigeons, I still wouldn't like you." (619)

She later walks out on him, and he is killed trying to shake Macauley down for additional money.

Lastly, of course, we are told very early that Clyde's adultery with Julia Wolf was what caused the breakup between Mimi and him. William Kenney sums up his view of personal relationships in the novel by saying:

> Moreover, as if to right some strange balance, Hammett depicts in this novel a series of relationships in which the strongest emotion either partner seems capable of for the other is contempt.[27]

I would add that the feeling of contempt is joined by the feeling of hate and the desire to survive financially. Though the novel deals explicitly only with the murders of two people—Julia Wolf and Clyde—it implicitly pictures a society of cannibals. Hammett may or may not have remembered Melville's line from *Moby Dick*, "Oh horrible vultureism of earth! from which not the mightiest whale is free,"[28] but vultureism is what he renders.

One possible implication of Hammett's preoccupation with broken and alienated families is that, however incompletely or obliquely he articulates it, he perceived and gave warning to a birth of an attitude that Kenneth Keniston defines as part of a larger alienated pattern:

> Central to alienation is a deep and pervasive mistrust of any and all commitments, be they to other people, to groups, to American culture, or even to the self. Most basic here is the distrust of other people in general—a low and pessimistic view of human nature.[29]

Though set in New York City, *The Thin Man* was written by Hammett while living and working in Hollywood, and the insecurity, violence, and the failure to communicate on any level but the most primitive suggest his recognition that the Hollywood dream has become the American nightmare.[30] Philip Durham refers to *The Thin Man* as being "obviously written under Hollywood influence," by which he meant to imply that it was superficial.[31] But I think his comment carries more weight than he realized. The Packer story is exemplary of an aspect of America's historical move Westward in pursuit of the golden dream of success. The unconscionable rapacity of Packer mirrors what befalls the human race when it reaches the land of golden illusions. By letting the action speak for itself, Hammett raises the grim specter of what modern society has become.

Hammett reinforces his conception of a hollow world by emphasizing the problematic nature of identities in the novel. He presents us with a series of characters whose names turn out to be false. In *The Maltese Falcon . . .* [Hammett] employed deceptive images and details to illustrate that a character's outward appearance in no way reflected his true reality.[32] This same disjunction between one's appearance and one's real nature is embodied in *The Thin Man* by the uncertainty of one's name. Jorgensen is discovered to be Rosewater; Julia Wolf is Rhoda Stewart, finally Nancy Kane; Albert Norman turns out to be Arthur Nunheim; and Sparrow is discovered to be Jim Brophy. Climactically, the alive Clyde Wynant turns out to have been dead from the beginning. Ironically, almost all of the action in the novel emanates from the assumption that Wynant is alive, an assumption that proves as misleading and hollow of truth as everything else. Even when his body is discovered his identity is still obscured by the false signs of baggy clothes and a belt buckle carrying the initials of D.W.Q.

Undoubtedly, the greatest triumph of *The Thin Man* is its plot. For the first time, Hammett makes plot primary, and characterization secondary. As a mystery-detective plot it is a *tour de force*. The entire structure is built around the idea that the suspected murderer will be dead from the beginning, himself a victim of murder. The ingenuity of such an idea is well proven by its finding repeated use in later writers. Raymond Chandler employs this device in his first novel, *The Big Sleep* (1939), and Ross Macdonald repeats it with variation in *The Wycherly Woman* (1961) and *The Underground Man* (1971).

One point in using such a structure is to suggest the problematic nature of reality, a theme Hammett's novels all stress. The reader is consistently misled by red herrings, although Hammett plants enough clues that he cannot be accused of violating the fair-play doctrine. We are told early, for example, that Clyde supposedly gave Macauley power of attorney over his estate and though this turns out to be untrue, Macauley does possess that power. Therefore he has a motive for murder (603/626). Later we are told that Macauley had once lost a large amount of money on the stock market and therefore he has need of money (699-700). The main clue, of course, is the fact that no one sees Clyde through the first three-fourths of the novel; all we have are letters and telegrams supposedly from him. The triumph of the plot as a mystery plot is that these clues go almost unnoticed because everything else points to Clyde as the murderer of Julia Wolf. Only Nick's skepticism seems to point to other possibilities. When the truth is uncovered, we can see its probabilities, but throughout the novel we are taken in by Macauley's rendition of reality. He literally creates his own mystery fiction, planting clues (red herrings) and suggesting a host of possible alternatives for the police to examine.

Hammett is far more skillful in plotting *The Thin Man* than critics have hitherto realized. Aside from the ingenuity of its basic conception, the plot is shown to be an accurate reflection of Hammett's conception of mankind. It illustrates and gives resonance to Hammett's themes of greed and savagery.

If, for example, we examine Macauley's actions in the plot we note that all are precipitated by his greed and his instinct for self-survival. His murder of Julia Wolf is necessitated by his discovery that she has a lover—Face Peppler—who is about to be freed from jail. Knowing that she has always been frightened and uneasy over his murder of Wynant, he surmises that once she has a chance she will run away with Peppler, and perhaps reveal his crime. He therefore kills her to prevent discovery. Greed and financial self-survival drove him to murder Clyde, and here greed and self-survival drive him to kill her. Macauley had to kill Clyde, who had discovered that Macauley had been cheating him. Macauley's savage murder recalls Packer:

> "He'd been sawed up in pieces and buried in lime or something so there wasn't much flesh left on him, according to the report I got . . ." (713)

As Nick puts it, two of the murders were "obviously in cold blood" (721). Macauley's murder of Nunheim was another motivated by greed and the instinct for self-survival.

But the plot does more than simply unmask a villain because it shows that the villain survives only because of corresponding greed and savagery in those around him. In the last fourth of the novel, Hammett reverses our growing expectation that Macauley may have been lying all along by bringing forward two characters who claim they, too, have seen Clyde: Gilbert and his mother, Mimi. Gilbert lies to rise in his sister's eyes, as aforementioned, and his selfishness and meanness of spirit temporarily aid Macauley, first by directing attention away from himself, and secondly by giving him the idea to use Mimi's own greed and selfishness to cheat her out of most of her fortune. Hammett's point seems to be that Macauley almost gets away with everything because everyone else is corrupt as well. The implication we draw is that cannibals like Macauley can feast off of others because the world is so devoid of values that he can appear as a natural part of the landscape.

A plot such as this emphasizes the interdependence of the criminal and his society and suggests that a Macauley is only an exaggerated form of a general malaise. As Eric Fromm has argued, modern man is empty and selfless because he is alienated from himself by society's extreme marketing orientation. By portraying society as an unwitting accomplice to Macauley, Hammett suggests a very similar point. George Grella has commented that Hammett's works imply, but do not articulate fully, "an urban chaos, devoid of spiritual and moral values, pervaded by viciousness and random savagery."[33]

Seen this way, crime is not a temporary aberration but a ubiquitous fact. Wylie Sypher, in speaking of the nineteenth century and the modern existentialists, says that one question which these novelists pose is, "What does experience mean after the self has been diminished, or perhaps, has vanished?"[34] Though Hammett cannot rightly be called an existentialist, *The Thin Man* and even *The Glass Key*, can certainly be seen as a step in that direction. Hammett's rendering of Nick Charles, as well as the others in the novel, suggests that what he sees in the modern world around him is the loss of the authentic self. If, as Sypher argues, the existential question is "honesty," a searching for the authentic self,[35] can we not say that Hammett too has been concerned with this impulse in his creations Sam Spade and Ned Beaumont, and that Nick Charles *et al* embody the loss of this impulse? The comic tone of the novel masks the tragic vision lying beneath and lends to the events a sense of the absurd.

The Thin Man is Hammett's bleakest novel because it posits an entropic vision of man. The moral energy of his earlier heroes becomes squandered in the aimless motions of Nick Charles. The movement from the rough and brutally instinctive Op in *Red Harvest* to the cool and sophisticated Nick Charles is a drift towards inertia and *ennui*. Similar to Meursault in Camus' *The Stranger*, Nick is willing to surrender to a kind of comic neutrality, a distrust in actions that just six years ago had been his existence.[36] His will to act has been dissipated, and even when his analytic mind is forced into action and he discovers the truth, nothing changes. All will remain as it was. Hammett's heroes have been measured by what they *did*; identity was a matter of *doing*, a doctrine quite amenable to the existentialists. André Malraux, André Gide, and Camus were all admirers of Hammett.[37] Gide praised Hammett's rendering of deception in *Red Harvest* because he thought it was so truthful to experience.[38] What would probably be as satisfying to such writers is Hammett's portrayal of man's second fall, to use Heidegger's words, the fall from authenticity.[39]

Finally, even detective work in the novel is conceived as a matter of appearance, not truth. Nick's description of the way real detectives work defines the authenticity of guilt or innocence as largely a matter of probabilities:

"You find the guy you think did the murder and you slam him in the can and let everybody know you think he's guilty and put his picture all over newspapers, and the District Attorney builds up the best theory he can on what information you've got and meanwhile you pick up additional details here and there, and people who recognize his picture in the paper—as well as people who'd think he was innocent if you hadn't arrested him—come in and tell you things about him and presently you've got him sitting in the electric chair. (722)

This construct-a-villain approach works in this novel—Macauley is guilty—but the implication of such a doctrine is disturbing. Justice becomes a matter of good advertising and considerable luck; were police forces manned by people as intuitively bright as Charles turns out to be—he reconstructs the *gestalt* of the crime perfectly—then perhaps such an approach would be efficacious, but the novel makes it clear that the truth-conscious private eye is all but gone, and that it leaves at best, a Guild, and at worst, a brutal and stupid Andy.

The moral vision of *The Thin Man* is dark indeed. In it we sense most acutely the emptiness which underlies human existence. At his best, Charles is a residue of Hammett's earlier figures, hardboiled people who would sacrifice all for a piece of the truth. They, at least, had the inner strength to will their own worlds into being, even if it meant making them totally alien to the world around them. In its presentation of the loss of will and belief in truth and justice, *The Thin Man* represents Hammett's rendition of the end-game. [*The Armchair Detective* 8 (1974): 27-35]

NOTES

1. "Books," *New Statesman and Nation* (New Series), VII (May 26, 1934), p. 801. For a different view see Joseph Haas, Review of *The Big Knockover*, Chicago *Daily News*, June 18, 1966. Haas writes: "It seems probable that neither man was familiar with the works of the other, in those early years. What is likely is that their approaches were the products of two similar minds affected by comparable influence."

2. [In the original article, the information for this endnote is not supplied.]

3. [In the original article, the information for this endnote is not supplied.]

4. "Dashiell Hammett: Themes and Techniques," *Essays on American Literature in Honor of Jay B Hubbell*, ed. Clarence Gohdes (Durham: Duke Univ. Press, 1967), pp. 303-4.

5. See "The Gangster Novel: The Urban Pastoral," *Tough Guy Writers of the Thirties*, ed. David Madden (Carbondale: Southern Illinois Press, 1968), pp. 186-198; "Murder and The Mean Streets: The Hard-Boiled Detective Novel," *Contempora*, I.1 1970, republished in *The Armchair Detective*, V.1 (October, 1971), pp. 1-10; "The Literature of the Thriller: A Critical Study." Diss. Kansas, 1967.

6. "Dashiell Hammett's Private-Eye: No Loyalty Beyond the Job," *Commentary*, VII (May 1949), p. 472.

7. "Decline and Fall of the Whodunit," *Saturday Review*, XXXV (May 31, 1952), p. 31.

8. "The *Black Mask* School," *Tough Guy Writers*, p. 71. Durham's interest is more in what *The Thin Man*, as it was originally begun, might have become. Begun in 1930, written in the third person, set in San Francisco, and with a "modified Op" whose main characteristic was a ghost-like, un-touchable character. Hammett only completed 65 pages of this draft.

9. "The Dashiell Hammett Tradition and the Modern Detective Novel," Diss.

Michigan 1964, pp. 106-7.

10. Kenney, p. 107.

11. Kenney, p. 106.

12. Kenney, p. 106. See also Wayne Booth, *The Rhetoric of Fiction* (Chicago and London: University of Chicago Press, 1961), p. 225. Booth shows why it is almost impossible to have dramatic irony and mystification simultaneously.

13. Kenney, pp. 86-7, 84.

14. "The Poetics of the Private-Eye: The Novels of Dashiell Hammett," *Tough Guy Writers*, p. 101.

15. Edenbaum, p. 102.

16. (New York: Dell Publishing Co, Inc., 1970), p. 391.

17. Kenney, pp. 86-7.

18. Kenney, p. 94.

19. *The Thin Man*, collected in *The Novels of Dashiell Hammett* (New York: Random House, 1966), p. 162. All further references are from this edition and citations will appear in the text of the paper.

20. Reported in Orel, "The American Detective-Hero," *JPC*, II.3 (1968), p. 400.

21. "Cops, Robbers, Heroes and Anti-Heroes: The American Need to Create," *JPC* 1 (1967), p. 118.

22. "The Tough Hemingway and His Hard-Boiled Children," *Tough Guy Writers*, p. 21.

23. "The Writer as Detective Hero," *The Mystery Writer's Art*, ed. Francis M. Nevins, Jr. (Bowling Green Univ. Popular Press, 1970), p. 300.

24. Lillian Hellman, *An Unfinished Woman* (New York: Bantam Books, Inc., 1970), p. 167.

25. See Kenney, pp. 83-4. He makes the excellent point that the corruption of the family unit suggests the larger corruption of society as a whole. Cf. George Grella, "Murder and the Mean Streets: The Hard-Boiled Detective Novel," *TAD*, pp. 5-6.

26. Edenbaum, p. 102.

27. Kenney, p. 87.

28. Herman Melville, *Moby Dick*, ed. Charles Feidelson, Jr. (Indianapolis and New York: Bobbs-Merrill, Inc., 1964), p. 402.

29. *The Uncommitted*, p. 49.

30. See George Grella, "Murder and the Mean Street: The Hard-Boiled Detective Novel," p. 6. Speaking generally for Hammett, Chandler, and Macdonald, Grella makes the point that the hardboiled detective novel illustrates what happens when the "frontier" disappears and is replaced by the "urban jungle."

31. "The *Black Mask* School," *Tough Guy Writers*, p. 71.

32. See Walter Blair, "Dashiell Hammett: Themes and Techniques," p. 304-5.

33. Grella, "Murder and The Mean Streets," p. 5.

34. *Loss of the Self in Modern Literature and Art* (New York: Random House, 1962), p. 68.

35. Sypher, p. 66.

36. Summoning Camus here is not farfetched. See W.M. Frohock's *The Novel of Violence in America* (Dallas: Southern Methodist Univ. Press, 1950), p. 13. We are told Camus imitated James M. Cain in *The Stranger*; Cf. Robert Edenbaum, p. 94. He compares the Hammett hero to Camus' man without a memory in *The Rebel*.

37. [In the original article, the information for this endnote is not supplied.]

38. "An Imaginary Interview," tr. Malcolm Cowley, *New Republic*, CX (February 7, 1944), p. 186.

39. See Sypher's discussion of Heidegger's concept, p. 91, in *Loss of the Self in Modern Literature and Art.*

From *Beams Falling: The Art of Dashiell Hammett's Novels*

Peter Wolfe

Perhaps because readers hope to find in *The Thin Man* (1934) a positive encompassing morality and come away disappointed, Hammett's last novel is also his most controversial. Some have even denied the artistic basis of the controversy; [Robert B.] Parker, for instance, calls the novel "far and away Hammett's weakest effort."[1] Howard Haycraft's assessment is only a mite friendlier; though commending the novel for its humor, Haycraft judges it Hammett's "least typical and least important contribution."[2] The novel may have fared better in England. Perhaps anticipating disclaimers like those of the Americans Haycraft and Parker, Peter Quennell defended the work in his contemporary review. "It has every right to consideration on its literary merits,"[3] claims Quennell, whose fellow English critic, Julian Symons, echoed his praise nearly forty years later by calling the novel "a continually charming and sparkling performance."[4]

The book has many touches and trimmings indicative of Hammett's hand. As in all the other novels, it interrupts the action with a set piece (e.g., the Flitcraft story in *Falcon*) that illuminates the plot. It contains, in Dorothy Wynant, a debutante of twenty drawn to gangsters with the same force that compelled rich men's daughters in "The Gatewood Caper" and "$106,000 Blood Money." Dorothy also descends from Gabrielle Leggett Collinson in *Dain Curse*, another highly strung daughter of an eccentric inventor who fears that she's mad. But the novel resembling *Thin Man* most closely is the one standing closest to it in time, *Glass Key*. From *Key* comes the New York City setting, the physical cruelty, a title character who, with his mustache and tall, bony frame, looks like an aged, gaunt Ned Beaumont (or Dashiell Hammett), and the motif of hypergamy, or marrying above one's social class, as a symptom of social change: in Nora, Nick Charles, who may be the son of a Greek immigrant, has married the daughter of an industrial tycoon. (Another barrier that may come from *Glass Key* is that of age; in marrying Nora, who is fifteen years his junior, Nick follows a pattern formed by the newspaper publisher, Hal Mathews, Paul Madvig, and perhaps Beaumont.)

Contrasts between *Glass Key* and *Thin Man* clarify the later work as well as do comparisons. The sparkle and charm noted by Symons argue that Hammett followed his darkest novel with his lightest, most glittering one. Trim and mobile, *Thin Man* is both a murder mystery and a sophisticated comedy in the manner of a Philip Barry play; the New York holiday setting, witty repartee, and rich characters all invoke Barry's *Holiday*. [A.] Alvarez reads the work as more of a social critique than a detective novel: "The main interest is its view of New York just after the crash, with its nervy, slanderous parties, sporadically violent speakeasies, disintegrating boozing, and permanent hangovers."[5] It is easy to support this reading, the novel's steadiest presence being its aura of cosmopolitan glamor. The many phone calls to the Charleses' elegant hotel suite, the taxi rides through the humming city during Christmas week, and the hearty cheer with which the Charleses enjoy themselves all exude fun and bounce. The vacationing couple stay up till four or five o'clock in the morning. Interspersing bright conversation, they also eat Japanese food, go to a play, hear a private piano recital in Greenwich Village, and attend the opening of the Radio City Music Hall. While Nick is stalking a murderer or simply walking the celebrated Schnauzer, Asta, Nora will get her hair done, go to an art gallery, or shop at expensive stores like Saks or Lord and Taylor. The fun and festivity generated by this free spending put the Charleses at the center of New York City at its busiest, happiest season. . . .

[While] Brilliant in spots, *Thin Man* falters as an organic whole. It is hard to make sense of the novel's structure: the sophisticated comedy doesn't join hands with the murder case, and the undertones get lost in the wisecracks and cocktails. *Thin Man* undermines itself. Though its mode is comic, it suggests tragic depths. Unfortunately, to sound these depths is to destroy the novel's holiday glamor. The novel's leading ideas don't make our job any easier. Pointing to the numerous aliases adopted by the characters, [George J.] Thompson cites "the problematic nature of identities in the novel":

> Jorgensen is discovered to be Kellerman; Julia Wolf is Rhoda Stewart, finally Nancy Kane; Albert Norman turns out to be Arthur Nunheim; and Sparrow is discovered to be Jim Brophy. . . . Ironically, almost all the action in the novel emanates from the assumption that Wynant is alive, an assumption that proves as misleading and hollow of truth as everything else.[6]

The large helping of sex served up in the novel, while introducing excitement, is usually rank. Nora's question about the Wynant-Jorgensen set, "Are they the first of a new race of monster?" could be answered by references to illicit sex: Mimi's mention of "my beautiful white body" and the erection Nick gets while wrestling her to the sofa in Chapter 25 lend erotic force to "those couple of afternoons we killed" he refers to in Chapter 6. But Mimi isn't the only one in the family with sexual designs on Nick. Both she and her son Gilbert believe Dorothy to be in love with him. Add to this maimed love triangle Gilbert's incestuous craving for Dorothy, the bigamy of Jorgensen-Kelterman, and Dorothy's claim that she needs a pistol to ward off her step-father's sexual advances, and Nick's estimate of the family, "They're all sex-crazy," makes good sense. (Gilbert, who asks Nick about incest, tells Dorothy that he's been seeing their father in order to win her attention, which he believes has been shunted to Nick.)

The problem of stable identities and the sexual tangle at the Courtland merge with Hammett's picture of family life, suggesting, says Thompson, "the almost total alienation of modern man."[7] Marriages crack all through *Thin Man*: Wynant and Mimi get divorced before the time of the book; Sid Kelterman walks out on two wives; the stockbroker, Harrison Quinn, wants to leave his wife for Dorothy; even the Charleses are celebrating Christmas away from home. Now the motifs of married sex and multinymity as functions of a shaky identity meet in the central chapter of this thirty-one-chapter work. They meet in the figures of little Arthur Nunheim, or Albert Norman, and the outsized woman he lives with, Miriam. The travesty of marriage Miriam and Nunheim (no home) have been enacting ends when a police investigation breaks their domestic routine. Shaken by the presence of the police, Miriam throws a greasy frying pan at Nunheim before walking out on him. Then Nunheim slips away, to be murdered only hours later. Is Hammett saying, through this brief domestic sequence, what he said in the Packer story—that the collapse of the family brings on death? We can't say, because Nunheim-Norman is too minor a figure to carry a large share of the thematic load. Yet, by walking into the book in Chapter 16, he gets this load heaped on his back. He sags under it, never to reappear.

If Nunheim is too shadowy, the culprit, Macaulay, reflects even worse judgment and technique. "The murderer is the most weakly drawn character in the novel," complains [William Patrick] Kenney, and Thompson agrees, calling Macaulay "the weakest villain Hammett ever created."[8] These judgments hit home. In fact, the title of the novel could refer to the insubstantial Macaulay, whose personality and role in the plot do lack force. Above all, he displays no traits that show him capable of sawing a friend's corpse to pieces; his being a poor shot with firearms denoting fear of, not attraction to, violence. Besides, Hammett doesn't give him a motive for murder, neither his law practice nor his home in fashionable Scarsdale appearing to need a fast infusion of Wynant dollars.

Hammett's treatment of Macaulay's guilt, as distinct from his character, shows skill and tact. After mentioning Macaulay on the first page, Hammett portrays him consistently as a man with something to hide. Every action that Macaulay engineers refers back to his guilt. To watch Hammett placing his clues is to watch a master of literary detection at his craft. First, we only have

Macaulay's word for it that Wynant left New York in October to work on an invention; the only other person who has seen the thin man since his alleged departure, Julia Wolf, can't refute the story. Then, Macaulay protects himself by distracting the investigation. By spreading the falsehood that Julia pinched $4000 belonging to Wynant, he makes the police think she was killed for the money, none of which was found at her death-site. He continues to shunt suspicion away from himself by diverting the attention of the police. The story he makes up about an important message lying between some pages of a nonexistent book at Julia's, by wasting the time and energy of the police, cools the trail to himself. Some of his ruses he directs to Nick, whom he fears more than the police, having worked with him in the past. To quiet these fears, he plans to kill Nick. First, he makes Nick believe that the police suspect him of murdering Julia and that Nick can relieve the pressure by apprehending Wynant, the real murderer. To banish any worries Nick may have about his own safety, Macaulay paints himself as a man of good will who has run out of patience. Refusing to protect Wynant, his treacherous client-friend, with any more stalls, he wants action. But the action he wants consists of luring an unsuspecting Nick to Scarsdale to be butchered.

Nick can handle Macaulay. Though retired six years from sleuthing, he has retained the sleuth's mentality and code of survival. Lacking the tough, knowing manner of Spade and the nervous intensity of Beaumont, he can carouse or work (his refusal of a drink in Chapter 27 proves that, though a hard drinker, he is no alcoholic). He also has the knack of defusing danger with wit. Waking up to the sight of Shep Morelli holding a pistol, he begins wisecracking immediately: "Do you mind putting the gun away?" he asks Morelli. "My wife doesn't care, but I'm pregnant." Wise-cracks make up a big part of his verbal strategy. Often, he will joke either to hide the truth that he is fencing hard with an interlocutor or to hold back facts. He holds back more than he tells. At different points he is told, "I never know when you're lying," "You're the damnedest evasive man," and "You'll never talk yourself into any trouble." He won't. He makes very few mistakes. Yet he can reply fully and accurately when he wants. Asked by Gilbert about the sensation caused by being stabbed, he explains what it feels like to be wounded by a knife *and* a bullet.

Like Agatha Christie's Hercule Poirot, he has a nose for lies, both their meaning and their cause. On the other hand, his suspiciousness hasn't jaded him. At times, his morality is more compassionate than legalistic. Righting wrongs and catching crooks must give way to deeper, more delicate needs at times. His respect for the feelings of Gilbert shows in his speedy rejection of Lt. Guild's suggestion that the boy lead the police to his father: "You can't ask that of him, Guild. It's his own father," says Nick protectively; betraying his father could haunt Gilbert for the rest of his life. This ripe heart knowledge typifies Nick. He knows he will miss life's richness by keeping his guard up all the time. Yet he can be whatever he has to be. He doesn't sacrifice logic for sentiment, and his tour of duty as a detective has honed his instinct for falling beams. He saved Macaulay's life when the two men fought together in the war; Macaulay showed his gratitude by getting Nick some jobs back in his sleuthing days. But Nick won't let this background of mutual service or his liking of Macaulay, of whom he said in Chapter 2, "We had always gotten along nicely," stop him from arresting the lawyer. Hadn't the lawyer plotted to murder *him*?

In his farewell to literary detection, Hammett portrays the sleuth as a God figure; Nick saves Macaulay's life in the trenches and then takes it away after discovering the lawyer's guilt. Nor does he restrict his powers to crime-stopping. A brilliant talker, he controls conversations in which two subjects are being discussed at the same time and in which no speech answers the previous one. He pries things from Dorothy that she won't tell her family. He always comes back with a witty, tension-relieving answer to Nora's embarrassing questions. As has been said, he has taught her how the accidental and the oblique can bolster their marriage. Nora learns fast. Right after Dorothy starts talking about the psychological impact of childhood experience, Nick denies the importance of early influences. But without discounting other possibilities created by the subject; on the same page, Nora, alert to nuances, addresses him as "son," and minutes later, following her lead, Nick calls her "Mamma." The bond between them has been strengthened as smoothly as either could wish.

This bond needs all the help it can get to withstand the void threatening it. Perhaps Thompson is right to call *Thin Man* "a continuation and logical extension of the themes and concerns of the preceding novels."[9] Hammett's lightness of touch in his last book has not disguised his awareness of evil. Granted, the frolic and fun of *Thin Man* robs Hammett's career of a sense of artistic growth or deepening of vision. But other American writers of the century have also ended their careers on an artistic tailspin; Raymond Chandler's *Playback* (1958) and the late works of both Sinclair Lewis and John Dos Passos betray a weakening of intellectual fiber. The outlook put forth by *Thin Man* is less weak than it is modulated. Though kept on a tight rein, depravity stalks the novel. Nearly all the characters live for money and/or sex. The guests at the Courtland and Normandie, despite their fine manners and stylish clothes, reappear at the brawling speakeasy, the Pigiron Club. Furthermore, the emotions displayed in this gangster dive match those seen at the chic residences. The following description of Mimi as an enraged wildcat, as she fights off Nick in her suite, unleashes a ferocity that smashes all differences created by money and social rank:

> Mimi's face was becoming purple. Her eyes protruded, glassy, senseless, enormous. Saliva bubbled and hissed between clenched teeth with her breathing, and her red throat—her whole body—was a squirming mass of veins and muscles swollen until it seemed they must burst.

Hammett can be faulted for resisting the implications of this brilliant description. Though he saw lust, cruelty, and betrayal in Mimi Wynant and the others, he shied away from his vision. No demonic creator, he both shunned self-inquiry and refused to follow his inventiveness to its dark source after it abandoned Marxist writ. The sense of guilt and dread (Henry James's "black merciless things") that goads all creative artists dried his genius rather than feeding it. Though he calls attention to mysteries relating to matters of deep human concern, he never unveils them. The metaphysical issues called forth in *Falcon* and *Glass Key* and the ancient taboos grazed in *Thin Man* all get whipped into the froth of social comedy, where their terror fades. Hammett's primitivism survives chiefly as stylistic flourish.

This escapist way of dealing with his vision made fiction-writing more of a denial than a fulfillment for Dashiell Hammett. The Marxist implications of his stance must have made him smile thinly. He had reached an artistic dead-end. After *Thin Man*, he had nowhere either to grow into or to hide. [Bowling Green U Popular P, 1980: 148-49, 158-63]

NOTES

1. Robert B. Parker, "The Violent Hero, Wilderness Heritage and Urban Reality," Diss., Boston University, 1971, p. 118.

2. Howard Haycraft, *Murder for Pleasure: The Life and Times of the Detective Story* (1941; rpt. Biblo and Tannen, New York: 1974), p. 171.

3. Peter Quennell, "Books," *New Statesman and Nation*, 26 May 1934, p. 78.

4. Julian Symons, *Mortal Consequences* (New York: Harper and Row, c. 1972), p. 140.

5. A. Alvarez, "The Novels of Dashiell Hammett," *Beyond All This Fiddle* (New York: Random House, c. 1969), p. 210.

6. Ibid., pp. 187-88.

7. Ibid., p. 170.

8. William Patrick Kenney, "The Dashiell Hammett Tradition and the Modern Detective Novel," Diss., University of Michigan, 1964, p. 106; Thompson, p. 170.

9. Ibid., p. 169.

General Studies

From *Murder for Pleasure:
The Life and Times of the Detective Story*

Howard Haycraft

For all his wide and undeniable influence and achievements, S.S. Van Dine was essentially a developer, an adapter and polisher of other men's techniques, rather than a true innovator. In this, though scarcely otherwise, his position was not unlike that of Conan Doyle a generation earlier. By contrast, his almost immediate chronological follower, Dashiell Hammett, acknowledged founder of the realistic or "hard-boiled" division of detective writing, must be called a *creator* of the first rank, deserving to sit with such diverse comrades-at-arms as E.C. Bentley, Francis Iles, and the small handful of others who brought something really new to their chosen field of effort. Van Dine's Philo Vance novels—to continue the comparison—were epochal in the sense that they raised the detective story to a new peak of excellence and popularity in the land of its birth; they were American in the narrow sense that their milieu and subject matter were American; yet in method and style they departed no whit from the well established English tradition. On the other hand, Hammett's lean, dynamic, unsentimental narratives created a definitely *American style*, quite separate and distinct, in fact, that to this day certain short-sighted formalists refuse to admit they are detective stories at all! (But with such narrow parochialism the truly eclectic student can have no traffic.) In no slight degree the circumstances of this achievement arose from Hammett's own career, on which he has drawn copiously for material and inspiration. . . .

Hammett had been writing for the pulp market (he is the most notable of the numerous "alumni" of *Black Mask*) and reviewing detective fiction for the New York *Post* for some time before he published his first novel, in 1929. It was called *Red Harvest* and was a loosely constructed blood-and-thunder yarn with more gangsterism than detection, even of the Hammett definition, in it. *The Dain Curse*, published the same year, showed a substantial improvement and crystallization of his talent and technique. He reached his zenith (and one of the all-time high points in the detective story) with *The Maltese Falcon* (1930). This novel holds the unusual distinction of being the only contemporary detective story to date to be included in the carefully selected Modern Library series. *The Glass Key* (1931), ranked by most critics as only below *The Maltese Falcon* (though it is Hammett's own first choice among his books), was a worthy successor. But *The Thin Man* (1932) [sic], the most popular of his works, paradoxically marked (in the opinion of the initiated) a distinct softening of the author's talents. A film version with William Powell and Myrna Loy in the leading roles was sensationally successful and has been followed by a number of cinematic sequels with the same actors. The affluence which the series has brought Hammett is probably the reason that he has produced no published work in many years. Nevertheless, *The Thin Man*, while his least typical and least important contribution, is not without significance on its own account, as one of the first works to bring humor, and of a distinctly native brand, to the detective story in this country.

Because of their startling originality, the Hammett novels virtually defy exegesis even to-day—though their external pattern is by now all too familiar by process of over-much imitation. As straightaway detective stories they can hold their own with the best. They are also character studies of close to top rank in their own right, and are penetrating if often shocking novels of manners as well. They established new standards for realism in the genre. Yet they are as sharply stylized and deliberately artificial as Restoration Comedy, and have been called an inverted form of romanticism. They were commercial in inception; but they miss being Literature, if at all, by the narrowest of margins.

The Bookman's comment in 1932 that "it is doubtful if even Ernest Hemingway has written more effective dialogue" may seem a trifle over-enthusiastic to-day, but only a little. And Hammett's talents in this direction are, if anything, exceeded by his ability to delineate character by sharp, frugal, telling strokes admirably suited to the form. He is at his best in depicting his central figures, invariably private inquiry agents (drawn from life, he has intimated): brutal, grasping, lecherous "heels"; each, however, with his own hard and distinct code of Hemingwayesque courage and fatalism and a twisted sort of personal integrity incomprehensible to conventional minds. His secondary characters are not always realized with equal care, but some of them (such as the tormented baby-faced gunman of *The Maltese Falcon* or the gorilla, Jeff, in *The Glass Key*) give new and unforgettable inflections to the word "sinister."

The action of the novels is machine-gun paced and so violent that, in the first two books particularly, it occasionally defeats its purpose by exhausting the reader's receptive and reactive capacities. Some of the incidents, also, by the extremity of their sadism, tend to stand out too strongly from the main thread of the story and thus to imperil the unity and balance of the novel as a whole: too often they are merely stunts in realistic narration and definitely impede the progress of the plots in which they occur. (This is no moralistic objection, but a statement of the recognized fact that artistic excesses bring their own retribution.) The prose, except for the few such moments of intemperance, is economical, astringent, and muscular, while the Hammett vocabulary, as might be expected, is consistently and quite properly for the *mores* depicted blunt and outspoken. In fact, *The Thin Man*'s lively success in the bookstores is commonly ascribed in publishing circles to the inclusion of a single usage seldom seen in polite print. But it would be an error and an injustice to dismiss Dashiell Hammett's novels as merely salacious or sensational—even though their author wrote with a keen eye to the box-office and a not-too-reluctant use of some of the more dubious tricks of the trade. For the tremendous impact and virility he achieved transcend the means employed.

Dashiell Hammett is currently in Hollywood, writing for the moving pictures, for which in the past he has expressed no high regard. He is married and has two daughters. He does most of his writing at night and sometimes works on a scenario as long as thirty-six hours at a stretch. With his slender six feet in height, crest of prematurely gray hair, small dapper mustache, and poker-features, he might serve as the physical model for one of his own detectives. As enigmatic in many ways as his fictional heroes, he has surprised his associates in recent years by the indubitable sincerity of his interests in social and political movements of a Left-wing nature. No great admirer of his own detective stories, he hopes eventually to sever his moving picture connections and write "straight" plays and novels. There is no doubt of his ability to do so if he may find the time and inclination for at least an occasional book in the *Maltese Falcon* and *Glass Key* tradition. But should he never write another detective story, it is already safe to say that no other author of modern times—certainly no other American—has so basically changed and influenced the form.

Like all originators, Dashiell Hammett has suffered at the hands of his imitators. But the circumstance does not and should not obscure what he has done to give the American detective story a nationality of its own. [Appleton-Century Co., 1941: 169-173]

From "The Simple Art of Murder"

Raymond Chandler

In *The Long Week-end*, which is a drastically competent account of English life and manners in the decades following the First World War, Robert Graves and Alan Hodge gave some attention to the authors of detective stories, whose books sold into the millions, and in a dozen languages. These were the people who fixed the form and established the rules and founded the famous Detection Club, which is a parnassus of English writers of mystery. Its roster includes practically every important writer of detective fiction since Conan Doyle.

But Graves and Hodge decided that during this whole period only one first-class writer had written detective stories at all. An American, Dashiell Hammett. Traditional or not, Graves and Hodge were not fuddy-duddy connoisseurs of the second rate; they could see what went on in the world and that the detective story of their time didn't; and they were aware that writers who have the vision and the ability to produce real fiction do not produce unreal fiction.

How original a writer Hammett really was it isn't easy to decide now, even if it mattered. He was one of a group—the only one who achieved critical recognition—who wrote or tried to write realistic mystery fiction. All literary movements represent the whole movement; he is usually the culmination of the movement. Hammett was the ace performer, but there is nothing in his work that is not implicit in the early novels and short stories of Hemingway.

Yet, for all I know, Hemingway may have learned something from Hammett as well as from writers like Dreiser, Ring Lardner, Carl Sandburg, Sherwood Anderson, and himself. A revolutionary debunking of both the language and the material of fiction had been going on for some time. It probably started in poetry; almost everything does. But Hammett applied it to the detective story, and this, because of its heavy crust of English gentility and American pseudo-gentility, was pretty hard to get moving.

I doubt that Hammett had any deliberate artistic aims whatever; he was trying to make a living by writing something he had firsthand information about. He made some of it up; all writers do; but it had a basis in fact; it was made up out of real things. The only reality the English detection writers knew was the conversational accent of Surbiton and Bognor Regis. If they wrote about dukes and Venetian vases, they knew no more about them out of their own experience than the well-heeled Hollywood character knows about the French Modernists that hang in his Bel-Air chateau or the semi-antique Chippendale-cum-cobbler's bench that he uses for a coffee table. Hammett took murder out of the Venetian vase and dropped it into the alley; it doesn't have to stay there forever, but it looked like a good idea to get as far as possible from Emily Post's idea of how a well-bred debutante gnaws a chicken wing.

Hammett wrote at first (and almost to the end) for people with a sharp, aggressive attitude to life. They were not afraid of the seamy side of things; they lived there. Violence did not dismay them; it was right down their street. Hammett gave murder back to the kind of people that commit it for reasons, not just to provide a corpse; and with the means at hand, not hand-wrought dueling pistols, curare, and tropical fish. He put these people down on paper as they were, and he made them talk and think in the language they customarily used for these purposes.

He had a literary style, but his audience didn't know it, because it was in a language not supposed to be capable of such refinements. They thought they were getting a good meaty melodrama written in the kind of lingo they imagined they spoke themselves. It was, in a sense, but it was much more. All language begins with speech, and the speech of common men at that, but when it develops to the point of becoming a literary medium it only looks like speech. Hammett's style at its worst was as formalized as a page of *Marius the Epicurean*; at its best it could say almost anything. I believe this style, which does not belong to Hammett or to anybody, but is the American language (and not even exclusively that any more), can say things he did not know how to say, or feel the need of saying. In his hands it had no overtones, left no echo, evoked no image beyond a distant hill.

Hammett is said to have lacked heart; yet the story he himself thought the most of is the record of a man's devotion to a friend. He was spare, frugal, hard-boiled, but he did over and over again what only the best writers can ever do at all. He wrote scenes that seemed never to have been written before.

With all this, Hammett did not wreck the formal detective story. Nobody can; production demands a form that can be produced. Realism takes too much talent, too much knowledge, too much awareness. He may have loosened it up a little here, and sharpened it a little there. Certainly all but the stupidest and most meretricious writers are more conscious of their artificiality than they used to be. And he demonstrated that the detective story can be important writing. *The Maltese Falcon* may or may not be a work of genius, but an art which is capable of it is not "by hypothesis" incapable of anything. Once a detective story can be as good as this, only the pedants will deny that it *could* be even better.

Hammett did something else; he made the detective story fun to write, not an exhausting concatenation of insignificant clues. Without him there might not have been a regional mystery as clever as Percival Wilde's *Inquest*, or an ironic study as able as Raymond Postgate's *Verdict of Twelve*, or a savage piece of intellectual double-talk like Kenneth Fearing's *The Dagger of the Mind*, or a tragi-comic idealization of the murderer as in Donald Henderson's *Mr. Bowling Buys a Newspaper*, or even a gay Hollywoodian gambol like Richard Sale's *Lazarus #7*.

The realistic style is easy to abuse: from haste, from lack of awareness, from inability to bridge the chasm that lies between what a writer would like to be able to say and what he actually knows how to say. It is easy to fake; brutality is not strength, flipness is not wit, edge-of-the-chair writing can be as boring as flat writing; dalliance with promiscuous blondes can be very dull stuff when described by goaty young men with no other purpose in mind than to describe dalliance with promiscuous blondes. There has been so much of this sort of thing that if a character in a detective story says "Yeah," the author is automatically a Hammett imitator.

And there are still a number of people around who say that Hammett did not write detective stories at all—merely hard-boiled chronicles of mean streets with a perfunctory mystery element dropped in like the olive in a Martini. These are the flustered old ladies—of both sexes (or no sex) and almost all ages—who like their murders scented with magnolia blossoms and do not care to be reminded that murder is an act of infinite cruelty, even if the perpetrators sometimes look like playboys or college professors or nice motherly women with softly graying hair.

There are also a few champions of the formal or classic mystery who think that no story is a detective story which does not pose a formal and exact problem and arrange the clues around it with neat labels on them. Such would point out, for example, that in reading *The Maltese Falcon* no one concerns himself with who killed Spade's partner, Archer (which is the only formal problem of the story), because the reader is kept thinking about something else. Yet in *The Glass Key* the reader is constantly reminded that the question is who killed Taylor Henry, and exactly the same effect is obtained—an effect of movement, intrigue, cross-purposes, and the gradual elucidation of character, which is all the detective story has any right to be about anyway. The rest is spillikins in the parlor. [*Atlantic Monthly* December 1944: 57-59]

Dashiell Hammett's Private Eye:
No Loyalty Beyond the Job

David T. Bazelon

The figure of the rough and tough private detective—or the "private eye," as we have come to call him with our circulating library knowingness—is one of the key creations of American popular culture. He haunts the 10-cent thrillers on the newsstands, he looks out at us grimly from the moving-picture screen, his masterful gutter-voice echoes from a million radios: it is hard to remember when he was not with us. But he is only some twenty years old. His discoverer—his prophet—is Dashiell Hammett.

In the chief critical history of the detective story written by a fellow-believer—Howard Haycraft's *Murder for Pleasure* (1941)—Dashiell Hammett is placed centrally in "the American Renaissance of the late twenties and early thirties." Except for the fact that this "Renaissance" started a bit late and ended a bit soon, it coincides with a much larger cultural and social impulse that (except for the Depression and the consequent preparation for war) was the most significant feature of the inter-war period. Culturally, this impulse would include, defined in the most general way, the productions of Hemingway, Faulkner, Dos Passos, Farrell; the critical work of Edmund Wilson; the "brain trust" aspect of the New Deal; and the whole complex of expression connected with the diffusion of Marxist ideas and the growth of political consciousness.

But what began as a revolt of the individual sensibility against the whole ideological pattern allied with American participation in World War I (the great "debunking") ended in bureaucracy, Stalinism, proletarian literature, lots and lots of advertising-Hollywood-radio-popular-magazine jobs, and—another war.

The relation between Popular Frontism and popular culture is not accidental; the kind of mind that is able to construct commercial myths without believing in them is the same kind of mind that needs to construct one great myth in which it can believe, whether it is the myth of Abraham Lincoln-Franklin Roosevelt-Walt Whitman-John Henry, or the myth of the Socialist Fatherland, or some incongruous mixture of the two. And the tenacity with which the creator of popular culture holds to this myth—in the face of all the facts which precisely his "sophisticated" mind might be expected to understand—is the measure of the corruption that this one great "ideal" is supposed to cover. Nor is it accidental that these members of the "working class," when threatened with the loss of their fantastically lucrative jobs, should be able to speak in all sincerity of being threatened with starvation because of their political convictions. For what holds this uneasy psychic structure together for the living individual is that American Nirvana—the Well-Paying Job. In America, a good job is expected to be an adequate substitute for almost anything; in an industrial society, the job is the first and last necessity of life. And American society is not only more industrialized than any other, it also embodies fewer traditional elements that might contradict the industrial way of life.

The ascendancy of the job in the lives of Americans—just this is the chief concern of Dashiell Hammett's art. When tuberculosis forced him to return to writing, it was his job experience that he drew upon; and his knowledge of the life of detectives could fit easily into a literary form that had at least as much in common with a production plan as with art. As soon as he got a "better" job, he stopped writing. And, as we shall see, the Job determines the behavior of his fictional characters just as much as it has set the course of his own life.

The most important fact in Samuel Dashiell Hammett's biography is that he worked off and on for eight years as an operative for the Pinkerton detective agency. Hammett claims that he was pretty good as a detective. (He was involved in several "big" cases, including those of Nicky Arnstein and "Fatty" Arbuckle.) We may take him at his word, since detective work is the only job—including his writing—at which he ever persevered.

Hammett seems to have come from a farm—his place of birth is specified only as St. Mary's County, Maryland, and the date is May 25, 1894. But he received his slight education in Baltimore, leaving school—the Baltimore Polytechnic Institute—at the age of thirteen. His jobs, in more or less chronological order, were: newsboy, messenger boy, freight clerk, stevedore, railroad laborer, detective. During World War I, he served in Europe as a sergeant in the Ambulance Corps and contracted tuberculosis. He spent two years in hospitals; and his disease finally forced him to abandon his career as a private investigator. Until he began to write in 1922, he worked as advertising manager for a small store in San Francisco.

Apart from one tubercular hero and one dipsomaniac (both of whom are also investigators), Hammett's fictional characters are derived almost entirely from his own experience as a detective.

His first detective stories, built around the nameless figure of the "Continental Op," were published in pulp magazines—*Black Mask, Sunset,* and the like. Hammett was one of a group of detective-story writers who had begun producing violent, realistic material in opposition to the refined puzzles of such old hands as S. S. Van Dine. These postwar stories signified a sharp turn from the genteel English tradition toward the creation of a "lean, dynamic, unsentimental" American style (although, as George Orwell has demonstrated, the English too were solving imaginary crimes in new ways and in new settings). Hammett took the lead in this development.

He published five novels between 1929 and 1933. Together with the short stories written concurrently and earlier, these novels constitute almost the total body of his work. He has been phenomenally successful: his books are still being reprinted and most of his old stories have been dug up and republished. But he has written almost nothing in the last fifteen years. Since 1932 he has wanted to write a play, to begin with, and then go on to "straight" novels; he has said that he does not admire his detective stories. Hammett has been in Hollywood off and on since the early Thirties.

There is an obvious coincidence between the beginning of Hammett's sojourn in Hollywood and the de facto end of his literary effort. Moreover, his job in the West Coast magic factories (at a reported $1,500 a week) is not strictly a writing one; he is employed as a trouble-shooter, patching up scripts and expediting stories, often when the film is already before the cameras. Until 1938, Hammett seems to have been exclusively occupied with his joy-ride on the Hollywood gravytrain, but in that year—it was the height of the Popular Front period—he was seized by "political consciousness." Already forty-four, he had spent six of his best years in Hollywood instead of writing his play, and thus was more or less ready for religion.

Unlike many victims of the Popular Front, Hammett went on following the Communists—up hill and down dale: Popular Front—No Front—Second Front. We can only assume that his need is great. During the war, he was president of the League of American Writers and as such occupied himself lining up talent behind war activities in general and the second front in particular. He also joined the army. At present he serves as head of the New York branch of the Civil Rights Congress, a Stalinist "front" organization; most recently, his name turned up as a sponsor of the Cultural and Scientific Conference for World Peace, held in New York in March.

The core of Hammett's art is his version of the masculine figure in American society. The Continental Op constitutes the basic pattern for this figure, which in the body of Hammett's work undergoes a revealing development.

The older detectives of literature—exemplified most unequivocally by the figure of Sherlock Holmes—stood on a firm social and moral basis, and won their triumphs through the exercise of reason. Holmes, despite his eccentricities, is essentially an English gentleman acting to preserve a moral way of life. The question of his motives never arises, simply because it is answered in advance: he is one of the great army of good men fighting, each in his own way, against evil. Who needs a "motive" for doing his duty? (Holmes's love for his profession is never contaminated by any moral ambiguity: he is not fascinated by evil, but only by the intellectual problem of overcoming evil.) With Hammett, the moral and social base is gone; his detectives would only be amused, if not embarrassed, by any suggestion that they are "doing their duty"—they are merely *doing*.

The Op is primarily a job-holder: all the stories in which he appears begin with an assignment and end when he has completed it. To an extent, *competence* replaces moral stature as the criterion of an individual's worth. The only persons who gain any respect from the Op are those who behave competently—and all such, criminal or otherwise, are accorded some respect. This attitude is applied to women as well as men. In *The Dain Curse,* the Op is attracted deeply only to the woman who has capacity and realism—and he fears her for the same reason. So Woman enters the Hammett picture as desirable not merely for her beauty, but also for her ability to live independently, capably—unmarried, in other words.

But the moral question is not disposed of so easily. Hammett's masculine figures are continually running up against a certain basic situation in which their relation to evil must be defined. In *Red Harvest,* for instance, the detective doing his job is confronted with a condition of evil much bigger than himself. He cannot ignore it since his job is to deal with it. On the other hand, he cannot act morally in any full sense because his particular relation, as a paid agent, to crime and its attendant evils gives him no logical justification for overstepping the bounds of his "job." Through some clever prompting by the Continental Op, the gangsters—whose rule is the evil in *Red Harvest*—destroy each other in their own ways. But it becomes a very bloody business, as the title suggests. And the Op's lost alternative, of perhaps having resolved the situation—and performed his job—with less bloodshed, grows in poignancy. He begins to doubt his own motivation: perhaps the means by which a job is done matters as much as the actual accomplishment of the job.

One of the most suggestive aspects of this situation is that the Op's client hinders rather than aids him in resolving the evil. For the client is the capitalist who opened the city to the gangsters in the first place, to break a strike. (This ambiguous relation to the client is characteristic in that it further isolates the detectives; suspicion is imbedded like a muscle in Hammett's characters, and lying is the primary form of communication between them. In two of the novels, the murderer is an old friend of the detective.) If the Op were not simply *employed*—that is, if he were really concerned with combating evil—he would have to fight against his client directly, to get at the evil's source. As it is, he confines his attention to his "job," which he carries out with an almost bloodthirsty determination that proceeds from an unwillingness to go beyond it. This relation to the job is perhaps typically American.

What is wrong with the character of the Op—this American—is that he almost never wrestles with personal motives of his own. The private eye has no private life. He simply wants to do his job well. One might think he was in it for the money—but his salary is never made known, is apparently not large, and he isn't even *tempted* to steal. Each story contains at least one fabulously beautiful woman—but the Op goes marching on. If he is a philosopher of some peculiarly American *acte gratuit,* a connoisseur of crime and violence, we never know it, since we are never permitted to know his thoughts. So, while this character often holds a strong primitive fascination because he represents an attempt at a realistic image of a human being who succeeds (survives not too painfully) in an environment of modern anxiety, he is, ultimately, too disinterested—too little involved—to be real.

It is interesting, in view of the importance of job-doing to the detective, to remark the reasons for this lack of personal motivation. What the Op has as a substitute for motives is a more or less total projection of himself into the violent environment of crime and death. And by "projection" I mean that he surrenders his emotions to the world outside while dissociating them from his own purposeful, responsible self; he becomes a kind of sensation-seeker. So, despite all the *Sturm und Drang* of his life, it remains an essentially vicarious one, because the moral problem—the matter of individual responsibility or decision-making in a situation where society has defaulted morally—is never even faced, much less resolved. The question of doing or not doing a job competently seems to have replaced the whole larger question of good and evil. The Op catches criminals because it is his job to do so, not because they are criminals. At the same time, it is still important that his job is to catch criminals; just any job will not do: the Op has the same relation to the experience of his job, its violence and excitement, the catharsis it affords, as has the ordinary consumer of mass culture to the detective stories and movies he bolts down with such regularity and in such abundance. His satisfactions require a rejection of moral responsibility—but this in itself requires that he be involved in a situation charged with moral significance—which exists for him solely that it may be rejected.

Hammett must have felt the lacks in the Op, for the detective figures that follow—Sam Spade in *The Maltese Falcon*, Ned Beaumont in *The Glass Key,* and Nick Charles in *The Thin Man*—all represent attempts to give his character a more genuine human motivation. And this attempt to intensify the meaning of his detective was also, naturally, an effort on Hammett's own part to express himself more deeply.

"Spade had no original. He is a dream man in the sense that he is what most of the private detectives I worked with would like to have been and what quite a few of them in their cockier movements thought they approached. For your private detective does not—or did not ten years ago when he was my colleague—want to be an erudite solver of riddles in the Sherlock Holmes manner; he wants to be a hard and shifty fellow, able to take care of himself in any situation, able to get the best of anybody he comes in contact with, whether criminal, innocent bystander or client." This statement of Hammett's in his 1934 introduction to *The Maltese Falcon* could have applied equally to the Op, except that Spade is more fully realized.

Spade differs from the Op primarily in the fact that he has a more active sexual motive of his own. This sexual susceptibility serves to heighten, by contrast, his basic job-doing orientation. So when Spade, in conflict, chooses to do his job instead of indulging in romantic sex, he takes on more dramatic meaning than does the hero of the Op stories. That is, a new, definite motive has been admitted to the public world, and its relations to that world explored dramatically. But Spade *always* chooses to be faithful to his job—because this means being faithful to his own individuality, his masculine self. The point of the character is clear: to be manly is to love and distrust a woman at the same time. To one woman, Spade says, "You're so beautiful you make me sick!"

The very center of Spade's relation to women resides in a situation where the woman uses her sex, and the anachronistic mores attached to it, to fulfill a non-sexual purpose of her own, usually criminal. It is this situation in *The Maltese Falcon,* coming as the climax of Spade's relation to Brigid O'Shaughnessy, that is the supreme scene of all Hammett's fiction. Its essence is stated very simply by Spade as he answers Brigid's—the woman's eternal—"If you loved me you would . . ." "I don't care who loves who," he says. "I'm not going to play the sap for you."

In his great struggle with Brigid, Spade must either deny or destroy himself. Because of the great distance between his *self* (summed up in a masculine code grounded in a job) and *others* whom he loves and does things for (women or clients), Spade is seldom able to act "normally" in significant situations. His choice is usually between being masochistic or sadistic—unless he simply withdraws his inner sentient self from the objective situation. It is his job that so alienates him from life—and yet it is his job also that gives him his real contact with life, his focus. If his emotions released their hold on his job, he would find himself adrift, without pattern or purpose. On the other hand, the job is obviously a form of—not a substitute for—living. This dissociation of the form of one's life from the content of actual life-gratifications is symbolized excellently by the fact that the Maltese Falcon—around which so much life has been expended and disrupted—turns out to be merely a lead bird of no intrinsic interest or value.

Ned Beaumont of *The Glass Key* is Hammett's closest, most serious projection, and the author himself prefers *The Glass Key* to all his other books—probably because it was his chief attempt at a genuine novel.

Loyalty is the substitute for job in *The Glass Key*. And the factors of masculinity are a little more evenly distributed among the several characters than in Hammett's more purely detective-story writing. Beaumont is not a professional sleuth, although he occupies himself with getting to the bottom of a murder. Furthermore, the book ends not in the completing of a job but with the hero and heroine planning marriage. We never know whether Beaumont's motive in solving the murder is loyalty, job-doing, or love. However, because the motivation is more complex, though confused, it is superior to that in Hammett's other work.

Beaumont is Hammett's only *weak* hero. He gambles irrationally, gets nervous in a crisis, and seems to be tubercular. The issue of the masculine code is therefore presented in him more sharply and realistically. Unlike the Op, Beaumont is directly involved in evil since he is sidekick to a political racketeer.

His relation to the woman involved is ignored over long stretches of the novel, and when Beaumont ends up with Janet Henry we are surprised because unprepared emotionally—although the development is logical in the abstract. It makes sense as consequence rather than as conscious purpose. All in all, *The Glass Key* is an expressive but very ambiguous novel. And this ambiguity reflects, I think, Hammett's difficulty in consciously writing an unformularized novel—that is, one in which an analysis of motives is fundamental.

The ambiguity is also reflected in the style, which is almost completely behavioristic. "He put thoughtfulness on his face"—and one doesn't know whether he is thoughtful or not. We are given various minute descriptions of the hero's breathing process, the condition of his eyes, etc. Hammett employs the technique, I presume, as expertly as it can be. But it is a poor one to begin with, being too often a substitute for an analysis of consciousness—being, that is, the *distortion* of such an analysis. (There is only one story in which Hammett shows us the processes of thought in his characters—*Ruffian's Wife*—and it is an embarrassing failure.) But just as consciousness is a weakness for Hammett the man (his conscious mind has been dominated by mere formulas—Stalinism, the detective story, etc.), so analysis of consciousness would appear the same for Hammett the artist. And, of course, he is not wrong. Consciousness is either accepted as an essential, growing factor in the structure of one's life, or else it suffers continual distortion—not by accident, but inevitably.

Beaumont's friend, Paul Madvig, is also his boss and his superior in strength and manliness—almost, indeed, a homosexual love object. The factors that make Beaumont succeed where Madvig fails—in getting Janet Henry—are therefore extremely important: Beaumont has more awareness of the pretensions of higher society; he banks more on cunning than on pure power; he prefers silence to lying; he does not protect the girl's father-murderer but fights him. Beginning with more weakness than Madvig, with defects in his male armor, he is eventually a more successful male because of his capacity to approach the objects of his desire indirectly—to work upon their relations in the real world rather than remaining fixed on the intrinsic qualities that his desire attributes to them. This factor of cunning and restraint, of knowing when to talk and when to shut up, when to fight, when to run, appears, then, as the final fruit of Hammett's brief but not unrewarding engagement in literature. The private investigator's shrewdness emerges finally as more important—more reliable in a pinch—than his toughness (which in Ned Beaumont is reduced to the power to endure rather than the power to act aggressively).

Now such an indirect road to satisfaction must be supplemented by consciousness—by which I mean a comprehensive hypothesis as to the nature of real life, based on as accurate as possible an understanding of the environment—or else it is likely to become frustrating beyond endurance. We can assume this alliance between our deep desires and a carefully defined world *on paper,* intellectually; but can it be *lived*? Or, a less ambitious question, can it subserve the creation of an aesthetically unified novel?

In the case of Hammett, the answer apparently is no—not without great distortion. For Hammett, in *The Glass Key*, got only as far as the experience of the vital need of knowing (beyond the horizon of the job). He then collapsed—quite completely. Instead of following his literary problem where it was leading him, he preferred to follow his new-found Hollywoodism down whatever paths of pleasure it might take him. He postponed the attempt to resolve those problems with which life had presented him. But it was, it could be, only a postponement, and after a few years he came upon Stalinism—that fake consciousness, fake resolution, perfect apposite of Hollywoodism—and crossed the t's of his lost art.

Nick Charles, the hero of *The Thin Man,* spends more time drinking than solving crimes. If he does his job at all, it is only because Nora, his wife, eggs him on for the sake of her own excitement. Nick is as indulgent of his wife's whims as he is of the bottle's contents. Ned Beaumont's weakness, which was at least to some degree a product of moral consciousness, becomes in Nick Charles the weakness of mere self-indulgence, the weakness of deliberate *unconsciousness;* thus literal drunkenness becomes a symbol of that more fundamental drunkenness that submerges the individual in commercialized culture and formularized "progressive" politics. *The Thin Man* was very successful, as I have noted. It is a very amusing detective comedy. But whatever the book was publicly, to Hammett himself it must surely have been an avowal of defeat. He had to give up Ned Beaumont, because Ned Beaumont was almost a human being and *The Glass Key* was almost a novel. It is Nick Charles who survives best in the atmosphere in which Hammett has stifled his talent. [*Commentary* May 1949: 467-72]

The Thin Man

A. Alvarez

I had better admit straight away that I find most detective stories unreadable. I haven't the knack of skimming simply for clues and the plot. So for the sake of the crossword-puzzle interest of solving the things, it never seems worth while wading through all that terrible prose, the type-casting of the characters and the inane exchange of clichés that passes for dialogue in the average Agatha Christie. On the old issue of "Who Cares Who Killed Roger Ackroyd?" I'm on

Edmund Wilson's side. With one exception. Wilson also thought nothing of Dashiell Hammett—or nothing, at least, of *The Maltese Falcon*, which was the only one he claimed to have read. I suppose he was irritated by the way Hammett was taken up by the intellectuals during the thirties: Gide, Sinclair Lewis, Robert Graves—Hammett had powerful friends.

Yet reading his complete novels in a splendid new one-volume collected edition, thirty-five years after they first appeared, he seems to have deserved them. His books tell you more about the United States than many with more highminded intentions, like Upton Sinclair's. They also have that air of moral lobotomy that seems so to preoccupy us nowadays. Above all, with their elegant plots and stripped, clean writing, they have their own unwavering kind of perfection. Only one of them fails: *The Dain Curse*, which is wandering, melodramatic, a bit silly and, with its supernatural trimmings, not at all typical. Though it was published second, my guess is that it was an apprentice work, written earlier and rushed into print only after the success of *Red Harvest*.

This quirky perfection is appropriate, for Hammett was in all ways an odd phenomenon, stylishly original yet without a trace of the literary about him. Born in Maryland in 1894, he left school at fourteen and wandered through the usual grinding odd jobs—messenger boy, newsboy, clerk, timekeeper, yardman, machine operator, stevedore—finally landing up as a private eye for the famous Pinkerton's Detective Agency. He served as a sergeant in the First World War, but it ruined his health and for some time after he was in and out of hospitals. Though he never fully recovered, he went back to Pinkerton's until the vast success of his novels (four of them were made into films) gave him his freedom. The whole of his collected works was published in the space of five years: *Red Harvest* appeared in February 1929, *The Dain Curse* six months later; in February 1930 came *The Maltese Falcon*, *The Glass Key* in April 1931, and *The Thin Man* in January 1934. According to his friend Lillian Hellman, who has written a brief foreword to this collection, he started another novel but never finished it. For the last twenty-seven years of his life he published nothing. He was a sergeant again in the Second World War and did not die until 1961.

It is a curious history: a lifetime's literary output which did not begin until he was thirty-five years old and had already finished when he was forty; obscurity before it, silence after. It is almost as if he weren't interested in writing as such, only in making his fortune; and when that was done he retired, as though from a business. Yet that explanation clearly won't do when faced by the purity and concentration of his style. Nor will the classical Freudian line: the laconic, tough-guy hero—who was utterly Hammett's invention, however much he has since been copied—was a compensation for his own failing health. The books are neither that simple nor that self-satisfied, and have to do with a good deal more than toughness.

They also have little to do with conventional detective routine: crime, complication of the suspects and clues, and final neat solution by the omniscient, omnipotent sleuth. In Hammett's books the actual finding of the murderer is almost by the way. When Nick Charles does a particularly slick bit of summing-up at the end of *The Thin Man*, his wife gets the last word: "That may be," Nora said, "but it's all pretty unsatisfactory." Hammett seems to have felt that way too. As often as not he gets the straight who-done-itry out of the way early and then goes on to something else, or at least to further, casual who-done-its which add up to something else. The crime puzzle matters less than the mentality, the habit of crime. Even in *The Thin Man*, which is smarter, more deliberately sophisticated, and also more conventional than the rest (its hero, like Hammett himself, has already made his pile and given up sleuthing), the main interest is its view of New York just after the crash, with its nervy, slanderous-parties, sporadically violent speakeasies, disintegrating boozing and permanent hangovers. It might have been written by some sour-mouthed Scott Fitzgerald who was never for a moment taken in by the dizzy glamour of it all.

But his best novels, *Red Harvest* and *The Glass Key*, are not really detective stories at all. They are political; they are about what happens and how it feels when the gangsters take over. *Red Harvest*, for example, is set in an ugly Western mining town which is virtually owned by one man:

> For forty years old Elihu Willson . . . had owned Personville, heart, soul, skin and guts. He was president and majority stockholder of the Personville Mining Corporation, ditto of the First National Bank, owner of the *Morning Herald* and *Evening Herald*, the city's only newspapers, and at least part owner of nearly every other enterprise of any importance. Along with these pieces of property he owned a United States senator, a couple of representatives, the governor, the mayor, and most of the state legislature. Elihu Willson was Personville, and he was almost the whole state.

That ironic acceptance of how things are dictates Hammett's tone and pervades the whole story, however savage it becomes. Willson has had trouble from the Wobblies; to break their strikes he has imported gunmen. But the hoods have found the pickings too good to leave, and gradually they have slid out of his control. So Willson reluctantly allows a private eye in on the act. He, the narrator, is forty, overweight, thick with booze, and more or less without principles.

With a kind of blank cunning, like a good poker-player, he sets the gangs against each other. There are twenty murders before the place is finally tidied up. Only one is a normal "mystery," and that is cleared up early. The real interest is in the effect of all this carnage on the narrator:

> This damned burg's getting me. If I don't get away soon I'll be going blood-simple like the natives . . . I've arranged a killing or two in my time, when they were necessary. But this is the first time I ever got the fever . . . Look. I sat at Willson's table tonight and played them like you'd play trout, and got just as much fun out of it. I looked at Noonan and knew he hadn't a chance in a thousand of living another day because of what I had done to him, and I laughed,

and felt warm and happy inside. That's not me . . . After twenty years of messing around with crime I can look at any sort of murder without seeing anything in it but my bread and butter, the day's work. But this getting a rear out of planning deaths is not natural to me.

This has less in common with Agatha Christie than *The Revenger's Tragedy*. The killings are not a game or a puzzle or a joke. Instead, they are at one with the obsessional, illicit drinking, the drug-taking, the police beatings-up—all casual symptoms of prevailing corruption.

You have only to compare this with factual histories of prohibition and its legacy (see *Murder, Inc.*, 1951, by Burton B. Turkuis, Assistant D.A. of New York) to see that Hammett exaggerated nothing; indeed, he may even have toned down the realities. Yet his massacres are intriguing neither as social history nor because they cater so nicely to our sadistic fantasies—as do his imitators, in descending order from Raymond Chandler to Mickey Spillane. The fascination of Hammett's writing is that it makes the killing somehow different: accepted, habitual, part, as he says, of "the day's work." It has the ordinariness of real nihilism. And this makes him seem peculiarly close to us, though we now accept violence on a grander scale and expect our politicians not to be owned by gangsters but themselves to behave like gangsters.

God forbid I should foist any large moral significance on thrillers dealing mostly with American small-town politics. But Hammett has a genius, and part of it lies in his ability to make corruption seem normal without ever quite endorsing it. His heroes have all undergone that brutalizing which Lawrence called "the breaking of the heart"; and obscurely they know it. Hence the conventional barriers are down between the goodies and baddies. Those laconic, wise-cracking investigators may see all, know all, and handle themselves with startling confidence, but they are essentially no better, no worse, than the crooks they outwit. The narrator in *Red Harvest* becomes "blood-simple"; Ned Beaumont, in *The Glass Key*, is an underworld figure, henchman of a political boss; Sam Spade in *The Maltese Falcon* and Nick Charles in *The Thin Man,* in their controlled, cynical, alcoholic ways, both qualify as psychopaths. All are liars when it suits them, all are indifferent to murder, all are marginally corrupt. They win out only because they are more able, more canny and above all, more thorough-going with their contempt. Such toughness makes them seem impregnable, but it is also a burden. At moments, fatigue and distaste for themselves come over them like a sickness. It is as though the habitual violence pulled them psychically apart and they then had to reassemble themselves through booze and cunning and patience. You can sense Hammett's own illness through all that hardboiled glitter.

It is his steady refusal to expect anything beyond the immediate, and usually rather nasty, situation, or to presume on any values anywhere, that makes for the curious distinction of his style: the wit, the flair for essential details, the suppressed, pared-down, indifferent clarity. His achievement is to have evolved a prose in which the most grotesque or shocking details are handled as though they were matters of routine, part of the job. Hammett, too, was a writer of considerable deliberation and skill, but he made his taut style, like his ear for gangsterese, sound as though it were something he had come by in the grind of being a Pinkerton's agent. He seems less to have evolved his style than to have earned it.

Maybe this is what makes him so sympathetic. At the moment, the serious arts are faced with gloomy choices: either they are tense with despair at the confusion of all the values on which they were traditionally based, or they are anxiously and suicidally scrambling aboard the pop wagon. Dashiell Hammett, who had no cultural pretensions at all, provides a hardminded alternative: his books have artistic concentration without literariness, they achieve their purity from their absence of values. They are meticulous, witty, authentic and utterly nihilistic. It may not be high art, but it is a relief. [*Spectator* 11 February 1966: 169-170]

The Poetics of the Private Eye:
The Novels of Dashiell Hammett

Robert I. Edenbaum

[The daemonic agent] will act as if possessed. . . . He will act part way between the human and divine spheres, touching on both, which suggests that he can be used for the model romantic hero, since romance allows its heroes both human interest and divine power. His essentially energic character will delight the reader with an appearance of unadulterated power. Like a machiavellian prince, the allegorical hero can act free of the usual moral restraints, even when he is acting morally, since he is moral only in the interests of his power over other men. This sort of action has a crude fascination for us all; it impels us to read the detective story, the western, the saga of space exploration and interplanetary travel.
                                        —Angus Fletcher, *Allegory*

Raymond Chandler, Dashiell Hammett's major successor in the tradition of the tough detective novel, Howard Haycraft, a historian of the form, and David T. Bazelon, a far from sympathetic critic, all agree that Hammett shaped the archetype and stereotype of the private-eye. Hammett's third novel, *The Maltese Falcon*, heads any list of tough guy novels of the thirties. The pre-eminence and popularity of that novel is not only due to its date of publication at the very start of the new decade, nor to the fact that eleven years later John Huston turned it into "the best private-eye melodrama ever made," according to James Agee (*Agee on Film*). And it is not only the vagaries of camp taste that have made Humphrey Bogart's Sam Spade a folk-hero a third of a century later. Sam Spade of *The Maltese Falcon* (1930), together with the nameless Continental Op of the earlier novels, *Red Harvest* and *The Dain Curse* (both 1929), and to a lesser extent Ned Beaumont of *The Glass Key* (1931) and Nick Charles of *The Thin Man* (1934) constitute a poetics of the tough guy hero of novel, film, and television script from 1929 to the present.

The characteristics of Hammett's "daemonic" tough guy, with significant variations in the last two novels, can be schematized as follows: he is free of sentiment, of the fear of death, of the temptations of money and sex. He is what Albert Camus calls "a man without memory," free of the burden of the past. He is capable of any action, without regard to conventional morality, and thus is apparently as amoral—or immoral—as his antagonists. His refusal to submit to the trammels which limit ordinary mortals results in a godlike immunity and independence, beyond the power of his enemies. He himself has under his control the pure power that is needed to reach goals, to answer questions and solve mysteries, to reconstruct the (possible) motivations of the guilty and innocent alike. Hammett's novels—particularly the first three, with which this essay will be primarily concerned—represent a "critique" of the tough guy's freedom as well: the price he pays for his power is to be cut off behind his own self-imposed masks, in an isolation that no criminal, in a community of crime, has to face.

The Maltese Falcon is the most important of the novels in the development of the poetics of the private-eye because in it Hammett is less concerned with the intricacies of the detective story plot than with the combat between a villain(ess) who is a woman of sentiment, and who thrives on the sentiment of others, and a hero who has none and survives because he has none. As a result of that combat itself, the novel is concerned with the definition of the private-eye's "daemonic" virtue—with his invulnerability and his power—and with a critique of that definition.

The word "combat" has to be qualified immediately, for there can be unequal combat only when one antagonist holds all the cards and the other is always victim; when the one manipulates and the other is deceived; when the actions of the one are unpredictable and the responses of the other stock. These terms would seem to describe the villain and his victim in Gothic fiction from *The Mysteries of Udolpho* to *The Lime Twig*. But Hammett, in *The Maltese Falcon*, reverses the roles. Brigid O'Shaughnessy, the murderer of Sam Spade's partner Miles Archer, is the manipulated, the deceived, the unpredictable, finally, in a very real sense, the victim. Customarily in the detective story, the solution to the mystery—for example, the identity of the murderer—is known only to the murderer himself; terror makes everyone victim but the murderer, for only the murderer, the unpredictable element, can know what will happen next. In the first few pages of *The Maltese Falcon* Miles Archer is murdered, apparently by Floyd Thursby. Thursby is killed; that is apparently a mystery (though it takes no great imagination to settle on the young hood Wilmer as the likely culprit). The ostensible mystery, then, is why Thursby killed Archer, and why he in turn was killed. In the last pages of the novel, however, the reader (and Brigid O'Shaughnessy) discovers that he (and she) has been duped all along, for Spade has known from the moment he saw Archer's body that Brigid is the murderer. Spade himself, then, is the one person who holds the central piece of information; he is the one person who knows everything, for Brigid does not know that he knows. And though Spade is no murderer, Brigid O'Shaughnessy is his victim.

Once the reader knows, finally, that Spade has known all along that Miles Archer, with his pistol tucked inaccessibly under his arm, would not have gone up a dark alleyway with anyone but a girl as beautiful as Brigid, and therefore must have gone with *her*, he can make sense out of an apparently irrelevant anecdote that Spade tells Brigid early in the novel. The story, about a case Spade once worked on, concerns a man named Charles Flitcraft who had disappeared without apparent motive. The likely possibilities—as nearly always in Gothic fiction, sex and money—are eliminated beyond doubt. The mystery is cleared up when Spade finds the missing man. Flitcraft's life before his disappearance had been "a clean orderly sane responsible affair," Flitcraft himself "a man who was most comfortable in step with his surroundings." The day of his disappearance, on his way down a street, a beam had fallen from a building under construction and missed killing him by an inch. At that moment Flitcraft "felt like somebody had taken the lid off life and let him look at the works." He left his old life on the spot, for "he knew then that men died at haphazard like that, and lived only while blind chance spared them." Flitcraft spends several years living under that Dreiserian philosophy, working at a variety of jobs, until he meets another woman identical to his first wife except in face, marries her, has children identical to those by his first wife, leads a life identical to the one he had led before his black epiphany. Spade had returned to the first Mrs. Flitcraft to tell her what he had learned. Mrs. Flitcraft had not understood; Spade had no trouble understanding. Brigid O'Shaughnessy, despite her fascination with Spade's story almost against her will (she is trying to find out what he intends to do in her case) understands no more than Mrs. Flitcraft did.

Flitcraft moves from a life—and a commensurate philosophy—in which beams do not fall, to one in which beams do, back to one in which they don't. There can be no doubt which of the two Spade subscribes to: "Flitcraft *knew* then that men died at haphazard" (my emphasis). That commonplace enough naturalistic conception of the randomness of the universe is Spade's vision throughout. The contrast is of Spade's life (that of the private-eye) in which beams are expected to fall, and do fall, and that of the suburban businessman, in which they do not—or, at least, do not until they do. Since they did stop in the years between, Flitcraft merely adjusted himself back to a world where they did not. In Spade's world, of course, they never stop falling. If Brigid were acute enough—or less trammelled by conventional sentiment—she would see in the long, apparently pointless story that her appeals to Spade's sense of honor, his nobility, his integrity, and finally, his love, will not and cannot work. That essentially is what Spade is telling her through his parable. Brigid—totally unscrupulous, a murderess—should understand rather better than Mrs. Flitcraft, the bourgeois housewife. But she doesn't. She falls back on a set of conventions that she has discarded in her own life, but which she naively assumes still hold for others'. At the end of the novel, Brigid is not merely acting her shock at Spade's refusal to shield her; that shock is as genuine as Effie Perine's at Spade for that same refusal—and as sentimental. Paradoxically, in *The Maltese Falcon* the good guy is a "blonde satan" and the villain is as innocent as she pretends to be. For that matter Gutman, Cairo, even Wilmer, are appalled by Spade, and in their inability to cope with him are as innocent as Brigid.

This reading of the Flitcraft story accounts for Spade's over-riding tone of mockery with Brigid whenever she appeals to his gallantry and loyalty based on her trust and confidence in him. His response to her talk of trust is, "You don't have to trust me . . . as long as you can persuade me to trust you." But, as we have seen, that is impossible from the very start, and Spade's saying so is a cruel joke on an unsuspecting murderer. To Brigid, Spade is "the wildest person I've ever known," "altogether unpredictable." Had she understood the Flitcraft story, she would have known that he is not unpredictable at all, but simply living by Flitcraft's vision of meaninglessness and the hard knowingness that follows from that vision. Spade is in step with his surroundings as much as Flitcraft is in step with his. Except for a brief (but important) moment at the end when he is nonplussed by Effie, Spade is never surprised by anyone's actions as Brigid is continually surprised by his. Spade several times picks up mockingly on Brigid's words "wild and unpredictable." She asks at another point what he would do if she were to tell him nothing about the history of the falcon and the quest for it; he answers that he would have no trouble knowing "what to do next." Sam Spade (cf. Humphrey Bogart) never has to hesitate about what to do next. Brigid, of course, has no idea what he will do. When a thousand dollar bill disappears from the envelope holding Gutman's "payment" to Spade, the detective takes Brigid into the bathroom and forces her to undress so that he can make sure she does not have it hidden on her person. Brigid, incredulous, responds with the appropriate clichés: "You'll be killing something." "You shouldn't have done that to me, Sam . . ." But Spade will not be stopped by "maidenly modesty," for he knows that Gutman is testing him to see what he will do. The fat man finds out; Brigid still does not, and learns only when it is too late.

The rejection of the fear of death, perhaps the most obvious characteristic of the tough guy in general, is but another aspect of the rejection of sentiment.

Spade fully expects those falling beams, and thus detective work is as much a metaphor for existence as war is in *The Red Badge of Courage* or *A Farewell to Arms*. In an exchange with the driver of a rented car on its way to one unknown destination in the unending series that is the fictional detective's life, the driver comments on Miles Archer's death and on the detective business.

> "She's a tough racket. You can have it for mine."
> "Well [Spade answers], hack-rivers don't live forever."
> "Maybe that's right . . . but just the same, it'll always be a surprise to me if I don't."

The driver is a working class Flitcraft; Spade, on the other hand, is heading towards another potential falling beam—though, in fact, the trip turns out to be a wild-goose chase planned by Gutman. And the final sentence of the dialogue—"Spade stared ahead at nothing . . ."—bears a double force.

Hammett's reversal of the trap of naturalism gives his heroes a kind of absolute power over their own destiny, a daemonic power, in Angus Fletcher's useful phrase. To stare into nothing and know it; to be as dispassionate about death as about using others—Wilmer, Cairo, *or* Brigid—as fall-guy: all this means that Spade can rob a Gutman of his ultimate weapon, the threat of death. When Gutman threatens Spade, the detective can argue that the fat man needs him alive; Gutman returns that there are other ways to get information; Spade, in his turn, insists that there is no terror without the threat of death, that he can play Gutman so that the fat man will not kill him, but that if need be he can *force* Gutman to kill him. Who but the tough guy can *make* the beam fall? In that lies the tough guy's power to set his own terms in life and death, a power that is the basis of his popularity in detective and other fiction.

To a generation of readers suckled on the violence of Mickey Spillane and Ian Fleming, it will hardly come as a shock to learn that detectives are as unscrupulous and amoral as "the enemy," as Spade calls them. In this book, though, Hammett seems to be consciously defining the nature of that unscrupulousness through Spade's relationship with Brigid, a relationship which itself becomes the major subject of *The Maltese Falcon* and itself exemplifies the terms of the detective's existence in the novel and in the fiction that ultimately derives from it. The dialogue between Sam Spade and Brigid does much of the work of developing that definition. For example, at one point Brigid says that she is afraid of two men: Joel Cairo and Spade himself. Spade answers, with his total awareness of what she means and what she is, "I can understand your being afraid of Cairo . . . He's out of your reach" (that is, because he is homosexual). And she: "And you aren't?" And he: "Not that way." Under the terms I am suggesting, this exchange must be read as follows: she says she is afraid of him; he says that that's not true because he's not out of her reach; he's right, she's not afraid of him; she should be because he *is* out of her reach. If she thinks him unscrupulous it is because she thinks he is after her and/or her money. She "seduces" him, thinking it will make a difference, but it doesn't. As soon as he climbs out of bed in the morning he steals her key to ransack her apartment, to find further evidence of her lies, though once again the reader doesn't know what he finds until the very end. The fact that Spade does not "cash many checks for strangers," as his lawyer puts it, is the key to his survival, and it leaves him outside the pale of tenderness.

One further key to Hammett's demolition of sentiment is the all but passionless figure of Sam Spade and one further indication of the price immunity exacts is Effie Perine, the archetypal tough guy's archetypal secretary. Spade pays Effie the highest compliment of all in the classic line, "You're a damned good man, sister," but unlike many of her later peers Effie is not tough. In the course of the novel Spade baits Effie again and again by asking what her "woman's intuition" tells her about Brigid O'Shaughnessy; Effie is "for her"; "that girl is all right." The point is not simply that Effie is wrong. Even at the end, knowing that she has been wrong all along, that Brigid has murdered one of her bosses, she responds as a woman, with a woman's (from Hammett's point of view?) sentimental notions, with appalled distaste for *Spade*. The last word in the novel is Effie's. She has learned of Brigid's arrest through the newspapers; Spade returns to his office.

> Spade raised his head, grinned, and said mockingly: "So much for your woman's intuition."
>
> Her voice was as queer as the expression on her face. "You did that, Sam, to her?"
>
> He nodded. "Your Sam's a detective." He looked sharply at her. He put his arm around her waist, his hand on her hip. "She did kill Miles, angel," he said gently, "offhand, like that." He snapped the fingers of his other hand.
>
> She escaped from his arm, as if it had hurt her. "Don't, please, don't touch me," she said brokenly. "I know—I know you're right. You're right. But don't touch me now—not now."

Effie's response amounts to a definition of sentiment: the impulse that tells you to pretend that what you know to be true is not true, to wish that what you know has to be, did not have to be. In the vein of the romanticism of action that becomes doing what everything sensible tells you you cannot do. You're right, you're right, but couldn't you better have been wrong? As Hammett has made sufficiently clear in the course of the book, and particularly in the final confrontation with Brigid, exactly the point about Spade—and about the tough guy in general—is that he could not have.

The confrontation of Spade and Brigid rather than the doings of Gutman, Cairo, and Wilmer, who are disposed of perfunctorily offstage, is the climax of the novel. Spade makes Brigid confess to him what, as we have seen, he has known all along—that she is Miles Archer's murderer; then he tells her, to her horror, that he is going to "send her over." His theme throughout this sequence is, "I won't play the sap for you." Though he says, "You'll never understand me" (anymore than Mrs. Flitcraft understood her husband), he goes on, in an astonishing catalogue, to tote up the balance sheet on the alternatives available to him. He ticks off the items on one side: "when a man's partner is killed he's supposed to do something about it"; "when one of your organization gets killed it's bad business to let the killer get away with it"; a detective cannot let a criminal go anymore than a dog can let a rabbit go; if he lets her go, he goes to the gallows with Gutman, Cairo, and Wilmer; she would have something on him and would eventually use it; he would have something on her and eventually she couldn't stand it; she might be playing him for a sucker; he could go on "but that is enough." On the other side of the ledger is merely "the fact that maybe you love me and maybe I love you."

The tabulation of pros and cons suggests that Spade is a bookkeeper calculating the odds for getting away with breaking the law. But that is inaccurate, for his final statement demolishes his own statistics and suggests that something else is at stake: "If that [all he has been saying] doesn't mean anything to you forget it and make it this: I won't because all of me wants to say to hell with the consequences and do it—and because—God damn you—you've counted on that with me the same as you counted on that with the others." The rejection of sentiment as motivating force, i.e., of sentimentality, is at the heart of the characterization of Sam Spade and of the tough guy in general. It is not that Spade is incapable of human emotions—love, for example—but that apparently those emotions require the denial of what Spade knows to be true about women and about life. The sentiment Spade rejects is embodied in all three women in *The Maltese Falcon*—Brigid, Iva Archer, and Effie: murderer, bitch, and nice girl, respectively. It is in this theme itself, paradoxically, that *The Maltese Falcon* has been weakened by the passage of time. As one reads the novel now, Spade himself still retains his force; he is still a believable, even an attractive (if frightening) character. Brigid, on the contrary, is not. (Just so, Hemingway's assertion of Jake Barnes' stoical mask in *The Sun Also Rises* still works, but the attack on Robert Cohn's romanticism seems to be beating a dead horse.) And yet it is the pitting of Brigid's sentimental platitudes against Spade's mocking wisecracks that may make this book the classic it is. This theme, too, signals a reversal in the naturalistic novel, for the tough guy in the tradition of Sam Spade can no longer be the victim of sentiment (cf., for example, Dreiser's Hurstwood or Clyde Griffith, or a Hemingway character defeated by the death of the woman he loves). On the contrary, he hedges himself so thoroughly against betrayal that he lives in total isolation and loneliness. Spade is last seen shivering (temporarily) in revulsion as Effie Perine sends the moral slug Iva in to him. The attractions of Brigid given up to the law, the possibilities of Effie lost, Spade is left with only Iva—or an unending string of Iva's successors.

The Hammett detective most pure, most daemonic, is the Continental Op of the first two novels, his purity indicated even in his namelessness. The Op, perhaps more than Spade, is free of sentiment, of the fear of death, of a past, of the temptations of sex and money. Like Spade he is capable of anything that his opponents are in the pursuit of his goals; in *Red Harvest* he goes further than Spade ever does in his responsibility for setting criminals against one another murderously. The Op in *Red Harvest* is much like Mark Twain's mysterious stranger that corrupts Hadleyburg: the stranger drops the bag of "gold" in the laps of the townsmen and watches them scramble; and so the Op in Personville (pronounced Poisonville). Both manipulate matters with absolute assurance and absolute impunity (cf. Spade as well). In *Red Harvest* twenty-five people are killed, not counting an additional unspecified number of slaughtered hoodlums, yet the only mishaps to befall the Op are to have a hand creased by a bullet and an arm stunned by the blow of a chair-leg. His powers come to seem almost supernatural, his knowledge of the forces that move men (sex and money) clairvoyance. His single-minded mission is to clean up the corruption no matter what the cost in other men's lives. The Op's own explanation of his motives—like those voiced to Gutman by Spade, a kind of personal grudge against those who have tried to get him—is not particularly convincing. It is tempting to say that the Op's apparently personal response to being picked on is the equivalent of the response of Hemingway's characters when they are picked off, but Hemingway's characters do have identifiable human emotions, whether disgust, or relief from disgust, or love; Hammett's, because of the purely external mechanistic method, do not. The superhuman is so by virtue of being all but nonhuman.

Red Harvest offers a perfect role for the Hammett private-eye. Elihu Willsson, aristocratic banker-boss of Poisonville, gives the Continental Detective Agency in the person of the Op ten thousand dollars to clean up the town because Willsson thinks the local gangsters responsible for the murder of his son. After the Op discovers that the crime was one of passion (if passion bought and sold) unrelated to the bootlegging-gambling-political corruption of the town, Willsson tries to dismiss the Op, who refuses to be dismissed, "Your fat chief of police tried to assassinate me last night. I don't like that. I'm just mean enough to want to ruin him for it. Now I'm going to have my fun. I've got ten thousand dollars of your money to play with. I'm going to use it opening Poisonville up from Adam's apple to ankles." Ten thousand dollars of *your* money to play with—there is the role of invulnerable power with the most possibilities open. The Op almost seems to forget he has the money; aside from his day-to-day expenses, all he uses of it is $200.10 that he reluctantly pays Dinah Brand for information. Hammett seems to want to establish the financial freedom of his character: with ten thousand dollars in hand how can the Op be suborned? Once that immunity is established it does not matter how (or whether) the money is spent.

The Op's immunity from temptation indicates something of the allegorical nature of these novels. Rather than being amoral, they establish moral oppositions of the simplest kind: if the proletarian novel is a version of pastoral, in William Empson's witty formulation, the tough detective novel is a version of morality, with allegorical combat between the forces of good and evil, and the most obvious of object lessons. Don't be a sucker for sex (read "love"): better Spade with Iva than Spade with Brigid. Don't be a sucker for money: it leaves you wide open for the crooks and the cops. Myrtle Jennison (a minor character in *Red Harvest*) was once as beautiful as Dinah Brand: now she's bloated with Bright's Disease (and Dinah herself dies of an ice-pick wound). Twenty-five men, slaughtered, were once alive (*Red Harvest*). And so on.

The morality of Hammett's detectives is basically defensive, as it must be in the Gothic world posited. As I indicated earlier, in the traditional Gothic novel (and as well in the naturalistic novel in this century) corruption and evil stem from two sources of power, two kinds of end—money and sex. Innocence (virginity in the older Gothic) is eternally threatened, usually for money; sex is used to gain money, and is in turn corrupted by money. Sexual and financial power are at most equatable, at least inextricable, for it is money which makes sex purchasable and sex which makes money attainable. The Op functions as a monkish ascetic who in order to survive must stay clear of money and sex, the only real temptations. Presumably he could walk off with Elihu Willsson's ten thousand, but of course he is no more tempted to abscond than he is to seduce Dinah Brand (he is just about the only male in the novel who doesn't). He unfixes a prizefight, lets Dinah win a pile of money, but does not himself bet. When Dinah, puzzled, questions him, he claims he was not sure his plan would work; but there is no evidence that that is anything but bluff. Dinah no more understands the Op's immunity to cash than Brigid understands Spade's to love. For Dinah, trying to get money out of the Op in exchange for the information she has on the inner workings of Poisonville, "It's not so much the money. It's the principle of the thing." The Op, refusing, parodies her with her own words: "It's not the money . . . It's the principle of the thing." Everything about Dinah, particularly her body, can be bought; nothing about the Op can be, by money or sex or sentiment. In self-defense he must be untouchable; otherwise his invulnerability would be compromised.

Like Spade, the Op in his immunity from temptation becomes god-like, perhaps inseparable from a devil, his concern not a divine plan but a satanic disorder. "Plans are all right sometimes . . . And sometimes just stirring things up is all right—if you're tough enough to survive and keep your eyes open so you'll see what you want when it comes to the top." The Op's way of unravelling the mess in Poisonville is to "experiment," in his word, to see if he can pit one set of crooks against another, when he unfixes the prizefight, for example. The result, in that case and always, is more murder and further chaos impending. Dinah Brand's irony—"So that's the way you scientific detectives work"—is Hammett's as well. The Op's metaphor makes him the same kind of godlike manipulator the naturalist novelist himself becomes in *his* experiments with the forces that move human beings to destruction. The stranger in "The Man That Corrupted Hadleyburg" may drop the bag of money in the town, but it is Mark Twain who drops the stranger there; and Hammett the Op in

Poisonville. The bitter enjoyment may be Hammett's and Mark Twain's as well as their characters'.

Ultimately the Op does discover that he is paying the price for his power—his fear that he is going "blood simple like the natives." "Play with murder enough and it gets you one of two ways. It makes you sick or you get to like it," he says as he tabulates the sixteen murders to that moment. The blood gets to the Op in both ways. He finds that he cannot keep his imagination from running along murderous lines on the most common of objects; he carries an ice-pick into Dinah's living room, and Dinah asks why.

> "To show you how my mind's running. A couple of days ago, if I thought about it at all, it was as a good tool to pry off chunks of ice." I ran a finger down its half-foot of round steel blade to the needle point. "Not a bad thing to pin a man to his clothes with. That's the way I'm betting, on the level. I can't even see a mechanical cigar lighter without thinking of filling one with nitroglycerine for somebody you don't like. There's a piece of copper wire lying in the gutter in front of your house—thin, soft, and just enough to go around a neck with two ends to hold on. I had one hell of a time to keep from picking it up and stuffing it in my pocket, just in case—"
> "You're crazy," [Dinah says].
> "I know it. That's what I've been telling you. I'm going blood-simple."

Out of his head on the gin and laudanum which he takes to relieve his own morbidity, the Op wakes the next morning to find his hand around the ice-pick buried in Dinah's breast. It is not surprising that not only the authorities but one of the other operatives sent down from San Francisco and the Op himself think he may be Dinah's murderer. If the Op, like all men, is capable of all things, then he is capable of unmotivated murder. If the calculatedly nonhuman yields to human emotion and human weakness, defenses are down; loss of control and near destruction follow. The point would seem to be, don't let your defenses down. No one, including the detective, is exempt from the possibility of crime. Thus, in *The Dain Curse* and *The Thin Man* the murderer turns out to be an old friend of the detective; in *The Maltese Falcon* it is the girl the detective loves (or may love); in *The Glass Key* a father (and U. S. Senator) murders his own son; and in *Red Harvest* there is no one who might not be a killer—and most of them are, given those twenty-five some odd murders.

In *The Rebel* (Vintage Books) Albert Camus offers a brilliant analysis of the implications of the fear of emotion in the tough guy novel. The concomitants of the rejection of sentiment is the rejection of psychology itself and of everything that comprises the inner life in favor of the hedges themselves.

> The American novel [the tough novel of the thirties and forties, Camus explains in a note] claims to find its unity in reducing man either to elementals or to his external reactions and to his behavior. It does not choose feelings or passions to give a detailed description of . . . It rejects analysis and the search for a

fundamental psychological motive that could explain and recapitulate the behavior of a character . . . Its technique consists in describing men by their outside appearances, in their most casual actions, of reproducing, without comment, everything they say down to their repetitions, and finally by acting as if men were entirely defined by their daily automatisms. On this mechanical level men, in fact, seem exactly alike, which explains this peculiar universe in which all the characters appear interchangeable, even down to their physical peculiarities. This technique is called realistic only owing to a misapprehension . . . it is perfectly obvious that this fictitious world is not attempting a reproduction, pure and simple, of reality, but the most arbitrary form of stylization. It is born of a mutilation, and of a voluntary mutilation, performed on reality. The unity thus obtained is a degraded unity, a leveling off of human beings and of the world. It would seem that for these writers it is the inner life that deprives human actions of unity and that tears people away from one another. This is a partially legitimate suspicion . . . [but] the life of the body, reduced to its essentials, paradoxically produces an abstract and gratuitous universe, continuously denied, in its turn, by reality. This type of novel, purged of interior life, in which men seem to be observed behind a pane of glass, logically ends, with its emphasis on the pathological, by giving itself as its unique subject the supposedly average man. In this way it is possible to explain the extraordinary number of "innocents" who appear in this universe. The simpleton is the ideal subject for such an enterprise since he can only be defined—and completely defined—by his behavior. He is the symbol of the despairing world in which wretched automatons live in a machine-ridden universe, which American novelists have presented as a heart-rending but sterile protest (pp. 265-66).

Camus' analysis isolates both the success and the sadness of the tough novel. The success is that of the serious novel in general in that the correlation between the "voluntary mutilation" performed on reality by the author and that of the characters is complete; technique is subject matter in Hammett as much as in Joyce (though the analogy ends there). The excision of mind and emotion in tough dialogue, the understatement, the wise-guy joke-cracking cynicism—all the characteristics of Hammett's particular stylization—are matter as much as method. The sadness lies in the thinness of the world that remains and in the terror that is the common denominator of all men, who must fear all other men and themselves, and whose primary occupation would seem to be the development and maintenance of a reflexive self-defense. Finally, the detective's motives are as hidden as the murderer's and as indeterminable. The inner world is so thoroughly left to shift for itself (if it exists at all) that there is some question as to whether Hammett's characters are more than Camus' "wretched automatons"—with credits to Hollywood for the terrorless charms of Bogart, Greenstreet, *et al.*

The Dain Curse is one of the more interesting of Hammett's novels, in part because it is concerned with the implications and consequences of the mechanistic method and the mechanical world, with the difficulty of discovering, not only the motives of the actors, but the actual events that took place. As a result *The Dain Curse* is by far the most complicated of the novels. It consists of three

separate plots concerning the events surrounding the drug-addict Gabrielle
Leggett, events which eventually include the deaths of her father, mother, step-
mother, husband, doctor, and religious "counselor," among others. In the first
sequence, an apparently trivial theft of a batch of inexpensive diamonds leads
to several murders and to incredible disclosures about the history of Edgar
Leggett and his two wives, the Dain sisters Alice and Lily, a history that
includes, for example, Alice's training of the three-year-old Gabrielle to kill
Lily. In the second sequence, her father and aunt/step-mother dead, Gabrielle,
a virtual prisoner in the quack Temple of the Holy Grail, is involved in another
round of deaths, and the Op does battle with a man who thinks he is God and
with a spirit that has weight but no solidity. In the third, after still more murders
and maimings—a total of nine, plus three before the time of the novel—the Op
discovers that there was, as he had suspected, a single mind behind the many
criminal hands at work in all three apparently unrelated sequences of events.
The man the Op has known for several years as Owen Fitzstephan is actually a
Dain, a mastermind whose prime motive is—love for Gabrielle.

After the second part, the Op gives the still-unsuspected Fitzstephan his
reconstruction of the events at the Temple of the Holy Grail, then adds,

> "I hope you're not trying to keep this nonsense straight in your mind. You know
> damned well all this didn't happen."
> "Then what did happen?" [Fitzstephan asks]
> "I don't know. I don't think anybody knows. I'm telling what I saw plus the part
> of what Aaronia Haldorn [the woman who runs the Temple, and, it is later
> disclosed, Fitzstephan's mistress and tool] told me which fits in with what I saw.
> To fit in with what I saw, most of it must have happened very nearly as I've told
> you. If you want to believe that it did, all right. I don't. I'd rather believe I saw
> things that weren't there."

And again the Op asks, "You actually believe what I've told you so far?"
Fitzstephan says that he does, and the Op answers, "What a childish mind
you've got," and starts to tell the story of Little Red Riding-Hood. In these
novels there is no question of the complexity of, say, the relativity of guilt, for
there is no ambiguity in human actions. As I have suggested, the allegory is
fairly simple. The complexity is in the mystery of motive which results in the
thorough-going ignorance that even the detective must admit to. What, finally,
does move any human being—here, a criminal—to act? Put together a gaggle
of the criminal and semi-criminal, the tempted and the merely self-interested,
and it may be nearly as difficult to find out what happened as why. Similarly in
The Thin Man Nora Charles is thoroughly dissatisfied with Nick's "theories" and
"probablys" and "maybes" in his reconstruction of the events surrounding the
death of Clyde Wynant. To the Op "details don't make much difference,"
details, that is, such as whether Joseph Haldorn really came to think himself
God or merely thought he could fool everyone into thinking he was God. All

that matters is that Joseph "saw no limit to his power." The same impossibility of determining truth recurs at the end of the novel: is Fitzstephan a sane man pretending to be a lunatic or a lunatic pretending to be sane? It's not clear whether the Op himself thinks Fitzstephan sane. That again is a detail that doesn't make much difference, especially since people are capable of anything. Fitzstephan, like Haldorn, saw no limit to his power. The exact terrors of the curse are irrelevant; he is lost in any case.

In *The Dain Curse* Hammett once again explores the detective's mask by means of a woman's probing, but the Op's motives are no more susceptible to analysis than the criminals'. Gabrielle wants to know why the Op goes to the trouble of convincing her that she is not degenerate or insane, cursed by the blood of the Dains in her veins. She asks the questions the reader might ask: "Do I believe in you because you're sincere? Or because you've learned how—as a trick of your business—to make people believe in you?" The Op's response—"She might have been crazy, but she wasn't so stupid. I gave her the answer that seemed best at the time . . ."—doesn't answer the question for the reader any more than it does for the girl. Is it only a trick of his business or does he have a heart of gold beneath his tough exterior? Gabrielle is asking unanswerable questions, finally, because the removal of one mask only reveals another beneath. That may amount to saying that the toughness is not a mask at all, but the reality.

In their next encounter Gabrielle asks specifically why the Op went through the ugliness of supervising her withdrawal from drugs. He answers, with exaggerated tough guy surliness, "I'm twice your age, sister; an old man. I'm damned if I'll make a chump of myself by telling you why I did it, why it was neither revolting nor disgusting, why I'd do it again and be glad of the chance." By refusing to expose himself he is suggesting that he is exposing himself. Certainly his words suggest love for the girl, but he's hardly to be believed. He pretends to be hiding his sentiments under his tough manner, but it is more likely that he is pretending to pretend. Gabrielle has been the object of the "love" of a whole series of men: of the insane passion of Owen Fitzstephan and the only less insane of Joseph Haldorn, the High Priest and God of the Cult of the Holy Grail; of the petty lechery of her lawyer, Madison Andrews; and of the fumbling, well-meant love of Eric Collinson, who gets himself (and nearly Gabrielle) killed as a result. This view of love as destructive force, as we have seen, is an essential part of the occasion for the tough role. The Op, like Spade, has to think himself well out of it, though the reader does not have to agree.

In the last of this series of interviews in which Gabrielle, acting as the reader's friend, tries to comprehend the Op's tough guy role, the girl accuses the detective of pretending to be in love with her during the previous talk.

> "I honestly believed in you all afternoon—and it *did* help me. I believed you
> until you came in just now, and then I saw—" She stopped.
> "Saw what?"

"A monster. A nice one, an especially nice one to have around when you're in trouble, but a monster just the same, without any human foolishness like love in him, and—What's the matter? Have I said something I shouldn't?"

"I don't think you should have," I said. "I'm not sure I wouldn't trade places with Fitzstephan now—if that big eyed woman with the voice [Aaronia Haldorn] was part of the bargain."

"Oh, dear!" she said.

It's tempting to take the Op at his word here, at least, and believe that he has been hurt by Gabrielle's unwittingly cruel words. But the pattern I have been developing makes it difficult to accept the Op's sensitivity about his toughness. It is more reasonable to assume that he is telling her, once again, what she wants to hear, suggesting that she is in some way unique in his life. If no sentiment whatever is involved in his actions, he is the monster she calls him. And, in fact, that is the case with the Op as with Sam Spade. Seen as figures in stylized romance, both men may be seen as daemons; as characters in realistic fiction they are monsters both.

The Glass Key is Hammett's least satisfactory novel, perhaps precisely because it is not allegorical Gothic Romance, lacking as it does a godlike Spade or Op. It may be the case, as David T. Bazelon writing in *Commentary* suggests, that Hammett was trying to write a book closer to a conventional novel, one in which characters are moved to action for human reasons such as loyalty and love. But Hammett's mechanistic method is unchanged and, as a result, it is still impossible to tell what is under Ned Beaumont's mask. Does Ned take the punishment he does out of loyalty to the political boss Paul Madvig, because Madvig picked him out of the gutter fifteen months earlier? Perhaps the reader's sense of propriety or decency fills in that answer, but there is no evidence that it is accurate. It can be argued, on the contrary, that Ned takes the vicious beatings, not out of loyalty but out of indifference to death (to falling beams, if you will). He "can stand anything [he's] got to stand," a gangster's sadism no more and no less than his (apparent) tuberculosis or a purely fortuitous traffic accident in a New York taxi. But "standing" punishment stoically (or suicidally) is not loyalty, not a basis for positive action; and without some clarification of motive, the sense of Ned's activities is merely muddle.

In a sequence that goes on for four brutal pages Ned tries repeatedly to escape his enemies despite being beaten after each attempt. But nothing stops him; as soon as he regains consciousness, he goes to work on the door again. It is tempting, once again, to take this behavior (which includes setting fire to the room) as motivated by loyalty, by Ned's overwhelming desire to warn Paul. But nothing of the sort is possible, for Hammett's descriptions of Ned's actions make it clear that most of his behavior—both his attempts to escape and to kill himself—are instinctual. He remembers nothing beyond his first beating, we are told. Action is determined mechanistically—or animalistically.

Ned's motives are essential to make sense of the climax of the novel when

Ned allows Janet Henry, Paul's ostensible fiancée, to go off with him. His response to her "Take me with you" is hardly romantic: "Do you really want to go or are you just being hysterical? . . . It doesn't make any difference. I'll take you if you want to go." Yet there are indications earlier that Hammett wants to suggest the development of some kind of love between the two, growing out of their original mutual dislike, a love about which Paul Madvig has no doubt. The men have a falling out when Paul accuses Ned of lying to him because of Ned's own interest in Janet; at the end of the novel, Paul is confronted with the couple going off together. The question remains whether Paul was right in the first place, whether Ned acted out of desire for the girl rather than loyalty to Paul, or for neither reason. But there is no basis for judgment, by Janet *or* the reader. Motives are once again indeterminable, but in this book it is necessary that they be determined. The result is not the richness of fruitful ambiguity but the fuzziness of inner contradiction.

The title of this novel, from a dream recounted to Ned Beaumont by Janet Henry, suggests once again the fear of unhedged emotion and thus of all human relationships despite the matching of Ned and Janet with which it ends. In the dream Janet and Ned are starving and come upon a locked house within which they can see food—and a tangle of snakes. To open the door there is a glass key; to get access to the food is to release the snakes. The fragile key breaks as the door opens, and the snakes attack: apparently to get at the heart's need is to open a Pandora's box. Given the tawdriness of the "love" relations in *The Glass Key*—Taylor Henry's unscrupulous use of Opal Madvig's love, Janet Henry's of Paul's—there is not much chance that Ned and Janet will escape the snakes ("I'll take you if you want to go"). Once again in these novels it would seem that the only safety is in not letting down your guard in the first place: do without the food and you escape the snakes.

It is perhaps significant that Ned Beaumont is not actually a detective, though he functions as one in trying to clear up the mystery of the murder of Taylor Henry. However, there is a professional detective in the novel, Jack Rumsen, who is interesting for his unHammett-like behavior; it is not Sam Spade or the Op who would say to a man trying to solve a crime, "Fred and I are building up a nice little private-detective business here . . . A couple of years more and we'll be sitting pretty. I like you, Beaumont, but not enough to monkey with the man who runs the city." That modification of the private-eye character in the direction of the cynicism and timidity of self-interest prepares the way for Hammett's last novel, *The Thin Man*, published three years later. Nick Charles is the least daemonic of Hammett's heroes, but then he's only an ex-detective. However indifferent he may have been to death in the past, now he wants to be left out of danger, to be able to enjoy his wife, her wealth, and his whiskey. Nick Charles and his boozing is what happens to the Op/Spade when he gives up his role as ascetic demi-god to become husband, man of leisure, investor in futures on the stock market.

The Thin Man is perhaps less concerned with murder and the private-eye than with the people around the murder—with a wide range of social types spiritually sibling to the Alfred G. Packer of the long entry Gilbert Wynant reads in *Celebrated Criminal Cases of America*. The man-eaters Mimi, Dorothy, and Gilbert Wynant; Christian Jorgensen, Herbert Macauley, the Quinns, the Edges; as well as underworld characters like Shep Morelli and Julia Wolf are little less cannibalistic than Packer. Nick Charles has no interest in their problems; it is his wife who drags him into the search for the missing Wynant against his will. The martini-for-breakfast cracking wise of William Powell and Myrna Loy more than anything else accounts for the popularity of *The Thin Man*. Despite Nick Charles' tough manner, Hammett's tough guy had been retired for good before this book appeared.

In Hemingway's story "In Another Country" the Italian major whose wife has just died fortuitously of a cold says, "[A man] must not marry. He cannot marry . . . If he is to lose everything, he should not place himself in a position to lose that. He should not place himself in a position to lose. He should find things he cannot lose." Knowing that, and despite that knowledge, Hemingway's characters of course always put themselves in a position to lose. They continually fall in love, knowing just how vulnerable that makes them, and they continually lose. Their hard exterior is merely a mask for the fine sensibility on a perpetual quest for good emotion. Hammett, in his best novels, literalizes the Hemingway mask and produces "monsters" who take the major's advice. The Hemingway mask is lifted every time the character is alone; he admits his own misery to himself—and to the reader—and exposes his inner life. The Hammett mask is never lifted; the Hammett character never lets you inside. Instead of the potential despair of Hemingway, Hammett gives you unimpaired control and machinelike efficiency: the tough guy refuses "to place himself in a position to lose." For all (or most) intents and purposes the inner world does not exist: the mask is the self. It is that "voluntary mutilation" of life that is the subject matter of these novels as much as Hemingway's stoical mask is of his. Hammett uses the relationships of Sam Spade with Brigid O'Shaugnessy, of the Continental Op with Dinah Brand and then with Gabrielle Leggett as proving grounds to indicate just how invulnerable his tough guys are. In each case the woman tries to find out what the man is; in each case the toughness is tested—and found not wanting. In the fantasy of detective novel readers and movie-goers who are themselves victims of a machine-ridden universe, loneliness is not too high a price to pay for invulnerability. [*Tough Guy Writers of the Thirties*. Ed. David Madden. Southern Illinois UP, 1968: 80-103]

Dashiell Hammett and the Continental Op

Steven Marcus

I was first introduced to Dashiell Hammett by Humphrey Bogart. I was twelve years old at the time, and mention the occasion because I take it to be exemplary, that I share this experience with countless others. (Earlier than this, at the very dawn of consciousness, I can recall William Powell and Myrna Loy and a small dog on a leash and an audience full of adults laughing; but that had nothing to do with Hammett or anything else as far as I was concerned.) What was striking about the event was that it was one of the first encounters I can consciously recall with the experience of moral ambiguity. Here was this detective you were supposed to like—and did like—behaving and speaking in peculiar and unexpected ways. He acted up to the cops, partly for real, partly as a ruse. He connived with crooks, for his own ends and perhaps even for some of theirs. He slept with his partner's wife, fell in love with a lady crook, and then refused to save her from the police, even though he could have. Which side was he on? Was he on any side apart from his own? And which or what side was that? The experience was not only morally ambiguous; it was morally complex and enigmatic as well. The impression it made was a lasting one.

Years later, after having read *The Maltese Falcon* and seen the movie again and then reread the novel, I could begin to understand why the impact of the film had been so memorable, much more so than that of most other movies. The director, John Huston, had had the wit to recognize the power, sharpness, integrity, and bite of Hammett's prose—particularly the dialogue—and the film script consists almost entirely of speech taken directly and without modification from the written novel. Moreover, this unusual situation is complicated still further. In selecting with notable intelligence the relevant scenes and passages from the novel, Huston had to make certain omissions. Paradoxically, however, one of the things that he chose to omit was the most important or central moment in the entire novel. It is also one of the central moments in all of Hammett's writing. I think we can make use of this oddly "lost" passage as a means of entry into Hammett's vision or imagination of the world.

It occurs as Spade is becoming involved with Brigid O'Shaughnessy in her struggle with the other thieves, and it is his way of communicating to her his sense of how the world and life go. His way is to tell her a story from his own experience. The form this story takes is that of a parable. It is a parable about a man named Flitcraft. Flitcraft was a successful, happily married, stable, and utterly respectable real estate dealer in Tacoma. One day he went out to lunch and never returned. No reason could be found for his disappearance, and no account of it could be made. "'He went like that,' Spade said. 'like a fist when you open your hand.'"

Five years later, Mrs. Flitcraft came to the agency at which Spade was working and told them that "she had seen a man in Spokane who looked a lot like her husband." Spade went off to investigate and found that it was indeed Flitcraft. He had been living in Spokane for a couple of years under the name of Charles Pierce. He had a successful automobile business, a wife, a baby son, a suburban home, and usually played golf after four in the afternoon, just as he had in Tacoma. Spade and he sat down to talk the matter over. Flitcraft, Spade recounts, "had no feeling of guilt. He had left his family well provided for, and what he had done seemed to him perfectly reasonable. The only thing that bothered him was a doubt that he could make the reasonableness clear" to his interlocutor. When Flitcraft went out to lunch that day five years before in Tacoma, "he passed an office-building that was being put up. . . . A beam or something fell eight or ten stories down and smacked the sidewalk alongside him." A chip of smashed sidewalk flew up and took a piece of skin off his cheek. He was otherwise unharmed. He stood there "scared stiff," he told Spade, "but he was more shocked than really frightened. He felt like somebody had taken the lid off life and let him look at the works."

Until that very moment Flitcraft had been "a good citizen and a good husband and father, not by any outer compulsion, but simply because he was a man who was most comfortable in step with his surroundings. . . . The life he knew was a clean orderly sane responsible affair. Now a falling beam had shown him that life was fundamentally none of these things. . . . What disturbed him was the discovery that in sensibly ordering his affairs he had got out of step, and not into step, with life." By the time he had finished lunch, he had reached the decision "that he would change his life at random by simply going away." He went off that afternoon, wandered around for a couple of years, then drifted back to the Northwest, "settled in Spokane and got married. His second wife didn't look like the first, but they were more alike than they were different." And the same held true for his second life. Spade then moves on to his conclusion: "He wasn't sorry for what he had done. It seemed reasonable enough to him. I don't think he even knew he had settled back into the same groove that he had jumped out of in Tacoma. But that's the part of it I always liked. He adjusted himself to beams falling, and then no more of them fell and he adjusted himself to their not falling." End of parable. Brigid of course understands nothing of this, as Spade doubtless knew beforehand. Yet what he has been telling her has to do with the forces and beliefs and contingencies that guide his conduct and supply a structure to his apparently enigmatic behavior.

To begin with, we may note that such a sustained passage is not the kind of thing we ordinarily expect in a detective story or novel about crime. That it is there, and that comparable passages occur in all of Hammett's best work, clearly suggests the kind of transformation that Hammett was performing on this popular genre of writing. The transformation was in the direction of literature. And what the passage in question is about among other things is the ethical irrationality of existence, the ethical unintelligibility of the world. For Flitcraft the falling beam "had taken the lid off life and let him look at the works." The works are that life is inscrutable, opaque, irresponsible, and arbitrary—that human existence does not correspond in its actuality to the way we live it. For most of us live as if existence itself were ordered, ethical, and rational. As a direct result of his realization in experience that it is not, Flitcraft leaves his wife and children and goes off. He acts irrationally and at random, in accordance with the nature of existence. When, after a couple of years of wandering aimlessly about, he decides to establish a new life, he simply reproduces the old one he had supposedly repudiated and abandoned; that is to say, he behaves again as if life were orderly, meaningful, and rational, and "adjusts" to it. And this, with fine irony, is the part of it, Spade says, that he "always liked," which means that part that he liked best. For here we come upon the unfathomable and most mysteriously irrational part of it all—how despite everything we have learned and everything we know, men will persist in behaving and trying to behave sanely, rationally, sensibly, and responsibly. And we will continue to persist even when we know that there is no logical or metaphysical, no discoverable or demonstrable reason for doing so.[1] It is this sense of sustained contradiction that is close to the center—or to one of the centers—of Hammett's work. The contradiction is not ethical alone; it is metaphysical as well. And it is not merely sustained; it is sustained with pleasure. For Hammett and Spade and the Op the sustainment in consciousness of such contradictions is an indispensable part of their existence and of their pleasure in that existence.

That this pleasure is itself complex, ambiguous, and problematic becomes apparent as one simply describes the conditions under which it exists. And the complexity, ambiguity, and sense of the problematical are not confined to such moments of "revelation"—or set pieces—as the parable of Flitcraft. They permeate Hammett's work and act as formative elements in its structure, including its deep structure. Hammett's work went through considerable and interesting development in the course of his career of twelve years as a writer. He also wrote in a considerable variety of forms and worked out a variety of narrative devices and strategies. At the same time, his work considered as a whole reveals a remarkable kind of coherence. In order to further the understanding of that coherence, we can propose for the purposes of the present analysis to construct a kind of "ideal type" of a Hammett or Op story. Which is not to say or to imply in the least that he wrote according to a formula, but that an authentic imaginative vision lay beneath and informed the structure of his work.

Such an ideal-typical description runs as follows. The Op is called in or sent out on a case. Something has been stolen, someone is missing, some dire circumstance is impending, someone has been murdered—it doesn't matter. The Op interviews the person or persons most immediately accessible. They may be innocent or guilty—it doesn't matter; it is an indifferent circumstance. Guilty or innocent, they provide the Op with an account of what they know, of what they assert really happened. The Op begins to investigate; he compares these accounts with others that he gathers; he snoops about; he does research; he shadows people, arranges confrontations between those who want to avoid one another, and so on. What he soon discovers is that the "reality" that anyone involved will swear to is in fact itself a construction, a fabrication, a fiction, a faked and alternate reality—and that it has been gotten together before he ever arrived on the scene. And the Op's work therefore is to deconstruct, decompose, deplot, and defictionalize that "reality" and to construct or reconstruct out of it a true fiction, i.e., an account of what "really" happened.

It should be quite evident that there is a reflexive and coordinate relation between the activities of the Op and the activities of Hammett, the writer. Yet the depth and problematic character of this self-reflexive process begin to be revealed when we observe that the reconstruction or true fiction created and arrived at by the Op at the end of the story is no more plausible—nor is it meant to be—than the stories that have been told to him by all parties, guilty or innocent, in the course of his work. The Op may catch the real thief or collar the actual crook—that is not entirely to the point. What is to the point is that the story, account, or chain of events that the Op winds up with as "reality" is no more plausible and no less ambiguous than the stories that he meets with at the outset and later. What Hammett has done—unlike most writers of detective or crime stories before him or since—is to include as part of the contingent and dramatic consciousness of his narrative the circumstance that the work of the detective is itself a fiction-making activity, a discovery or creation by fabrication of something new in the world, or hidden, latent, potential, or as yet undeveloped within it. The typical "classical" detective story—unlike Hammett's—can be described as a formal game with certain specified rules of transformation. What ordinarily happens is that the detective is faced with a situation of inadequate, false, misleading, and ambiguous information. And the story as a whole is an exercise in disambiguation—with the final scenes being a ratiocinative demonstration that the butler did it (or not); these scenes achieve a conclusive, reassuring clarity of explanation, wherein everything is set straight, and the game we have been party to is brought to its appropriate end. But this, as we have already seen, is not what ordinarily happens in Hammett or with the Op.

What happens is that the Op almost invariably walks into a situation that has already been elaborately fabricated or framed. And his characteristic response to his sense that he is dealing with a series of deceptions or fictions is—to use the words that he uses himself repeatedly—"to stir things up." This corresponds integrally, both as metaphor and in logical structure, to what happened in the parable of Flitcraft. When the falling beam just misses Flitcraft, "he felt like somebody had taken the lid off life." The Op lives with the uninterrupted awareness that for him the lid has been taken off life. When the lid has been lifted, the logical thing to do is to "stir things up"—which is what he does.[2] He actively undertakes to deconstruct, decompose, and thus demystify the fictional—and therefore false—reality created by the characters, crooks or not, with whom he is involved. More often than not he tries to substitute his own fictional-hypothetical representation for theirs—and this representation may also be "true" or mistaken, or both at once. In any event, his major effort is to make the fictions of others visible as fictions, inventions, concealments, falsehoods, and mystifications. When a fiction becomes visible as such it begins to dissolve and disappear, and presumably should reveal behind it the "real" reality that was there all the time and that it was masking. Yet what happens in Hammett is that what is revealed as "reality" is a still further fiction-making activity—in the first place the Op's, and behind that yet another, the consciousness present in many of the Op stories and all the novels that Dashiell Hammett, the writer, is continually doing the same thing as the Op and all the other characters in the fiction he is creating. That is to say he is making a fiction (in writing) in the real world; and this fiction, like the real world itself, is coherent but not necessarily rational. What one both begins and ends with then is a story, a narrative, a coherent yet questionable account of the world. This problematic penetrates to the bottom of Hammett's narrative imagination and shapes a number of its deeper processes—in *The Dain Curse*, for example, it is the chief topic of explicit debate that runs throughout the entire novel.

Yet Hammett's writing is still more complex and integral than this. For the unresolvable paradoxes and dilemmas that we have just been describing in terms of narrative structure and consciousness are reproduced once again in Hammett's vision and representation of society, of the social world in which the Op lives. At this point we must recall that Hammett is a writer of the 1920s and that this was the era of Prohibition. American society had in effect committed itself to a vast collective fiction. Even more, this fiction was false not merely in the sense that it was made up or did not in fact correspond to reality; it was false in the sense that it was corrupt and corrupting as well. During this period every time an American took a drink he was helping to undermine the law, and American society had covertly committed itself to what was in practice collaborative illegality.[3] There is a kind of epiphany of these circumstances in "The Golden Horseshoe." The Op is on a case that takes him to Tijuana. In a bar there, he reads a sign:

**ONLY GENUINE PRE-WAR AMERICAN AND
BRITISH WHISKEYS SERVED HERE**

He responds by remarking that "I was trying to count how many lies could be found in those nine words, and had reached four, with promise of more," when he is interrupted by some call to action. That sign and the Op's response to it describe part of the existential character of the social world represented by Hammett.

Another part of that representation is expressed in another kind of story or idea that Hammett returned to repeatedly. The twenties were also the great period of organized crime and organized criminal gangs in America, and one of Hammett's obsessive imaginations was the notion of organized crime or gangs taking over an entire society and running it as if it were an ordinary society doing business as usual. In other words, society itself would become a fiction, concealing and belying the actuality of what was controlling it and perverting it from within. One can thus make out quite early in this native American writer a proto-Marxist critical representation of how a certain kind of society works. Actually the point of view is pre- rather than proto-Marxist, and the social world as it is dramatized in many of these stories is Hobbesian rather than Marxist.[4] It is a world of universal warfare, the war of each against all, and of all against all. The only thing that prevents the criminal ascendancy from turning into permanent tyranny is that the crooks who take over society cannot cooperate with one another, repeatedly fall out with each other, and return to the Hobbesian anarchy out of which they have momentarily arisen. The social world as imagined by Hammett runs on a principle that is the direct opposite of that postulated by Erik Erikson as the fundamental and enabling condition for human existence. In Hammett, society and social relations are dominated by the principle of basic mistrust. As one of his detectives remarks, speaking for himself and for virtually every other character in Hammett's writing, "I trust no one."

When Hammett turns to the respectable world, the world of respectable society, of affluence and influence, of open personal and political power, he finds only more of the same. The respectability of respectable American society is as much a fiction and a fraud as the phony respectable society fabricated by the criminals. Indeed he unwaveringly represents the world of crime as a reproduction in both structure and detail of the modern capitalist society that it depends on, preys off, and is part of. But Hammett does something even more radical than this. He not only continually juxtaposes and connects the ambiguously fictional worlds of art and of writing with the fraudulently fictional worlds of society. He connects them, juxtaposes them, and sees them in dizzying and baffling interaction. He does this in many ways and on many occasions. One of them, for example, is the Maltese Falcon itself, which turns out to be and contains within itself the history of capitalism. It is originally a piece of plunder, part of what Marx called the "primitive accumulation"; when its gold encrusted with gems is painted over it becomes a mystified object, a commodity itself; it is a piece of property that belongs to no one—whoever possesses it does not really own it. At the same time it is another fiction, a representation or work of art—which turns out itself to be a fake, since it is made of lead. It is a rare avis indeed. As is the fiction in which it is created and contained, the novel by

Hammett.

It is into this bottomlessly equivocal, endlessly fraudulent, and brutally acquisitive world that Hammett precipitates the Op. There is nothing glamorous about him. Short, thickset, balding, between thirty-five and forty, he has no name, no home, no personal existence apart from his work. He is, and he regards himself as, "the hired man" of official and respectable society, who is paid so much per day to clean it up and rescue it from the crooks and thieves who are perpetually threatening to take it over. Yet what he—and the reader—just as perpetually learn is that the respectable society that employs him is itself inveterately vicious, deceitful, culpable, crooked, and degraded. How then is the Op to be preserved, to preserve himself, from being contaminated by both the world he works against and the world he is hired to work for?

To begin with, the Op lives by a code. This code consists in the first instance of the rules laid down by the Continental Agency, and they are "rather strict." The most important of them by far is that no operative in the employ of the Agency is ever allowed to take or collect part of a reward that may be attached to the solution of a case. Since he cannot directly enrich himself through his professional skills, he is saved from at least the characteristic corruption of modern society—the corruption that is connected with its fundamental acquisitive structure. At the same time, the Op is a special case of the Protestant ethic, for his entire existence is bound up in and expressed by his work, his vocation. He likes his work, and it is honest work, done as much for enjoyment and the exercise of his skills and abilities as it is for personal gain and self-sustainment. The work is something of an end in itself, and this circumstance also serves to protect him, as does his deliberate refusal to use high-class and fancy moral language about anything. The work is an end in itself and is therefore something more than work alone. As Spade says, in a passage that is the culmination of many such passages in Hammett—

> "I'm a detective and expecting me to run criminals down and then let them go free is like asking a dog to catch a rabbit and let it go. It can be done, all right, and sometimes it is done, but it's not the natural thing."

Being a detective, then, entails more than fulfilling a social function or performing a social role. Being a detective is the realization of an identity, for there are components in it which are beyond or beneath society—and cannot be touched by it—and beyond and beneath reason. There is something "natural" about it. Yet if we recall that the nature thus being expressed is that of a man hunter, and Hammett's apt metaphor compels us to do so, and that the state of society as it is represented in Hammett's writing reminds us of the state of nature in Hobbes, we see that even here Hammett does not release his sense of the complex and the contradictory, and is making no simple-minded appeal to some benign idea of the "natural."

And indeed the Op is not finally or fully protected by his work, his job, his vocation. (We have all had to relearn with bitterness what multitudes of wickedness "doing one's job" can cover.) Max Weber has memorably remarked that "the decisive means for politics is violence." In Hammett's depiction of modern American society, violence is the decisive means indeed, along with fraud, deceit, treachery, betrayal, and general, endemic unscrupulousness. Such means are in no sense alien to Hammett's detective. As the Op says, "detecting is a hard business, and you use whatever tools come to hand." In other words, there is a paradoxical tension and unceasing interplay in Hammett's stories between means and ends; relations between the two are never secure or stable. And as Max Weber further remarked, in his great essay "Politics as a Vocation": "The world is governed by demons, and he who lets himself in for . . . power and force as means, contracts with diabolic powers, and for his action it is not true that good can follow only from good and evil only from evil, but that often the opposite is true. Anyone who fails to see this is, indeed, a political infant." Neither Hammett nor the Op is an infant; yet no one can be so grown up and inured to experience that he can escape the consequences that attach to the deliberate use of violent and dubious means.

These consequences are of various orders. "Good" ends themselves can be transformed and perverted by the use of vicious or indiscriminate means. (I am leaving to one side those even more perplexing instances in Hammett in which the ends pursued by the Op correspond with ends desired by a corrupted yet respectable official society.) The consequences are also visible inwardly, on the inner being of the agent of such means, the Op himself. The violence begins to get to him:

> I began to throw my right fist into him.
> I liked that. His belly was flabby, and it got softer every time I hit it. I hit
> it often.

Another side of this set of irresolvable moral predicaments is revealed when we see that the Op's toughness is not merely a carapace within which feelings of tenderness and humanity can be nourished and preserved. The toughness is toughness through and through, and as the Op continues his career, and continues to live by the means he does, he tends to become more callous and less and less able to feel. At the very end, awaiting him, he knows, is the prospect of becoming like his boss, the head of the Agency, the old Man, "with his gentle eyes behind gold spectacles, and his mild smile, hiding the fact that fifty years of sleuthing had left him without any feelings at all on any subject." This is the price exacted by the use of such means in such a world; these are the consequences of living fully in a society moved by the principle of basic mistrust. "Whoever fights monsters," writes Nietzsche, "should see to it that in the process he does not become a monster. And when you look long into an abyss, the abyss also looks into you." The abyss looks into Hammett, the Old Man, and the Op.

It is through such complex devices as I have merely sketched here that Hammett was able to raise the crime story into literature. He did it over a period of ten years. Yet the strain was finally too much to bear—that shifting, entangled, and equilibrated state of contradiction out of which his creativity arose and which it expressed could no longer be sustained. His creative career ends when he is no longer able to handle the literary, social, and moral opacities, instabilities, and contradictions that characterize all his best work. His life then splits apart and goes in the two opposite directions that were implicit in his earlier, creative phase, but that the creativity held suspended and in poised yet fluid tension. His politics go in one direction; the way he made his living went in another—he became a hack writer, and then finally no writer at all. That is another story. Yet for ten years he was able to do what almost no other writer in this genre has ever done so well—he was able to really write, to construct a vision of a world in words, to know that the writing was about the real world and referred to it and was part of it; and at the same time he was able to be self-consciously aware that the whole thing was problematical and about itself and "only" writing as well. For ten years, in other words, he was a true creator of fiction. [*Partisan Review* 41 (1974): 366-377]

NOTES

1. It can hardly be an accident that the new name that Hammett gives to Flitcraft is that of an American philosopher—with two vowels reversed—who was deeply involved in just such speculations.

2. These homely metaphors go deep into Hammett's life. One of the few things that he could recall from his childhood past was his mother's repeated advice that a woman who wasn't good in the kitchen wasn't likely to be much good in any other room in the house.

3. Matters were even murkier than this. The Eighteenth Amendment to the Constitution was in effect from January 1920 to December 1933, nearly fourteen years. During this period Americans were forbidden under penalty of law to manufacture, sell, or transport any intoxicating liquor. At the same time, no one was forbidden to buy or drink such liquor. In other words, Americans were virtually being solicited by their own laws to support an illegal trade in liquor, even while Congress was passing the Volstead Act which was intended to prevent such a trade.

4. Again it can hardly he regarded as an accident that the name Hammett gives to the town taken over by the criminals in *Red Harvest* is "Personville"—pronounced "Poisonville." And what else is Personville except Leviathan, the "artificial man" represented by Hobbes as the image of society itself.

Homage to Dashiell Hammett

Ross Macdonald

I have been given some space to speak for the hardboiled school of mystery writing. Let me use it to dwell for a bit on the work of Dashiell Hammett. He was the great innovator who invented the hardboiled detective novel and used it to express and master the undercurrent of inchoate violence that runs through so much of American life.

In certain ways, it must be admitted, Hammett's heroes are reminiscent of unreconstructed Darwinian man; *McTeague* and *The Sea Wolf* stand directly behind them. But no matter how rough and appetent they may be, true representatives of a rough and appetent society, they are never allowed to run unbridled. Hammett's irony controls them. In fact he criticized them far more astringently and basically than similar men were criticized by Hemingway. In his later and less romantic moments Hammett was a close and disillusioned critic of the two-fisted hard-drinking woman-chasing American male that he derived partly from tradition and partly from observation, including self-observation.

Even in one of his very early stories, first published by Mencken in *Smart Set*, Hammett presents a character who might have been a parody of the Hemingway hero, except that he was pre-Hemingway. This huge brute is much attached to his beard. To make a short story shorter, the loss of his beard reveals that he used it to hide a receding chin and makes him a public laughing-stock. This isn't much more than an anecdote, but it suggests Hammett's attitude towards the half-evolved frontier male of our not too distant past. Shorn and urbanized, he became in Hammett's best novels a near-tragic figure, a lonely and suspicious alien who pits a hopeless but obstinate animal courage against the metropolitan jungle, a not very moral man who clings with a skeptic's desperation to a code of behavior empirically arrived at in a twilight world between chivalry and gangsterism.

Like the relationship of Charles Dickens and Wilkie Collins, the Hemingway-Hammett influence ran two ways. Hammett achieved some things that Hemingway never attempted. He placed his characters in situations as complex as those of life, in great cities like San Francisco and New York and Baltimore, and let them work out their dubious salvations under social and economic and political pressures. The subject of his novels, you might say, was the frontier male thrust suddenly, as the frontier disappeared, into the modern megalopolis; as Hemingway's was a similar man meeting war and women, and listening to the silence of his own soul.

Hammett's prose is not quite a prose that can say anything, as Chandler overenthusiastically claimed it could. But it is a clean, useful prose, with remarkable range and force. It has pace and point, strong tactile values, the rhythms and colors of speech, all in the colloquial tradition that stretches from Mark Twain through Stephen Crane to Lardner and Mencken, the Dr. Johnson of our vernacular. Still it is a deadpan and rather external prose, artificial-seeming compared with Huck Finn's earthy rhetoric, flat in comparison with Fitzgerald's more subtly colloquial instrument. Hammett's ear for the current and the colloquial was a little too sardonically literal, and this is already tending to date his writing, though not seriously.

Analysis of any kind is alien to this prose. Moulding the surface of things, it lends itself to the vivid narration of rapid, startling action. Perhaps it tends to set too great a premium on action, as if the mind behind it were hurrying away from its own questions and deliberately restricting itself to the manipulation of appearances. It is in part the expression of that universally-met-with American type who avoids sensibility and introspection because they make you vulnerable in the world. At its worst such prose can be an unnecessary writing-down to the lowest common denominator of the democracy. But at its best it has great litotic power, as in some of Hemingway's earlier stories, or in the haunting chapter where Sam Spade makes devious love to Brigid by telling her the story of Flitcraft:

> "A man named Flitcraft had left his real-estate office, in Tacoma, to go to luncheon one day and had never returned. He did not keep an engagement to play golf after four that afternoon, though he had taken the initiative in making the engagement less than half an hour before he went out to luncheon. His wife and children never saw him again. His wife and he were supposed to be on the best of terms. He had two children, boys, one five and the other three. He owned his house in a Tacoma suburb, a new Packard, and the rest of the appurtenances of successful American living."

Sam Spade is Flitcraft's spiritual twin, the lonely male who is not at ease in Zion or in Zenith. He is inarticulate about himself, like Babbitt is aware only of a deep malaise that spurs him on to action and acquisition. *The Maltese Falcon* is a fable of modern man in quest of love and money, despairing of everything else. Its murders are more or less incidental, though they help to give it its quality of a crisis novel. Its characters act out of the extreme emotions of fear and guilt and concupiscence, anger and revenge; and with such fidelity to these passions that their natures almost seem co-terminous with them.

Driven by each and all of them, Sam Spade strips away one by one the appearances which stand between him and the truth, and between him and the complete satisfaction of his desires. His story ends in drastic peripeteia with the all but complete frustration of his desires. His lover is guilty of murder; the code without which his life is meaningless forces him to turn her over to the police. The black bird is hollow. The reality behind appearances is a treacherous vacuum. Spade turns for sardonic consolation to the wife of his murdered partner (whose name was Archer). It is his final reluctant act of animal pragmatism.

Probably Hammett intended the ultimate worthlessness of the Maltese falcon to be more than a bad joke on his protagonist. I see it as the symbol of a lost tradition, representing the great cultures of the past which have become inaccessible to Spade and the men of his time. It represents explicitly the religious and ethical developments of the Mediterranean basin, Christianity and knight-errantry. Perhaps it stands for the Holy Ghost itself, or rather for its absence.

In any case the bird's lack of value implies Hammett's final comment on the inadequacy and superficiality of Sam Spade's life and ours. If only his bitterly inarticulate struggle for self-realization were itself more fully realized, the stakes for which he plays not so arbitrarily lost from the beginning (a basic limitation of the detective story is that its action is preordained, in a sense, by what has already happened), Sam Spade could have been a great indigenous tragic figure. Maybe he is. I think *The Maltese Falcon*, with its astonishing imaginative energy persisting undiminished after a third of a century, is tragedy of a new kind, deadpan tragedy. [*Self-Portrait: Ceaselessly Into The Past.* Ed. Ralph B. Sipper. Capra Press, 1981: 109-112]

Finding out about Gender in Hammett's Detective Fiction: Generic Constraints or Transcendental Norms?

David J. Herman

In the violent world of Dashiell Hammett, a man's virility is, more often than not, judged by the size of his pistol. When the "Whosis Kid" is faced down by his recalcitrant French partner, for instance, "[h]is bony hands pushed his coat and rested where his vest bulged over the sharp corners of his hip-bones" (*CO* 224). In *The Maltese Falcon*, moreover, the effeminate Joel Cairo revealingly "carries a smaller gun than the one Thursby and Jacob were shot with" (*MF* 213). Hammett's treatment of Wilmer in the same novel, however, records the slippage between sign and signified that undermines this entire system of phallic correspondences. When we discover that Wilmer's "[b]lack pistols were gigantic in his small hands" (199), the discrepancy between symbol and fact becomes palpably apparent. Indeed, Sam Spade, in front of the hotel detective, draws attention to and, in effect, parodies Wilmer's effort to substitute his pistols for a phallus: "What do you let these cheap gunmen hang out in your lobby for, with their tools bulging in their clothes?" (108).[1] Later in the novel, though Wilmer's "pockets bulged more than his hands need have made them bulge" (137), Wilmer ultimately proves "impotent" in Spade's strong grip (138). But Hammett's parodic reproduction of Wilmer's bulging "heaters" amounts to *self*-parody; in this rare instance Hammett attains some ironic distance from his own tendency to describe, say, Tom-Tom Carey by the way "[t]he bulge shows" when he sits down (*BK* 414). In turn, this double metonymy, by which Hammett substitutes a gun for a phallus and a phallus for virility and power, finds its classic expression in "The Big Knockover." In that story, "Angel" Grace Cardigan, discriminating between the Op and full-blown criminals, says somewhat wistfully: "If you were a gun, I'd—. . . . " (*BK* 380).

Angel's elliptic comment raises the question of exactly where women fit into a world in which masculine sexuality is deeply bound up with the capacity for violence—a world in which masculinity itself totemically resides in pistols, sleek and explosive instruments of death. Granted, as Paul Fussell notes in *The Great War and Modern Memory*, relations between the sexes have long been figured in terms of "assaults," "attacks," and "encounters" (270). But in Hammett's fiction, violence functions not just as the vehicle but also as the tenor of the metaphoric equation between sexuality and aggression: it is not simply that figures of battle are applied to sexual experience, but that sexuality itself reduces to some sort of primordially violent energy.

In his economy of sexuality and violence, Hammett's women characters necessarily take on a highly ambivalent status. They are at once fetishized and abominated—objectified as the Other and then, because so objectified, infused with all the threatening power of the alien, the inassimilable. Because Hammett in his women characters often combines voluptuousness with viciousness, ripe sexuality with rapacious self-interest, Hammett's texts not only figure what William Marling specifies as "the Hammett succubus," but also embody in general the dynamic that de Beauvoir, in *The Second Sex*, describes as "[t]he man's hesitation between fear and desire [in his dealings with women], between the fear of being in the power of uncontrollable forces and the wish to win them over" (152).[2]

In order to explain the negative, misogynistic phase of this essentially manic response to women, de Beauvoir discusses cultural traditions that encourage the Western male to see "himself as a fallen god," and to view himself as "fallen from a bright and ordered heaven into the chaotic shadows of his mother's womb"—to imagine himself as, and resent, being "imprisoned by woman in the mud of the earth" (146). Here in fact the applications of de Beauvoir's theory of misogyny overlap with those of Paul Ricoeur's theory of Evil. For if women in Hammett's fiction at some level incur the sort of metaphysical resentment that de Beauvoir associates with misogynistic thinking, Hammett's women characters also incur the equally metaphysical "dread" with which Ricoeur associates the notion of "impurity" and, by extension, the idea of Evil.

As Ricoeur says in *The Symbol of Evil*, "[d]read of the impure is like fear, but already it faces a threat which, beyond the threat of suffering and death, aims at the diminution of existence, a loss of the personal core of one's being" (41). The dreaded object, in a macabre re-articulation of the Sublime, threatens to overwhelm and disintegrate the dreading subject.[3] By the same token, James F. Maxfield notes that "[s]exual desire is possibly the greatest threat to the Hammett hero's invulnerability" (111), and Dennis Dooley describes as a "familiar pattern" in Hammett's fiction the way "a man, in fact a series of men, [gets] exploited by a woman who has found their weak points" (38). We thus see how women in Hammett's texts become quite literally the source of an impurity that, unless contained and purged, threatens to engulf in Evil—to negate or abolish—the "personal core" or identity of the detective.[4] This inherently irrational dread of contamination does much to explain, in general, the overdetermined character of gender in Hammett's work—and *ipso facto* the violence with which Hammett's detective often responds to women. In particular, such dread helps us account for the ambivalent repugnance that the Op manifests toward Jeanne Delano, who attempts to seduce him in "The Girl with the Silver Eyes": "'You're beautiful as all hell!' I shouted crazily into her face, and flung her against the door" (*CO* 176).

Yet as it turns out, the polysemousness of Hammett's own texts is precisely what lets "Evil" into Hammett's fictional world. The detective's very desire to purify himself of woman, it seems, is what most contaminates him, inscribing the dreaded object within the dreading subject—such that "male" and "female" cease to designate discrete entities. For by attributing androgynous features to certain of his women characters, at least in his early works, Hammett in effect blurs the differences between the sexes. In this way, Hammett, by complicating his oftentimes reductive vision of women, distends his own misogynist paradigm. Androgyny in Hammett's texts tends to neutralize, at one level, that conflict between men and women which, at another level, is one of Hammett's most abiding themes. Images of androgyny therefore make Hammett's early texts work against themselves; such images shatter that hall of mirrors in which violence replicates sexuality and sexuality, violence.

I shall turn to the issue of Hammett's later texts in a moment. But first, by abandoning the quasi-religious vocabulary ("dread," "Evil," "contamination") that I have thus far borrowed from de Beauvoir and Ricoeur, in order to align Hammett's treatment of women with the larger tradition of writing about gender, I believe that I can specify more precisely the self-divided nature of Hammett's early texts. In this connection, we need a vocabulary that, unlike de Beauvoir's and Ricoeur's, resists naturalizing or even eternalizing contingent social categories. This alternative vocabulary, I submit, will allow us to isolate one of the most interesting features of Hammett's work taken as part of the *genre* of so-called hard-boiled detective fiction: namely, the way Hammett's texts make explicit, or rather formalize, the internal contradictions of the ideology they ostensibly confirm.

The ideology that I have in mind is one that ascribes a particular, and immutable, role to gender. Through this ideology, gender ceases to be merely a means by which to divide social functions—a criterion for the appropriateness for either sex of a given activity or attitude. Gender becomes instead a kind of epistemological framework, in terms of which the world itself is made intelligible. Hammett's texts thus conflate gender construed as, on the one hand, a socially useful category, and gender construed as, on the other hand, what Kant would call a transcendental condition of knowledge, a condition for our being able to know anything at all. The upshot of Hammett's thus conflating the social with the transcendental is that, in the author's works, gender roles come to provide a sort of syntax for interpretation as such—interpretation in turn being the *raison d'être* of the detective. If a woman is almost always the crux of Hammett's mysteries, therefore, her presence is neither accidental nor a function of popular taste alone, but rather a sort of necessary constraint of the hard-boiled genre itself. In this genre, the world as a whole becomes decipherable only when looked upon from a deeply sexist vantage-point.

What I mean is that in Hammett and by extension male detective fiction generally, notions of gender in effect become interpretive axioms, syntactic laws subsisting at the same level of unquestioned generality occupied by natural laws. These axioms or laws constitute a syntax in the strict sense that they prescribe what sorts of propositions about the world are well-formed and therefore meaningful, and what sorts of propositions are ill-formed and therefore meaningless. My argument is that we can isolate pressure-points at which Hammett's interpretive syntax yields meaningful and relevant propositions about gender that do not however meet Hammett's own syntactic requirements for meaningfulness or relevance. One such proposition, crucial for my case, is that distinctions in gender are not absolute; this proposition is, as we shall see, at once implied and proscribed by Hammett's assumptions about gender. Indeed, by thus locating where Hammett's axioms of gender generate mutually incompatible claims, we are able to reverse the movement towards ideology that Hammett's own texts enact. We can demystify the transcendental pretensions of gender taken as syntax, and instead account for it as a social category with particular social uses, specific to a particular place and time.

My idea is therefore to substitute a variable for Hammett's immutable interpretive syntax, and to show how Hammett's very attempt to make gender roles constant is what plunges them into variability from the start. I contend, further, that in this connection the images of androgyny in Hammett's texts provide us with a significant analytic tool. In the first place, Hammett's androgynous images show just where the author's naturalization or rather transcendentalization of gender breaks down. Whereas the generic constraints under which Hammett operates serve to divide up experience into what should and should not be counted meaningful or important—what sorts of things should or should not be regularly factored into, say, our notion of "the feminine"—androgyny, *also* implicit within the hard-boiled genre, produces just the opposite effect. Androgyny liberates Hammett's texts from their own overrestrictive classification of what kinds of claims not just about gender, but by extension about the world itself, are in principle meaningful. In other words, images of androgyny in Hammett de-naturalize gender into a social category, and they achieve this by unmasking Hammett's own attempts to make that social category natural to the order of things.

In the second place, however, images of androgyny provide a heuristic tool to the extent that they do not appear in Hammett's later works—works such as *The Glass Key* and *The Thin Man*. I wish to argue that androgyny effectively drops out of Hammett's later novels because the author's interpretive syntax itself changes. Hammett's misogynistic reduction of women to a single female type, in which good and evil are indissolubly united, gives way in the later works to a broader spectrum of women characters. In *The Thin Man*, this spectrum ranges from the pathologically deceitful, and literally hysterical, Mimi Wynant to the detective's own resilient and resourceful wife, Nora Charles. Since the later Hammett can distribute positive and negative characteristics *between* different women, the author's notion of the feminine comes to include the sort of unequivocal strength and decency that Hammett formerly reserved for the masculine alone. Certain women can now be genuinely caring and helpful, just as certain others remain through and through malign and destructive. By the same token, Hammett is no longer driven toward androgyny by the exaggerated limitations he himself places on what statements can count as meaningful ones about women. The scope of claims that bear on women expands to include claims that, before, could be relevant only vis-à-vis men; and Hammett thus need no longer create *ersatz* men, androgynes, in efforts to capture with an impoverished interpretive syntax the recalcitrant complexities of gender.

We can put the matter this way precisely because the later Hammett reincorporates into his women characters an element of contingency or variability—one woman is not by definition the same as the next—gender in the later novels ceases to do the sort of transcendental work it did in the early works. Married, Nick Charles can no longer simply assume women to be duplicitous. No longer an interpretive syntax, gender itself becomes something that needs to be constantly interpreted.

I

In "Further Notes toward a Recognition of Androgyny," Carolyn Heilbrun provides a rough, somewhat over-general formulation of what the term "androgyny" itself signifies: "a condition under which the characteristics of the sexes and the human impulses expressed by men and women are not rigidly assigned" (143). By amassing evidence from a broad range of Hammett's works, however, I wish now to work past Heilbrun's definition inductively—to arrive at a more nuanced and precise conception of how androgyny functions in Hammett's texts. First, I shall catalogue what amount to Hammett's syntactic laws of gender: those fundamental axioms about women whose permutations Hammett's male detective must master in order not just to interpret, but also to survive the world around him. I shall discuss, second, how Hammett's androgynous images disrupt this interpretive syntax; the images of androgyny suggest how survival to some extent depends on the detective's being able to permute Hammett's axioms in fundamentally incoherent ways. In the final part of my paper I shall attempt to show that Hammett's characterization of women does in fact undergo development, and that the absence of androgyny in the later works represents not an increased conservatism about gender, but rather an interpretive code according to which gender itself becomes multiple and complex. On the later Hammett's own terms, male and female no longer signify an irreducible binary opposition, but instead an unstable manifold of contingent possibilities.

Curiously, Hammett sometimes seems to lack much in the way of a descriptive vocabulary for women. In "The Big Knockover," having almost perfunctorily listed Nancy Regan's blue eyes, red mouth and white teeth, and having even gone to the length of mentioning that "she had a nose," the Op says this: "Without getting steamed up over the details, she was nice" (*BK* 255). Later on, when he once more encounters Nancy, the Op again relies heavily on the banal and nondescript "nice": "I have already said that she was nice. Well, she was. And the cocky little blue hat that hid all her hair didn't handicap her niceness any tonight" (382). A moment later, the Op similarly remarks in Nancy "a blue-eyed, white-toothed smile that was—well—nice" (382). What here amounts to a kind of linguistic entropy indicates not so much Hammett's desire to avoid provocative description as a breakdown in the Op's capacity to imagine women. And for a detective whose very longevity hinges on successful sleuthing amid deceptive surfaces, the Op's inability to describe in much concrete detail the appearance of a beautiful woman suggests not simple carelessness, but rather powerful forces that inhibit and deflect the *modus operandi* of his psyche.

It is unwise, however, to conduct an argument solely in negative terms; and when we move to the descriptive vocabulary that Hammett *does* develop in connection with women, we discover a system of polarities and ironic tensions in which women at once attract and repulse, both threaten and allure.

In "The Tenth Clew," for instance, Hammett in the first place ironically names Creda Dexter, whose own account of her relations with Leopold Gantvoort proves, in the end, to be far from credible. Irony also lends a double-edgedness to Hammett's descriptions of Creda's appearance and manner. On the one hand, Creda has all the sensuality and grace of a pampered cat:

With the eyes for a guide, you discovered that she was pronouncedly feline throughout. Her every movement was the slow, smooth, sure one of a cat; and the contours of her rather pretty face, the shape of her mouth, her small nose, the set of her eyes, the swelling of her brows, were all cat-like. And the effect was heightened by the way she wore her hair, which was thick and tawny. (*CO* 18)

On the other hand, as O'Gar says to the Op: "'A sleek kitten—that dame! Rub her in the right way, and she'll purr pretty. Rub her the wrong way—and look out for the claws!'" (20). Similarly, after Creda discloses Madden Dexter's real identity, Hammett says this of Creda: "No sleek kitten, this, but a furious, spitting cat, with claws and teeth bared" (42). Granted, Hammett's use of animals as analogues for people fits him squarely into the naturalistic tradition, which, drawing from Social Darwinism, transforms the idea of survival of the fittest into a sort of mythic resource for realizing characters. Hammett's use of animals in characterizing women, however, stems not just from naturalistic but also from specifically misogynistic impulses. Perpetually oscillating between the sensual refinement and wild ferocity of a cat, Creda Dexter represents what Dennis Dooley identifies as the single female type that, with slight variations, occurs throughout Hammett's corpus: "A maddening blend of innocence and manipulation, vulnerability and villainy, sometimes she gets to him and sometimes the Op manages to keep her head in his cold eye" (59).

On certain occasions, in fact, women in Hammett's fiction pass from sensuality to truculence in the blink of an eye. In "The Gutting of Couffignal," for example, Hammett provides this description of the Princess Zhukovski, whose instantaneous transmutation the author himself links up with traditional ways of imaging and *eo ipso* containing women:

Her strong slender body became the body of a lean crouching animal. One hand—claw now—swept to the heavy pocket of her jacket. Then before I could have blinked an eye—though my life seemed to depend on my not batting it—the wild animal had vanished. Out of it—and now I know where the writers of old fairy stories got their ideas—rose the princess again, cool and straight and tall. (*BK* 29)

Arguably, it is these same "writers of old fairy stories" who provoke Gilbert and Gubar's comment in *The Madwoman in the Attic* that "male-engendered female figures as superficially disparate as Milton's Sin, Swift's Chloe, and Yeats's Crazy Jane have incarnated man's ambivalence not only toward female sexuality but toward their own (male) physicality" (12). Hammett's image of the bestialized-then-idealized "princess" reveals the extent to which this ambivalence informs traditional ideas of women's mutability—their radical instability and unpredictability even from one moment to the next.

On other occasions, though, as in Elvira in "The House in Turk Street," a woman's sensual appeal co-exists in time with, and thus becomes indistinguishable from, the physical threat that she poses

Smoke-gray eyes that were set too far apart for trustworthiness—though not for beauty—laughed at me; and her red mouth laughed at me, exposing the edges of little sharp animal teeth, She was beautiful as the devil, and twice as dangerous. (*CO* 101)

Similarly, in "The Whosis Kid," Ines Almad, whom the Op portrays as "beautiful—in a wild way" (*CO* 200), derives from the sparring match between the Op and the jealous "Billie" a sadistic and nearly orgasmic pleasure: "Her eyes were shiny behind their heavy lashes, and her mouth was open to let white teeth gleam through" (212). Summing her up afterwards, the Op provides this list of characteristics, which uneasily co-exist in one and the same person: "She was an actress. She was appealing, and pathetic, and anything else that you like—including dangerous" (217).[5]

Indeed, in "The Golden Horseshoe," Hammett localizes in female sexuality itself the menacing aspect that, for the detective, makes women's sensual appeal highly unsettling. Here, Hammett's descriptions of Kewpie[6] suggest how woman's power is threatening precisely because it is hidden or latent—both figuratively and anatomically speaking. When the Op suggests to Kewpie that her lover, Ed, is going to "ditch" her, Kewpie reacts in this way:

Her right shoulder was to me, touching my left. Her left hand flashed down under her shirt skirt. I pushed her shoulder forward, twisting her body sharply away from me. The knife her left hand had whipped up from her leg jabbed deep into the underside of the table. A thick-bladed knife, balanced for accurate throwing. (*CO* 72)

Hammett in the first place emphasizes the proximity of Kewpie's "thick-bladed" knife to her genitalia, whose attraction the Op in turn registers by mentioning "her short skirt." In this way Hammett has the Op gravitate toward Kewpie sexually at the same time that she objectifies, in Freudian terms at least, some deep-seated fear of castration by women.[7] Moreover, Hammett evokes in his description of Kewpie the suggestion that women, because of the inaccessible internality that they represent to the male detective's probing mind, always have the potential to lash out like Kewpie does. For when Kewpie "slid her knife back in its hiding place under her skirt and twisted around to face me" (*CO* 73), one senses that this "hiding place" continues to haunt the wary detective, at once stimulating and defeating his attempt to interpret when and where danger may strike next. Women quite literally embody pockets of psychological and, as it were, topographical turbulence that, again and again, interrupt and deflect the detective's interpretive enterprise.

On still other occasions, however, the ironic discrepancy between the benign and malignant aspects of a single woman can be so vast as to produce tremendous cognitive dissonance; it is this dissonance that, in effect, Hammett uses to justify or at least rationalize the misogyny that informs his vision of women in general. Thus, again in "The House in Turk Street," Hammett in his portrait of Mrs. Quarre plays off the nostalgia and sentimentality surrounding the image of "the mother" in contemporary or at least recent American culture.[8] Noting that Mrs. Quarre "was a very fragile little old woman, with a piece of gray knitting in one hand, and faded eyes that twinkled pleasantly behind goldrimmed spectacles" (*CO* 94), the Op goes on to record this about Mrs. Quarre and her husband: "These folks weren't made to be lied to" (94). So much does the Op wish to believe in this scene of domestic tranquillity that, when that scene is belied by the feel of a gun against the back of his neck, the Op seems to be struck by how surreal the experience is: "And looking at [the Quarres], I knew that something cold *couldn't* be against the back of my neck; a harsh voice *couldn't* have ordered me to stand up. It wasn't possible!" (*CO* 96).

Eventually, though, Hammett himself shatters all grounds for sentimentality about motherhood, because Mrs. Quarre, not only part of a crime-ring, finally presents this appearance to the Op:

> I looked at the old woman again, and found little of the friendly fragile one who had poured tea and chatted about the neighbors. This was a witch if there ever was one—a witch of the blackest, most malignant sort. Her little faded eyes were sharp with ferocity, her withered lips were taut in a wolfish snarl, and her thin body fairly quivered with hate. (*CO* 115)

In a world in which even kindly old mothers can at a moment's notice display the fierceness of a wolf, a man in approaching a woman must proceed along lines of suspicion, distrust and unremitting vigilance. Like the Op's when he is in the company of Princess Zhukovski, or Kewpie, one's life depends on one's not batting an eye in the presence of a woman.

This necessity, it is true, reappears in "The Whosis Kid" in a more generalized form: it is not just women, but all perceptual data that, for the sleuth, require constant interpretation, awareness uninterrupted by the smallest gap in consciousness. While struggling to discern whether the Whosis Kid's shape, in passing through a doorway, has darkened the luminous face of the watch upon which the Op has his eyes riveted, the Op describes how "I couldn't afford to blink. A foot could pass the dial while I was blinking. I couldn't afford to blink, but I had to blink. I couldn't tell whether something had passed the watch or not" (*CO* 234). In a world in which information means survival, any sign is potentially a sign of danger, and can itself dangerously mean more than one thing.

On the one hand, Hammett's emphasis on the necessity of constant interpretation may indeed reflect the sorts of generic and thematic constraints that D.A. Miller discusses in *The Novel and the Police*. Examining novels in which the police are marginalized and alternative sources of investigation and crime-solving brought to the fore, Miller describes how "[i]n the same move whereby the police are contained in a marginal pocket of representation, the work of the police is superseded by the operations of another, informal, and extralegal principle of organization and control" (3). This displacement, in turn, eventually opens up a cognitive space for novels in which the narrative techniques themselves—the meticulous recording of detail, the penetration into characters' motives and thoughts, etc—"usurp" the power of the police (21). As Miller puts it, "[W]henever the novel censures policing power, it has already reinvented it, in *the very practice of novelistic representation*" (20). Similarly, to the extent that Hammett marginalizes and disempowers the police in his texts, he seems to reinscribe the policing function itself in the detective's consciousness, and to substitute the detective's interpretive energies for more overt and public forms of policing activity.

But on the other hand, I do not think that we can merely subsume Hammett's treatment of women under Miller's explanatory model. The threat posed by women in Hammett's texts seem to be at the very least irreducible to the threat posed by ambiguous information in general. In fact, the reverse inference seems to me more compelling: that the problem of ambiguous information is reducible to the categories in terms of which Hammett accounts for gender. This is because Hammett's assumptions about women are, *relative to the elaboration of his own plots*, a pre-given frame of reference—a syntax—within whose boundaries danger as such takes on concrete, recognizable shape. I mean that on Hammett's own terms women occupy a different order of explanation than that occupied by the male detective's threatening, naturalistic environment as a whole. Gender roles in Hammett are conceptually prior to the contingencies of experience: gender is destiny.

I think that I can substantiate these rather large claims in the following way. Granted, Hammett's women characters are part of the sometimes deadly play of signs that, on Miller's model, tends to internalize within the detective himself the tense vigilance associated with policing. But we cannot *a fortiori* explain away the threatening equivocality that Hammett ascribes to women. For in Hammett's works, women who do not veer back and forth between the extremes of sensual passivity and fierce aggressiveness cannot subsist; such women are, often in highly unsubtle fashion, erased from the text; and thus Hammett indirectly confers duplicity on the women who do negotiate through the treacherous circumstances and dangerous liaisons into which he leads them. Implicitly, Hammett's view is that, prior to his being able to discover anything else about a given case, the detective can know beforehand that only a "red-haired she-devil" like Elvira in "The House in Turk Street" could survive amid the violence that comprehends and structures male-female relationships. And as if arguing with a grotesquely foregone conclusion, Hammett proves this general interpretive rule by killing off all possible exceptions to it.

Consider Hammett's treatment of Mrs. Ashcraft in "The Golden Horseshoe." Although a relatively minor character, Mrs. Ashcraft is one of the most unequivocally attractive women in all of Hammett's fiction. When we first meet her, the Op describes how

> Mrs. Ashcraft received us in a drawing-room on the second floor. A tall woman of less than thirty, slimly beautiful in a gray dress. Clear was the word that best fit her; it described the blue of her eyes, the pink-white of her skin, and the light-brown of her hair. (*CO* 55)

A moment later the Op mentions how "[h]er eyes lighted up happily, but she didn't throw a fit. She wasn't that sort" (56). Indeed, the Op remarks explicitly that "I liked this Mrs. Ashcraft" (56). But in attributing such positive features to this mild and unassuming woman, it is as if Hammett is providing a *rationale* for her brutal murder:

> Mrs. Ashcraft was dead. . . . Her body was drawn up in a little heap, from which her head hung crookedly, dangling from a neck that had been cut clear through to the bone. Her face was marked with four deep scratches from temple to chin. . . . Bedding and pajamas were soggy with the blood that the clothing piled over her had kept from drying. (*CO* 65)

Similarly, although, Dinah Brand in *Red Harvest* is a prostitute, the Op achieves with her a certain straightforward intimacy; they seem to communicate well with one another. The Op and Dinah feel comfortable enough together to exchange witty repartees about Dinah's household etiquette. At one point, while the Op and Dinah conduct a vigil outside, "[t]he girl shivered with her cheek warm against mine" (130). Again, however, the Op's sense of connection with a woman seems to lend a kind of inexorability to that woman's brutal murder. And given the Op's troubled dreams, in which he feels embarrassed by physical contact with Dinah (150); indeed, given the Op's uncertainty about whether or not he himself actually plunged the ice-pick into her left breast (151), Hammett suggests that violence between the sexes—whether it issues from the woman or from the man—is ineradicable because it is built into the very nature of experience. Male-female violence seems part of a tragic pattern of external circumstance precisely because, for Hammett, such violence precedes external circumstance as its immutable condition, its transcendental explanation.

II

I have thus far attempted to enumerate inductively the misogynist axioms, as it were, on which Hammett bases his model for understanding gender and, by extension, the contingencies of experience. Positively, these axioms ascribe limitless duplicity and cruelty to women; negatively, the laws imply that there cannot be, in the world as it is, a woman who has the detective's best interests at heart or who even maintains indifference towards him. But is it the case that Hammett's interpretive syntax bodes ill for any effort to rethink gender roles in non-conflictual terms? My view is, rather, that Hammett's pessimistic model tends to undermine itself from within.[9] In Hammett, the tragic necessity of violence between the sexes is undercut by the possibility that, at some fundamental level, the masculine and the feminine mirror or replicate one another. At this level, misogyny gives way to androgyny; and by blurring the boundaries between the sexes Hammett implicitly removes the basis on which men, distancing themselves from women, at times try to reduce and demean them. Indeed, through the mechanisms of androgyny, the violence that pervades relations between Hammett's men and women shows itself to be reflexive and, in effect, suicidal. Hammett's texts thus parody the misogynistic vision that simultaneously shapes and informs them.

Significantly, Hammett's representations of women prove contrary to expectations that have been built up around androgyny itself. Cynthia Secor, for instance, voices her "apprehensiveness" about the revolutionary potential of the concept by noting that "[a]ndrogyny, as the term is used in our patriarchal culture, conjures up images of the feminized male . . . and of the perfect marriage in which the female has been acquired by the male in order to complete himself. . . . There is no comparable imagistic tradition of the masculinized female" (166). Daniel A. Harris elaborates on this argument thus:

the myth of androgyny has been created by man, and its design is the co-option, incorporation or subjugation of women: in seeking "feminine" elements with which to complete himself, the man reduces woman to merely symbolic status, plays parasite, and paradoxically demands from the creature he has thus mentally enslaved his own freedom. (172)

In Hammett, however, the image of the masculinized female occurs with much greater frequency than that of the feminized male.[10] Accordingly, Hammett's women characters do not so much "complete" their male counterparts as they are completed by them. And the interpretive crux that women constantly pose to the male detective can therefore be specified in terms that at least partially demarcate the problem at hand: women on the one hand mark the limits of the detective's identity—the threshold beyond which the detective feels compelled to ward off what threatens him—and on the other hand they remind him of his deep complicity with that by which he feels most threatened.

As before, however, I wish to translate this sort of language into somewhat less portentous and thus more useful terms. I wish to demonstrate in this connection how Hammett's works themselves de-naturalize the very categories of masculine and feminine—the brute facts of gender, so to speak—on which the author's interpretive syntax is based. As we shall see, what is controversial or constructed and what is indisputable or natural about gender roles ceases to be, on Hammett's own terms, easy to distinguish.

In the first place, it is significant that, by making the Op a short and pudgy character, Hammett brings to the fore the *size* of certain of the women he meets.

Of the Princess Zhukovski in "The Gutting of Couffignal," for instance, the Op observes that "[s]he was tall, I am short and thick. I had to look up to see her face . . . " (*BK* 10). Likewise, Big Flora in "The Big Knockover," although her "voice was deep but not masculine" (*BK* 397), seems to have the physique of a man—and of a strong man at that:

> She stood at least five feet ten in her high-heeled slippers. They were small slippers, and I noticed that her ringless hands were small. The rest of her wasn't. She was broad-shouldered, deep-bosomed, thick-armed, with a pink throat which for all its smoothness was muscled like a wrestler's and a handsome, brutal face. . . . From forehead to throat her pink skin was underlaid with smooth, thick, strong muscles. (*BK* 397)

Even Dinah Brand, who it is true seems to be "popping open" with feminine sexuality (*RH* 30), cuts an imposing and somewhat masculine figure when juxtaposed to the Op: "She was an inch or two taller than I, which made her about five feet eight. She had a broad-shouldered, full-breasted, round-hipped body and big muscular legs" (*RH* 30).

But it is not by size alone that Hammett suggests androgyny. In "The Golden Horseshoe," Kewpie, whom the Op meets "hustling drinks" in a bar in Tijuana, appears thus: "Her short hair was brown and curly over a round, boyish face with laughing, impudent eyes" (*CO* 58). Even her grin "was as boyish as the straight look in her brown eyes" (58). Similarly, when we first meet her, Effie Perine in *The Maltese Falcon* not only has eyes that are "brown and playful in a shiny boyish face" (1), Effie also seems to have an uncommonly vivid sense of how Spade will respond to Brigid O'Shaugnessy: "You'll want to see her anyway: she's a knockout" (1). Passing from Spade's inner to his outer office, Effie seems to pass as well from one set of sexual possibilities to another, and she adjusts herself to conventions that constrain her to address "Miss Wonderly" with professional tact and reserve: "Will you come in . . . " (*MF* 1).

In "The Scorched Face," further, Myra Banbrock meets this description:

> Myra—20 years old; 5 feet 8 inches; 150 pounds; athletic; brisk, almost masculine manner and carriage; bobbed brown hair; brown eyes; medium complexion; square face, with large chin and short nose; scar over left ear, concealed by hair; fond of horses and all outside sports. (*BK* 76)

In describing Ruth, Myra's younger sister, Hammett also mentions that Ruth is "quiet, timid, inclined to lean on her more forceful sister" (*BK* 76). Arguably, Hammett here employs the technique that, in *Swann's Way*, Proust uses to describe "beneath the mannish face" of M. Vinteuil's daughter "the finer features of a young woman in tears" (87). But whereas Proust so laminates Mlle. Vinteuil that beneath "her thick, comfortable voice" it seems "as though some elder and more sensitive sister, latent in her" were blushing at her younger sibling's "thoughtless, schoolboyish utterance" (87), Hammett in "The Scorched Face" objectifies masculine and feminine impulses—the animus and anima, as it were—and distributes them between the two Banbrock sisters. Thus, where Proust's method is psychological, capturing through an image or figure of speech the interior states and composite sexuality of one woman, Hammett's method is in effect allegorical, embodying in separate characters dialectically opposed psychic forces. And Hammett's allegory continues when, as the story progresses, Ruth finally shoots herself, whereas Myra, after her participation in orgies of an unspecified nature, "had none of the masculinity that had been in her photographs and description" (107)—integrating within herself, presumably, the aggressiveness and passivity once divided between her and Ruth.

We thus have at least an initial indication of the scope of androgyny in Hammett: from the author's rather vague attributions of "boyishness" to figures like Kewpie, and his ascriptions of masculine stature to figures like Big Flora, to his suggestion of a female masculinity not co-extensive with mere physical appearance, an androgyny of impulse of which androgyny of appearance is but one symptom. Certainly we might at this point undertake a more exhaustive list of the symptoms and motivations of androgyny in Hammett's corpus, as well as a thoroughgoing account of why Hammett himself apparently wants to drive a wedge between women's transgression of convention (as symptom) and women's transgression of nature (as cause). But what I wish to stress here is simply that Hammett, by describing women in a way that places them on a continuum with men, produces a series of propositions whose status is of a very special sort.

Hammett's propositions about androgyny, on the one hand, do not consist with the author's own rules for forming meaningful or relevant propositions about gender. Those rules, as I have indicated, posit an absolute antagonism of interest between men and women. Yet Hammett's female androgynes, by definition, share what on Hammett's own terms would be deemed masculine interests. Hence, if he is to avoid abrogating the rules for valid interpretation, if he is to work within the syntax that so far has allowed him to interpret and survive a hostile environment, the misogynist detective cannot afford to enter the logical space in which propositions about androgyny subsist. But on the other hand, neither can the detective afford *not* to enter this logical space, for it is the space in which interpretation itself unfolds. Simply by recording propositions about androgyny in the first place, the detective thereby includes those propositions in the domain of evidence. In turn, this domain, because it is just the set of all possible clues, thereby proves itself not only meaningful or rule-governed, but moreover relevant to the detective's particular interests. If the *misogynist* detective must in principle disallow the very possibility of androgyny, therefore, in fact, the misogynist *detective* cannot disallow this possibility, on pain of closing off the avenue of evidence that he must always keep open, or else perhaps die.

To put this last point in slightly different terms, the detective belies his own misogynistic interpretive code, which he views as necessary for survival, just by including reports of evidence that destroy the very basis of misogyny, but that the detective *also* views as necessary for survival. This, I submit, is the double-bind or rather antinomy into which Hammett's own interpretive syntax leads him. And again we should take our cue from Kant: as Kant asserts in the first *Critique*, should any theoretical syntax or model lead to an antinomy of the kind that I have detailed, this very fact provides us with sufficient grounds for rejecting that theoretical model from the start.

I wish to close off my discussion by arguing that in Hammett's last two novels, *The Glass Key* and *The Thin Man*, the author does in fact circumvent what might now be termed the antinomy of androgyny, precisely by rejecting, at least in part, his own earlier misogynistic model—a model in relation to which androgyny is, as I just suggested, at once a species of insuperable counterevidence and an inescapable consequence or corollary. In the later Hammett's treatment of women, uncontestable grounds for hating *certain* women are mitigated by equally irrefutable grounds for not hating others. As a result, Hammett's later texts imply that the detective must treat women case by case, and resist, on pain of manifest error, making any general claim about what women in essence are like.[11] Hammett's treatment of women in the later works, therefore, becomes deliberately fragmentary and particularized: it is as if each woman merits a theory in her own right. Gender no longer provides an interpretive syntax, but instead cries out for one.

Indeed, in *The Glass Key*, Hammett comes close to stating outright the view of women on which the author's later novels are premised. When Janet Henry comes to Ned Beaumont's apartment in hopes of convincing Beaumont that his friend Paul Madvig is indeed guilty of murder, and in hopes of justifying in this way her own semi-deceitful conduct toward Madvig, Hammett completes the scene in this manner:

> [Janet] sighed and stood up holding out her head. "I'm sorry and disappointed, but we needn't be enemies, need we?"
> [Beaumont] rose facing her, but did not take her hand. He said: "The part of you that's tricked Paul is my enemy."
> She held her hand there while asking: "And the other part of me, the part that hasn't anything to do with that?"
> He took her hand and bowed over it. (146)

Granted, the view that a woman has "parts," which sometimes consist but ill with one another, is not unique to the later Hammett. But the explicit discussion of this view by a female character herself *is* unprecedented in Hammett. We here see Hammett's fiction thematize and so transcend itself. For as Hammett himself represents them, women now have, it seems, the power to eschew enemies and establish allegiances by conscious choice, instead of being driven by some irrational mechanism that bestows upon women's every kindness, and every woman's kindness, a baleful duplicity.

I do not mean to overstate my case, however: plenty of evidence of a misogynist interpretive scheme can be found in both *The Glass Key* and *The Thin Man*. Consider this description of Lee Wilshire in the former novel, a description that brings to mind the sort of threat associated with Kewpie's anatomy in "The Golden Horseshoe": "She put a hand inside her dress and brought it out a fist. She held the fist up close to Ned Beaumont's face and opened it" (18). Consider, too, Hammett's account of Eloisa Matthews, whose quasi-nymphomaniacal response to Beaumont represents at the same time a brutal disregard of her weak husband's feelings:

> [Mr. Matthews] said: "Darling, won't you come to bed? It's midnight."
> . . . . She did not look up from the fire until [Beaumont] had put [a drink] in her hand. When she looked up she smiled crookedly, twisting her heavily rouged exquisite thin lips sidewise. Her eyes, reflecting red light from the fire, were too bright.
> . . . . She lifted her glass and said, cooing: "To my husband!" (125-26)

In *The Thin Man*, further, the way Miriam Nunheim and her husband settle verbal disputes suggests that violence and chaos are the invariable concomitants of marriage: "She swung her arm and let the skillet go at his head. It missed, crashing into the wall. Grease and egg-yolks made fresher stains on wall, floor, and furniture" (110). Hammett's treatment of Miriam seems calculated to warrant both Studsy Burke's later claim that "somebody could do something with that cluck if they took hold of her right," and also Shep Morelli's reply to Studsy: "[Yes,] by the throat" (158).

What is more, Hammett's treatment of Mimi Wynant in the same novel suggests how even the later Hammett, though ultimately placing in question the brute facts or rather primitive terms of a misogynist syntax, cannot wholly exorcise the misogynistic *Weltanschauung* by whose spell he remains, at the same time, profoundly fascinated. It is not only that Mimi beats her daughter Dorothy, both in private (44) and in public (164); Nick Charles also justifies his own mistrust of Mimi by telling Dorothy: "She hates men more than any woman I've ever known who wasn't a Lesbian. . . . Mimi hates men—all of us—bitterly" (173). And Hammett's misogyny vis-à-vis Mimi seems to extend itself to women as a group, when Nick Charles advises the police thus:

> the chief thing . . . is not to let [Mimi] tire you out. When you catch her in a lie, she admits it and gives you another lie to take its place and, when you catch her in that one, admits it and gives you still another, and so on. Most people—*even women*—get discouraged after you've caught them in the third or fourth straight lie and fall back on either the truth or silence, but not Mimi. She keeps trying and you've got to be careful or you'll find yourself believing her, not because she seems to be telling the truth, but simply because you're tired of disbelieving her. (177, my emphasis)

In fact, when we witness Mimi's hysterical fit a moment later, Hammett uses Mimi's *physical* monstrousness to figure, as in his account of the Princess Zhukovski in "The Gutting of Couffignal," women's mythic capacity to transform themselves, instantaneously, into something not only alien, but also hostile to men:

> Mimi's face was becoming purple. Her eyes protruded, glassy, senseless, enormous. Saliva bubbled and hissed between clenched teeth with her breathing, and her red throat—her whole body—was a squirming mass of veins and muscles swollen until it seemed they must burst. Her wrists were hot in my hands and sweat made them hard to hold. (186)

Are we to say, then, that the later Hammett seems to have progressed not at all past the visceral misogyny evident in his early works?

The thing to keep in mind here is that other women characters in the later novels do not merit the sort of treatment Hammett gives to figures like Eloise Matthews, Miriam Nunheim and Mimi Wynant. We have for instance Mrs. Madvig in *The Glass Key*, a woman whom Ned Beaumont insists on calling "Mom" (21, 107, 187). Paul's mother, in return, shows genuine affection towards Beaumont: "Her eyes were as blue and clear and young as her son's—younger than her son's when she looked up at Ned Beaumont entering the room" (21). Again, after Beaumont and Paul have exchanged words and made an irreparable split, Mrs. Madvig tries to bring about a reconciliation between the two men she seems to love equally (188). And unlike Mrs. Quarres in "The House in Turk Street," Mrs. Madvig does not undergo any wolfish transmutations, but continues to exert a benign, if ineffectual, influence on affairs throughout the novel.

One could also use Opal Madvig in *The Glass Key* and Dorothy Wynant in *The Thin Man* to make a (perhaps slightly weaker) case for a change of interpretive schemes or syntaxes in Hammett's last two novels. These two women parallel one another to the extent that their youth accounts for the partly compromising situations in which they sometimes find themselves. Opal Madvig seems to be guilty of, if anything, a too-intense, somewhat misplaced idealism. After all, it is her devotion to the murdered (or else accidentally killed) Taylor Henry that prompts her to league herself with Shad O'Rory and Mr. Matthews in their smear campaign against Opal's father, Paul, whom Opal genuinely believes to have murdered Taylor. Opal, in any event, never proves herself worthy of Beaumont's distrust, and he continues to manifest toward her the same sort of candid affection he displays at the opening of the novel (24-6).

Further, Dorothy Wynant, though guilty once of lying in order to get Nora's and Nick's attention and sympathy (*TM*, 21-22), and in general more given to the histrionic than the factual, shows herself at the same time to be up against considerable odds: her brutalization by an uncaring mother; her fear that she, like her father may be insane (14); and an older, darker victimization at which

Hammett twice hints (47, 188), but which he never reveals. Hammett's inclusion of extenuating circumstances in his treatment of Dorothy suggests that, in the author's own view, we must not be too quick to judge her. At the very least, we can make for Dorothy the same sort of negative claim that we can make for Opal, but that we could not make for the early Hammett's women characters: at no time does Dorothy pose a threat to, or exert a destructive influence on, Hammett's male detective; and yet neither does Hammett kill off these women as aberrations that prove, in grisly fashion, a misogynist rule.

But the strongest case for a global change in Hammett's interpretive syntax—a shift whose effects we can begin to register by superimposing Hammett's later on his earlier representations of women—the strongest case for such a shift can be made vis-à-vis Nora Charles, with whom the detective actually allies himself by marriage in *The Thin Man*. I might mention in passing the issue of how this novel domesticizes the genre of hard-boiled detective fiction, producing startling and unresolved tensions between sexist individualism and a sort of comic nuptial harmony. What I wish to focus on here specifically, however, are the kinds of attributes Hammett confers on Nora Charles herself.

Capable of keeping her nerve even while Shep Morelli brandishes his gun at her, and capable of maintaining interest in the serious, manly business of detection, Nora does not *ipso facto* exhibit androgynous features, physical or otherwise—as would have been the case were *The Thin Man* driven by the (monolithically) sexist logic of the early Hammett. Through Nora, it seems, Hammett begins to dissociate strength and seriousness from masculinity, and by extension to undo the whole nexus of assumptions according to which certain attributes remain invariably gender-specific. Or rather does Hammett's treatment of Nora initiate this transvaluation of gender only to reverse it? After all, John Guild, the official police detective assigned to the Wynant case, early on in the novel does praise Nora's poise and bravery in this way: "'Jesus,' he said, 'there's a woman with hair on her chest'" (37).

In my view, however, Hammett as it were desublimates this suggestion of Nora's androgyny in two ways. First, Hammett places the suggestion in indirect discourse and thus ascribes it to a de-privileged point of view—the view not only of a policeman, but moreover of a policeman who comically insists on informing Nick "that's a fine woman you have there" every time he happens to see Nora. Second, Hammett phrases the suggestion in blatantly figurative terms. What the detective would have reported before in an apparently neutral observation-language—a discourse internal to the process of interpretation itself—now gets objectified in language set off by quotation marks—a discourse of limitation, bias, even farce. The early Hammett's own over-restrictive assumption that women cannot show "masculine" strength without at the same time literally being masculine—this assumption now becomes the stuff of mockery or, more precisely, self-parody.

But we need not resort to such micro-narratological analysis to see how Hammett's treatment of Nora in *The Thin Man* is a large-scale transformation in the author's own interpretive syntax. Throughout the novel, Hammett's portrayal of Nora suggests that we cannot, as we could in the early works, make an unproblematic inference from distinctions of gender to distributions of labor—including, most importantly, *interpretive* labor. Nora constantly strains against the conventions that, within the hard-boiled genre as such, make the business of detection a specifically male enterprise. For instance, it is Nora who first sees and then points out to Nick the newspaper account of Julia Wolf's murder (9). Further, when Nora poses questions to Nick about the murder ("Do you suppose [Clyde Wynant] killed her?" . . . . "Was she in love with him or was it just business?" (10-111), Nora's discourse becomes coextensive with the discourse of interpretation itself. Hammett forces the reader here and throughout the novel to identify with Nora, whose reading-position, as it were, mirrors our own: we too must read in the interrogative mode. It is therefore characteristic of Nora that she likes solving jigsaw puzzles (133). And when Nora theorizes that Clyde Wynant is "shielding somebody else" (208)—though as it turns out she is mistaken—Nick thinks her insights important enough to mention Nora's theory to Detective Guild (228). Overall, we see that the process of interpretation takes place *between* Nora and Nick, in the give-and-take of question and answer, hypothesis and argument. Interpretive acumen ceases to be gender-specific.

Indeed, Nora provides Nick with information that he could not have obtained at all without Nora's manifest skill at observing and interpreting. We learn, for example, that Nora has feigned sleep while actually watching goings-on at the Wynant's apartment (191). In response to the other possible clues that Nora at this time also gives to Nick, Nick himself, twice, expresses a sort of admiring surprise: "Well, well" (191). Far from being congruent with distinctions of gender, therefore, the distribution of interpretive labor now seems to depend on what one happens to be in the position to hear or observe at any given time. Hammett thus reincorporates contingency into the notion of gender itself; in turn, successful interpretation requires that the male detective not prematurely exclude women's perspectives on the larger contingency of which both men and women are a part. As Nick tells Nora, in a statement no doubt meant to be patronizing, but whose irony ultimately doubles back on Hammett himself: "I don't see how any detective can hope to get along without being married to you . . . " (191-2).

One will perhaps have observed that my analysis has virtually trailed off into a discussion, *in seriatim*, of particular women in Hammett's last two novels. At the risk of appearing to rationalize a blinkered or narrowly inductive approach, however, I contend that Hammett's later treatment of women itself warrants the case-by-case procedure I have finally adopted in this paper. For in Hammett's later works, gender no longer functions (completely) as a transcendental condition for our being able to know anything at all about particular men and women. Rather, it is particular men and women with whom we are bound to concern ourselves, and whose variability from one instance to the next becomes the only thing we can assume. Not only are we to resist seeking in gender a transcendental condition for understanding the world; this need for de-transcendentalizing gender becomes, as it were, the only gender-specific assumption that we are entitled to make. In other words, by extending the concepts the later Hammett himself sets into play, we infer that any given woman deserves our special effort *not* to think of her behavior as being motivated by eternalized gender categories. I do not mean to imply that Hammett's fiction entirely lives up the imperative of particularism that I have, for the purposes of argument, abstracted from Hammett's later texts; even *The Glass Key* and *The Thin Man*, to the extent that these texts provide grounds for misogyny at all, of course bear the pernicious impress of a sexist syntax. But I do mean to assert that, relative to the early works, Hammett's treatment of women in the late works can be mapped out along a vector of change. Whereas Hammett begins by subsuming interpretation under the rule of gender, he ends by subsuming gender, at least in part, under the rule of interpretation. [*Genre* 24 (Spring 1991): 1-23]

NOTES

1. Note too how Wilmer stares at Spade's and the hotel detective's (phallic) neckties (108). With Hammett's description of Wilmer's hands, moreover, compare the "flaccid bluntness" of Cairo's hands (47).

2. The same dynamic, of course, is implicit in Nina Auerbach's exploration of the paradox that "[w]hile right-thinking Victorians were elevating woman into an angel, their art slithered with images of a mermaid" or else a demon (6 and *passim*). What is more, Viola Klein identifies in Freud, at what might be termed the meta-theoretical level, a similar, sometimes paradoxical ambivalence toward women: "on the one hand the wonder at the 'enigmatic' woman, the approach to feminine psychology as a 'riddle' to be solved, and a theory which views the development of femininity as a particularly 'difficult and complicated process'; on the other hand there is contempt . . . for her inferior intellectual capacities, her greater vanity, her weaker sexual instincts, her disposition to neuroses and hysteria, and for her constitutional passivity" (84).

3. In "The Hammett Succubus," moreover, William Marling, discussing Kenneth Rayner Johnson's *The Succubus* (1979), asserts that "[t]he cause of [the protagonist's] fear is the female antagonist, the 'succubus' of the title; as in other popular novels of detection, *she threatens the protagonist's sense of discrete self*" (67, my emphasis).

4. It would be interesting in this connection, too, to consider Hammett's various statements of the detective's "code" as a sort of purifying ritual (or rather litany) aimed to dispel precisely that dread which Ricoeur associates with the fear of Evil. In "The Gutting of Couffignal," for instance, it is to a *woman*, Princess Zhukovski, that the Op must explain his code. When the threat of contamination is greatest, it seems, the detective must ritualistically or perhaps apotropaically recite, to himself and in the face of the threatening object, the ascetic code that allows him to negotiate circumstances rife with Evil.

5. Note how Ines' and Elvira's roles in the two stories are the same: they both seduce men and then lead them on to steal from their employers either money or assets.

6. It is interesting to note that Webster's *Ninth New Collegiate Dictionary* defines "Kewpie" thus: "used for a small chubby doll with a topknot of hair."

7. Kewpie's "thick-bladed knife" also carries phallic connotations, of course. To the extent that the Op feels intensely threatened by a woman so equipped, Hammett's representation of Kewpie suggests that images of androgyny in Hammett owe much to the late nineteenth-century, "pessimistic" version of androgyny that is discussed by A.J.L. Busst. See note 9.

8. My sense of this sentimentalization of motherhood derives from a lecture given by Paul Fussell, in the fall of 1986, concerning the effects of WWI on chivalry and perceptions of motherhood.

Note too that movies of the early '30s, such as *The Public Enemy* and *Little Caesar*, rely on the image of the frail and loving, if perhaps naive, old mother. The *Public Enemy* ends with ironic (and, to the modern sensibility, comic) counterpointing between Tom Powers' return home in the form of a sort of brutalized mummy and his mother's joyous preparations upstairs in the bedroom for her son's "homecoming." Similarly, in *Little Caesar*, Joe Massera, Rico's best friend, shares a touching and nostalgic moment with his mother—a moment that, we are to assume, has something to do with Joe's abandonment of a life of crime.

9. Although, as we shall see, it does not fully accounct for the manifestations of androgyny in Hammett's works, A.J.L. Busst's account of "The Image of the Androgyne in the Nineteenth-Century" suggests how images of androgyny may *not* in fact undermine the pessimism that informs Hammett's view of relations between the sexes and perhaps of the world in general. Busst describes how late in the nineteenth century the hermaphrodite symbolized generally the decay of earlier ideals, and in particular the advent of "vices" such as sadism and masochism. As Busst puts it, "a sadistic woman, in as far as she dominates her male victim, may be considered virile, since she exhibits strength . . . and her ability to indulge in her vice depends to a large extent on the male's abdication of his own virility, his masochistic willingness to be ruled—even tormented—by the female. . . . His refusal to assert himself often indicates awareness of the vanity of all action, which must accompany loss of convictions in a world without values, where good is often indistinguishable from evil" (in *Romantic Mythologies*, 56). However, as I shall explain, I believe that images of androgyny in Hammett's texts can be linked with the project of interpretation in general, such that Busst's basic opposition between "optimistic" and "pessimistic" uses of the androgyne holds valid only for androgyny taken in its narrower sense.

10. Joe Cairo in *The Maltese Falcon* is a notable exception. However, Raymond Chandler's male characters—including figures like Lindsay Mariott in *Farewell, My Lovely*, Leslie Murdock in *The High Window*, and, most interestingly, Philip Marlowe himself—are in general much more aptly described as androgynous than Hammett's. Indeed, in order to get a sense of Chandler's subtlety and sophistication in this respect, one might note how, in *The Big Sleep*, Chandler figures Arthur Gwynn Geiger's androgyny by the use of significant details in descriptions of Geiger's house. Geiger, who is like Caesar, "a husband to women and a wife to men" (61), has in his house a "near, fussy, womanish" bedroom in which "a man's brushes" rest beside "perfume on the triple-mirrored dressing table" (24). Similarly, "a man's slippers" are visible "under the flounced edge of the bed cover" (24).

11. In this connection, the later Hammett's treatment of women seems to bear important resemblances to (American) philosophical pragmatism. James's and particularly Dewey's pragmatism, as Richard Rorty discusses in both *Philosophy and the Mirror of Nature* and *Consequences of Pragmatism*, also replaces the search for enduring essences with an emphasis on provisional, deliberately anti-systematic explanations of the world. Note, too, the internal evidence for a pragmatist orientation in Hammett. For example, the famous story about Flitcraft in *The Maltese Falcon* concerns a man who changes his name to Charles (Sanders) Pierce, and in *The Thin Man* we discover that Gilbert Wynant is "writing a book on Knowledge and Belief" (86). Moreover, in the latter novel's closing pages, in which Nick explains to Nora how he arrived at the conclusion that Herbert Macaulay is the culprit, Hammett seems to underwrite a basically pragmatist analysis of notions like evidence and truth.

WORKS CITED

Auerbach, Nina. *Woman and the Demon: The Life of a Victorian Myth*. Cambridge: Harvard UP, 1982.

Blair, Walter. "Dashiell Hammett: Themes and Techniques." In *Essays on American Literature in Honor in Jay B. Hubbell*. Ed. Clarence Gohdes. Durham: Duke UP, 1967.

Busst, A.J.L. "The Image of the Androgyne in the Nineteenth Century." In *Romantic Mytholgies*. Ed. Ian Fletcher. London: Routledge and Kegan Paul, 1967.

Chandler, Raymond. *The Big Sleep*. New York: Vintage Books, 1988.

De Beauvoir, Simone. *The Second Sex*. Trans. H. M. Parshley. New York: Alfred A. Knopf, 1949.

Dooley, Dennis. *Dashiell Hammett*. New York: Frederick Ungar Publ. Co., 1984.

Eliade, Mircea. "Mephistopheles and the Androgyne, or the Mystery of the Whole." In *The Two and the One*. Trans. J.M. Cohen. London: Harvill P, 1965.

Freud, Sigmund. "Femininity." In *New Introductory Lectures on Psychoanalysis*. Trans. and Ed. James Strachey. New York: W.W. Norton and Co., 1965.

Fussell, Paul. *The Great War and Modern Memory*. London: Oxford UP, 1975.

Gilbert, Sandra M. and Susan Gubar. *The Madwoman in the Attic: The Woman Writer in the Nineteenth-Century Imagination*. New Haven: Yale UP 1979.

Gregory, Sinda. *Private Investigations: The Novels of Dashiell Hammett*. Carbondale: Southern Illinois UP, 1985.

Hammett, Dashiell. *The Big Knockover*. Ed. Lillian Hellman. New York: Vintage Books, 1972.

___. *Continental Op*. Ed. Stephen Marcus. New York: Vintage Books, 1974.

___. *The Glass Key*. New York: Vintage Books, 1972.

___. *The Maltese Falcon*. New York: Vintage Books, 1984.

___. *Red Harvest*. New York: Vintage Books, 1972.

___. *The Thin Man*. New York: Alfred A. Knopf, 1933.

Harris, Daniel A. "Androgyny: The Sexist Myth." *Women's Studies*, vol. 2, no. 2 (1974): 171-84.

Heilbrun, Carolyn. "Further Notes toward a Recognition of Androgyny." *Women's Studies*, vol. 2, no. 2 (1974): 143-50.

Kant, Immanuel. *Critique of Pure Reason*. Trans. Norman Kemp Smith. New York: St. Martin's Press, 1965.

Klein, Viola. *The Feminine Character: History of an Ideology*. Urbana: U. of Illinois P, 1946; 2nd ed., 1971.

Marling, William. "The Hammett Succubus" *Clues* 3 (1982): 66-75.

Maxfield, James F. "Hard-Boiled Dicks and Dangerous Females: Sex and Love in the Detective Fiction of Dashiell Hammett." *Clues* 6 (1985): 107-23.

Miller, D. A. *The Novel and the Police*. Berkeley: U of California P, 1988.

Nye, Russell. *The Unembarassed Muse: The Popular Arts in America*. New York: The Dial Press, 1970.

Proust, Marcel. *Remembrance of Things Past*. Trans. C. K. Scott Moncrieff. New York: Random House, 1934.

Ricoeur, Paul. *The Symbolism of Evil*. Trans. Emerson Buchanan. New York: Harper and Row, Publishers, 1967.

Rogers, Katharine M. *The Troublesome Helpmate: A History of Misogyny in Literature*. Seattle: U of Washington P, 1966.

Rorty, Richard. *Consequences of Pragmatism*. Minneapolis: U of Minnesota P, 1982.
___. *Philosophy and the Mirror of Nature*. Princeton: Princeton UP, 1979.

Secor, Cynthia. "Androgyny: An Early Reappraisal." *Women's Studies*, vol. 2, no. 2 (1974): 161-170.

Dangerous Romance as Prelude to Love: Hammett's *Woman in the Dark*

Larry Anderson

Commentators generally agree that Dashiell Hammett's relationship with Lillian Hellman served as a turning point, for better or worse, in both his life and his writing. One critic, in fact, says that the change in his writing "can be seen in the marked shift in tone between his previous novels, together with the unfinished manuscript [of *The Thin Man*] and the final version of *The Thin Man*" (Hamilton 124). Others have also pointed out the differences between *The Thin Man* and Hammett's earlier works (Schoper; Marcus; Marling). Changes like these usually do not happen quickly, without developing through intermediate stages. The time period between his meeting Lillian Hellman and before publication of *The Thin Man* seems to have been such a stage of development. During this time was published what can be seen as a transitional novella, *Woman in the Dark: A Novel of Dangerous Romance*. Robert Parker points out in his introduction to the story that the work was serialized in three parts in April 1933, two years after Hammett had met Hellman, one year before *The Thin Man* came out. Of the style, Parker says that "it is very much Hammett . . . . yet it also shows us Hammett's view of life in transition" (v). Just what view undergoes a transition is suggested by Cynthia Hamilton: "The companionship [Hammett] found with Hellman changed his mind about the possibility of relationships being both positive and close" (124). Typically, Hammett's characters do not find positive or close relationships; they tend to isolate themselves, chiefly because of their inability to trust anyone. As Stephen Marcus puts it: "In Hammett, society and social relations are dominated by the principle of basic mistrust" (373-74). As a result, Hammett's fictional world contains few meaningful relationships. Although the two central characters in *Woman in the Dark* are individuals to be sure, such basic mistrust is *not* evident; indeed, the question of trust is never really an issue. If anything, the characters in *Woman in the Dark* rely on a fundamental type of trust, generated out of sheer pragmatic necessity.

More than anything else, *Woman in the Dark* is a story of relationships; Parker goes further, characterizing the work as sentimental, and saying that it is "more of a love story than Hammett usually wrote" (ix). I would question whether there is enough evidence to call it a love story; let us consider it a *prelude* to a love story, which then requires that we take a closer look at the two characters involved in this rather curious relationship, Luise Fischer and Brazil.

The opening scene of Part One, "The Flight," and its characterization of both Luise and Brazil, will put most readers on very familiar Hammettian territory. An injured woman is being battered by the forces of nature; her lack of control is reinforced through Hammett's masterful use of synecdoche and personification. The opening sentence places Luise in a position of vulnerability: "Her right ankle turned under her and she fell" (3). Having been betrayed by her ankle, she cries out, but the wind "made a whisper of her exclamation and snatched her scarf away" (3). She loses her step, her voice, and her protection. As she tries to stand, she is challenged by both the terrain and the weather: she "rose with her back to the wind, leaning back against the wind's violence and the road's steep sloping" (3-4). It's almost as if the wind and the road are conspiring against her.

But she manages to move on, and after crossing a wooden bridge she is confronted by a sign at a fork in the road. We are told that she does not look at the sign but rather looks around her, shivering. Nature seems to direct her: "Foliage to her left moved to show and hide yellow light. She took the left-hand fork" (4). And so she arrives at Brazil's house, literally being blown in:

> She opened the door. The wind blew it in sharply, her hold on the latch dragging her with it so that she had to cling to the door with both hands to keep from falling. . . . She forced the door shut and, still leaning against it, said: "I am sorry." She took pains with her words to make them clear notwithstanding her accent. (4-5)

The vulnerability, the penitential posture, the obvious mysteriousness, and the touch of the exotic with the accent, all combine to invite us into the dark, hard-boiled world we expect. However, this portrayal of Luise as vulnerable, as being at the mercy of surrounding forces, will turn out to be false.

We eventually learn that Luise is running away from a man named Kane Robson, a wealthy landowner, who had brought her home with him from Switzerland a couple of weeks ago. The decision to be Robson's mistress was not a difficult one for her to make: "'I was without any money at all, any friends. He liked me and he was rich.' She made a little gesture with the cigarette in her hand. 'So I said Yes.'" (60). But it did not take long for Luise to tire of the situation, as she later tells her lawyer: "I could stand him no longer. We quarrelled and I left" (61). This is what leads to the opening scene of the story.

Brazil is also just what we would expect from Hammett. His voice, in response to Luise's first knock, is masculine, hoarse, and unemotional (4). As she enters, Brazil is seated by a hearth cleaning the bowl of a pipe with a knife: "His copperish eyes were as impersonal as his hoarse voice. . . . He did not rise from his chair. The edge of the knife in his hand rasped inside the brier bowl of his pipe" (5). His face, "not definitely hostile or friendly," is sallow and heavily featured (5). During the ensuing conversation, Brazil several times wanders over to the door, opens it, and glances outside, apparently for no reason; he later explains that he suffers from claustrophobia, as a result of a long stretch in prison for manslaughter. A month ago he rented this house—from Kane Robson—in order to figure things out. As he tells Luise: "That's what I came up here for—to try to get myself straightened out, see how I stood, what I wanted to do" (24-25). We have in the character Brazil what could very well be one of Hammett's hard-boiled detectives: the impersonal eyes, the hoarse voice, the inscrutable face with just the hint of unhealthiness, and the somewhat mysterious background.

Brazil, like Luise, has been damaged, and both their lives are in transition. Each in a sense is leaving behind one kind of life, looking for another. However, the two differ in the ways in which they respond to the forces around them. It is in the manner of their responses to the upcoming events that their relationship becomes defined. This character analysis must proceed, then, accompanied by a plot analysis.

The fictional world of *Woman in the Dark* consists of a series of intrusions, and the individuals who populate this world can only react, as quickly and forcibly as they can, to each intrusion as it comes. To use the words of Brazil, when in trouble "you have to take your chances . . . . And the best you can expect is the worst of it" (42). Brazil certainly seems to have taken this motto as his guiding philosophy of life. But in Luise Fischer we have someone who stands in contrast to Brazil and his motto; at least, she seems to have higher expectations than he. Hammett gives us a picture of life in a world of events motivated by human evil, as opposed to the existential vision commonly ascribed to his work (e.g., Hamilton; Marcus; Marling; Ruehlman). Into the lives of Luise and Brazil comes the force of human evil in the form of Kane Robson, and from the opening scene until the finale, everything that happens does so as a result of Robson's influence. There is nothing random about the events that embroil Brazil and Luise; it is not a matter of "cosmic chaos" (Hamilton 129), or existential traps. One human being intrudes his desires into the lives of others and, temporarily, determines the paths those lives will take.

Luise's arrival at Brazil's house is the first of six intrusions that divide Part One into six rapidly-paced scenes. Shortly after Luise arrives and receives help with her ankle (from the mysterious Evelyn, a girl/woman who apparently regularly spends time with Brazil), there is another knock on the door. Two men, Kane Robson and Dick Conroy, are looking for Luise to return her to Robson's house up on the hill. When Luise makes it clear that she will not return with them, they politely leave, telling her to call on them if she needs any help. After they leave, the telephone intrudes, warning Evelyn that her father is coming looking for her. The father, Grant, does show up a little later, after Evelyn has rushed off. After Grant departs unsatisfied, Brazil rushes off to see if Evelyn made it home all right. With Luise alone in the house, Robson and Conroy again intrude, drunk, planning on taking Luise by force. Brazil returns, intruding on their plan, in time to chase them off. Later the telephone intrudes again; this time it's Evelyn, warning Brazil that Robson is swearing out a warrant for his arrest.

Robson's will is behind not only his two visits, but also every other one as well. The first telephone call comes from Evelyn's step-mother, warning her that her father is on the way. Someone called to tell him that Evelyn was at Brazil's; this happens *after* the first visit by Robson and Conroy. Brazil at one point asks Luise if she thinks Robson made the call to Evelyn's father. She in turn wonders aloud if Robson would know that Evelyn's father did not want her seeing Brazil, to which Brazil responds: "In a place like this, everybody knows all about everybody" (19). The implication is clear.

If Robson did not make the call, then we are left with the coincidence that has Robson and Conroy showing up at just the time when Brazil is gone. Yes, an existential interpretation of Hammett's fictional world would accept all such events as simply random, with no other explanation necessary, or possible. But in the context of the entire story, and Brazil's earlier comment about expecting the worst of things, we *need* to see Robson behind these events.

The second telephone call we know is motivated by Robson. When Brazil catches Robson and Conroy trying to take Luise by force, he punches Conroy in the face. As Conroy falls his head hits the stone fireplace, apparently fracturing his skull. Robson later calls the local justice of the peace—who happens to be Grant, Evelyn's father (oh, happy coincidence!)—to swear out a warrant for Brazil's arrest. Evelyn overhears this, and calls Brazil to warn him. His response is not that of an impersonal, stoic, masculine, hard-boiled hero:

His face was pasty, yellow, glistening with sweat on forehead and temples, and the cigarette between the fingers of his right hand was mashed and broken. . . . "That damned fireplace. I can't live in a cell again!" (26)

Part One amounts to a tightly orchestrated series of events, not planned out by Robson in their entirety from the beginning, but planned nonetheless, each step of the way. It has the feel of a game of checkers, both sides reacting to the previous move, making short-term plans along the way. Robson moves, Luise and Brazil react. This pattern continues into Part Two.

Part Two, "The Police Close In," picks up where Part One ends, with Brazil having just received his telephone call. Luise asks him what he is going to do, to which he responds adamantly, "They've got me . . . and I can't live in a cell again!" (30). During the ensuing conversation, we learn a little more about why Brazil had gone to prison: "It was a drunken free-for-all in a roadhouse, with bottles and everything, and a guy died. I couldn't say they were wrong in tying it on me" (29). Brazil accepted the blame for the death in the roadhouse, and will apparently accept responsibility for Conroy's death, should he die. Since Brazil is on record as a killer, he is convinced that this time he will be convicted of murder. If Conroy lives, Brazil is convinced they will hold bail and get him on assault with intent to kill. This sets him into a panic: his voice rises, his eyes jerk around toward the door, and then "he raise[s] his head with a rasping noise in his throat that might have been a laugh" (30) and says, "Let's get out of here. I'll go screwy indoors tonight" (30). So he and Luise drive off to the city.

This scene begins to clarify the relationship between Luise and Brazil, and the contrast between them. In Part One we are unsuspectingly drawn into what seems to be a very familiar Hammettian landscape—the vulnerable, somewhat mysterious, somewhat exotic woman, and the very masculine, stoic man. She needs his help, and he is able to provide it by chasing off Robson and Conroy. But now Brazil finds himself in a position similar to Luise's: he too is fleeing from Kane Robson. Their reasons for running are different, but Luise and Brazil seem to be gaining an understanding of one another. Earlier in the evening, when Grant bursts in looking for Evelyn, Luise vouches for the fact that the girl is not in the house, to which Grant scoffs, "Bah! The strumpet's word confirms the convict's!" (17). Near the end of Part One, just prior to Brazil's telephone call, Luise asks him if people talk about her. He says they do, and that they say the worst. She then ask him what *he* thinks. He replies, "I can't very well go around panning people" (26). Brazil knows he is also the kind of person that people talk about. When he suggests that they get out of the house, Luise agrees: "'Yes,' she said eagerly, putting a hand on his shoulder, watching his face with eyes half frightened, half pitying. 'We will go'" (30). She understands and appreciates his fear.

What is unusual in this developing relationship is the lack of duplicity that we so often find in conversations between Hammett's "typical" characters. Brazil speaks from the heart about his time in prison and what it's done to him; Luise accepts the fact that she made a mistake moving in with Robson, and displays no indignation at learning that people refer to her as a strumpet and worse. Perhaps what we are seeing here is a writer's continued movement through the genre he helped define and then expand. According to Bernard Schoper, an advance in the development of the detective story in America resulted when writers began paying attention to character development along with detection. Schoper describes this as "moving from simply puzzles to people" (175). In *Woman in the Dark*, we seem to have *all* people and *no* puzzles. Our center of consciousness, Luise, is not an investigator or detective, but the type of character the detective usually pursues. Furthermore, the main characters are not trying to solve a puzzle of any sort; they are simply trying to outpace Robson's machinations. It is not even a mystery why Robson is doing what he's doing. In Part One, when he and Conroy have Luise alone for those few minutes, he tells her, "wagg[ing] his head up and down, grinning," that "I haven't got my money's worth out of you yet" (19). Later, when Luise and Robson have the chance to talk privately, she asks him, "You want me back, knowing I despise you?", to which he replies, grinning, "I can get fun out of even that" (66). We understand perfectly well the motives of the selfish man with money. The only mystery—such as it is—is the rather melodramatic one presented to the readers concerning the nature of the peculiar relationship developing between Luise and Brazil.

The leitmotif of intrusions continues through Part Two. Luise and Brazil intrude on friends of his, Donny Link, a former cellmate, and his wife Fan. After getting something to eat, Luise and Brazil find themselves alone in the bedroom. She offers herself as payment for the help he's given. Just as Brazil prepares to accept payment, Donny intrudes to tell them that the lawyer is on his way over. Suddenly, the police intrude, and Brazil makes his escape out the window. Except for one brief moment, it is the last we see of him until the end of the novella. As was the case in Part One, characters act by reacting to intrusions, seen most graphically in Brazil's jump out the window.

The relationship between Luise and Brazil further evolves during Part Two. During the drive to the city, Brazil once again seems back in control; even a passing police car does not faze him. He tells Luise, "I'm all right outdoors. It's walls that get me" (32). He is able to stop his habit of opening the door and glancing out. As he and Luise are walking into the Link's dining room for breakfast, they pass the apartment's front door:

> In the passageway Brazil turned and took a tentative step toward the front door, but checked himself when he caught Luise Fischer's eye and, grinning a bit sheepishly, followed her and the blonde woman [Fan] into the dining room. (39)

With Luise's help, he seems to be making progress, though not enough to keep himself from running when the police show up.

The police take Luise to the station, where she waits for someone from Mile

Valley (the small town where Robson lives) to bring her back on suspicion of theft. Once again, behind the scenes, Robson has been busy. He has pressed charges, accusing Luise of stealing from him the rings she is wearing, rings that he had, in fact, given to her. In this fictional world human evil, personified in Kane Robson, is ever-present, and once again it seems to put Luise in a position of vulnerability. She is escorted and locked up by city police, then handed off to Mile Valley police, who retrace the route she and Brazil had taken that morning. Where Part One ends with panic for Brazil, Part Two ends with a sense of panic for Luise—she has heard that Brazil had been shot and captured. She digs her fingers into one officer's arm as she tries to elicit information from them. She insists that she must know; they begin to explain, but then interrupt themselves, saying that the District Attorney would not want them discussing the case. Once again Luise is at the mercy of the forces surrounding her.

As Part Three, "Conclusion," opens up, Luise and her "captors" (57) arrive at the Mile Valley police station. Harry Klaus, the lawyer contacted by Donny Link, is waiting for her. Luise may not be in control, but that does not make her a victim. The strong character we have seen earlier standing up to Kane Robson we see again during a conversation with Klaus.

He of course wants to know her entire story. As she begins talking, Klaus calmly starts moving his hand up Luise's leg. She at first seems to pay no attention to his advances and continues with her story: "'He [Robson] brought me over here then and'—she put the burning end of her cigarette on the back of his hand—'I stayed at his—'" (61). At this point, Klaus understandably yanks his hand away, sucking on the burned area, wanting to know what she thought she was doing. If she does not like something, he tells her, she should just say so. As is the case throughout the novella, Luise deals firmly and directly with any situation facing her. She does not back down from Robson, or Brazil, or Klaus. She may at times seem vulnerable, but she can still exert as measure of control. This will be dramatically borne out as the story reaches its climactic close.

After leaving the police station, Klaus and Luise go to a tavern for something to eat. As they are sitting there, in walks Robson, who comes over and requests a private conversation with Luise. He promises to tell the police that the problem with the rings was all a mistake if she will go back with him. Once again, Luise will not be bullied, and shows herself to be her own person.

> "I am not a fool," she said. "I have no money, no friends who can help me. You have both, and I am not afraid of you. I try to do what is best for myself. First I try to get out of this trouble without you. If I cannot, then I come back to you." (67)

This is the clearest, most succinct expression of Luise's philosophy of life. Brazil, we have seen, has no expectations but the worst, and runs from confrontation. Luise, on the other hand, while not necessarily expecting the best, certainly does not expect the worst. She will do what is best for herself, first without the assistance of someone like Robson. If that does not work, then she—being not the fool—will be ready to use Robson to help herself. When Robson retorts that he may not *take* her back at that point, she merely shrugs her shoulders. As she said, she is not afraid of him, and is capable of taking care of herself. We readers have seen nothing throughout the story in either her words or actions to cause us to dispute this contention.

The plot becomes a bit ungainly at this point. Hammett needs to reveal two pieces of information, and does so in an almost clumsy manner. Klaus and Luise drive back to the city the next morning, to the Link apartment, apparently to await word concerning Brazil. As they enter the apartment, who should be there but the mysterious girl/woman Evelyn, explaining through sobs that the police showed up yesterday because of her. Evelyn's father, Grant, caught Evelyn trying to call Donny to see what had become of Brazil; Grant, an unwitting tool of Robson's, sent the police.

We also learn from Donny that Brazil is in a hospital outside of town, supposedly being treated for D.T.'s. He was shot in the side, but is being cared for by a trustworthy doctor. However, when Donny mentions the doctor's name, Luise puts her hand to her throat and demands that he repeat the name. She knows the doctor, met him once at Robson's house; he was with Robson at the tavern the previous night. She figures the doctor was there to find out what Robson wanted him to do with Brazil. They decide to get Brazil out of the hospital.

When they get to his room, they find two men already there, one of them the policeman who arrested Luise the day before. They let Donny and Luise say hello to Brazil and then chase them out. But Luise has made a decision; as she has done throughout, she confronts the forces around her and responds forcibly. She borrows ten dollars from Donny and buys a one-way ticket to Mile Valley. While waiting for the train she calls Robson: "Well, you have won. You might have saved yourself the delay if you had told me last night what you knew. . . . Yes. . . . Yes, I am" (72-73). We cannot be entirely certain what she means by conceding victory to Robson. Has she turned her back on Brazil? Is she simply doing what she vowed earlier, taking care of herself? The Romantic in me wants to hope that she is giving herself up in order to save Brazil, but there is no indication of that.

Before dealing with the climactic final scene of the story, I want to return to the evolving relationship between Brazil and Luise, considering it specifically from the perspective of the "dangerous romance" of the subtitle. Each of the three parts of the novella contains one scene of physical romance—of sorts— between Luise and Brazil, the middle one standing at the structural center of the story. These three scenes deserve further scrutiny.

The first physical contact comes near the end of Part One, after Brazil has rescued Luise from the drunken Robson and Conroy. He has just told her that he rented the house in order to figure out what to do with his life. She asks him if he has. He replies:

> "Have I found out where I stand, what I want to do? I don't know." He was
> standing in front of her, hands in pockets, glowering down at her. "I suppose I've
> just been waiting for something to turn up, something I could take as a sign which
> way I was to go. Well, what turned up was you. That's good enough. I'll go along
> with you."
>   He took his hands from his pockets, leaned down, lifted her to her feet, and
> kissed her savagely. (25)

Brazil is the hard-boiled man taking his romance on his own terms. But Luise
Fischer is not one to let others deal with her on their terms: "For a moment she
was motionless. Then she squirmed out of his arms and struck at his face with
curved fingers. She was white with anger." Her blow is unsuccessful; Brazil
pushes it down, carelessly. "If you don't want to play," he tells her, "you don't
want to play, that's all." Furiously, she retorts, "That is exactly all" (25). This
sounds fair to Brazil—they both know where they stand. Their conversation
continues, almost as if nothing had happened, with Luise asking if the people
really talk about her as a strumpet. This business-like relationship begins to
change quickly, though, with the telephone call warning Brazil that the police
are looking for him.

When he explains the call, Luise "came to him with her hands out" (29). She
"stood close to him and took one of his hands" (29). She tries to bolster his
mood, reminding him that it was an accident, not his fault. He then explains his
previous conviction for manslaughter; they decide to drive to the city. In spite
of the tension created between them, Brazil and Luise find themselves falling
into a relationship, an *actually* romantic one. Romance is not savage, is not
taken, in the manner in which Brazil had tried with his savage kiss. Romance
is standing close, holding hands, bolstering the other's mood. Romance then
becomes a motivating force; it provides new motivation—concern for the
other—for responding to surrounding events. This overriding concern for the
other is one of the potential dangers of romance.

The physical romance that occurs in Part Three (I will deal with the scene in
Part Two last) happens during the brief hospital visit. As Luise and Donny enter
the room, Brazil partially raises himself and extends a hand toward Luise; she
walks over, takes his hand, and apologizes. He replies, "Hard luck, all right.
And I'm scared stiff of those damned bars" (71). At this point, Luise leans over
and kisses Brazil. The police try to shoo Donny and Luise out of the room, but
she kisses Brazil one more time. He, in the best tradition of melodrama, tells
Donny to look after her. Donny, of course, promises to do so.

Interestingly, this scene does not reveal any of Luise's thoughts—we have
only her actions, which consist of the two kisses. It stands as a counterpoint to
the scene in Part One, where Brazil reaches down and plants a savage kiss on
Luise. In the hospital, she is the one bending over and planting tender kisses on

him. By this point in the story, we have a positive view of her decision to return to Robson; that is, we are prepared to see that Luise is thinking more of Brazil than of herself. Their developing relationship moves Luise to action: she immediately calls Robson and concedes victory. Her concern for Brazil has placed her in a potentially dangerous situation.

The center of the story is the scene in the Link's bedroom, just before the police arrive, forcing Brazil to jump out the window. Luise has been in the shower, and returns to the bedroom to find Brazil already there, standing, of course, by the window looking out. She seems to know what she wants to do: "She shut the door slowly and leaned against it, the faintest of contemptuous smiles curving her mobile lips" (41). Brazil does not turn around, does not move. She sits on the edge of the bed, her face "proud and cold," and speaks, beginning with perhaps the most meaningful statement a character in Hammett's world can make:

> "I am what I am, but I pay my debts." This time the deliberate calmness of her voice was insolence. "I brought this trouble to you. Well, now, if you can find any use for me—" She shrugged. (41)

Our narrator tells us that Brazil turns away from the window without haste and says, "O.K." This scene is beginning to look like a standard hard-boiled sex-as-payment scene, with Luise finally giving Brazil what he apparently wanted back in Part One:

> He stood close to her for a moment, looking at her with eyes that weighed her beauty as impersonally as if she had been inanimate. Then he pushed her head back rudely and kissed her.
> She made neither sound nor movement of her own, submitting completely to his caress, and when he released her and stepped back, her face was as unaffected, as masklike, as his. (42)

This language echoes that in Part One, but in this case it applies to both of them; they are alike—cold, impersonal, unaffected. As is the case in most of Hammett's fictional world, not much separates the good guys from the bad, since the world has a corrupting influence on all. William Ruehlman makes this point about Hammett's detective stories, arguing that in each case the Op and the adversary become one; in taking the enemy down, the Op takes himself down as well (67). Luise, in this central scene, seems to be stepping down to Brazil's level.

But the scene is not over. Brazil backs away from Luise and shakes his head, telling her she's no good at her job, an ironic reference to the community's opinion of her. The romance now takes over:

> And suddenly his eyes were burning and he had her in his arms and she was clinging to him and laughing softly in her throat while he kissed her mouth and

cheeks and eyes and forehead. (42)

Hammett, though, is teasing us. Donny intrudes at this point to announce that the lawyer is on his way—the mood is broken. Luise barely has enough time to ask Brazil if they can leave, saying she does not like these people, before the police come ringing the doorbell.

It seems clear that Luise and Brazil are developing a meaningful relationship, at least as meaningful as one can be in the fictional world created by Hammett. Can it succeed? We come to the final scene of the story.

Luise, in pale negligee and slippers, is sitting erect in Robson's mansion. It is midnight. We have apparently entered in the middle of a conversation, for Robson has paused to let the clock strike. He is rebuking Luise: "And you are making a great mistake, my dear, in being too sure of yourself" (73). Luise replies with her usual torpor: "She yawned. 'I slept very little last night,' she said. 'I am too sleepy to be frightened'" (73). This snippet of conversation reinforces our judgment that Luise is here on her terms. Then, as in Part One, events happen rapidly.

Robson arises to go upstairs and check on "the invalid" (73). Conroy is upstairs, we learn, under the care of a nurse, who at that moment comes into the room panting, and announces that Conroy seems to be regaining consciousness. Robson, after telling the nurse to phone Dr. Blake, states that he will stay with Conroy while the nurse is on the phone. Luise wants to go with him; he tells her no; she insists. Robson shrugs and goes upstairs. Luise, in her slippers, cannot ascend as quickly as Robson, and she arrives in Conroy's room "in time to catch the look of utter fear in Conroy's eyes, before they closed, as his bandaged head fell back on the pillow" (74). Robson, sighing, tells Luise that Conroy has just passed out again. As they stand staring at each other, the Japanese butler enters, announcing that a Mr. Brazil is here to see Fraulein Fischer.

This seems to play into Robson's hands: "Into Robson's face little by little came the expression of one considering a private joke" (74). He tells the butler to bring Brazil into the living room and to then phone the sheriff. The butler leaves and the nurse returns; Luise tells her to stay with Conroy, then goes downstairs to see Brazil.

Brazil's reason for sneaking out of the hospital is clear: "His face was a ghastly yellow mask in which his eyes burned redly. He said through his teeth: 'They told me you'd come back. I had to see it.' He spit on the floor." He then reaches for the one invective he knows will hurt Luise: "Strumpet!" (75). Luise stamps her foot and calls Brazil a fool. She begins to say something—we anticipate an explanation of why she returned to Robson—when she sees the nurse on her way to a neighbor's house to use the telephone. This immediately sends Luise into action. She kicks off her slippers, runs upstairs, and finds Robson attempting to suffocate Conroy. As she throws herself at Robson's legs, she screams for Brazil.

As in Part One, Brazil has shown up at just the right time, this time to help Luise pull Robson off Conroy. Conroy manages to sputter that Robson hit him over the head the other night with a piece of wood; Robson, behind everything else, was even the cause of Conroy's fractured skull. All three of them—Robson, Luise, Brazil—are on the floor as the police arrive. Luise has her arm around Brazil, wiping his face with her handkerchief. He speaks his final words of the story: "The guy was screwy, wasn't he?" To which Luise replies, "All men are" (76). She then removes Robson's only hold over her, the rings, and places them by Robson's feet.

In the introduction to the novella, Parker criticizes the ending: "the happy ending seems a bit forced, as if Hammett, in order to bring Brazil and Luise together after all, might have bent his hard-eyed gaze away for a moment" (ix-x). But are they together "after all"? Readers naturally fill in gaps as they read; they expect closure, and will create it if it is not provided by the author. Parker, in criticizing Hammett for bending away his "hard-eyed gaze," confuses reader with writer. Readers help construct the fiction they read (e.g., Bleich, Crosman, Iser, Holland). Parker has bent *his* hard-eyed gaze away and attributed the result to Hammett.

We find ourselves confronted, then, with the following question: did Hammett anticipate his readers constructing a sentimental ending out of its ambiguity? Certainly all artists recognize the dangers of ambiguity; writers in particular have always made use of this rhetorical device. Hammett, however, was working within a genre, and keenly aware of it. One way to stretch a genre would be to work against its received expectations; in *Woman in the Dark* Hammett is reaching for an ending that confounds rather than satisfies the expectation that loose ends get tied up.

I have tried to argue that Luise's motivation is noble, that she sacrifices herself for Brazil. But we cannot be so sure about Brazil's motives. While Hammett uses a third person point of view, it is limited, selectively, to Luise. When we examine Brazil's actions, we see him as being quite single-minded: he will not return to prison. That is why he leaves his house and drives to the city; that is why he jumps out the window; it would be the simplest explanation for his behavior in the final scene. He knows he faces prison if Conroy dies. When he responds to Luise's call, his instincts take over, as we have seen happen throughout the story, and he lunges at Robson. All he can say at the end—revealing his lack of understanding of human motivation—is that Robson is screwy, which is what he said about Evelyn's father, Grant, in Part One, and himself in Part Two. While he does display anger after arriving at Robson's house, we have little basis for seeing Brazil as acting from a sense of romance.

To see this novella as having a sentimental, happy ending requires three assumptions on our part. First, we assume that Conroy will clear Brazil, and that Robson will be charged with attempted murder. Second, we assume that the charges of theft against Luise will be dropped since she is leaving the rings. Third, we assume that Brazil will give Luise a chance to make the explanation she presumably started to make earlier, and will accept it. Given these assumptions, Luise and Brazil are together. I cannot help but recall, however, the conversation the two of them have in Brazil's car when they first drive to the city. At one point Luise asks him if he would fight if the police catch him. He replies, "I don't know. That's what's the matter with me. I never know ahead of time what I'll do" (32). This, more than anything else, defines Brazil's character: he is a reactive person. Luise, as has been the case throughout the story, finds herself finally in yet another potentially dangerous situation—a one-sided relationship. This is not yet a story of romance, though prelude it may be. [This essay was written specifically for this volume]

WORKS CITED

Bleich, David. "Epistemological Assumptions in the Study of Response." *Reader-Response Criticism: From Formalism to Post-Structuralism.* Ed. Jane P. Tompkins. Baltimore: Johns Hopkins UP, 1980. 134-63.

Crosman, Robert. "Do Readers Make Meaning?" *The Reader in the Text: Essays on Audience and Interpretation.* Ed. Susan R. Suleiman and Inge Crosman. Princeton: Princeton UP, 1980. 149-164.

Hamilton, Cynthia S. *Western and Hard-Boiled Detective Fiction in America.* Iowa City: University of Iowa Press, 1987.

Hammett, Dashiell. *Woman in the Dark: A Novel of Dangerous Romance.* New York: Alfred A. Knopf, 1988.

Holland, Norman. "Re-Covering 'The Purloined Letter': Reading as a Personal Transaction." *The Reader in the Text: Essays on Audience and Interpretation.* Ed. Susan R. Suleiman and Inge Crosman. Princeton: Princeton UP, 1980. 350-70.

Iser, Wolfgang. "Interaction Between Text and Reader." *The Reader in the Text: Essays on Audience and Interpretation.* Ed. Susan R. Suleiman and Inge Crosman. Princeton: Princeton UP, 1980. 106-19.

Marcus, Stephen. "Dashiell Hammett and the Continental Op." *Partisan Review* 41 (1974): 362-377.

Marling, William. *Dashiell Hammett.* Boston: Twayne, 1983.

Parker, Robert B. Introduction. *Woman in the Dark: A Novel of Dangerous Romance.* Dashiell Hammett. New York: Knopf, 1988. v-x.

Ruehlman, William. *Saint With a Gun: The Unlawful American Private Eye.* New York: NYU Press, 1974.

Schoper, Bernard A. "From Puzzles to People: The Development of the American Detective Novel." *Studies in American Fiction* 7 (1979): 175-189.

Additional Readings

Abramson, Leslie H. "Two Birds of a Feather: Hammett's and Huston's *The Maltese Falcon*." *Literature-Film Quarterly* 16 (1988): 112-18.

Adams, Donald K. "The First Thin Man." *Mystery and Detection Annual* 1 (1970): 160-77.

Anderson, Isaac. Review of *The Thin Man*. *New York Times* 7 January 1934: 18.

Anderson, John Robert. "'Hidden Fires': The Dimensions of Detection in American Literature and Film." Diss. Yale U, 1983.

_____. "The World of *The Maltese Falcon*." *Southwest Review* (Summer 1988): 76-97.

Babener, Liahna K. "California Babylon: The World of American Detective Fiction." *Clues* 1 (Fall-Winter 1980): 77-89.

Balmer, Edwin. "Our Literary Nudism." *Esquire* September 1934: 30, 89.

Bauer, Stephen F., Leon Balter, and Winslow Hunt. "The Detective Film as Myth: *The Maltese Falcon* and Sam Spade." *American Imago* 35 (Fall 1978): 275-96.

Benstock, Bernard. "Dashiell Hammett and Raymond Chandler: An Anatomy of the Rich." *All Men Are Created Equal: Ideologies, reves et realities*. Ed. Jean-Pierre Martin. Aix-en-Provence: Université de Provence, 1983. 181-189.

Bentley, Christopher. "Radical Anger: Dashiell Hammett's *Red Harvest*." *American Crime Fiction: Studies in the Genre*. Ed. Brian Docherty. New York: St. Martin's, 1988. 54-70.

Berger, Jurgen. "Herabsturzende Balken: Das Universum des Dashiell Hammett." *Die Horen* 38.4 (1993): 59-67.

Billi, Mirella. "Quel doppio gioco di Dashiell Hammett." *Il Ponte* 37 vii-viii (1981): 710-16.

Blair, Walter. "Dashiell Hammett: Themes and Techniques." *Essays on American Literature in Honor of Jay B. Hubbell*. Durham: Duke UP, 1967. 295-306.

Bonfantini, Massimo. "Pleiadi 18: Imparare semiotica dal Falcone Maltese."

Letteratura: Percorsi Possibili. Ed. Franca Mariani. Ravenna: Longo, 1983. 123-27.

Braun, Hans-Martin. *Prototypen der amerikanischen Kriminalzählung: Die Romane und Kurzgeschichten Carroll John Daly und Dashiell Hammett.* Frankfurt: Lang, 1977.

Burelbach, Frederick M. "Symbolic Naming in *The Maltese Falcon.*" *Literary Onomastic Studies* 6 (1979): 226-45.

Chiappini, Ligia. "A Questao de 'Grande Arte': Uma Faca de Dois Gomes." *Brasil/Brazil: Revista de Literatura Brasileira/A Journal of Brazilian Literature* 5.7 (1992): 47-60.

Cooper, James. "Lean Years for the Thin Man." *Washington Daily News.* March 11, 1957.

Crider, Allen Billy. "The Private-Eye Hero: A Study of the Novels of Dashiell Hammett, Raymond Chandler, and Ross Macdonald." Diss. The University of Texas at Austin, 1972.

Cuppy, Will. Review of *The Maltese Falcon. New York Herald Tribune* 23 February 1930: 17.

_____. Review of *Red Harvest. New York Herald Tribune* 17 February 1929: 10.

_____. Review of *The Thin Man. New York Herald Tribune* 7 January 1934: 11.

Day, Gary. "Investigating the Investigator: Hammett's Continental Op." *American Crime Fiction: Studies in the Genre.* Ed. Brian Docherty. New York: St. Martin's, 1988. 39-53.

Doogan, Michael G. "Dash-ing Through the Snow." *Armchair Detective* 22 (1989): 82-91.

Dooley, Dennis. "Time's Shadow: *The Thin Man* and Dashiell Hammett." *Gamut* 14 (Winter 1985): 34-44.

Durham, Philip. "The *Black Mask* School." *Tough Guy Writers of the Thirties.* Ed. David Madden. Carbondale: Southern Illinois UP, 1968. 51-79.

Fanning, Michael. "*The Maltese Falcon* and My Alligator, Academically Considered." *Clues* 5 (Spring-Summer 1984): 147-56.

Fiedler, Leslie A. *Love and Death in the American Novel.* New York: Stein and Day, 1966.

Gardner, Frederick H. "The Return of the Continental Op." *Nation* 31 October 1966: 454-56.

Gide, André. "An Imaginary Interview." Trans. by Malcolm Cowley. *New Republic* 7 February 1944: 184, 186.

Glover, D. "The Frontier of Genre: A Further to John S. Whitley's 'Stirring Things Up: Dashiell Hammett's Continental Op.'" *Journal of American Studies* 15 (August 1981): 249-52.

_____. "Sociology and the Thriller: The Case of Dashiell Hammett." *Sociological Review* 27 (February 1979): 21-40.

Gores, Joe. "A Foggy Night." *City of San Francisco* 4 November 1979: 29-32.

Grebstein, Sheldon. "The Tough Hemingway and His Hardboiled Children." *Tough Guy Writers of the Thirties.* Ed. David Madden. Carbondale: Southern

Illinois UP, 1968. 18-41.

Gregory, Sinda. "The Mystery of Mystery: The Novels of Dashiell Hammett." Diss. U of Illinois at Urbana-Champaign, 1980.

Grella, George. "Murder and the Mean Streets." *Contempora* 1 (1970): 6-15.

_____. "The Wings of the Falcon and the Maltese Dove." *A Question of Quality: Popularity and Value in Modern Creative Writing*. Bowling Green: Bowling Green UP, 1976. 108-14.

Grenier, Donald J. "Antony Lamont in Search of Gilbert Sorrentino: Character and Mulligan Stew." *Review of Contemporary Fiction* 1 (1980): 104-112.

Guetti, James. "Aggressive Reading: Detective Fiction and Realistic Narrative." *Raritan* 2 (1982): 133-54.

Haas, Joseph. "The Big Knockover." *Chicago Daily News* 18 June 1966.

Hagemann, E. R. "From 'The Cleansing of Poisonville' to *Red Harvest*." *Clues* 7 (Fall-Winter 1986): 115-132.

Hamilton, Cynthia S. *Western and Hard-Boiled Detective Fiction in America: From High Noon to Midnight*. Iowa City: U of Iowa P, 1987.

Handlin, Oscar. Review of *The Big Knockover*. *Atlantic* July 1966: 137-38.

Harred, Larry Dale. "The Artful Detectives of Dashiell Hammett, Raymond Chandler, and Ross Macdonald: The Uses of Literary Style." Diss. Purdue University, 1983.

Hellman, Lillian. Introduction to *The Big Knockover and Other Stories*. By Dashiell Hammett. New York: Random House, 1966.

_____. *Pentimento*. Boston: Little, Brown, 1973.

_____. *Scoundrel Time*. Boston: Little, Brown, 1976.

_____. *An Unfinished Woman*. Boston: Little, Brown, 1969.

Hulley, Kathleen. "From Crystal Sphere to Edge City: Ideology in the Novels of Dashiell Hammett." *Myth and Ideology in American Culture*. Eds. Regis Durand and Michel Fabré. Villeneuve D'Ascq: Université de Lille, 1976. 113-137.

Humm, Peter. "Camera Eye/Private Eye." *American Crime Fiction: Studies in the Genre*. Ed. Brian Docherty. New York: St. Martin's, 1988. 23-38.

Johnson, Diane. *Dashiell Hammett: A Life*. New York: Random House, 1983.

_____ and Carlos Losilla. "Hammett: Una biografia dificil." *Quimera: Revista de Literatura* vol 50: 38-45.

Kenney, William Patrick. "The Dashiell Hammett Tradition and the Modern Detective Novel." Diss. University of Michigan, 1964.

Krajewski, Bruce. "Play Hermeneutics Again, Sam." *Iowa Journal of Literary Studies* 6 (1985): 22-31.

Kress, Paul F. "Justice, Proof, and Plausibility in Conan Doyle and Dashiell Hammett." *Occasional Review* 7 (Winter 1977): 119-34.

Kuzmics, Helmut. "Der Schriftsteller als Soziologe: R. Chandlers und D. Hammetts 'hartgesottener Privatdetektiv' als Sozialcharakter." *Die Horen* 32.4 (1987): 101-11.

Lamanna, Richard Stephen. "The Art of Postmodern Detection: 'Realities,' Fictions and Epistemological Experience in the Mysteries of Dashiell

Hammett, Jorge Luis Borges, and Umberto Eco." Diss. University of South Florida, 1992.

Lamb, Margaret. "Expressionism and American Popular Literature: Hammett as a Continental Op-Eye." *Clues* 2 (Spring-Summer 1981): 26-34.

Layman, Richard. *Dashiell Hammett: A Descriptive Bibliography*. Pittsburg: U of Pittsburg Press, 1979.

Leenhouts, Annica. "'Taking What's Coming to You': Dashiell Hammett's *The Glass Key*." *Clues* 6 (Fall-Winter 1985): 73-84.

Legman, G. *Love and Death: A Study of Censorship*. New York: Breaking Point, 1949.

Leverence, John. Review of *The Continental Op*. *The Journal of Popular Culture* 9 (Winter 1975): 741-43.

Macdonald, Ross. "Down These Mean Streets a Man Must Go." *Antaeus* 25/26 (Spring-Summer 1977): 211-16.

_____. "The Writer as Detective Hero." *The Mystery Writer's Art*. Bowling Green: Bowling Green UP, 1970. 295-305.

MacLaren, Ross. "Chandler and Hammett." *London Magazine* March 1964: 70-79.

Magny, Claude-Edmonde. *The Age of the American Novel: The Film Aesthetic of Fiction Between the Two Wars*. Trans. Eleanor Hochman. New York: Frederick Ungar, 1972.

Mahan, Jeffrey H. "The Hard-Boiled Detective in the Fallen World." *Clues* 1 (Fall/Winter 1980): 90-99.

Marcus, Steven. "Dashing after Hammett." *City of San Francisco* 4 November 1975.

Margolies, Edward. *Which Way Did He Go?: The Private Eye in Dashiell Hammett, Raymond Chandler, Chester Himes, and Ross Macdonald*. New York: Holmes and Meier, 1982. 17-31.

Marling, William. *Dashiell Hammett*. Boston: Twayne, 1983.

_____. "The Hammett Succubus." *Clues* 3 (Fall 1982): 66-75.

_____. "The Style and Ideology of *The Maltese Falcon*." *Proteus* 6 (Spring 1989): 42-50.

Maugham, Somerset. "The Decline and Fall of the Detective Story." *The Vagrant Mood*. Garden City: Doubleday, 1953. 101-32.

Maxfield, James F. "Hard-Boiled Dicks and Dangerous Females: Sex and Love in the Detective Fiction of Dashiell Hammett." *Clues* 6 (Spring-Summer 1985): 107-23.

_____. "Le Belle Dame sans Merci and the Neurotic Knight: Characterization in *The Maltese Falcon*." *Literature-Film Quarterly* 17 (1989): 253-60.

Michaels, Leonard. "The Continental Op." *New York Times Book Review* 8 December 1974: 1, 20, 22, 26.

Miller, D.A. "The Language of Detective Fiction: The Fiction of Detective Language." *Antaeus* 35 (Autumn 1979): 99-106.

Morris, H.H. "Dashiell Hammett in the Wasteland." *Midwest Quarterly* 19 (Winter 1978): 196-202.

Moss, Leonard. "Hammett's Heroic Operative." *New Republic* 8 January 1966: 32-34.

Mundell, E.H. *A List of the Original Appearances of Dashiell Hammett's Magazine Fiction.* Kent: Kent State UP, 1968.

Müller, Wolfgang G. "Implizite Bewesstseinsdarstellung im behavioristischen Roman der zwanzinger und dreissiger Jahre: Hammett, Chandler, Hemingway." *Amerikastudien* 26 (1981): 193-211.

Nakjavani, Erik. "*Red Harvest*: Archipelago of Micro-Powers." *Clues* 4 (Spring-Summer 1983): 105-13.

Naremore, James. "Dashiell Hammett and the Poetics of Hard-Boiled Detection." *Art in Crime Writing: Essays on Detective Fiction.* Ed. Bernard Benstock. New York: St. Martin's, 1983. 49-72.

Nevins, Francis M. "Social and Political Images in American Crime Fiction." *Armchair Detective* 5 (1971): 61-78.

Nolan, William. "A Decade of Dash; or the Further Adventures of the Hammett Checklist." *Armchair Detective* 17 (Fall 1984): 360-367.

_____. "Setting the Record Straight on *Dashiell Hammett: A Life.*" *Armchair Detective* 17 (Winter 1984): 34-38.

_____. "Shadowing the Continental Op." *The Armchair Detective* 8 (1974): 121-32.

Nye, Russell. *The Unembarrassed Muse: The Popular Arts in America.* New York: Dial, 1970.

O'Brien, Geoffrey. *Hardboiled America: The Lurid Years of the Paperbacks.* New York: Van Nostrand Reinhold, 1981.

Palmer, Jerry. *Thrillers: Genesis and Structure of a Popular Genre.* London: Edward Arnold, 1978.

Parker, Robert B. "The Violent Hero, Wilderness Heritage and Urban Reality: A Study of the Private Eye in the Novels of Dashiell Hammett, Raymond Chandler and Ross Macdonald." Diss. Boston University, 1971.

Paterson, John. "A Cosmic View of the Private Eye." *Saturday Review* 22 August 1953: 7-8.

Pattow, Donald. "Order and Disorder in *The Maltese Falcon.*" *Armchair Detective* 11 (1978): 171.

Pettengell, Michael John. "Naturalism in American Hard-Boiled Fiction: The First Four Decades." Diss. Bowling Green State University, 1990.

Phelps, Donald. "Dashiell Hammett's Microcomos." *National Review* 20 September 1966: 941-42.

Porter, J.C. "End of the Trail: The American West of Dashiell Hammett and Raymond Chandler." *Western Historical Quarterly* 6 (1975): 411-24.

Powell, Robert S. "Including Murder: An Unpublished Hammett Collection." *Clues* 2 (Fall-Winter 1981): 135-42.

Puertolas, Soledad. "Los detectives de Hammett." *Rev. de Occidente* 44 (1985): 164-177.

Raubicheck, Walter. "Dashiell Hammett and the Tradition of the Detective Story." Diss. New York University, 1984.

_____. "Stirring It Up: Dashiell Hammett and the Tradition of the Detective Story." *Armchair Detective* 20 (Winter 1987): 20-25.

Redman, Ben Ray. "Decline and Fall of the Whodunit." *Saturday Review* 31 May 1952: 8-9, 31-32.

Reeves, W.V. "The Mutation of The Maltese Falcon." *American Notes and Queries* 18 (1979): 21-24.

Reilly, John M. "The Politics of Tough-Guy Mysteries." *University of Dayton Review* 10 (1973): 25-31.

_____. "Sam Spade Talking." *Clues* 1 (Fall-Winter 1980): 119-125.

[Review of *Red Harvest*]. *Boston Evening Transcript* 6 April 1929: 3.

[Review of *Red Harvest*]. *Springfield Republican* 10 February 1929: 7e.

[Review of *The Dain Curse*]. *Springfield Republican* 4 August 1929: 7e.

[Review of *The Maltese Falcon*]. *Times Literary Supplement* 14 Aug 1930: 654.

[Review of *The Maltese Falcon*]. *New York Times* 23 February 1930: 28.

[Review of *The Maltese Falcon*]. *New Statesman* 9 August 1930: 576.

[Review of *The Glass Key*]. *Books* 26 April 1931: 13.

[Review of *The Glass Key*]. *Boston Evening Transcript* 9 May 1931: 2.

[Review of *The Glass Key*]. *Times Literary Supplement* 21 March 1931: 201.

[Review of *The Thin Man*]. *Boston Evening Transcript* 31 January 1934: 2.

[Review of *The Thin Man*]. *Nation* 4 April 1934: 395.

[Review of *The Thin Man*]. *Times Literary Supplement* 14 June 1934: 426.

[Review of *The Thin Man*]. *Saturday Review* 30 June 1934: 773.

Ruehlmann, William. *Saint With a Gun: The Unlawful American Private Eye.* New York: New York U P, 1974.

Ruhm, Herbert. "In Rats' Alley." *Carelton Miscellany* 8 (Winter 1967): 118-22.

Sale, Roger. "The Hammett Case." *New York Review of Books* 6 February 1975: 20-22.

Sanderson, Elizabeth. "Ex-detective Hammett." *Bookman* January/February 1932: 516-18.

Santraud, Jeanne-Marie and Jean Rouberol. *Deux regards sur l'Amerique: Dashiell Hammett et Walker Percy.* Paris: Sorbonne, 1986.

Saporta, Marc. "Dashiell Hammett: Condemnation en appel." In *Deux regards sur l'Amerique: Dashiell Hammett et Walker Percy.* Ed. Jeanne-Marie Santraud and Jean Rouberol. Paris: Sorbonne, 1986. 25-50.

Scher, Saul N. "*The Glass Key*: The Original and Two Copies." *Literature-Film Quarterly* 12 (1984): 147-59.

Schickel, Richard. "Dirty Work." *Book Week* 28 Aug 1966: 14-15.

Schopen, B.A. "From Puzzles to People: The Development of the American Detective Novel." *Studies in American Fiction* 7 (1979): 175-89.

Schulman, Robert. "Dashiell Hammett's Social Vision." *Centennial Review* 29 (Fall 1985): 400-19.

Skinner, Robert E. *The Hard-Boiled Explicator: A Guide to the Study of Dashiell Hammett, Raymond Chandler, and Ross Macdonald*. Metuchen: Scarecrow, 1985.

Staalesen, Gunnar. "Tarzan pa en stor rod scooter: Den hardkokte privatdetektiven som litteraer typ." *Vinduet* 35.3 (1981) 38-44.

Symons, Julian. *Critical Observations*. London: Ticknor and Fields, 1981.

_____. *Dashiell Hammett*. San Diego: Harcourt, 1985.

_____. "Tough Guy at the Typewriter." *Times Literary Supplement* 5 June 1981: 619-20.

Thompson, George J. "The Problem of Moral Vision in Dashiell Hammett's Detective Novels." Diss., U of Connecticut-Storrs, 1972.

_____. "The Problem of Moral Vision in Dashiell Hammett's Detective Novels." *Armchair Detective* 6 (1972): 153-56.

_____. "The Problem of Moral Vision in Dashiell Hammett's Detective Novels. Part 2, *Red Harvest*: The Pragmatic and Moral Dilemma." *Armchair Detective* 6 (1972): 213-25.

_____. "The Problem of Moral Vision in Dashiell Hammett's Detective Novels. Part 3, *The Dain Curse*." *Armchair Detective* 7 (1973): 32-40.

_____. "The Problem of Moral Vision in Dashiell Hammett's Detective Novels. Part 4, *The Maltese Falcon*: The Emergency of the Hero." *Armchair Detective* 7 (1973): 178-92.

_____. "The Problem of Moral Vision in Dashiell Hammett's Detective Novels. Part 5, *The Glass Key*: The Darkening Vision." *Armchair Detective* 7 (1973): 270-80.

_____. "The Problem of Moral Vision in Dashiell Hammett's Detective Novels. Part 7, Conclusion." *Armchair Detective* 8 (1974): 124-30.

Tuska, Jon. *The Detective in Hollywood*. New York: Doubleday, 1978.

Vielledent, Catherine. "Le tough Guy et le deni des profundeurs." *Revue Francaise d'Etudes Americaines* 12 (Nov 1987): 553-64.

Vincent, Marcelle. "L'Universe de Dashiell Hammett." In *Deux regards sur l'Amerique: Dashiell Hammett et Walker Percy*. Ed. Jeanne-Marie Santraud and Jean Rouberol. Paris: Sorbonne, 1986. 51-58.

Ward, Katherine. "Clients, Colleagues, and Consorts: Roles of Women in American Hardboiled Detective Fiction and Film." Diss. Ohio State University, 1989.

Whitley, John S. *Detectives and Friends: Dashiell Hammett's "The Glass Key" and Raymond Chandler's "The Long Goodbye."* Exeter: American Arts Documentation Centre, 1981.

_____. "Stirring Things Up: Dashiell Hammett's Continental Op." *Journal of American Studies* 14 (1980): 443-55.

Wolfe, Peter. "Sam Spade—Lover." *Armchair Detective* 11 (1978): 366-71.

Index

About the Editor

CHRISTOPHER METRESS is Assistant Professor of English at Samford University in Birmingham, Alabama. His essays on American and British literature have appeared in such journals as *Studies in the Novel, Essays in Literature, South Atlantic Quarterly*, and *English Literature in Transition*. He is currently working on a study of Southern literature and the civil rights movement.

ISBN 0-313-28938-7

HARDCOVER BAR CODE